Since 1969, Antonia Fraser has written many acclaimed historical works which have been international bestsellers. These include the biographies *Mary Queen of Scots* (James Tait Black Memorial Prize), *Cromwell: Our Chief of Men* and *King Charles II*, and *The Gunpowder Plot: Terror and Faith in 1605* (St Louis Literary Award; CWA Non-Fiction Gold Dagger). Four highly praised books focus on women in history: *The Weaker Vessel: Woman's Lot in Seventeenth-Century England* (Wolfson Award for History, 1984), *The Warrior Queens: Boadicea's Chariot* (1988), *The Six Wives of Henry VIII* (1992) and *Marie Antoinette: The Journey* (Enid McLeod Literary Prize, Franco-British Society, 2001). Antonia Fraser is the editor of the series *Kings and Queens of England* (Weidenfeld & Nicolson), and wrote the volume *King James VI of Scotland, I of England*. She is married to Harold Pinter and lives in London. Antonia Fraser was made CBE in 1999, and awarded the Norton Medlicott Medal by the Historical Association in 2000. Her latest book, *Love and Louis XIV: the Women in the Life of the Sun King*, is published by Phoenix.

By Antonia Fraser

Mary Queen of Scots

Cromwell: Our Chief of Men

King James VI of Scotland, I of England
(*Kings and Queens* series)

King Charles II

The Weaker Vessel: Woman's Lot
in Seventeenth-Century England

The Warrior Queens: Boadicea's Chariot

The Six Wives of Henry VIII

The Gunpowder Plot: Terror and Faith in 1605

Marie Antoinette: The Journey

Love and Louis XIV: the Women in the
Life of the Sun King

The Weaker Vessel
Woman's Lot in Seventeenth-century England

ANTONIA FRASER

Volume One

PHOENIX

This edition produced for The Book People Ltd,
Hall Wood Avenue, Haydock, St Helens WA11 9UL

First published in Great Britain in 1984
by William Heinemann
First published in paperback in 1993
by Mandarin Paperbacks

Paperback edition published in 2002
by Phoenix,
an imprint of Orion Books Ltd,
Orion House, 5 Upper St Martin's Lane,
London WC2H 9EA

A CIP catalogue record for this book is available from the British Library.

ISBN 978 1 4072 1530 3

Printed and bound in Great Britain by
Clays Ltd, St Ives plc

The Orion Publishing Group's policy is to use papers that are natural, renewable
and recyclable products and made from wood grown in sustainable forests. The
logging and manufacturing processed are expected to conform to the environmental
regulations of the country of origin.

www.orionbooks.co.uk

for
LECTISSIMA HEROINA ELIZABETH LONGFORD

Contents

Author's Note

'*Were* there any women in seventeenth-century England?' This question was put to me by a distinguished person (male) when I told him the proposed subject of my new book; like another jesting interlocutor, he did not stay for an answer, but vanished up the steps of his club. This book is in part at least an attempt to answer that question.

Wherever possible I have quoted the voices of women themselves, in letters, in the few but poignant diaries, and in the reports of others. Obviously there are enormous difficulties with the written record where women of this period are concerned, in view of the fact that the vast majority below the gentry class were, through no fault of their own, illiterate. Nevertheless I have battled to breach the walls of this artificial silence. Indeed, if I have had a bias, it has been towards the unknown rather than the known; believing strongly in what we owe to 'the number who lived faithfully a hidden life, and rest in unvisited tombs', in the words of George Eliot's moving conclusion to *Middlemarch*.

The idea of writing such a book first came to me in 1970 when I was working on a biography of Oliver Cromwell; it occurred to me that a study of women in the English Civil War would produce some interesting results, in view of the spirited nature of the women in question, whether petitioning, defending castles or fighting alongside their husbands – a variety of activities, none of them particularly passive. Working on a life of Charles II, following these women through to the next generation, did nothing to diminish my ardour, but did show me how much more complicated the subject was than I had supposed.

After ten years of working on the seventeenth century I felt more enthusiasm than ever. But I did come to the conclusion that I must confine my study to England alone; although I had at an early stage wistfully contemplated including Scottish women, until the many differences in the laws as well as the society of the two nations convinced me that this was a separate subject. I also realized how important it was to take the hundred odd years from the death of Queen Elizabeth I to the accession of Queen Anne as a whole, if only to explore to what extent woman's position in society did or did not improve with the passage of time.

This, then, is a study of woman's lot: it is not intended as a dictionary of female biography in the seventeenth century, nor for that matter as an encyclopedia of women's topics. I have selected those characters who interested me; omissions were not only inevitable, if the book was not to be of mammoth size, but also deliberate.

Obviously, no one writes in a vacuum, and to boast of being unswayed by the currents of opinion swirling about in one's own time would be, like most boasts, foolish. During the twelve years in which I have been taking notes towards this book, the growth of feminism both as a force and an influence has been a spectacular phenomenon. But this book is, I hope, a historical work, not a tract. After all, to write about women it is not necessary to be a woman, merely to have a sense of justice and sympathy; these qualities are not, or should not be, the prerogative of one sex.

I have taken the usual liberties in correcting spelling and punctuation where it seemed necessary to make sense to the reader today. For the same reason I have ignored the fact that the calendar year was held to start on 25 March during this period, and have used the modern style of dates starting on 1 January throughout. This is an age which presents considerable problems to the writer, where the nomenclature of women is concerned. On the one hand, many of the them bore the same Christian name: in a host of Marys, Elizabeths and Annes, one learns to be grateful for the odd Jemima. On the other hand, equally confusingly, women at this period changed their surnames with frequency, due to marriage and remarriage. Sometimes, therefore, it has proved convenient to use a pet-name or diminutive consistently for a particular character; sometimes I have used the same surname or rank for a woman throughout the book (as for example Margaret 'Godolphin', antedating her marriage, and Margaret 'Duchess' of Newcastle, despite the changes in her husband's title). My aim in all this has been clarity for the reader.

I wish to thank the Marquess of Bath for permission to quote from the Longleat MSS, and Miss Jane Fowles, Librarian and Archivist to the Marquess of Bath; Miss Cathleen Beaudoin, Reference Librarian of the Public Library, Dover, New Hampshire, for letting me see the Jon Scale MS on Quaker women; and the Wardens, Melvin and Sandra Roberts, of the Religious Society of Friends, Nottingham Meeting, for permission to quote from the letter of Isabel (Fell) Yeamans. I am grateful to the staff of numerous libraries, principal among them the Bodleian Library, the British Library, the Institute of Historical Research, the London Library and the New York Public Library.

I should also like to express my thanks to the following, who helped me in a variety of different ways over the years, from answering queries to conducting stimulating conversations: Dr Maurice Ashley; Professor John Barnard; Mr G.P. Bartholomew; Dr Chalmers Davidson; Mr Fram Dimshaw; Lt. Col. John Dymoke of Scrivelsby; Mr Peter Elstob; Miss Jane Ferguson, Librarian to the Royal College of Physicians, Edinburgh; Mr John Fowles; Ms Valerie Fildes; Reverend Mother M. Gregory IBVM; Pauline Gregg; Mrs Cicely Havely; Mr Cyril Humphris; P.J. Le Fevre; Sir Oliver Millar; Mr G.C.E. Morris; Sir Iain Moncrieffe of that Ilk; Mr Richard Ollard; Professor Elaine Pagels; Mr Derek Parker; Professor J.H. Plumb; Mr Anthony Powell; Dr Mary Prior; the Duke of Rutland; Ms Sally Shreir; Lady Anne Somerset; Emma Tennant; Miss Dorothy Tutin;

Brigadier Peter Young.

Over the years I have much appreciated professional support from my publishers on both sides of the Atlantic, John Curtis of Weidenfeld and Nicolson and Robert Gottlieb of Knopf. In addition, I am deeply indebted to my daughter Flora Powell-Jones for her assiduous researches; to Mrs Hatherley d'Abo who showed herself a heroine typing the manuscript; to Linden Lawson of Weidenfeld's for patient editorial overseeing; to Dr Malcolm Cooper for the Chronology and to Gila Falkus for the Index.

Lastly I would like to acknowledge with affection and gratitude three early readers of the book: my mother, to whom it is justly dedicated; my daughter Rebecca; and my husband, who was, as he is fond of pointing out, 'the first'.

ANTONIA FRASER
All Hallows Eve, 1983

Chronology of Important Events 1603–1702

(20 September); Parliament signs Solemn League and Covenant with Scots; first meeting of the Westminster Assembly

1644 Battles of Cheriton (29 March), Marston Moor (2 July), Lostwithiel (2 September) and second Newbury (27 October)

1645 Introduction of the Self-Denying Ordinance and formation of the New Model Army; Battle of Naseby (14 June); execution of Laud

1646 Charles I surrenders to the Scots; end of the First Civil War

1647 Charles I imprisoned at Carisbrooke

1648 Start of the Second Civil War; Battle of Preston (17 August); end of the Second Civil War; Pride's Purge

1649 Execution of Charles I; formation of the Commonwealth; Cromwell's expedition to Ireland

1650 Cromwell leads campaign against Scots; Battle of Dunbar (3 September)

1651 Battle of Worcester (3 September); escape of Charles II

1652 Start of the First Dutch War

1653 Dissolution of the Rump Parliament; the Barebones Parliament; Cromwell becomes Lord Protector

1654 End of the First Dutch War

1658 Death of Cromwell

1660 Declaration of Breda; Restoration of Charles II; Act of Indemnity and Oblivion; marriage of the Duke of York and Anne Hyde

1661–5 Enactment of the 'Clarendon Code'; Corporation Act (1661); Act of Uniformity (1662); first Conventicle Act (1664); Five Mile Act (1665)

1662 Marriage of Charles II and Catherine of Braganza; foundation of the Royal Society

1665 The Great Plague; start of the Second Dutch War

1666 The Fire of London

1667 End of the Second Dutch War; fall of Clarendon

1670 Enactment of the second Conventicle Act

1672 Charles II's Declaration of Indulgence; start of the Third Dutch War

1673	The First Test Act; marriage of the Duke of York and Mary of Modena
1674	End of the Third Dutch War
1677	Marriage of Princess Mary and William of Orange
1678	The Popish Plot
1682	The Rye House Plot
1685	Death of Charles II; accession of James II; the Monmouth Rebellion; the Bloody Assizes
1687	James II dismisses Parliament and issues his first Declaration of Indulgence
1688	James II's second Declaration of Indulgence; imprisonment of the Seven Bishops; birth of James's son; overthrow of James II and arrival of William and Mary
1689	Start of joint rule of William III and Mary II; Bill of Rights and Toleration Act passed; start of the War of the Grand Alliance
1694	Death of Mary II; Triennial Act passed
1697	End of the War of the Grand Alliance
1701	Act of Settlement passed
1702	Death of William III; accession of Anne

How Weak?

I t was a fact generally acknowledged by all but the most con-
tumacious spirits at the beginning of the seventeenth century
that woman was the weaker vessel; weaker than man, that is.

The phrase had originated with Tyndale's translation of the
New Testament into English in 1526 and was given further
prominence by the King James Bible. St Peter, having advised
wives in some detail to 'be in subjection to your own husbands',
urged these same husbands to give 'honour unto the wife, as
unto the weaker vessel, and as being heirs together of the grace
of life', founding his remarks on those of St Paul, in his Epistle to
the Ephesians.

By 1600 the phrase was freely employed – by Shakespeare
amongst others – to denote either a particular female or the
female sex as a whole. Throughout the century following, the
words of St Peter, founded on those of St Paul, might form part
of the Protestant marriage service as an alternative to a sermon:
so that there was a fair chance that most women would listen to
them at least once – on the most important day of their life, their
wedding-day.

Man then was the stronger, woman the weaker vessel. That
was the way God had arranged Creation, sanctified in the words

of the Apostle. About the precise nature of this female 'weakness' there was however a good deal less agreement.

Was woman *morally* weaker than man? And if she was accepted as such – for Eve's audacious behaviour in the Garden of Eden certainly seemed to hint at some innate tendency to depravity in the female sex – what followed? Many of those of both sexes who accepted woman's innate moral inferiority deduced from this that man had a particular duty to protect the weaker sex. Furthermore, it could be argued that for man, the stronger vessel, to sin was a good deal worse than for woman, the weaker – her own frail nature, while inevitably leading her towards temptation in that fatal way she had inherited from her 'Grandmother Eve', also to a certain extent excused her.†

It was a point made by the Rev. Robert Wilkinson in a wedding sermon of 1607, 'The Merchant-Royal or Woman a Ship', which provided a classic exposition of the duties of the married state: where sin was concerned 'he that imposeth so much upon the Weaker Vessel, importeth much more to the stronger'. Equally if a husband was exacerbated by a particular fault of his wife's: 'Yet you must remember she is the Weaker Vessel: God therein exerciseth your wisdom in reforming, and your Patience in bearing it ...'[2]

Few however would have gone as far as the sultry and intelligent Emilia Lanier, who at the beginning of the century dared to pursue the question of 'my Grandmother Eve's' feminine frailty to its logical conclusion:

> But surely Adam cannot be excused,
> Her fault though great, yet he was most to blame;
> What weakness offered, strength might have refused,
> Being Lord of all, the greater was his shame.[3]

The majority of those who accepted the notion of woman's moral inferiority simply concentrated on the eternal vigilance

† Prayers for women's use, composed by either sex, often referred apologetically to 'my Grandmother Eve'. Men in the seventeenth century were not, it seemed, descended from Eve.[1]

necessary to keep the devil from tempting the woman and causing her to fall – yet again. As William Perkins wrote in 1608, on the vexed subject of witchcraft: 'the woman being the weaker sex, is sooner entangled by the devil's illusions with this damnable art than the man'.[4] Witchcraft and sorcery represented perhaps the extreme forms of the devil's attentions to womankind: Elizabeth Josceline, laying down precepts for her unborn child in 1622, expressed the more conventional view that a girl would inevitably be in greater danger from the sin of pride than a boy; to her hypothetical daughter she wrote: 'thou art weaker and thy temptations to this vice greater'.[5]

If morally weaker, was woman necessarily spiritually *inferior?* From the notion of woman's susceptibility to temptation, certain propagandists did slide casually towards the notion of woman as inherently evil – tempted as it were in advance of her birth, born already beguiled. Joseph Swetnam provided a notorious example of this in *The Arraignment of Lewd, Idle, Froward and Unconstant Women*, first printed in 1615. 'Then who can but say, that Women spring from the Devil,' he inquired, 'whose heads, hands, hearts, minds, and souls are evil?'[6] This type of fulmination, however, tended to elicit a fierce barrage of objections, and although Swetnam's book had gone through six editions by 1702, his views were violently attacked.

These interesting discussions concerning woman's possible spiritual inferiority were rooted in uncertainty rather than bigotry. The question of the female soul was crucial. Once again, the notion that women were actually born without souls represented the extreme view, generally denounced whenever it was stated.[7] For example, in 1646 George Fox, the founder of the Society of Friends, met some people in Nottingham 'that held women have no souls, adding in a light manner, no more than a goose'. He reproved them by adducing the text of the Magnificat: how could the Virgin Mary's soul magnify the Lord if she did not possess one?[8]

The equality of the male and female soul was another matter. At the beginning of the seventeenth century it was by no means taken for granted that the respective souls which dwelt in the bodies of men and women were identical. It was for this reason that William Austin, in a book of 1637 praising the female sex, took so much trouble to stress the point: 'in that the soul there is neither hees nor shees'.[9] It was significant that throughout the seventeenth century educators and other friends of the female cause felt the need to state and restate the principle: God 'gave the feeblest woman as large and capacious a soul as that of the greatest hero', declared Richard Allestree in 1673 in *The Ladies Calling*, a best-selling guide to conduct.[10] Despite St Peter's statement that the strong and weak vessels were 'heirs together of the grace of life', not everyone agreed with Allestree even then. In 1600 there would have been a good many who instinctively flinched from such a proposition.

Perhaps the idea of the woman as merely physically weaker was the simplest notion to entertain, as Rosalind, in man's apparel in the Forest of Arden, knew it was her duty to check her tears and 'comfort the weaker vessel [her Cousin Celia] as doublet and hose should show itself courageous to petticoat'. It is true that women were regarded as more susceptible to ailments than men; the midwife Jane Sharp, in a popular book of 1671 based on forty years' experience in her profession, pleaded for greater medical care for women for that very reason.[11] Obviously the general sufferings of women in childbirth, although not strictly speaking produced by disease, and the high rate of maternal mortality encouraged this view.

Yet there was an unexpected corollary to the notion of woman's physical weakness, her 'fairness', her 'softness' – for as the century wore on, phrases like 'the softer sex' – used by John Locke for example – and 'the fair sex' hung delicately like perfume in the air. By the 1690s in the popular *Ladies Dictionary*, females were referred to unhesitatingly as 'being made of the softest mould'.[12] The identification during this period of outward beauty with inward beauty, reaching its extreme form in the doctrines of the 'Platoniques', took the argument further. If women were indeed softer, physically 'smoother' as William Austin had it, might they not also be softer and smoother in spirit? Better than men?

In a very different context, to present woman as physically

inferior to the male was to ignore one potentially menacing aspect of her strength well known at the beginning of the seventeenth century. This was woman's carnality. 'Though they be weaker vessels, yet they will overcome 2, 3 or 4 men in satisfying of their carnal appetites' – thus the Elizabethan musician Thomas Wythorne.[13] Female sexual voracity was a subject of frequent comment. It was axiomatic that a woman who had once experienced sex would wish to renew the pleasure as soon as possible and as often as possible – hence the popular concept of the 'lusty widow'. The relative facts concerning the male and female orgasm being well understood, women were regarded in an uneasy light for being undeniably weaker – yet in certain circumstances insatiably stronger.

Where intelligence was concerned, there was a great deal more unanimity. At the time of the death of Queen Elizabeth I, almost everyone of both sexes agreed that the female intelligence was less than that of the man: women themselves were wont to refer as a matter of form to the strength of their passions, apt to rule over their weaker reason. The intellectual – and childless – Duchess of Newcastle was described in an elegy on her death as being the exception to the rest of 'her frail sex... who have Fruitful Wombs but Barren Brains'. The Duchess herself subscribed to one contemporary supposition that the female brain was somehow biologically different: 'mix'd by Nature with the coldest and softest elements'.[14]

And yet... there was something troubling here too, which could not be altogether overcome by referring automatically to clever women as having a masculine intelligence. The great Queen who died in 1603 had played that game herself with consummate skill, describing herself in a famous passage as having the body of a weak and feeble woman but the heart and stomach of a king – that is her masculine counterpart. As the century progressed, obstinate voices would point out that women were not actually intellectually inferior to men – merely worse educated. Other voices would be raised to the effect that if woman's intelligence was really inferior, she might logically need more, not less education than a man.

For those who pondered on such subjects, it must have been a relief to come to the absolute certainty of the English common law, or as a cynical assessment of women's position, *The Lawes Resolutions*, put it, 'The common law here shaketh hand with divinity.'[15] Under the common law of England at the accession of King James I, no female had any rights at all (if some were allowed by custom). As an unmarried woman her rights were swallowed up in her father's, and she was his to dispose of in marriage at will. Once she was married her property became absolutely that of her husband. What of those who did not marry? Common law met that problem blandly by not recognizing it. In the words of *The Lawes Resolutions*: 'All of them are understood either married or to be married.'[16] In 1603 England, in short, still lived in a world governed by feudal law, where a wife passed from the guardianship of her father to her husband; her husband also stood in relation to her as a feudal lord. This had serious consequences for those wives foolish enough to be detected plotting to kill their husbands: for the act thus counted as treason. Like servants who plotted the death of their master, the wife was subject to the death penalty in its severest form – being burnt alive.

Here was the weak vessel with a vengeance – weak at law. Yet even here there was a respite. The wealthy widow might or might not be racked with lust as the popular imagination believed (one of those 'young brisk widows who cannot be satisfied without that Due Benevolence which they were wont to receive from their Husbands').[17] Her position was none the less, as we shall see, in many ways enviable. City wives were particularly well treated: by the Custom of London a wife had the right to one third of her husband's property at death, and if there were no children, their one third share also. The potential strength in the position of the wealthy widow, if her settlement was unencumbered, her children free from restricting guardianship, may stand as one example of those possibilities which did exist for womankind in the real world, outside the dream or nightmare of her theoretical weakness...

For it is at this point that we notice history holding the door ajar; through this door we glimpse prophetesses, business-women, nuns, blue-stockings, radicals, female labourers, prosti-tutes and courtesans, good women, holy women, the immoral and the amoral, criminals, wayward heiresses, unhappy wives, purposeful mothers, heroines – great ladies who defended besieged houses and castles in the Civil War and others, no less brave, who fought as soldiers themselves – nurses, midwives, adventuresses, educators, and that new breed, the actress.

The contemplation of these faces, in their variety and vitality, whether suffering or triumphant, summons questions to the lips. Now the sound of the female voice too is heard: the writers including poets and playwrights, the diarists – the first diary by a British woman was written at the turn of the sixteenth century by Lady Margaret Hoby[18] – the memorialists, the letter-writers from the sublime and literary to the humble, the latter all the more fiercely poignant for being so often without name or number; Dante's *la gente perduta*,[9] a phrase which can cover too easily 90 per cent of English womanhood in the first half of the seven-teenth century.

Were these vessels all really so weak as society ostensibly sup-posed? What kind of lives did women really lead in England between the death of one Queen Regnant and the accession of another?

PART ONE

As It Was – This Blessed Knot

'Marriage, O Lord, is thine own holy and sacred ordinance:
Thou sawest in thy wisdom, that it was not fit for mankind
to be alone. Upon this, it was thy pleasure to appoint this
blessed knot...'

SAMUEL HIERON, *Prayer for those intending marriage,* 1613

CHAPTER ONE

A Wife Sought for Wealth

'House and possessions, wealth and riches, land and living is that, that most men regard, and look after: yea men are wont to seek wives for wealth. But saith Solomon, as a good name, so a good wife, a wise and a discreet woman is better than wealth; her price is far above pearls...'

THOMAS GATAKER, 'A Good Wife Gods Gift', 1624

Let us begin with a wedding. That was after all how most women in the early seventeenth century were held to begin their lives 'All the Time of your Life you have been gathering for this Day', Honoria Denny was told at her wedding to James Lord Hay at Twelfth Night in 1607, 'therefore learn to practise now that [which] you learned before; that is, to honour, to love and to obey...'[1] Thus was Honoria, only daughter and heiress of Lord Denny, dispatched into the arms of her bridegroom with the aid of a masque devised by Thomas Campion and a prolonged banquet.

It was all held in the presence of the King. James I enjoyed these pretty wedding celebrations of a young couple, particularly when as on this occasion he had acted as matchmaker. In the course of the masque, characters such as Flora, Night, Hesperus and Zephyrus emitted suitably nuptial sentiments, to the dulcet sounds of violins, a harpsichord, the odd double sackbutt and several bandoras (an early form of guitar or banjo) twanged by 'two Sylvans'.[2] The King looked on with sentimental satisfaction. James Hay, a good-natured but extravagant young man, was the first of his favourites at the English court: King James sought to cure his financial problems with the aid of Honoria Denny's rich expectations. Although the bride's father had for some years opposed the match – for exactly the same reason as the King was promoting it – he had finally succumbed to royal blandishments which included a title and the grant of a patent. So the new Lord Denny handed over Honoria.

At the wedding ceremony, the Rev. Robert Wilkinson, chaplain to the Prince of Wales and rector of St Olave's Church, chose to denounce marriages based on mercenary considerations in the course of his sermon. It was 'the Manner of the World', he proclaimed angrily, to seek wives 'as Judas betrayed Christ, with a *Quantum Dabis?* (How much will you give?)' Later, for the benefit of the young couple – and the world in general – he had printed 'what so lately sounded in your ears'.³ This sermon was reprinted in a collection entitled *Conjugal Love* as late as 1725. Despite the genesis of the Hay marriage, Wilkinson's words would not have echoed ironically in the ears of his fashionable audience in 1607, or plagued the consciences of his readers in the ensuing decades.

Throughout the seventeenth century marriages for money were regularly denounced from the pulpit, and in guides to behaviour of all types. The Puritan handbooks in particular pointed to the perils inherent in such money-based matches. In another wedding sermon of 1624, 'A Good Wife Gods Gift', the Puritan divine Thomas Gataker was as firm as the royal chaplain had been: 'House and possessions, wealth and riches, land and living is that, that most men regard, and look after: yea men are wont to seek wives for wealth. But saith Solomon as a good name, so a good wife, a wise and a discreet woman is better than wealth; her price is far above pearls: For house and possessions are the inheritance of the fathers; but a prudent wife is of the Lord.'⁴

At the same time in real life, the inquiry '*Quantum Dabis?*', far from being regarded as the cry of Judas, was a question seldom off the lips of any respectable and dutiful father. A girl brought with her a dowry, or 'portion' as it was termed; in return she would be promised a 'jointure', something to support her should she survive her husband. An heiress not only brought with her a larger portion at the time of her marriage; her jointure would also be larger, since there was considered to be some mathematical relationship between the size of the dowry and the size of the jointure. That however lay ahead – it was always possible she would predecease her husband. At the time of the marriage it was more relevant that, in the words of *The Lawes Resolutions* (an exposition of the law concerning the female sex printed in 1632 but thought to have been written by two lawyers at the end of the sixteenth century), 'That which the husband hath is his own' and 'That which the wife hath is the husband's.'⁵ Marrying an heiress, or at least a bride with a decent portion, was therefore a recognized – and respectable – path to material advancement at this date, one which a good parent did not hesitate to recommend to his offspring.

Henry, fifth Earl of Huntingdon, laying down some ground rules by which his son Ferdinando might choose a wife in about 1613, advised him not to bother too much about her exact rank, since he was 'already allied to most of the nobility'; the boy would do better to 'match with one of the gentry where thou mayest have a great portion'. The true interests of a noble family were at stake: 'without means thy honour will look as naked as trees that are cropped'. Oliver Cromwell, by birth a member of the gentry, set to with a will to secure an heiress – Dorothy Mayor – for his unsatisfactory elder surviving son Dick; he regarded getting the best terms out of Dorothy's father as a kind of holy task, devoting a great deal of correspondence and worry to it at two crucial periods in his political career. At one point there was a question of £2,000 in cash being handed over: 'I did insist upon that ... The money I shall need for my two little wenches.'⁶ In other words, as the pattern of the prudent Puritan father, Cromwell wished to do his best by Dick, in order to promote the interests of his own unmarried daughters Mary and Frances.

A coarser view was expressed by Richard Lane. Hearing that his friend Christopher Lord Hatton had a mistress, he gave the following advice: 'Well Kitt, do anything but marry her, and that too if she have money enough; but without it you shall never have my consent, since this is to reduce you to a filthy dowlas [very coarse linen] and bread and cheese, which, whilst the love lasts, is fancied partridge and pheasant, but when that is gone (and we know it will go) then it turns to cheese again; and what will you do then?'[7]

It is true that the seventeenth century also witnessed a cautious development of the law of equity in the Court of Chancery, where an heiress's financial interests were concerned. A judgment of 1638, for example, indicated that where a deceased person's estate was 'thrown into Chancery' for administration, the interests of any married woman who might be amongst his beneficiaries obtained indefeasible protection. (Previously, although the dating of the change cannot be pinpointed precisely, the Court of Chancery had followed the common law courts in upholding the doctrine of conjugal unity where finance and property were concerned.)[8] But this modest and gradual amelioration of the female lot at law applied of course only to those few women whose affairs somehow reached the august precincts of Chancery. Where the majority of women were concerned, their lives were lived within the depressing and total restrictions of the common law.

So, in an age before the English had properly discovered the rumbustious sport of fox-hunting, heiresses were hunted as though they were animals of prey. But these vulnerable creatures, unlike foxes, were neither wily nor predatory. For the most part they were very young. The age of consent for a girl was twelve (fourteen for a boy),[9] but the exciting whiff of a glittering match particularly if the girl was an orphan, was often scented long before that; then the chase was on. The mention of 'unripe years' might mean the postponement of such routine accompaniments to the marriage as consummation; but the contract itself was made, even though a bride was theoretically entitled to her own choice of husband at the age of consent, without a previous betrothal to inhibit her.

The peculiarly confused state of the laws of England concerning valid marriages and the marriage ceremony before the Hardwicke Act of 1753, helped to make the chase still more exciting when much was at stake. Throughout the seventeenth century a girl might well have been forced into a marriage against her will, by parental pressure, or even outright violence from a stranger, and have found herself thereby robbed of her freedom and her money.

Under these circumstances, the heiress's lot could hardly be described as invariably happy, despite the fact that her hand was so avidly coveted by her male contemporaries. Moreover, where the law was concerned, there was yet another sinister rider on the subject of adultery. *The Lawes Resolutions* had something pithy to say about that too: adulterous wives, if convicted, lost their 'dower'; men, on the other hand, could commit adultery with impunity where finance was concerned. 'They may lope over ditch and Dale', for the fortunate male there would still be no 'forfeiture'.[10] This provision relating to the adulterous wife was particularly ominous where an heiress was concerned. Married when still virtually a child for her 'house and possessions', a wife sought 'for wealth' in Gataker's phrase, it might be easy and even natural for her to look elsewhere for affection. But the consequences, as we shall see, could be disastrous.

On Michaelmas Day 1617, ten years after the wedding of Honoria Denny and James Hay, King James presided over another magnificent nuptial celebration. The bride was Frances Coke, daughter of the great jurist Sir Edward Coke. She was fourteen years old. The bridegroom, Sir John Villiers, was twenty-six. In this case it was not upon him but upon his younger brother George Villiers, recently created Earl of Buckingham, that the King's affections were passionately focused. (As for Honoria, she was by this time dead, during her brief life having fulfilled one normal female destiny by providing her husband with a male heir – and property; the spendthrift Lord Hay was on the verge of taking a seventeen-year-old girl, Lucy Percy, as his second wife; at their wedding the King would be once again 'exceeding merry'.)[11]

At Frances Coke's marriage, James I himself gave away the bride. Splendid court festivities ensued and the King rounded off his own enjoyment of the proceedings by sending a directive to the newly married pair to the effect that they should be in no hurry to end their wedding-night. He intended to visit them personally, lying in bed, sometime after noon the next day, to hear details of what had transpired. Such visits were a royal hobby: in 1612 James had paid a similar visit to 'two young turtles' (doves), his sixteen-year-old daughter Elizabeth and her husband the Elector Palatine.[12]

Yet what a world of trouble, pain and unhappiness lay behind the formal proceedings by which the fourteen-year-old Frances Coke was wedded and bedded with Sir John Villiers![13] It is true that Frances herself was quite beautiful enough – if not sufficiently docile – to be compared to a turtle-dove. As one of the late flowers of the Jacobean court, Ben Jonson would hail her:

> Never yet did Gypsy trace
> Smoother lines in Hands or Face;
> Venus here doth Saturn move
> That you should be Queen of Love...[14]

John Villiers, on the other hand, shortly to be ennobled as Viscount Purbeck, the name by which he is known to history, was nobody's idea of an appealing bridegroom. The man suffered from periodic fits of insanity of a manic nature which might lead him to smash glass and 'bloody' himself. The matching of this disparate pair had nevertheless become the dearest project of the bride's father, Sir Edward Coke.

Coke, in political disgrace, saw in the alliance of his child with the all-powerful Buckingham-Villiers clique a means back into the King's favour. The Villiers family was at this point headed by an ambitious matriarch Lady Compton, mother of both Villiers and Buckingham, now the wife of the wealthy Sir Thomas Compton. Having persistently married for money herself, Lady Compton intended her sons to do likewise. For her part, she saw in Frances Coke's enticing portion and still more savoury expectations just the kind of fortune her son needed.

As it happened, Frances Coke's expectations owed much to her mother as well as to her father. Elizabeth Lady Hatton had been the young rich widow of Sir William Hatton when she married the elderly Coke a few months after Hatton's death in 1597. (Lady Hatton was generally known by the title of her first husband even after she married Coke.) From Hatton Elizabeth had received endowments including Corfe Castle in Dorset and Hatton House in London, with its tranquil garden containing fishponds, fountains, arbours and a dovecot. Much of this might accrue to John Villiers if he married Frances; and then there was the question of the additional fortune, of Queen Elizabeth's favourite, Christopher Hatton, which Sir William had inherited from his uncle.

Unfortunately for the smooth resolution of Coke's plan, neither Lady Hatton nor for that matter Frances Coke happened to represent that kind of modest submissive female, full of 'bashful shamefastness' which was the masculine ideal of the time.[15] Lady Hatton had no particular wish to fall in with Coke's plans, having come to dislike her second husband; in any case, quite reasonably, she did not regard John Villiers as a suitable bridegroom for the child described by a contemporary as 'the Mother's Darling'. Furthermore Lady Hatton detested the ambitious Lady Compton, with whom she had recently quarrelled.[16]

Coke, however, paid no attention to his wife's objections, and as for Frances's feelings, they were judged to be quite irrelevant. Negotiations with the Villiers family went on apace. 'I would have been pleased to have taken her in her smock', declared Sir John Villiers gallantly of the lovely Frances; in fact the bride was to be dressed a great deal more richly, metaphorically speaking. Coke proposed a down payment of £10,000, and an allowance of £1,000, with the magnificent prospect of her Hatton expectations to come.[17]

Lady Hatton's next move was swift. Her pleas being unavailing, she suddenly removed Frances by coach to Oatlands, near Weybridge, which had been rented for the summer by one of her cousins. Here Lady Hatton tried to get Frances personally committed to another suitor, Henry Earl of Oxford (an official betrothal in those days – or 'spousals' in front of witnesses – having arguably the validity of a marriage).[18] To help matters along Lady Hatton first forged some love letters from Lord

Oxford and then obliged her daughter to sign a document pledging herself to him entirely: 'and even if I break the least of these [vows]' it ran, 'I pray God Damn me Body and Soul in Hell fire in the world to come'. It was signed by Frances on 10 July 1617 'in the presence of my dear mother Eliza Hatton'.[19] Presumably as the result of the forged letters, Frances herself now felt a clear preference for Lord Oxford over Sir John Villiers.

The great Sir Edward Coke was not, however, so easily outwitted. Arming himself with a search warrant of sorts – its validity was very doubtful – he arrived at Oatlands to reclaim his daughter. When he was refused admittance, Coke simply battered down the door and then searched the house from top to bottom until he found Frances and her mother cowering in a dark closet. A physical tug-of-war between the rival parents ensued. Coke won. Frances was dragged weeping away.

Now it was Lady Hatton's turn. In hysterics, she got a warrant from the Council, signed by the Lord Keeper Bacon (whom she had woken in the middle of the night), and set off to rescue her daughter with men and pistols. In return Coke summoned his wife for kidnapping and counterfeiting the Oxford engagement and planning to seize the girl again. Lady Hatton was more than equal to this one: 'Who intended this [i.e. force]? The Mother. And wherefore? Because she was unnaturally and barbarously secluded from her daughter – and her daughter forced against her will contrary to her vows and liking to the will of him she disliked.'[20]

The Council felt some cautious sympathy for the plight of Lady Hatton and Frances – the caution being due to the fact that King James was absent in Scotland and his reaction to the prospective match was as yet unknown. When the King returned, making it clear that in his eyes Buckingham could do no wrong, the Council attempted to strike some kind of compromise which would soothe the outraged Lady Hatton and yet not risk offence to the favourite. So Frances was officially restored to Hatton House, and there amidst its arbours and fountains, it was ordained – perhaps rather optimistically – that Sir John Villiers should be allowed to win her hand for himself. Even more optimistically, his mother should be allowed to support him.

But Frances was not to be wooed. Lady Hatton, maintaining her opposition to the match to the last, was finally put under house arrest at the lodging of an alderman of the City of London. Lord Oxford, nervously aware of Frances's preference for his suit, backed away at the prospect of Buckingham's powerful displeasure. Even so, the fourteen-year-old Frances would not give in.

In the end she was 'tied to the Bedposts and whipped' – possibly more than once – 'till she consented to the Match'. Only now did Frances surrender and write a pathetic dictated letter to her mother, saying that she was a mere child, 'not understanding the world nor what is good for myself'; besides, Sir John Villiers was a gentleman and she saw no reason to dislike him. She ended with an ironic postscript: 'Dear mother, believe there has no violent means been used to me by words nor deeds.'[21]

This then, was the grotesque preamble to the ceremony on Michaelmas Day – 29 September – at which the King presided so magnificently, drinking many a health to the bride and inquiring so eagerly after the details of the wedding-night the next morning. Lady Hatton, the mother of the bride, still under house arrest, was at first refused permission to attend and then ordered to do so – at which she declined to come, saying she was sick.

A marriage begun with such a gorgeous sham of a ceremony was not necessarily doomed by the standards of the age. It was Buckingham's – and Coke's – cold ruthlessness in condemning Frances to such a demonstrably unsuitable bridegroom, which led to the next fatal episode in the heiress's story. Lady Hatton still refused to bestow certain Dorset properties on her new son-in-law, as a result of which the King felt obliged to create Villiers Viscount Purbeck to atone (the title being derived from those properties he had not yet acquired). As Viscount and Viscountess Purbeck, the newly wedded pair might be hoped to sparkle, he as Master of the Robes to the Prince of Wales, she as one of the reigning beauties of the court.

Instead, Purbeck's madness grew steadily worse. (It is interesting to note that Richard Napier, the clergyman-physician who began to treat Purbeck in 1622, seriously blamed his mother for his condition.) He was already 'weak in mind and body; when his worst fits were on him, he needed to be restrained from doing violence to himself.'[22] Buckingham's reaction was brilliantly rapacious. Announcing that his brother was mad, he proposed to take Purbeck's estates into his own care to administer them – which of course had the effect of denying Frances altogether the use of what had once been hers.

At the same time, Frances's beauty brought its own natural temptations, all the harder to resist in view of the unsatisfactory nature of her husband. 'You will turn all Hearts to Tinder', wrote Ben Jonson of his 'Queen of Love'. One heart in particular Frances's charms burnt up – that of Sir Robert Howard. Handsome and unmarried, Howard was ten years Frances's senior. Their adulterous liaison was not a very well-kept secret. It was said afterwards that Howard had been seen coming by water in the evenings to visit Lady Purbeck at York House, 'there being a private and secret passage to her chamber'; he would also be seen slipping away early the next morning.[23]

Adultery was at that date still officially a matter for the church courts (even though the common law was beginning to establish its jurisdiction in certain cases).[24] An ordinary couple so convicted could expect to perform some form of humiliating and arduous penance at least. However, cuckoldry was hardly unknown at the Jacobean court and under normal circumstances Lady Purbeck and Sir Robert Howard might have been left more or less free to pursue their liaison. The circumstances were made abnormal by two things: first, Buckingham's determination to secure Lady Purbeck's fortune on behalf of his mad brother; second, Lord Purbeck's presumed inability to beget a child – certainly he was unable to do so while living under restraint, apart from his wife.

Frances's petitions concerning her poverty after Buckingham seized Purbeck's estates make piteous reading: she could not even get 'relief in her necessities'; she declared herself 'most barbarously carried by force into the open street'. Buckingham in reply merely suggested that Frances's conduct had been the cause of Purbeck's madness. Frances really had no alternative but to declare herself willing to return to her unsatisfactory husband; 'though you may judge what pleasure there is in the conversation of a man in the distemper you see your brother in'. Otherwise she would be completely poverty-stricken, despite the injustice of the situation: 'for you know very well I came no beggar to you, though I am like so to be turned off'.[25]

Even the King seems to have felt that Buckingham had gone rather far on this occasion, for he intervened. Frances secured an annual income on condition that she left Purbeck for good – which of course also meant abandoning the estates to Purbeck, or rather Buckingham.

Frances now became pregnant by Sir Robert Howard. Given the lack of any effective form of birth control at the time, this development was perhaps inevitable, but it did undoubtedly complicate her cause. For one thing the law of the time, so cruel to wives, was very much softer towards children born – if not necessarily conceived – within wedlock. If the husband was testified to have been 'within the four seas' (i.e. not in foreign parts) at the time, the child was deemed to be his. The hysteria of the Villiers family at the prospect of Frances's pregnancy – which they maintained could not possibly be attributed to Lord Purbeck – was made still worse by the fact that Buckingham had at this point no male heir; a Purbeck son might actually inherit from his legal uncle Buckingham as well.†

Frances first of all denied that she was pregnant. When the story leaked out to Buckingham, via a necromancer called Dr Lambe, whom Howard and Frances had rather unwisely consulted, Frances bolted. Under the assumed name of Mistress Wright, she gave birth in lodgings to a baby which was secretly baptized as 'Robert Wright'.[26] Nevertheless she still swore when taxed that the baby was her husband's child. Afterwards Frances justified this guilty flight by saying that it had been caused by a brutal gynaecological 'search' of her person, at the hands of midwives employed by her mother-in-law. Given the latter's character, that was quite believable. Frances's explanation for the

†Divorce – keeping the bride's dowry, which was the aim of the Buckingham family – was virtually impossible at this date, as will be described in Chapter 15.

conception of her baby demanded more of an act of faith: she explained that Lord Purbeck had somehow eluded his captors for a short period, in the course of which a secret encounter with his wife had resulted in her pregnancy.

Here was an adultery with a fortune at stake. Frances and Robert Howard were called in front of the Court of High Commission; on and off the proceedings would continue for three years before both were found guilty and condemned to public penance. Frances throughout behaved with characteristic defiance. Some of her sayings have a biblical ring. In front of the court, 'with bitter revilings', she called on the prelates concerned 'that they should make their own Wives set the good example, by swearing that they were free from all Faults'.[27]

One of the last acts of James I, who died in the spring of 1625, was to sign a warrant by which Frances, her baby, its nurse and her other servants, were committed to the care of Alderman Barkham of the City of London, the same kind of house arrest to which Lady Hatton had been subjected. Unfortunately the new King, Charles I, was equally intoxicated by the personality of Buckingham; Howard received a coronation pardon but by 1627 there seemed no way in which Frances could avoid carrying out her destined penance. As well as paying a £500 fine, on a Sunday she was to walk barefoot and dressed in a white sheet from St Paul's Cross to the Savoy, and there stand at the door of the church for all to see.

But Frances still did not see fit to perform her penance. With the connivance of the Ambassador of Savoy she managed to escape, dressed as a page-boy. She was next heard of living with her lover Robert Howard on his Shropshire estates. It was not until the mid 1630s that the guilty pair felt it was safe to return to the capital – by which time an assassin had removed Buckingham from their path, and his mother was dead. Their return was however, a misjudgement. Frances was imprisoned once more on the old warrant and placed in the Westminster prison known as the Gatehouse.

This time it was a venal turnkey who enabled the dauntless Lady Purbeck – still determined not to perform her penance – to escape. She headed for France. Sir Robert Howard had also been confined, but in June 1635 was released on his promise not to 'come at' Lady Purbeck. Promptly breaking his promise, Howard was happily reunited with his mistress in Paris. Both became Catholics. Now perhaps, with French society ready to receive them, the couple might be allowed to rest. It is good to know that Sir Kenelm Digby, meeting the notorious Lady Purbeck in Paris, discovered in her 'Prudence, sweetness, goodness, honour and bravery' beyond any other woman he knew: '*vexatio dat intellectum*'. He was full of indignation that this enchantress should be obliged to live in exile.[28]

Frances Purbeck's adventures were however not concluded. King Charles I, in an unwise gesture, attempted to have the writ served on her in Paris, which aroused French nationalist fury. Then Frances withdrew into a nunnery, but finding it not to her liking, resumed her life in Paris, where she lived in considerable penury. By 1640 she was back in England petitioning for the return of her marriage portion from Buckingham's sister Lady Denbigh; only to find whatever estates she had secured sequestrated by Parliament in 1644. Frances Lady Purbeck died in June 1645 at Oxford, where the King was then holding his court and Parliament; she was buried in St Mary's Church. Sir Robert Howard, who had stuck to his mistress through all these traumatic events with admirable constancy, remained a bachelor until after her death, marrying for the first time at the age of fifty-eight.

The story of Frances Coke had a curious postscript. Lord Purbeck married again but never succeeded in begetting legitimate issue. The love-child Robert Wright, or Robert Villiers as he was alternatively termed, did make some claim to the title; but his real political sympathies were elsewhere. Under the Commonwealth he abandoned the Royalist name of Villiers for Danvers, that of his wife, daughter of one of the judges who tried Charles I. After the Restoration he became involved in an anti-governmental conspiracy and fled the country. But his widow, children and grandson resumed the claim to the Purbeck title, and also that of Buckingham after the second Duke of Buckingham's death, in a long-running *cause célèbre*.[29] The claim only ended properly in 1774 with the death of the last male descendant of that doomed union between Frances Purbeck, the wife sought 'for wealth', and Robert Howard, who sought her for love.

Mary Blacknall, heiress to a large amount of property in Berkshire including the Abbey of Abingdon, was, unlike Frances Coke, an orphan.[30] The lack of a father to hector her was however not necessarily to her advantage. In the first half of the seventeenth century the Court of Wards still engulfed heirs to the Crown's tenants-in-chief who inherited at the age of fourteen (if a girl) or twenty-one (if a boy). It was the right of the Court of Wards to sell off these orphans in marriage, the Crown receiving a fat fee in return; the Master of Wards could be just as unsympathetic a matchmaker as Sir Edward Coke, indifferent to the feelings of his wards where pecuniary concerns were at stake.

The Court of Wards and its procedure was one of the abuses of the Crown's position most resented on the eve of the Civil War: swept away by Parliament in 1645, it was officially abolished at the Restoration. Before that date interested relatives sometimes bought the wardship of a child back from the Crown. It would be nice to relate that this argued concern for the orphan's free choice of a spouse, but in most cases the transaction was once again financial. The relatives hoped themselves to benefit from administration of the properties and, sooner or later, the arrangement of a match.

This was the fate of Mary Blacknall. Four of her maternal relations – Richard Libb, Charles Wiseman and two Anthony Blagroves, father and son – paid a £2,000 fine to the Crown for the lease of her lands. Ostensibly they were securing for Mary not only a good education, outside the impersonality of the Court of Wards, but also freedom of choice of bridegroom when she reached the age of fourteen and was free from their guardianship. But somewhere along the way, three out of her four guardians forgot these fine feelings and married Mary off when she was ten to her first cousin, the son of Uncle Libb.

The fourth guardian, Uncle Wiseman, then proceeded to appeal to the Court of Wards on the grounds that Mary was under the age of consent. The appeal was successful. Orders were given that Mary should be delivered forthwith to the house of Sir John Denham, one of the barons of the Exchequer, at Boarstall; there she would be brought up with his own daughters. Despite her recent experiences, Mary was officially pronounced 'unmarried, unaffyed, and uncontracted'. At this point Uncle Wiseman evidently felt that he had frightened Uncle Libb sufficiently; the order was not enforced and Mary, remained with the Libbs – the possibility of a £5,000 fine hanging over the guardians' heads if they indulged in any further conspiracies before Mary reached the age of fourteen.

If not her Libb cousin, who was Mary to marry? The guardians set to with a will once more to see if some more congenial prospect could be envisaged. Of various offers made for Mary, that of Sir Edmund Verney on behalf of his son Ralph was held to be the best. So Mary was ordered to be delivered once more, this time to the house of Sir Francis Clarke, as the future bride of Ralph Verney. Sir Edmund Verney engaged himself to protect the guardians against any penalty imposed by the court, and also paid that half of the guardians' discharge to the Crown which remained outstanding. Still Mr Wiseman was not satisfied that Mary would retain her right of free choice at the age of fourteen; so Mary lingered on at the house of Mr Libb. Whereupon Sir Edmund Verney himself appealed to the Court of Wards, anxious that this prize should not slip through his – or rather his son's – fingers. The Court of Wards ruled in his favour. This time Mary really was delivered. And on 31 May 1629 Mary Blacknall was married to Ralph Verney.

There was still some explaining to do. First, Sir Edmund had to draft a letter for Mary to write to Mrs Wiseman: 'Good Aunt – Besides the desire I have to hear of your health and my uncle's, I think it fit to acquaint you that now I am married.' Since Aunt Wiseman's main preoccupation was to outwit Aunt Libb in the matter of the marriage – and Aunt Libb's plans for her son – Aunt Wiseman was not too much put out. She did hope however that the Wisemans would not be blamed 'when she [Mary] shall come to understand what she hath done': that was because Sir Edmund should have made a settlement for Mary before the marriage and had not yet done so. Aunt Libb on the other hand vowed that Aunt Wiseman would repent this matter as much as anything she did.

The second aspect of the affair was more serious. Mary referred in her letter to her marriage having been 'privately done' at her own request, to explain why the Wisemans had not been invited. Her mother-in-law wrote in the same vein: 'She desired so much to have it privately done ...'. Weddings at this date were not necessarily the grandiose court affairs of Honoria Denny and Frances Coke – nor the similarly celebratory if less magnificent occasions which in villages and country districts constituted one of the main features of social life. There was a good deal of vagueness as to what constituted a valid union in the first place.[31] It was naturally even more difficult to ascertain the validity of a marriage which had been 'privately done'. In the case of Mary Blacknall the obscurity of her wedding was surely deliberate. For on 31 May 1629 Mary Blacknall was still only thirteen years old. Once she was fourteen it would be theoretically possible for her to repudiate what had earlier been done in her name.

There is some evidence that efforts were made by her maternal relatives to persuade her to do so after her fourteenth birthday on 14 February 1630. How were the Verneys to prevent Mary from being once more wrested away? The obvious and natural solution was to persuade young Ralph Verney, by now a student at Magdalen Hall, Oxford, to win with soft words the prize which had hitherto been his solely in terms of a contract. Ralph was therefore tipped off that now, if ever, was the time for a gallant courtship of the young lady, 'rather than let slip this occasion, which if not now performed is not likely ever to be ended'.

Ralph Verney set to with a will. Shortly afterwards his tutor was hastily pointing out the inadvisability of total concentration on 'Hymen's Delights'; he must not neglect his work at university entirely for Mary's sake: 'the sweetness of a kiss will relish better after the harshness of a syllogism'. Happily for Mary, if not the tutor, Ralph preferred kisses to syllogisms. Mary Blacknall remained – or rather became in the fullest sense – his bride. Nearly twenty years later Ralph would refer to her as 'my dear, discreet and most incomparable wife'.[32]

We shall meet her again, this gallant supporter of her husband through all the tumult of war, exile and sequestration. At the present time it is enough to quote Ralph Verney's own description of his married life: 'We who ever from our very childhoods lived in so much peace, and christian concord...'[33] The practical common sense which dictated that, heiress as she might be, Mary must have her consent wooed not wrested from her, was responsible in no small measure for this happy union.

The worst of Mary Blacknall's fate was to be the object of gentlemanly bargaining among her adult relatives. The affair of the orphan Sara Cox represented an altogether darker aspect of the heiress's life. In August 1637 Sara Cox was fourteen years old. Being 'fatherless and motherless' and 'of a good portion' she had been made 'orphan of the City of London' (that is, placed under their guardianship).[34] She had then been sent to a well-known girls' boarding-school run by Mrs Winch at Hackney – a favourite area for such schools at the time, because although pleasantly rural, it was also convenient for the girls' parents many of whom were merchants and other dwellers in the City of London.

One of Sara's schoolfriends was called Katherine Fulwood. It was Katherine's brother, Roger Fulwood, who, hearing of Sara's 'good portion', conceived from afar the notion of transforming his fortunes by marrying her. Using Katherine as an intermediary, Roger tried to persuade Sara to share in this brilliant scheme – without success. On 22 August therefore, as Sara and a few of her schoolfriends were taking the air on Newington Common, an array of horsemen with drawn swords suddenly emerged. From out of the midst of her friends, Sara was seized and bundled off into a waiting coach. Here lurked Roger Fulwood. In this coach, Sara Cox, a latter-day Europa with Roger Fulwood as her bull, was 'carried off Screaming'.[35]

Her destination proved to be Winchester House in Southwark on the south bank of the Thames, residence of the Bishop of Winchester. At first her reception here seemed reassuringly respectable: for she found Roger's mother Lady Fulwood presiding, and spent the night under her protection. The next morning however matters took a grimmer turn. On the pretence of being shown over the Bishop's dwelling, Sara was inveigled into the chapel. Here, to her dismay, she found a waiting minister of religion and she was forthwith – and forcibly – married to Roger Fulwood in the presence of Lady Fulwood.

Worse followed. Lack of consummation being a well-known ground for establishing the nullity of a marriage, it was important to the Fulwoods that this enforced union should be seen to be a full one. So Sara's clothes were pulled off her and Sara herself was placed in bed with Roger Fulwood. (From what follows, it seems that this was done more as a formality than with the serious intent of consummating the marriage, but the experience must have been none the less terrifying for the fourteen-year-old Sara.)

Fortunately at this critical juncture the help of the law was at hand. Sara's abduction from Newington Common had led her friends to institute a furious search: that night Roger Fulwood and his accomplice, named Bowen, were at last located by the Lord Keeper's Sergeant-at-Arms and apprehended. Fulwood and Bowen, accompanied by Sara, were brought before the Lord Mayor of London at one o'clock in the morning. Poor Sara flung herself on her knees before him: 'she beseeching him ... and for God's sake, to deliver her out of the hands of these people'.[36]

The horrified Lord Mayor complied. Sara was given back into the custody of her friends. And now the full extent of Fulwood and Bowen's duplicity – and that of the Bishop of Winchester's housekeeper, one Nicholas Young – was known. The marriage licence for the wedding of Sara and Roger Fulwood had been secured on Young's false affidavit that the intended bride was neither heir nor ward. It was further affirmed that Sara had given her own consent to the match, because her friends had been planning to marry her off to a Dutch doctor – another fabrication.

The erring Roger Fulwood was arraigned for his life on 3 September: by an Act of the reign of Henry VII taking of women against their wills for 'the lucre of their substance' and either marrying them or 'defiling' them had been made a felony.[37] The events of this sordid abduction were outlined to King Charles I in a petition from the Lord Mayor on 17 September. The King's indignation was promptly expressed.

In the end Roger Fulwood and his friend Bowen did not pay the harshest penalties. Lady Fulwood weighed in with her own petition to the King at the beginning of November: on the one hand she complained that the matter was 'not nearly so barbarous as had been bruited' (presumably a reference to the fact that Sara had not actually been 'defiled' by Roger, whatever appearances might suggest); on the other hand she begged for mercy. On 25 November Fulwood and Bowen were both pardoned for their lives and for their estates, which as felons they had forfeited.[38]

Still the troubles of Roger Fulwood were not over. Obviously Sara's friends' chief concern was to secure a declaration of the nullity of this 'marriage' so that Sara's future prospects were not impaired. They were clearly reluctant to see Roger Fulwood leave prison until this matter had been settled in Sara's favour, for the following June Roger was still in prison, despite his pardon. He issued a desperate petition to the King: 'the said Sara and her friends desiring to question the said marriage', he had agreed in advance to give his consent to a suit of nullity, whenever it would be required by the court concerned. If he was not released now, he would have to lie in prison throughout the long vacation of the courts. Finally Roger offered a surety of £2,000 that he would consent to the annulling of the marriage when the time came, and was released.[39] Thus Sara Cox was officially restored to her maiden state.

This cautionary tale showed that young men who were 'wont to seek wives for wealth' needed to have the weight of the establishment, royal and legal, behind them. Roger Fulwood had transgressed not so much in his intention to marry an heiress — which was that of many respectable men of his time — as in the rash and violent manner in which he tried to carry it out. As a result, Sara Cox suffered a fearful ordeal at the hands of strangers; all because she epitomized that seventeenth-century object of desire, a young lady 'of a good portion'.

CHAPTER TWO

Affection Is False

~

'"Affection!" said the Queen, "Affection is false." Yet
her Majesty rose and danced; so did my Lady Marquess
of Winchester.'

ROWLAND WHYTE TO SIR ROBERT SIDNEY, JUNE 1600

'Poor greenheads', wrote the Puritan Daniel Rogers of those
who married purely for love: when a year or two had
passed and they had skimmed the cream of their marriage,
they would soon envy the good fortune of those whose union
was built on stronger foundations. In *Matrimoniall Honour* Rogers
even went so far as to argue that over-passionate marriages might
actually result in contaminated offspring: 'What a cursed posterity such are likely to hatch ... what woeful imps proceeded from
such a mixture.'[1]

During this period, the emotion we should now term romantic love was treated with a mixture of suspicion, contempt and
outright disgust by virtually all pundits. From the Puritans in
their benevolent handbooks of domestic conduct to the aristocrats concerned to see that society's pattern was reproduced in an
orderly fashion, that tender passion which has animated much of
the great literature of the world (including those plays of
Shakespeare and the Jacobean dramatists familiar to theatre audi-
ences of the time) received a hearty condemnation. Nor was this
a revolutionary state of affairs in seventeenth-century England,
the arranged marriage as opposed to the romantic union having
been preferred by most societies in the history of the world.

Only briefly at the court of Henrietta Maria did the cult of Platonic love (imported from the Queen's native France) hold sway. Then the elaborate paraphernalia of gallantry which attended this philosophy merely helped to underline the chasm which existed between the Queen's small coterie and the rest of the country. In his play of 1629, *The New Inn*, Ben Jonson cheerfully mocked the cult. Lady Frances Frampul was a 'Platonique' who desired nothing more than 'a multitude of servants', i.e. platonic admirers to worship at her shrine. Love itself was defined as

> ... a spiritual coupling of two souls
> So much more excellent, as it least relates
> Unto the body ...²

Outside this make-believe little court – and the realms of satire which fed upon it – public advocacy of romantic love was unknown.

James Houblon was the son of a Huguenot refugee who rose to wealth and success in the City of London, identified with the new Royal Exchange. He married, in 1620, an eighteen-year-old girl also of Huguenot descent, Marie du Quesne – 'in a happy day' as he later described it. When Marie died nursing a child of plague in 1646, she left her husband with seven young sons to bring up, her daughters being already married. (One of these sons, Sir John Houblon, was the first Governor of the Bank of England.) In his old age James Houblon was quite clear how his daughters should 'undertake the matching' of their children. 'Beg first the Assistance of God, and see that you match them in families that fear the Lord and have gotten their Estates honestly.' There was nothing here about inclination or susceptibility.³

It was not a question of rank. At roughly the same date as Jonson's play appeared, Henry, ninth Earl of Northumberland, was appalled to discover that his son, Algernon Lord Percy, had secretly engaged himself to Lady Anne Cecil, daughter of the Earl of Salisbury – and all for love!

It was true that in 1628 the families of Northumberland and Salisbury stood in roughly the same friendly relationship to each other as Montagues and Capulets in the opening scene of *Romeo and Juliet*. The 'ancient grudge' which existed between them, or as Lord Northumberland put it, the family wounds 'fresh smarting in my sides to this day', originated at the time of the Gunpowder Plot. Then Salisbury's father had been instrumental in having Northumberland imprisoned in the Tower of London for several years, although nothing had been proved against him; Northumberland had also been forced to pay an enormous fine. Twenty years later it was particularly galling for Northumberland to find that his son had secretly chosen a bride in whose veins ran the hated Cecil blood; which in Northumberland's opinion 'would not mingle [with his] in a basin, so averse was he from it'.[4]

The fact that Lord Percy had actually fallen in love with Lady Anne, far from being an extenuating circumstance, only made things worse. Lord Northumberland expostulated to Lord Salisbury: 'My son hath abused your Lordship, himself and me too. If I had had a daughter and your son had engaged himself in this sort, I should not have trusted his words ... *nulla fides est in amore* [there is no faith in love].' While it is difficult not to detect a note of gloomy satisfaction in his prediction of Anne Cecil's future: 'Poor lady, [she] I fear, will have the least good in the bargain, how so ever pleasing for the present. Loves will weave out and extinguish when the knot that ties them will not do so.'[5]

Lord Percy's reckless behaviour had also of course made it difficult for Lord Northumberland to strike that kind of hard bargain over the marriage settlement on which a father might pride himself – one excellent reason for distrusting love in the first place. Beauty, because it might incite a susceptible Romeo to love, as Lady Anne's beauty had won Lord Percy, was not to be trusted either. Joseph Swetnam, in that violent attack on women first printed in 1615, paid particular attention to the turpitude of beautiful women who represented traps for men. 'The fairest woman', he declared, had 'some filthiness' in her; beautiful women in general he compared to glow-worms, 'bright in the hedge, black in the hand'. Even the far more temperate Thomas Gataker referred to beauty as having 'a bait to entice' while adding that it had 'no hook to hold'.[6] Certainly Lord

Northumberland, who had already given his views on the likely impermanence of his son's 'hooked' affections, would also have agreed with Gataker that beauty was 'a bait to entice'. Throughout his negotiations with Lord Salisbury before the marriage finally took place, he constantly bewailed the expensive settlement he was obliged to make because 'the beauty of your daughter fettered my son'. (The marriage was however a happy one, cut short by Anne Cecil's death ten years later.)

Another celebrated infatuation of the time aroused echoes not so much of an ancient 'grudge' as of an ancient scandal. In 1634 the twenty-one-year-old William Lord Russell was described as being 'all in a flame of love' with the nineteen-year-old Lady Anne Carr.[7] Unfortunately this modest and charming young girl was the daughter of that notorious beauty of the Jacobean court, Frances Countess of Somerset, her father being Robert Carr, Earl of Somerset, yet another of the favourites of King James I. The fact that the ancient scandal – almost too light a word – concerned the bride's mother in this case made Anne Carr's descent even more unfortunate than that of Anne Cecil. Anne Cecil's grandfather might have had Lord Northumberland imprisoned, but Anne Carr's mother was a self-confessed murderess – and an adulteress too – who had spent some years in the Tower of London for conspiring to poison Sir Thomas Overbury.

'Cat will after kind' – so ran a popular saying of the day. There was a dire suspicion that a girl's moral character was inherited directly from her mother (it was the same kind of logic which held that all women were contaminated by their descent from Grandmother Eve). Anne Carr could be held to have been bred for depravity – for her maternal grandmother Katherine Countess of Suffolk had been another notorious woman.

Lord Russell's father, the Earl of Bedford, a leading Puritan, was of a notably harsh character. He had himself been present in the House of Lords on that fatal occasion in January 1616 when the lovely Countess of Somerset, all in black with 'cobweb lawn ruff and cuffs', had confessed her guilt 'in a low voice, but wonderful fearful'.[8] Only a few weeks earlier she had given birth to a child. That child was Anne Carr. Subsequently the Countess was imprisoned in the Tower of London. Who would welcome a girl of such flagrantly unfortunate antecedents as a daughter-in-law?

Yet this was the bride on whom William Lord Russell, 'a handsome genteel man' wrote the Rev. George Garrard, a contemporary observer, had set his heart. When William came back from the Grand Tour in 1634 he announced to his father that he would have Anne Carr or no one; this despite the fact that there was, in the words of the same observer, 'much looking on' the handsome and eligible young man – the names of the far more suitable Dorothy Sidney and Elizabeth Cecil (Anne Cecil's cousin) being mentioned in this connection.[9]

Lord Bedford utterly refused to entertain the idea of the marriage. With regard to Anne Carr he had given his son instructions 'to choose anywhere but there'. Equally William Russell refused to give way. Then Lord Bedford, faced with an only son who threatened not to marry at all, tried to scupper the match in another way by demanding a portion from the bride's father, which he believed Somerset – who was known to be financially embarrassed – would not be able to pay. Heroically, the Earl of Somerset decided that if 'one of the two must be undone', he would rather it was himself than his daughter, and he decided to pay the price asked.[10] Still the match lagged. Even King Charles I, on a visit to the Earl of Bedford at Woburn Abbey, failed to persuade the angry father to give way.

After four years of wrangling, the marriage finally took place in July 1637. It was a victory for love – not heredity – that Anne, Countess of Bedford and chatelaine of Woburn Abbey after her father-in-law's death, proved a pattern of gentle virtue; she was blessed with nine surviving children and enjoyed nearly fifty years of happy marriage. (Only her own life ended in a tragedy, as dramatic in its own way as her beginnings in the Tower of London – with the execution of her son William Lord Russell for treason – but to that we shall return.)

So for all the fulminations of fathers and the directives of handbooks, love, as it always has done, did find a way. What the prevailing climate of opinion on the subject did induce, however, was a distinct feeling of guilt on the subject, even when romantic love triumphed over such normal considerations as financial prudence and personal suitability.

Lettice Morrison was eighteen years old when she captured the heart of Sir Lucius Cary, later Viscount Falkland. The daughter of Sir Richard Morrison of Tooley Park, Leicestershire, she was an exceptional character, not only for her beauty, but also for a genuine love of study, which marked her out from most girls of her time: 'oft-times at a book in her Closet when she was thought to be in bed'. After Lettice Falkland's death, her chaplain wrote a eulogistic biography of her: here at last was one descendant of Eve who 'in her cradle' had 'strangled the serpent'.[11]

Scorning the contemporary fashion of wearing her hair 'in loose braids' in order to ensnare men, Lettice did none the less unwittingly ensnare Sir Lucius Cary; for she offered a far more unusual attraction than floating hair: a character which combined 'Piety, wisdom, quickness of wit, discretion, judgement, sobriety and gravity of behaviour'. Unfortunately, as her chaplain succinctly put it, Lettice brought with her no dowry beyond these 'riches'.[12] Such qualities might be portion enough for her lover, but her lover's father took a more worldly view and expressed strong disapproval. Father and son quarrelled. Even so Cary persisted in his suit – helped by the fact that he, not his father, had been made heir to his rich grandfather Lawrence Tanfield. Shortly after Easter 1630 Cary was married to this lovely but penniless girl. A short while after that Cary succeeded to the Falkland title; under which name his story, with that of the wife at his side, became woven into the political, religious and literary life of England on the eve of the Civil War; whether at his estate of Great Tew near Oxford, or in Parliament itself.

Despite Lettice's admirable character, Falkland's contemporaries were amazed that this 'incomparable young man' should marry in this rash way. Clarendon, who adored Falkland and thought that his death alone was enough to make the whole Civil War accursed, summed up the general feeling: Falkland had 'committed a fault against his father in marrying a young lady whom he passionately loved'.[13] Others, for whom mere love seemed an insufficient explanation, developed a theory that Falkland had married Lettice for her strong resemblance to her brother Henry, Falkland's friend, who had died young.

Interestingly, Falkland himself clearly felt a kind of honourable guilt about the whole matter. He was prepared to stand by his affections: at the same time he did not pretend he had behaved altogether correctly. According to Clarendon, he offered to resign the estate inherited from his grandfather and depend solely on maintenance from his father in order to atone 'for the prejudice he had brought upon his fortune, by bringing no fortune to him'. But his father's anger caused him to refuse this handsome offer.[14]

Had Falkland been influenced in his choice of Lettice Morrison by the example of his own mother? Elizabeth Tanfield, Viscountess Falkland, accorded the supreme compliment of having 'a most masculine understanding',[15] was one of those remarkable late Tudor women, educated in the great tradition of female learning of that time. Her accomplishments included a knowledge not only of French, Italian, Spanish, Latin and Greek but also of Hebrew and Transylvanian. Perhaps Falkland had early discovered in his mother the charms of the company of a well-educated woman.

Or was it on the contrary Lettice's natural seriousness – a sense of the sadness at the centre of things – which struck an answering chord in Falkland's heart? There had been a streak of melancholy in her make-up even as a girl, when some had criticized her 'lack of joy'. Aubrey tells us that during her married life she deliberately used her ready tears to obtain favours for her servants; but then Aubrey disapproved of a man of Falkland's reason and judgement being 'stormed' by a woman's tears for what he deemed an unworthy purpose.[16]

At the onset of the war, Falkland's own 'natural cheerfulness and vivacity' grew clouded. Having believed in the possibility of a simple Royalist victory, he watched instead the country being torn apart. Clarendon paints an unforgettable picture of the agonies of a man of conscience in a world of war: 'Often, after a deep silence and frequent sighs, he would, with a shrill and sad accent, ingeminate the word Peace, Peace.' Falkland was killed at the age of thirty-three at the first Battle of Newbury: he rode into the heart of the fighting – looking at last 'very cheerful', as he always did 'upon action'[17] – and was shot down.

Lettice Falkland never recovered from the blow. 'The same sword which killed *him*, pierced *her* heart also', wrote her chaplain. She lived another four years, spending her time in rigorous works of philanthropy, not all of which commended themselves to her friends. Her scheme for helping widows was one thing, but she was much criticized for encouraging layabouts by her charity.

'I know not their hearts', Lettice replied with spirit. 'I had rather relieve five unworthy Vagrants than that one member of Christ should go empty away.'[18] Her desire, as a Royalist, to help Roundhead prisoners in Royalist gaols aroused further suspicion.

Examples of her growing melancholia were more disquieting. Lettice became increasingly scrupulous in her piety, full of fears of the devil. Having already banned all rich clothing on her husband's death, and even looking-glasses, in order to extinguish personal vanity, she further abandoned that household pomp 'which her quality might have excused'. Lastly she turned on that very affection which had been the foundation stone of her own life. Urging other wives not to be too fond of their husbands, she insisted that there was 'no real comfort from any espousals but from those to Christ'.[19]

Lettice Viscountess Falkland died in 1647 at the age of thirty-five 'without twitch or groan or gasp or sigh' of what was surely a form of broken heart. (Her two surviving sons succeeded in turn to the title of their father.) It was notable that even in the elegy on her death the strange circumstances of her marriage, including Lord Falkland's waiving of a dowry, were solemnly commemorated:

> Nor did He wed her to join Fortunes and
> Lay Bags to Bags, and couple Lands to Land
> Such Exchange Ware he scorn'd, whose Noble eye
> Saw in her Virtues, Rich Conveniency.[20]

It would be quite wrong, however, to describe the general distrust of love among the upper classes as a purely masculine conspiracy. Those few women before the Restoration with the opportunity for self-expression did not hesitate to join in the chorus. Both Margaret Duchess of Newcastle and Dorothy Osborne, whatever the reality of their private lives, shuddered away from the concept of love, and above all from its devastating consequences.

The Duchess of Newcastle was that extravagantly dressed woman of letters who in later life would alternately fascinate and appal Restoration society. As a young woman, she prided herself on never having felt 'amorous love' for her husband. 'I never was infected therewith', she wrote. 'It is a disease, or passion, or both, I know only by relation.'[21] This was not a matter of mere cynicism towards the state of marriage – for the Duchess also prided herself with justice on her devotion to her husband; condemnation of 'amorous love' was a matter of principle.

William Cavendish, in turn Earl, Marquess and Duke of Newcastle, was over fifty and a grandee at the court of Charles I, when he began to woo Margaret Lucas, thirty years his junior, as his second wife. For all his seniority – he was well past middle age by the standards of the time – Newcastle displayed surprising vigour in his suit. It was his very enthusiasm which Margaret regarded with suspicion. First she was concerned that her own declarations should not be too explicit: 'I am a little ashamed of my last letter more than the others,' she wrote on one occasion, 'not that my affection can be too large but I fear I discover it too much in that letter, for women must love silently.' Then she was obsessed by the essentially ephemeral nature of any ardent protestation: 'If you are so passionate as you say,' she continued, 'and I dare not but believe [it], yet it may be feared it cannot last long, for no extreme is permanent.'[22]

Another lively and articulate young lady, Dorothy Osborne of Chicksands, never ceased to identify 'passion', that is, strong feeling, as the enemy of all mankind – and womankind in particular. Yet her beguiling and chatty love letters to William Temple, later an important diplomat in the reign of Charles II, seem to us to breathe a very romantic form of affection.[23] This was another star-crossed match, for Dorothy was the daughter of the Royalist Governor of Guernsey, while William Temple's father sympathized with Parliament. Even the lovers' first meeting was suitably exotic. On the Isle of Wight, on his way to France, Dorothy's brother rashly inscribed a piece of pro-Royalist graffiti on a window pane in hostile territory: Temple witnessed with admiration how the sister saved the brother from the consequences of his audacity by taking the responsibility for the inscription upon herself. Then family opposition to the marriage confined Temple and Dorothy to an apparently eternal courtship, while Temple travelled abroad, and pretty witty Dorothy was courted by a series of other men.

Through all this, the lovers remained true to each other. As this seventeenth-century Penelope rejected a number of eligible suitors, including the Protector's son, Henry Cromwell, she had to endure the vehement reproaches of her family, led by her youngest brother. Then Dorothy was struck down by that dreaded scourge of female beauty, smallpox, and much of her early physical charm vanished. Still William's fidelity held him to his vows. Finally in 1655 they were married.

The romantic elements in this story, including the constancy under trial of both parties, make an interesting contrast to Dorothy's oft-professed scorn for 'passion'. As much as Margaret Duchess of Newcastle, Dorothy prided herself that she had not been seared by that awkward emotion, amorous love. In her letters she was quick to denounce those who, by coming too close to its perilous flames, had been burnt or branded. When Lady Anne Blount, daughter of the Earl of Newport, ran off with one William Blunt (no relation), Dorothy bewailed her fate to Temple. She was also quite clear where the responsibility for Lady Anne's 'fall' lay.

'Ah! if you love yourself or me', she wrote to Temple, 'you must confess that I have reason to condemn this senseless passion; that whereso'ever it comes destroys all that entertain it; nothing of judgement or discretion can live with it, and [it] puts everything else out of order before it can find a place for itself.

What has it not brought my poor Lady Anne Blount to?', Dorothy went on. 'She is the talk of all the footmen and boys in the street, and will be company for them shortly, who yet is so blinded by her passion as not at all to perceive the misery she has brought herself to ...' As for William Blunt, Lady Anne's partner in the affair, 'if he had loved her truly he would have died rather than been the occasion of this misfortune to her'.[24] Once again we hear the Cassandra-like voice of Lord Northumberland, condemning his son's infatuation for Anne Cecil, because it would certainly lead to her undoing.

As it happened, Dorothy Osborne was probably right about the peripatetic Lady Anne Blount. By the next year William Blunt, her erstwhile partner, was petitioning against her, saying that she had only run off with him to obtain some money, so that she was presumably home again. The year after that Lady Anne had taken flight once more without her father's consent – this time with Thomas Porter, son of Endymion Porter, who had been Groom of the Bedchamber to Charles I. Yet Dorothy's own fear of 'this senseless passion' obviously runs deeper than mere condemnation of a flighty young lady's self-destructive behaviour.

There is a malaise here, seen again in her yearning for a peaceful life in another letter to Temple: 'Do you remember Herm [a Channel island]', she wrote, 'and the little house there? Shall we go thither? That's next to being out of the world. There we might live like Baucis and Philemon, grow old together in our little cottage, and for our charity to some ship-wrecked strangers obtaining the blessing of dying both at the same time.'[25] Some of this desire for an existence dominated by tranquillity – as opposed to some more excitable emotion – even with her lover, can of course be attributed to the troubled nature of the times. Nevertheless Dorothy and the rest of her generation, whatever the political strife about them, still drew back in apprehension from love itself, especially love in marriage.

'No passion could be long lived, and such as were most in love forgot that ever they had been so within a twelvemonth after they were married.'[26] The words are those of Dorothy's brother

Henry, trying to convince her that the very nature of this type of affection was to be impermanent. Dorothy, by her own account, was puzzled at the want of examples to bring to the contrary. Throughout the whole of Dorothy's correspondence, one detects a wistful hankering that Temple himself should somehow represent the settled convenient match of her family's desires. He did not. He represented something more dangerous. And in the end she married him.

At the marriage of William Herbert and Anne Russell in 1600, in the time of Queen Elizabeth, the traditional masque followed: 'delicate it was to see eight ladies so prettily and richly attired'. Mary Fitton, a lady-in-waiting, led the masquers. After they had finished, and it was time for each lady to choose another to tread the measure with her, Mary Fitton went up to the Queen and 'wooed her to dance'. The Queen asked Mary Fitton what allegorical character she represented; Mary Fitton replied that she was Affection.

'Affection!' said the old Queen. 'Affection is false.' Yet all the same Queen Elizabeth rose up and danced.[27] Many of the dancers in the pageantry of marriage in the seventeenth century believed that affection was false; yet trod to its measure all the same.

For love, like cheerfulness, kept breaking in, and ever with love came guilt. In July 1641 the fifteen-year-old Mary Boyle, daughter of the great Earl of Cork, made a match which at the time was conspicuous for its unworldliness. She married, very privately, Charles Rich, a 'very cheerful, and handsome, well-bred and fashioned person'. Then merely a younger son without prospects, he promised to make up for 'the smallness of his fortune' by the 'kindness' he would ever have for Mary. Previously 'unruly Mary', in her father's disapproving phrase, had rejected the suitor chosen by him in Ireland, the wealthy Mr Hamilton 'who professed great passion for her', on the grounds that her 'aversion for him was extraordinary'.[28]

It was unexpected that (by the deaths of several relations)

Charles Rich should eventually succeed to the title and property of the Earl of Warwick, establishing Mary Rich, Countess of Warwick, as the great lady her father had always intended her to be. Despite this fortunate occurrence, and despite an affection for her husband which persisted throughout their married life, Mary Countess of Warwick still felt it necessary to apologize for the circumstances of her marriage in her autobiography. 'My duty and my reason having frequent combats within me, with my passion', she wrote, she had acceded to the latter. In so doing she had gone against her father's wishes, and years later she still regarded this piece of defiance as 'an ill and horribly disobedient answer' for a daughter to give to a father.[29]

Not all stories where love and duty tugged in different directions ended as happily as that of Mary Countess of Warwick, especially when the financial arrangements could not be satisfactorily sorted out (finally the Earl of Cork did give his daughter her large dowry). From the Oxinden papers, the intimate records of a family living in East Kent, emerges the sad story of Dorothy Denne, who fell in love with a personable serving-man.[30] Dorothy Denne, an Oxinden cousin, was one of the five daughters of the Recorder of Canterbury; William Taylor worked for her brother Captain John Denne.

Propinquity led to a mutual attraction, but the question of privacy for the courtship was another matter. A rendezvous indoors was virtually impossible at a time when even the wealthy lived without any privacy in the modern sense. Under the circumstances ladies such as Mary Countess of Warwick and Dorothy Osborne turned to nature for spiritual retirement. Mary Warwick's 'wilderness', an artificial creation of trees and shrubs which she called her 'sweet place', was her favourite resort for meditation. Dorothy Osborne would dream of William Temple at night alone in the garden – 'a place to roam in without disturbance'; with the jasmine smelling 'beyond all perfume'.[31] Dorothy Denne and William Taylor too were compelled to turn to the outdoors, in a series of trysts.

Dorothy's letters, making the arrangements for them, can still be read: 'Friend', she begins, 'My sorrow and vexations [at not meeting] are as great as yours. I would fain speak with you there-fore any fair day about four o'clock in the afternoon, if you send Jack Munday or Jane to me … I will venture to speak with you in the orchard.' Somehow Dorothy and William were surprised at this rendezvous, possibly because William had told a 'lying … prating wench' (Dorothy's description) who was his offi-cial sweetheart about it. Great was Dorothy's lamentation, princi-pally on the subject of the scandal: 'I think there lives not a sadder heart than mine in the world, neither have I enjoyed scarce one hour of contentment since we happened to be disco-vered at our last meeting … If you had borne any true and real affection to me and valued my reputation you would never have run that hazard, knowing that a woman which has lost her good name is dead while she lives …'[32]

The romance continued, with Dorothy persistently preaching the superior claims of duty (and financial security) to those of passion, yet by her conduct encouraging very different expecta-tions in her admirer. She maintained that it would be 'a sin of a high nature' if she ran off with her William, and neither of them could expect the blessing of God on such an enterprise. She had heard that William might secure 'a gentlewoman worth a thou-sand pounds' as a wife: 'for the Lord's sake take her or any other, and make not yourself and me ever miserable'. As to William's romantic notions – 'You speak of having me without any clothes or one penny in my purse' – Dorothy made short work of them: 'people would think me either stark mad or a fool … to bring myself to beggary and contempt of all that know me'. Yet at the end of this long letter recommending prudence on both sides in a note in another hand – presumably William's: 'We did meet the same time.'[33]

Dorothy was appalled when news of their clandestine relation-ship began to leak out, which might mean that her father would reduce her inheritance; only God could protect them from the 'poverty and misery' which their sinful relationship deserved. At the same time Dorothy suffered agonies because of the news – reported maliciously by her maids – that William was courting another lady in the same village: 'They say it is a great disgrace for me to love such an unworthy fellow as you are ...' Nevertheless at the end of the letter Dorothy signed herself William's 'true and faithful yoke fellow so long as my life shall last'.[34]

William's letters have vanished but they must have been comparatively ardent since at one point Dorothy exclaimed: 'Dear Love, you write in such strains of rhetorick I know not well how to answer them. Your compliments term me a goddess ... I am not divine but a poor mortal creature, subject to all kinds of miseries, and I account myself the more miserable in losing thy sweet company.'[35] The end of the affair was, however, on a less elevated plane, since Dorothy eventually married a rich London draper named Roger Lufkin, whereupon William Taylor's mother tried unsuccessfully to blackmail Dorothy by producing the compromising correspondence. At least Captain John Denne, Dorothy's brother, still remembered William Taylor kindly in his will, while it is to William's mother's malevolence that we owe the preservation of Dorothy's agonized letters among the Oxinden papers.

Dorothy Denne accepted her destiny and made in the end a prudent match, the charms of William Taylor forgotten. The moral tale of Henry Oxinden of Barham's refractory daughter Peg demonstrated – from the point of view of the period – exactly what could happen to a young woman who refused to conform.[36] Peg had already declined one suitor produced by her father in 1647, when she was just over twelve. Henry Oxinden took her rejection ill, raging on in his letters that 'the folly of a girl' was preventing 'her own happiness' as well as making her 'assuredly miserable' in the future; he also punished Peg by denying her new clothes. Then Peg did worse still by selecting her own suitor, in the shape of John Hobart, son of a Lady Zouch by her first marriage; he was attending school at Wye nearby, and lodging at Barham.

Although the marriage did take place finally in 1649, Lady Zouch was quite as disapproving as Henry Oxinden. In vain her son pleaded for her forgiveness: 'I must confess that I have married one whom I have loved ever since I saw her', he wrote. Lady Zouch got her revenge by acting the tyrannical mother-in-law to Peg when the young couple came to lodge with her in London. As for Henry Oxinden, he continued to denounce Peg's 'neglective demeanour' to him, and when the marriage started – perhaps inevitably – to go badly, he took Lady Zouch's side. Peg, he decided, was growing 'too headstrong' and needed 'such a one as the lady [Zouch] to break her if possible of her wilful courses'. So Peg was not allowed to leave the house without permission, a sad fate for one who had led a comparatively unrestricted life in Kent. Poor Peg's troubles only increased when she became pregnant: she was still part of the Zouch household, Henry Oxinden insisting that she should not leave of her own accord, for then 'she would not have been allowed any maintenance by law'; a message also came from him, saying that Peg could expect nothing from her father. John Hobart's early love had clearly faded as well: Peg's husband, wrote an observer, minded her pregnancy 'as much as my cows calving'. No money was supplied for the lying-in or baby linen: 'she is as unprovided [for] as one that walks the highways'. Such was the unhappy end of Peg's defiance, based on impetuous affection.

Only at the bottom of society was some kind of proper independence enjoyed. Women of the serving or labouring classes were in theory subject to exactly the same pressures where love was concerned. 'This boiling affection is seldom worth anything' when making a choice of a husband, wrote Hannah Woolley in her commonsensical handbook for 'the Female Sex' which included 'A Guide for Cook-Maids, Dairy-maids, Chamber-maids, and all others that go to the service'.[37]

Nevertheless in practice these toiling females enjoyed a good deal more freedom of choice where their marriage partner was concerned than their well-endowed sisters, simply because they lived below the level where such considerations as portions and settlements could be relevant. With freedom of choice came obviously the freedom to marry for love, if so desired, simply because no one else's interests were at stake. Richard Napier was a consultant clergyman-physician who kept notebooks of his cases between 1597 and 1634; they reveal, according to their editor, many instances of romantic love (and its problems) 'among youth of low and middling parentage'.[38]

The lack of acute concentration on the matches made in the lower ranks of society did not of course mean that love suddenly became the paramount blinding emotion which guided them: the eternal practical consideration of the wherewithal on which to marry remained. This could take many different forms, according to the type of society in which a couple lived, urban or agricultural. The brother of Adam Martindale, a Nonconformist minister of Lancashire, disappointed his father grievously when he set his heart on 'a wild airy girl...a huge lover and frequenter of wakes, greens, and merry-nights, where music and dancing abounded', with a dowry of only £40 when he could have had a bride worth £140. Although the wild airy girl proved an excellent wife, the sense of disappointment remained.[39] (Perhaps only women of the vagrant classes enjoyed total freedom to follow their fancy – and they very often, so far as can be made out, did not bother to marry at all.) This lack of concentration did mean that women outside the propertied classes of the aristocracy and gentry married really quite late – according to recent research – at an average age between twenty-three and twenty-four.[40] Whatever the manifold disadvantages of the poor, that was another freedom they enjoyed, when one thinks of the ordeals of the wealthier young ladies, torn between 'duty and reason' and 'passion' in their early teens.

It was fashionable to gaze from outside at the innocence of the fresh country world, and marvel at it, as though with nostalgia for some lost paradise, as in the picture presented by the ballad of 'The Happy Husband-man':

> My young Mary do's mind the dairy
> While I go a howing and mowing each morn...
> Cream and kisses both are my delight
> She gives me them, and the joys of night.

A good deal of this was sentimental: Sir Thomas Overbury's 'fair and happy milkmaid', dressed without benefit of the silk-worm, being 'decked in innocence, a far better wearing', would with reason have envied the material lot of a court lady.[41] But there was one respect in which the milkmaid possessed an advantage to which the court lady could not aspire.

Robert Herrick wrote of the carefree celebrations of the country life:

> For Sports, for Pageantry and Plays,
> They hast their Eves, and Holidays:
> On which the young men and maids meet,
> To exercise their dancing feet.[42]

It is true that Herrick's young men and maids enjoyed a kind of guiltless freedom in the sphere of the affections unknown to their social superiors (even if it would never be expressed in literature or letter), especially when one bears in mind that this was a sphere in which enormous attention was not paid to the subject of the bride's virginity. Furthermore that simple betrothal before witnesses which constituted a valid precontract of marriage justified in many people's opinion full sexual intercourse.

Dorothy Osborne described how she would walk out of a hot May night to a common near her house, 'where a great many wenches keep sheep and cows, and sit in the shade singing of ballads'. When she walked over to them, she found their voices and appearance vastly different to 'some shepherdesses that I have read of'. But when she fell into discussion with them, she found that despite these deficiencies, they wanted 'nothing to make them the happiest people in the world but the knowledge they are so'.[43]

If not the happiest people in the world, Dorothy's wenches were, in the single instance of their emotional independence, ahead of the majority of their female contemporaries.

CHAPTER THREE

Crown to her Husband

~~~

'I with great thankfulness acknowledge she was my
crown and glory...'
DR ANTHONY WALKER, *The Holy Life of Mrs Elizabeth Walker*

'A virtuous woman is a crown to her husband'; so Elizabeth
Walker, wife of the minister Dr Anthony Walker, would
emphasize to her daughters, quoting from the Proverbs.
Samuel Hieron, a London preacher whose printed sermons were
so popular that they had run through eight editions by 1616,
referred to marriage as 'this blessed knot' appointed by God; a
'holy and sacred ordinance' since He had seen in His wisdom
'that it was not fit for mankind to be alone'. Woman was
intended to act as man's helpmate. Elizabeth Walker succeeded
triumphantly in this pious ambition according to her husband,
who wrote her *Holy Life* after her death: 'I with great thankfulness acknowledge she was my crown and glory...' Similarly, a
poetic obituary upon Mrs Anne Mors, a merchant's wife of
King's Lynn, referred to the support she had given her husband's
business in her lifetime:

> If women's soul be Planets in the air
> And rule like potent Constellations there
> Surely the Merchants' wives will there reside
> Darting kind beams their husbands' ships to guide...[1]

There were many other wives in the seventeenth century – not only among the ranks of the Puritans and the merchants – who were adjudged to have reached the status of an ideal wife; women whose funeral elegies might run like that of Lady Katherine Paston who died in 1637. On her monument it was written that her 'sad Consort' had 'reared this structure here':

> That future Ages might from it collect
> Her matchless merit, and his true respect.

The (extremely long) memorial to Elizabeth Cavendish, Countess of Bridgwater who died in 1663 at the age of thirty-seven and was described amongst other things as 'a most affectionate and observing wife to her husband, a most tender and indulgent mother to her children, a most kind and bountiful mistress to her family' (i.e. her household), ended: 'In a word she was so superlatively good, that language is too narrow to express her deserved character.'[2] There was indeed a remarkable unanimity in the nature of such tributes. For all the religious differences which bedevilled the structure of society, the qualities which went to make up a right royal 'crown to her husband' were not much in dispute.

Modesty, that preferred female attribute of the time – for all women, not only wives – received its due mention. Gervase Markham in *The English Huswife* of 1615 expected his 'compleat woman' to be 'of great modesty and temperance'; Thomas Fuller's *The Good Wife* of 1642 was also to be remarkable for her 'modest carriage' (although she could at the same time 'bind her children with a look' which might imply a slight contradiction in terms).[3] But if modesty and deference were to be displayed in theory, in practice a woman needed a formidable combination of organizing ability and sheer physical dexterity if she was to act as a proper crown to her husband.

Thus Gervase Markham's 'compleat woman' possessed skill in 'bakery, cookery, physic, banqueting stuff and distillation'. As to organization, the fact that the phrase 'the family' was so often applied to the household of the time, be it large or small, expresses the wide responsibilities of its effective ruler – the housewife. In 1631 in *The English Gentlewoman*, Richard Brathwaite wrote of 'the office of a Mistress' that 'winning Modesty' at all times should prevent its occupant from becoming an 'imperious Governess'. Instead, the mistress of a household should know 'when to put on a smooth brow, and to cherish industry with moderate bounty. Her discreet providence makes her family look with cheerful countenance ... The open field she makes her Gallery; her Labourers her living pictures.'[4] Modesty and submission might be persistently demanded – Elizabeth Walker was fond of quoting to her daughters another biblical precept: 'ye wives, be in subjection to your own husbands, even as Sarah obeyed Abraham, calling him Lord'[5] – but it was strength and executive ability – even perhaps a touch of the 'imperious Governess' – which were actually required in the 'compleat woman' if she happened to be a wife, as the great majority of women of this period were at one time or another during their lives.

To outsiders, the City wives with their rich costumes – grotesquely rich according to playwrights like Dekker who mocked them – affluent furnishings and groaning boards, were figures of fun. Even the old magnate James Houblon, larding his daughters with good advice, begged them to have a care not 'to puff up' their children with 'pride of apparel'.[6] It was a common-place to discuss the magnificence with which wealthy citizens adorned their homes, and at the same time to deride the social ambitions of their wives. Mocked as they might be, or lusted after (Pepys never failed to report a sighting of a pretty citizen's wife, including at church, if he had reason to suppose she might be available to his advances), the lives these women led ill accorded with the contemporary notion of the wife as modest silent help-mate. *Hic Mulier: Or, The Man-Woman*, in 1620, paid special atten-tion to 'the demy-Palaces of Burgers' which harboured vivacious painted wantons – 'these Apes of the City'. The citizens' wives, like all good women, were urged to bear in mind the following salutary quatrain:

Those Vertues that in women merit praise
Are sober shows without, chaste thoughts within,
True Faith and due obedience to their mate,
And of their children honest care to take.[7]

The fact was that strong independent characters were often concealed beneath the finery worn by the citizens' wives. What was more, this was in keeping with the true demands of such women's position, which entailed not only running their affluent household, but sometimes acting in virtual partnership with their husbands in business. Dekker, in *The Shoemaker's Holiday*, depicted Mrs Eyre, wife of the future Lord Mayor Simon Eyre, at work, bustling away amidst her husband's apprentices. The Custom of London gave to citizens' wives one third of their husband's estate on death, and also allotted to them a further one third if there were no children of the marriage; the last third was bestowed at the testator's wishes and so might also go to the widow. This meant that a merchant's wife never expected to be a mere cipher on his death (and as we shall see, this had an important influence on the remarriage of City widows). Nor did she behave as one in his lifetime. A traveller from the Continent noted about City wives: 'In all banquets and feasts they are shown the greatest honour; they are placed at the upper end of the table, where they are first served.' In mercantile society in cities elsewhere – nearly a million people at this period lived in towns other than London – in Bristol, for example, in 'the high and spacious Halls' of the Bristol merchants, wives were leading active lives in which submission, practically speaking, was the least of the qualities required.[8]

This was also true in the urban households lower down the social scale, those of the tradesmen and artisans where young (male) apprentices were taken. Here a wife, living above the shop, became her husband's active assistant, and effective partner; tales of wives beating apprentices were sufficiently common to prove that the weaker vessel could wield a strong arm on occasion, when she fancied she had the authority to do so. Young Valentine Pettit wrote a sad tale of Mrs Newman, the wife of the man to whom he was apprenticed, to his cousin Richard Oxinden. She was, he complained, 'a strange kind of woman' whose hold over her husband was so great that since his marriage he had terrorized his apprentices and would now 'beat them for any small occasion'.[9] There was clearly nothing very submissive about Mrs Newman.

Other tradesmen's wives deployed their energies more salubriously: borough records reveal them as energetic participants in their husbands' affairs, and in some minds they were rated their superiors: 'Your citizens' wives are like partridges, the hens are better than the cocks', was a contemporary comment.[10]

In the country the picture of industry – necessary industry – continued. Where rural practices were concerned, indeed, James Howell did not see why the country squires selling 'Calves and Runts' and their wives selling 'Cheese and Apples' should be held to be more 'gentle', that is refined, than the great merchant-adventurers of the town selling silks and satins, diamonds and pearls, with silver and gold. George Herbert's poem in memory of his mother gives a description of the life of the country clergyman's wife. The day began with some 'active kindling prayers' and a discreet toilette:

> ... as good women rightly use, she'd braid
> Her hair with simple art and sparing aid
> Of jewels ...

This was the prelude to a busy schedule:

> Then on her family forth she shone, and spent
> On kitchen, garden, house due management;
> To every thing its time and place disposed,
> And with her needlework the late day closed.
> Her life and household shared her constant plan,
> 'So many days for this' each task began.[11]

When a woman was married not to a clergyman but to a farmer her 'constant plan' would also include traditional and important responsibilities such as the garden and orchard and the poultry; many farmers' wives were also pig farmers. On the wife too fell the responsibility of training the servants, both male and female. (Dorothy Osborne's carefree shepherdesses might have to reckon with an irate farmer's wife, the reverse of modest in her carriage, if any of their charges strayed while they sang their ballads in the shade.)

John Banks, a Quaker farmer imprisoned for his religion at Carlisle in 1648, who described his separation from his wife as 'the greatest trial that ever I met with', specifically termed her 'a Meet-Help and a good Support to me' in his work; he worried how she would cope at harvest-time.[12] In fact it was not only the tasks close at home which fell to the woman: at harvest-time it was customary for all those capable to lend a hand, including the wives of husbandmen, who might generally tend the pigs and cows after their marriage, or work in the garden. Women could plough and sow; other specifically female tasks were 'weeding the corn' and shearing sheep. In his autobiography William Stout of Lancaster tells us that in the absence of his mother, his sister had to look after him as a child: 'our mother not only being fully employed in housewifery, but in dressing their corn for the market, and also in the fields, in hay and corn harvests, along with our father and the servants'.[13]

Dairy management was another traditional preserve of the farmer's wife, commemorated in Richard Brathwaite's picture of another busy woman like William Stout's mother:

> Oft have I seen her from the Dairy come
> Attended by her maids, and hasting home
> To entertain some guests of Quality.

The financial side of the farm's affairs was often undertaken by the wife; and it was frequently the wife on her own who performed the vital role of selling the farm's produce at the market. The fact that these activities were not without their attendant dangers is demonstrated by the awful story of Maud, the wife of another Quaker farmer, Thomas Collar of Woolavington.

Returning from the market at Bridgwater alone, Maud was struck and called 'ugly toad' by one Adrian Towes. Then he demanded her purse (presumably containing the farm's takings); finally he bullied her into kneeling and swearing on the Lord's blood that she was not a Quaker.[14]

The housewife, if she was literate, was not totally dependent on the traditional lore of domesticity handed down by word of mouth. There were some printed manuals (as there had been since the Middle Ages) and with the slow – the very slow – rise in female literacy, these increased. The desire to cash in on a famous name for commercial purposes being no modern phenomenon, these were generally launched with some fairly high-sounding credentials: *The Queen's Closet Opened*, for example, printed in 1655, attested to the universal lure of royalty even under Cromwell's Protectorate.[15] It offered 'Incomparable Secrets in Physick, Chirurgery, Preserving, Candying and Cookery as they were presented to the Queen [Henrietta Maria]. Never before Published. Transcribed from the true Copies of Her Majesties own Recipe books, by W.M., one of her late servants.' The author, while admitting that some might view 'with a kind of indignation' his action, as a servant who had been entrusted with 'so sacred a custody', in making these copies public, gave the classic defence that 'corrupt copies' of the same recipes were already circulating. He threw in for good measure the plea that any mistake should be overlooked, since he lived in the country and due to his age and infirmity had not been able to oversee the printing.

For all its boasted provenance *The Queen's Closet Opened* offers merely the conventional remedies of the time for the usual ills. Here is Dr Stephens' Water (a cordial frequently mentioned) and Dr Read's perfume against the plague – a fragrant mixture of red rose-water, treacle, cloves and angelica. Recipes for breaking the stone in the kidneys, for curing piles, for alleviating colic ('Take a turf of green grass and lay it to the Navel ...') jostle with purges, cordials to suppress Melancholy (borage and bugloss with juice of pippins) and other cordials for the heart. Some recommendations, like drinking a camomile infusion to induce sleep, still sound sensible to the modern ear; others, like swallowing the juice of sage or pimpernel to cure dumbness, must have needed a good deal of faith to make them work. However, 'The Lord Spencers Cherry Water' – a bottle of sack fortified by four pounds of crushed cherry-stones – certainly has a jolly sound, and one can well believe it might have cured fainting.

Elizabeth Talbot, Countess of Kent, author of *A Choice Manuall of Rare and Select Secrets in Physick and Chirurgery*, first printed after her death in 1651, was a daughter and co-heiress of the seventh Earl of Shrewsbury. In herself the Countess provided an interesting link with history: she was a granddaughter of that redoubtable bastion of Tudor womanhood, Bess of Hardwicke; her sister had been a god-daughter to Mary Queen of Scots, then a Shrewsbury captive; and both in childhood and later she herself was close to her unhappy cousin Lady Arbella Stuart. As a married woman, the Countess of Kent acted as a generous patron to Samuel Butler, but her outstanding role was as hostess and patron to the great Stuart jurist, John Selden.

A Choice Manuall was popular and ran through several editions.[16] Frequent remedies against the plague remind us that its outbreaks were not so much a dread as a reality in most people's lives: epidemics of varying severity occurred throughout the century, by no means confined to that notorious one of 1665. 'A Medicine for the Plague' begins well with 'Take a pint of Malmsie', before departing for the realms of spice and nutmeg. 'To break a Plague sore' involved the soberer process of roasting an onion and combining it with a white lily root. Another widespread scourge was the contagious disease known as 'The Itch'; for this a judicious mixture of unsalted butter and the juice of red sage, with additives of walnut and ginger, was recommended.

There is continuous mention of 'Melancholy' ('two spoonfuls of Sirrup of Gilliflowers … this will cheer the heart'), 'the Green Sickness' (from which the young were often considered to suffer), and 'fits of the Mother' (i.e. a form of hysterical convulsion to which all women were subject), not only in the Countess of Kent's manual but in other similar collections. These were the kind of sufferings, many of which would now be considered psychological in origin, which the mistress of a household would expect to combat with herbs, spices, wines and whatever else took her particular fancy.

In this connection 'The Countess of Kent's special Powder', otherwise known as 'Gascons powder', must have been a useful household requisite: a child of five troubled with much phlegm, a gentlewoman of forty troubled with 'crude and flatulous humours', a girl of about eighteen troubled with 'fits of the Mother', a young woman of twenty-four 'not without some suspicion of the Plague', were all cured by grains of this powder dissolved in assorted liquids. It was also said to be good against smallpox, measles, spotted or purple fever, 'good in swoonings and passions of the heart, arising from malignant vapours or old causes, as also in the Plague or Pestilent Fevers'. The Countess of Kent concluded with a sweeping recommendation worthy of her grandmother Bess: 'These and many other Experiments have I with good success tryed, and with Gods blessing recovered divers severall Patients.'[17]

Provision of her own necessities and medicines was only one part of the duty of the mistress of the household: the housewife in a financial position to do so must also act as 'An Over-seer for the poor'. 'She takes a Survey daily and duly of them,' wrote Richard Brathwaite, 'and, without any charge to the Hamlet, relieves them.' A good housewife, he concluded, would think 'that day wholy lost, wherein she doth not one good work at least'.[18]

That 'crown and glory' to her husband, Elizabeth Walker, was the daughter of a pharmacist in the City of London named Sadler, and was born in 1623 and married in 1650. Her husband in her biography did refer to the spiritual aspect of the marital partnership: let 'man and wife be meet helps to one another' in order to assist each other to reach Heaven. This was one refinement of the concept of the helpmate where Puritan thinking, with its stress on woman's spiritual capacity, was in advance of its time. However, Elizabeth Walker was aptly described by her husband as 'both Martha and Mary';[19] it was as Martha, with her conscientious housekeeping and her personally administered charities, that she exemplified the perfect wife of the time, whatever her religious persuasion.

True, it was as Mary that Mrs Walker began the day, at four o'clock in the morning, and sometimes as early as two or three, in order to obtain some hours of solitary meditation before the household was awake; in fact Mrs Walker was specially commended in the *Holy Life* for taking the trouble to light her own fire at that godly hour and not requiring some servant to do it for her! (The servants were first summoned at six for readings from the Bible, and prayers for the day-labourers came after breakfast.) After that Martha took over from Mary.

Indoors there was work with the needle, outdoors inspection of the dairy. Afternoons were spent visiting the sick, distributing salves and medicines. Mrs Walker would also visit women in childbirth, rising at any hour of the night, because of 'the commands of the Litany'. She was an excellent businesswoman, referred to jokingly by Dr Walker as 'my land-lady' because he allowed her £19 worth of rents to handle a year. And he took particular pride in his wife's skill at cookery; she was 'clerk of her little kitchen, if I may so speak', making her own pastry and cream cheeses.[20]

On the last wedding anniversary which they celebrated – honoured by the presence of 'three coronetted heads' – this prodigious caterer managed to envelop thirty-nine pies in one dish which she had made herself. Afterwards the fragments were used to feast the many poor families who thronged to the house, pretending to seek Dr Walker's advice, actually desiring Mrs Walker's food. At Christmas everyone was offered hospitality, rich and poor; people were even encouraged to bring their children, for whom there was a special table: 'Trouble not yourselves', she would say, 'I love to see this little fry.'[21]

Mrs Walker also concocted 'English wines' and ciders to give away to her friends as presents. One is relieved to discover that this latter-day saint, who as a minister's wife always wore black without a redeeming knot or ribbon of colour, reacted most humanly when all the guests' praise for the cider was directed towards her husband.

'His cider!', she would exclaim, according to Dr Walker half way 'betwixt jest and earnest', ''Tis my cider: I have all the pains and care, and he hath all the praise who never meddles with it.' But then on many counts Elizabeth Walker showed herself a woman of independent view. Dr Walker also tells us – 'however much it might lessen her in people's esteem' – that his wife was in the habit of observing that 'Blacks and Tawnys as well as Whites were descendants of the first Adam'.[22]

The household routine of Mary Rich, although on a far grander scale, particularly after she became Countess of Warwick, conformed to the same ideal. Here, like Mrs Elizabeth Walker, is Brathwaite's paragon of domestic energy. It is true that her autobiography was ostensibly written as a record of the 'providences' in her life after she had undergone a 'conversion' and embraced the stricter Puritan faith of her husband's family (charting spiritual progress in written form, what Isaac Ambrose called 'a Register of God's dealings', was a popular task with Puritan ladies).[23] However, so many of these 'providences' occurred within the household, such being the intimate pattern of her existence, that we have here a picture that is as much domestic as spiritual.

Even her avowedly spiritual writings have a charmingly domestic flavour, an appreciation of the small mercies of life in terms of the small beauties of the daily round: 'Upon walking in autumn among dead leaves', 'Upon seeing a silk worm spin', 'Upon seeing a hog lie under an acorn tree, and eat the acorns, but never look up from the ground to the tree from which they fell'. 'Upon a Hen of my Lady Essex Rich' described a chick which was hatched in the stillroom by her niece and afterwards 'this poor grateful creature' persisted in returning to the house to lay its eggs there (a lesson to those less thankful for benefits received). Fish, mowers in the fields, her pet dog, canary birds and linnets that learnt to sing like canaries, these were the kind of domestic sights seen at Leighs Priory, the Rich family property in Essex, which provoked edifying reflections from Mary.[24]

A typical day, on which Mary would rise at about six for two hours of solitary meditation, would include not only a lengthy ordering of her household with all its ramifications between breakfast and dinner, but also a visit to the sick servants, and another visit to the village girls' school. These activities were not purely gracious. On the contrary, the cure of the sick (as Mrs Walker had distributed salves) and the administration of medicines generally, were an important duty on a level with the relief of the poor; most of the remedies, of a herbal nature, being prepared at home in the stillroom.

As for education, Mary Warwick was in the habit of catechizing her maids daily and reading to them books of devotion, in addition to her diurnal visits to the village girls' school. The educative abilities of a mistress of a household – including those on a much smaller scale than Leighs Priory – were of enormous potential importance in an age when girls' schooling as such hardly existed since the disappearance of the Catholic convents in the previous century (the Leighs Priory neighbourhood being fortunate in their patrons). Obviously the Puritans, with their emphasis on Bible reading, had a particular incentive to increase the spiritual capacity of their dependants by teaching them to read: Mrs Walker had her maids read holy texts to her. But in general, as we shall see when we return to the subject of educational opportunities for women, any conscientious housewife would expect to exert some kind of good influence in this respect – that is, when she could read herself.

'Dost thou love me?', Elizabeth Walker would ask of her husband, smiling.

To which he would reply: 'Most dearly.'

'I know it abundantly,' she would answer, 'to my comfort; but I love to hear thee tell me so.'

On another occasion Dr Walker was telling Elizabeth why he loved her and began: 'First for conscience–'. She stopped him:

'I would have thee love me, not because thou must, but because thou *wilt*, not as a duty but delight. For,' she added, 'we are prone to reluctate against what is imposed, but to take pleasure in what we choose.'

'Our mutual compellation', wrote Dr Walker, 'was always "My dear", not spoken automatically nor as an empty compliment, but the sincere interpretation of the language of our hearts.'[25] This affectionate, even slightly flirtatious relationship between the Walkers, which emerges so beguilingly from the pages of the *Holy Life*, serves as a salutary reminder that the ground rules of seventeenth-century marriage, while they threw up a number of hard cases, did not preclude the formation of many very happy unions.

The intimacy which flourished in the 'sturdy oaken' matrimonial bedstead, destined to last 'one whole Century through' in Mary Evelyn's phrase in *Mundus Muliebris*, could be passionate and idyllic as well as fulfilling God's 'own holy and sacred ordinance'. (The importance of the marriage bed as a symbolic and enduring piece of furniture was attested by Henry Oxinden when he took the seventeen-year-old Kate Culling as his second wife, and had no bedstead of his own to share with her: he commissioned his cousin Eliza Dallison who lived in London to have a vast bed made, seven foot seven inches in breadth, six foot three inches long, with four posts at the corners one foot round. 'We would willingly have of the latest fashion,' he wrote, 'for this is all the beds we are like to make in our time.')[26] Marital sex, far from being frowned upon, was generally approved as leading to health and happiness in the husband; while the generally straightforward attitude of the time included the sensible notion that women too, once introduced to the pleasures of the marriage bed, could and would enjoy them.

'Dear Niece, Now that you know what's what, and the best and worst that man can do unto you, you will give me leave to wish you joy', wrote Lord Monmouth cheerfully to his niece Philadelphia Carey, now Lyttelton, shortly after her marriage. Philadelphia's sister was ill at Winchester: Lord Monmouth went on to suggest the same remedy for her: 'You may tell her that such an ingredient as you have had of late would do her more good than any physick she can take. But she is too good and too handsome to lack it long if she have a mind to it; and therefore she may thank herself if she continue to be ill. But you will be better to preach this doctrine to her than I, now that you have tried it yourself. Well, sweet niece, to leave raillery ..."[27]

Jane Sharp, the midwife, writing for popular consumption agreed with Lord Monmouth that the 'Green Sickness' which occurred in unmarried girls would be cured by the physical delights of marriage. What was more, this was an age when the possibility of the female orgasm was not only appreciated and encouraged, but also, in the rather muddled state of thinking on the subject of the procreative process, believed by some people to help it along. Jane Sharp, for example, writing quite frankly about the private parts of a woman's body such as 'a little bank called a mountain of pleasure near the well-spring', thought that a woman's imagination, when aroused, helped her to produce the seed. The French believed that the womb then opened to enable conception.[28]

The Puritan handbooks were equally forthright, seeing in marital sex part of the divine plan which helped to save the soul as well as keep the marriage together. As William Gouge wrote in *Of Domesticall Duties*: 'To deny this duty being justly required, is to deny a true debt and to give Satan a great advantage.' Milton, declaring that there was nothing inherently sinful about sex itself 'whatever hypocrites austerely talk', envisaged in *Paradise Lost* an Adam and Eve before the Fall who did not want for 'youthful dalliance as beseems Fair couple, linkt in happy Nuptial league'.[29]

There were prohibitions: excessive 'dalliance' even in marriage was to be avoided. Evelyn, in his advice to his son John on his wedding-night, particularly advised against the kind of 'intemperance' that would exhaust him (and might also create 'unfortunate expectations' in his bride ...). But then Evelyn also advised against making love on a full stomach, by day and in very hot or very cold weather: in short 'too frequent embraces dulls the sight, decays the memory, induces the gout ... and shortens life'.[30] The recommendation against sex in hot weather was general – in advice given in the almanacs the dog days of July and August were thought to be particularly hazardous. However, recent research into baptismal registers, while it does show a correlative drop in baptisms in May and June, has not yet pin-pointed the cause, which may have been simply due to the exhaustion of the harvest work. Even here the point was well taken, that 'if husband wont, another must'.[31] Although we must depend on guesswork, there is no reason to suppose that in a frank and earthy age these recommendations to sexual moderation in marriage were heeded by any who were not physically predisposed to it in the first place.

Married love is a more difficult subject to chronicle with certainty than the lack of it – if easier than married sex. Yet there are revealing vignettes such as that of Lady Oglander, the wife of Sir John Oglander, Deputy Governor of the Isle of Wight, who would rush eagerly out to meet her husband under the oaks on Matthew's Green when he returned to London from the Isle of Wight; merely to 'live lovingly' with his wife was Sir John Oglander's declared public ambition.[32] And true conjugal felicity can certainly be glimpsed obliquely through the conventional public tributes.

Sometimes it is the death of the beloved which provokes the revealing outburst, as when the Parliamentary lawyer Bulstrode Whitelocke wrote in his journal on 15 May 1649 (a time of extreme political tension for the new Commonwealth): 'This was the saddest day of all the days of my life hitherto; my brother William Willoughby brought me the direful news that my wife was dead.'[33] Anthony Ashley Cooper, later Earl of Shaftesbury, whose cool sense of intrigue enabled him to survive membership of Cromwell's Council of State into the high Whig politics of the next reign, made an advantageous marriage in February 1639 to Margaret, daughter of the Lord Keeper Coventry. His passionate encomium on her sudden death ten years later makes an extraordinary contrast with the taciturn jottings in his diary which precede it.[34]

'My wife, just as she was sitting down to supper, fell into an apoplectical convulsion fit: She recovered that fit after some time, and spoke and kissed me, and complained only in her head but fell again in a quarter of an hour, and then never came to speak again; but continued in fits and slumbers until next day. At noon she died.' Shaftesbury continued: 'She was a lovely beautiful fair woman, a religious devout Christian, of admirable wit and wisdom, beyond any I ever knew, yet the most sweet, affectionate and observant wife in the world. Chaste, without a suspicion of the most envious, to the highest assurance of her husband, of a most noble and bountiful mind, yet very provident in the least things, exceeding all in anything she undertook, housewifery, preserving, works with the needle, cookery, so that her wit and judgement were expressed in all things, free from any pride or forwardness. She was in discourse and counsel far beyond any woman.'

Ashley Cooper, who was now a childless widower, did not long remain so; but his entry for that day in April 1650 on which he made a second marriage – for sound political reasons – is once more extremely taciturn: 'I was married to Lady Frances Cecil, and removed my lodging to Mr Blakes by Exeter House.' This time the match seems to have remained one of pure political convenience, for when a few years later the new wife also died, there was no outburst and no eulogy.

Lady Essex Rich was that niece and ward of Mary Countess of Warwick who as a girl had kept the 'grateful hen'. She was married off by Mary, after due investigation of his moral suitability, to Daniel Finch, later second Earl of Nottingham. Lady Essex died not long after, leaving her husband with a single daughter. Finch wrote to the minister who had married them a distraught letter: 'for I have lost surely a better friend, a wife without her equal, one that I loved as myself, for she was willing even to die to wean me from this world ... that we might meet in a better, and live together eternally ... Henceforward I will not think she has gone from me, but that I am going to her ... no man can be so proud of what he has, as I am that I can say I once had the best woman in the world.'[35] Like Lord Shaftesbury, Finch married again shortly – to the heiress Anne Hatton – who presented him with an enormous family. But he called his eldest daughter by his second wife Essex – after she who had been 'the best woman in the world'.

Oliver Heywood, a Puritan minister, was even more explicit after the death of his first wife Elizabeth Augier, 'the mirror of patience and subjection in her relation, as a child, as a wife, and of tenderness and care as a sister, and as a mother'. He wrote: 'I want her at every turn, everywhere, and in every work. Methinks I am but half myself without her.'[36]

Letters too reveal affections beyond the normal conjugal respect which spouses were supposed to feel for each other.

On this evidence Brilliana Lady Harley, 'that noble Lady and Phoenix of Women', to whose heroic story we shall return, had enjoyed a married life abundant in tenderness at its inception. 'I pray you remember that I reckon the days you are away…', she wrote to Sir Robert Harley on 30 September 1625, when they had been married two years. Throughout his absences she expressed a constant wish to see him, culminating on 5 October 1627 with the cry: 'Believe me, I think I never missed you more than now I do, or else I have forgot what is past.'[37]

In 1642 Basil Lord Feilding, the Parliamentary commander, married as his third wife Elizabeth (Betty) Bourchier. The next year he succeeded to the title of his Royalist father, the Earl of Denbigh. It was no doubt an arranged match: despite his two previous marriages, the new Lord Denbigh was childless; Betty herself was a daughter and co-heiress of Henry Bourchier, fifth Earl of Bath. Nevertheless her letters breathe with her desire for him: 'My dear heart, my dear life, my sweet joy…', she begins, ending with 'PS A hundred, thousand kisses I give thee, as I might be so happy as this paper. I long much to see you.' Sometimes Betty becomes petulant: surely he doesn't really love her, otherwise he would come back and see her? At other times she is more resigned. In 1644 she writes: 'Dear Joy…I should have been glad to have been with you on the 8th July, because it is our wedding-day' but instead she will eat three cherry pies and drink her husband's health with his niece Su Hamilton. (For Lord Denbigh's own delectation Betty dispatched presents of cakes and candied flowers, borage and marigolds.) It is all summed up by another ecstatic postscript: 'Dear! how thy Betty loves thee!'[38]

It is good to be able to record that the loving Betty, unlike so many wives in the seventeenth century, lived to enjoy nearly thirty years of married life (although, like all the Earl of Denbigh's other wives, she was childless).

Lastly, in the private memoir written by Ann, wife of Sir Richard Fanshawe, can be found in a humbler prose form the kind of lyrical sentiments about love and separation which Richard Lovelace, the admired Cavalier poet of his generation, poured into his volume of 1649, *Lucasta:*

> ... Though seas and land betwixt us both,
> Our faith and troth
> Like separated souls
> All time and space controls:
> Above the highest sphere we meet
> Unseen, unknown, and greet as Angels greet.[39]

Ann, daughter of Sir John Harrison of Hertfordshire, described herself as being 'that which we graver people call a hoyting girl' (i.e. a hoyden) when she married Richard Fanshawe in 1644, he being a bachelor of thirty-five, and she a mere seventeen years old. She wrote the memoir after his death, in 1665, to be circulated in the family, and for the special attention of her only surviving son, so that he might understand the kind of man his father had been – and the kind of relationship of perfect trust which existed between them.[40] Fanshawe had been a man 'so reserved that he never showed the thought of his heart in the greatest sense, but to myself only', wrote his wife, but 'this I thank God with all my soul for, that he never discovered his trouble to me but went from me with perfect cheerfulness and content, nor revealed he his joys and hopes, but would say that they were doubled by putting them in my breast'.

Richard Fanshawe was a highly educated man, with a deep love of reading, especially history and poetry; he would even go for a walk with a book in his hand, generally poetry. He was a minor poet himself, a translator of Horace, and of Camoens's *The*

Lusiads from the Portuguese. Indeed his career, as a courtier-politician and diplomat in the Stuart cause, through good times and bad, fully justified his wife's description of it after his death as 'nearly thirty years suffering by land and sea, and the hazard of our lives over and over…' There were also 'seven years of imprisonment' as Lady Fanshawe phrased it: for Richard Fanshawe was captured after the fatal Battle of Worcester in 1651, which ended the cause of Charles II in England, and imprisoned at Whitehall. Although he was released on bail in November, it was not until 1658 that he was properly free once more and permitted to go abroad.

When the Fanshawes were married at Oxford in 1644, where the court then was, Richard had just been created Secretary for War to the Prince of Wales (the future Charles II, then a boy of fourteen); King Charles I hoped to use his son's position as a titular leader in order to pacify his squabbling rival commanders in the West. Clearly fierce love existed between the Fanshawes from the first, despite the seventeen-year gap in their ages and the allegedly austere nature of Richard. The first day they were parted after their marriage – Richard Fanshawe had to go to Bristol on the King's business – the 'reserved' husband was 'extremely afflicted even to tears, though passion was against his nature'. When he was able to send for Ann from Oxford, the letter of summons made her feel so faint with joy that she 'went immediately to walk, or at least to sit, in the air (being very weak) in the gardens of St John's College'.[41]

At Bristol, after Richard Fanshawe had joyfully hugged his young wife, he showed his trust in her practical sense by entrusting her with his store of gold. He told her: 'I know that thou that keeps my heart so well will keep my fortune, which from this time I will ever put into thy hands as God shall bless me with increase.' After this, Ann Fanshawe wrote, 'I thought myself a queen, and my husband so glorious a crown that I more valued myself to be called by his name than born a princess.'[42]

Equally clearly, it took a little time before the 'hoyting girl' realized the limits of the position of such a queenly wife, who could be trusted with her husband's fortune, but not his State secrets. Lady Fanshawe tells the story of how her kinswoman at the court – the Countess Rivers, an older woman – tacitly convinced her that in these troubled times it had become fashionable for women such as the beautiful Lady Isabella Thynne to display deep interest in matters of State and that to do so would make her even more beloved by her husband – 'if that had been possible' adds Lady Fanshawe quickly.[43] Impressed by this reasoning, the gullible girl proceeded to question her husband about his confidential business as Secretary for War, and in particular about the contents of a packet which had recently arrived from the Queen in France; all this was with a view to passing on the information to Countess Rivers.

So: 'When my husband returned from Council, after welcoming him home, as his custom ever was, he went with his handful of papers into his study for an hour or more. I followed him. He turning hastily said: "What wouldst thou have, my life?"' Ann Fanshawe then told him that she guessed he had the recent packet from the Queen in his hand and would like to know what was in it.

'He smiling replied, "My love, I will immediately come to thee. Pray thee go, for I am very busy." When he came out of his closet, I revived my suit. He kissed me and talked of other things.' At supper Ann declined to eat, although Richard carried on discoursing as usual, 'and drunk often to me, which was his custom'. Then it was time to withdraw. 'Going to bed, I asked again, and said I could not believe he loved me if he refused to tell me all he knew, but he answered nothing, but stopped my mouth with kisses, so we went to bed. I cried and he went to sleep … next morning very early, as his custom was, he called to rise, but begun to discourse with me first, to which I made no reply. He rose, came on the other side of the bed and kissed me, and drew the curtain softly and went to court.'

When Richard returned that night for dinner, Ann took his hand and accused him of not caring about seeing her so upset. 'To which he, taking me in his arms, answered, "My dearest soul, nothing upon earth can afflict me like that; and when you asked me my business, it was wholly out of my power to satisfy thee ... the trust I am in may not be revealed.'" He then assured her that in everything else 'my life and fortune shall be thine, and every thought of my heart'.

Richard Fanshawe kept his word, although some of the turns of fortune which he offered his wife might have broken the spirit of a lesser woman. In Galway they found themselves in a plague-ridden town, having narrowly escaped seizure in Cork at the time of Cromwell's campaign, as the Irish, 'stripped and wounded', were with 'lamentable shrieks' turned out of the town. On their subsequent sea journey to Spain at the request of Charles II, Ann Fanshawe, as a woman, was in danger of being taken as a slave by a Turkish man-of-war. While the master of their ship was parleying with the Turks, trying to convince them of his innocence, Ann was locked in her cabin. She stole out by bribing the cabin boy to let her have his clothes: 'I crept up softly and stood upon the deck by my husband's side as free from sickness and fear as, I confess, from discretion; but it was the effect of that passion I could never master.' When the danger had passed and Sir Richard realized who it was beside him, 'looking upon me he blessed himself and snatched me up in his arms, saying "Good God, that love can make this change!" And though he seemingly chid me, he would laugh at it as often as he remembered that voyage.'[44]

Leaving Spain for France, they were very nearly shipwrecked in the Bay of Biscay in a violent storm which lasted for two days and three nights, and ripped both sails and mast from the ship, so that crew and passengers thought all hope was lost. Afterwards, at Nantes, they had some white wine, butter, milk, walnuts and eggs, and 'some very bad cheese'. But, commented Ann: 'I am sure until that hour I never knew such pleasure in eating, between which we a thousand times repeated what we had spoke when every word seemed our last. We praised God; I wept, your father lifting then up his hands admired so great a salvation. Then we often kissed each other, as if yet we feared death ...'[45]

Richard Fanshawe had been made a baronet in 1650; after the Restoration he was made a Privy Councillor and appointed Ambassador first to Portugal and then to Spain (where he died, although his body was finally reburied in Ware Church near his home in Hertfordshire). Diplomacy apart, he enjoyed the role of ambassador, having a great taste for hospitality, 'and would often say it was wholly essential for the constitution of England. He loved and kept order with the greatest decency possible.' Here once more Ann Fanshawe was the perfect helpmate and house-keeper, as we can appreciate, reading between the lines of her own modest disclaimer: 'though he would say I managed the domestics wholly, yet I ever governed them and myself by his commands, in the managing of which I thank God I found his approbation and content'.[46]

When she tried to sum up her married life for her son, Lady Fanshawe wrote: 'Now you will expect I should say something that may remain of us jointly, which I will do, though it makes my eyes gush out with tears, and cuts me to the soul, to remember and in part express the joys I was blessed with in him.

'Glory to God we never had but one mind throughout our lives, our souls were wrapped up in each other, our aims and designs one, our loves one, and our resentments one. We so studied one the other that we knew each other's mind by our looks; what ever was real happiness, God gave it me in him ...'[47]

Fourteen years after her husband's death, when 'what ever was real happiness' had ended, Ann Lady Fanshawe was laid beside him, at the age of fifty-five, in the family grave at Ware. So for them both at last those lines which Richard Fanshawe had written half a century ago came true:

> White peace (the beautifullest of things)
> Seems here her everlasting rest
> To fix, and spreads her downy wings
> Over the Nest.[48]

CHAPTER FOUR

The Pain and the Peril

'My God and my Lord, my defender and protector,
receive I most humbly beseech thee my acknowledge-
ments of thy mercy, and my thanksgivings for my safe
deliverance from the pain and the peril of Childbirth ...'

PRAYER OF ELIZABETH VISCOUNTESS MORDAUNT
AFTER THE BIRTH OF HER SON JOHN, 1659

If we try to envisage the appearance of the women of the seventeenth century in relation to our own, we should allow of
course for the evil effects of diseases now vanished such as
smallpox, or dental decay in an age before competent dentistry.
Both of these depredations, taken for granted at the time, might
come as a shock to the curious time-traveller. But the fact that
most of the leading female characters of the seventeenth century
were in a state of virtually perpetual pregnancy would probably
come as a far greater surprise.

Let us take the reigning goddesses of the courts of Charles I,
Charles II and James II. Henrietta Maria, the exquisite sloe-eyed
pearly Queen of Van Dyck's portraits and the court masques of
Inigo Jones, was in fact pregnant almost without intermission
from the autumn of 1628 until January 1639, when she bore her
seventh child Katherine. After that, absence from the King's side
in wartime accounted for a gap, but a last child Henrietta-Anne
was born in 1644. Barbara Duchess of Cleveland, tempestuous
mistress of Charles II, and Lely's voluptuous beauty, produced
five children in as many years during the very height of her ascen-
dancy over the King's affections (as well as a sixth somewhat
later, about whose paternity there was undignified dispute). Mary

of Modena, second wife of James II, gave birth as Duchess of York to four children in four years between 1675 and 1678 and another in 1682. None of these survived. James ascended the throne in 1685. It was the birth of a son in 1688, after what was considered to be (by James's supporters) an alarmingly long gap, which precipitated the Protestant Revolution.

As the great ladies fructified, so did their humbler sisters. There too we should retain a floating image of motherhood. Once the blessed knot had been tied, a married woman was expected to shoulder forthwith that special burden of motherhood bequeathed to her by Grandmother Eve. It did not need the incentive of a royal succession (or a king's favour); the desire for children in marriage, as many children as possible, to be born as quickly as possible, was universal. Puritan doctrines emphasized the importance of God's ordinance to increase and multiply and cover the earth (which had the beneficial effect of increasing the number of the Elect).[1] At the other extreme, the Catholic Church had reaffirmed the teaching of St Thomas Aquinas, that the whole end of sex was procreation, at the Council of Trent in the previous century.

Most married couples, however, scarcely needed a scriptural or doctrinal backing to carry out such natural activity. Thus 'big-bellied' or 'great-bellied' women were considered to be the norm, the happy norm; indeed the very use of such a straightforward term as 'great-bellied' (the common phraseology of the time, being neither vulgar nor jocular) indicates the way in which perpetual gravidity was taken for granted during the long child-bearing years of a married female. Pregnant, 'she seems to me, Diana in her crescent majesty', wrote Nicholas Hookes, in *Amanda* in 1653, describing the various aspects of his loved one's beauty.[2]

Most of the admirable wives referred to in the last chapter spent their adult life, in addition to their other duties, bearing, rearing and – all too often – burying children, in a great cycle of birth and life, birth and death, but at any rate birth and birth and birth, which meant that they were generally either crescent or descendent.

Of Mrs Elizabeth Walker for example, her husband wrote that 'her posterity cannot choose but prosper'; he might have added – those of them that survived. In the course of her energetic and charitable life Mrs Walker gave birth to eleven children, and there were abortive or 'untimely' births in addition. Of these eleven, explained Dr Walker, 'I say nothing of the eight lost but only the last three.' These were all daughters. Little Mary died when she was six, but even at that tender age was established as a passionate reader, spending an hour or two every night at her books by candlelight; young Elizabeth died at the age of sixteen (the sins to which she used to confess were the sympathetic adolescent ones of lying in bed too long on Sundays and 'slubbering' over her duties). Mrs Walker's last daughter died in childbirth, although the baby – Johnny – for whom she gave her life, survived. To this beloved grandson, Mrs Walker in old age was wont to proffer a good deal of sage advice. 'Dear Johnny', she would write, 'let not the length [of this letter] be tedious unto thee ...' – twenty pages follow – but then we must remember that Johnny was the only 'posterity' left to her after eleven births, she who was used to declare that children were 'the nurseries of families, the church and the nation'.[5]

The background to the many dangerous adventures endured by Ann Lady Fanshawe was one of virtually unceasing pregnancy, child-nursing – and child-burying.[4] Her first son Harrison was born in February 1645 and died in March. The next year, when the Fanshawes had arrived in Jersey, in retreat from England with the Prince of Wales, was born Ann (the first of two daughters who bore their mother's name); she died when she was nine. A son (the first of two to be christened Henry) was born the year after, and died at the age of two. In 1648 – by which time Ann Fanshawe had been married four years – was born the first of three babies to be christened Richard; he died at the age of eleven. In 1650, while she was in Madrid on her husband's mission seeking aid, Lady Fanshawe gave birth to the first of her three daughters who would be called Elizabeth; the baby, whom Ann Fanshawe was carrying at the time of their perilous Irish experiences, died immediately. (It was also shortly after this that the Fanshawes were virtually shipwrecked on their way to Nantes.) The second Elizabeth was born the next year; she died at the age of five.

It was during the years of Richard Fanshawe's nominal captivity in England that Katherine, Margaret and Ann were born, all of whom survived; this was surely not unconnected with the fact that during these pregnancies Lady Fanshawe did not travel abroad. However, a fourth daughter Mary, who was born in 1656, died in 1660, and a son Henry, born in 1657, died in 1658. After the Restoration, when the Fanshawes' life was equally nomadic, if far more gloriously so, three more children were born. Elizabeth, born in 1662, survived, but the second Richard, born in 1663, died at birth; it was not until August 1665 that the third Richard Fanshawe, that surviving son for whom Ann wrote her memoir of her husband, was born in Madrid. The following June, when his son and heir was not yet a year old, Sir Richard Fanshawe himself died; among other problems faced by his widow in a foreign land was the task of conveying very young children homeward.

Not only Lady Fanshawe but very many of the married women whose deeds of heroism during the Civil War we shall consider, were struggling at the same time with the additional burden of repeated pregnancies. These include the wives of the Levellers – Mary Overton and Elizabeth Lilburne – whose sufferings were similar in kind to those of Mary Lady Verney or the Yorkshire heroine, Lady Cholmley, or her sister-in-law Dame Isabella Twysden, or Lucy Hutchinson, wife of the Roundhead Governor of Nottingham Castle, but whose privations through poverty and imprisonment were even worse.

It was the 'barren Hannah or childless Elizabeth', in Samuel Hieron's phrase, who bewailed her fate. Some real connection was seen between child-bearing and grace: for what was woman's best chance to redeem herself from the sin of Eve and restore herself to honour but by fulfilling this natural female role? This philosophy had the backing of the New Testament: 'Adam was not deceived, but the woman being deceived was in the transgression. Notwithstanding she shall be saved in child-bearing.'[5]

Conversely, infertility might come to be equated with sin. Thus Samuel Hieron's prayer for the barren woman began with an acknowledgement of the sinfulness which had brought the petitioner to such a state ('It is just, I confess, with thee, to punish my barrenness in grace, and my fruitlessness in holy things, with this want of outward increase'), before proceeding to the heartfelt plea: 'let me be as the fruitfall Vine on the walls of my husbands house, and let (at the least) one Olive plant spring out from me, to stand about this table ...'[6]

In 1644 Anne Murray was jilted by her lover Thomas Howard for the sake of a much richer bride, whom the unfaithful lover married 'privately' without letting Anne know. When the news leaked out, Anne's indignant maid Miriam lifted up her hands and cursed the new wife: 'Give her, O Lord, dry breasts and a miscarrying womb.' In her memoirs, Anne tells us that she reproved Miriam. However, she adds: 'But it seems the Lord thought fit to grant her [Miriam's] request, for that lady miscarried several children before she brought one to the full term, and that one died presently after it was born; which may be a lesson to teach people to govern their wishes ...'[7]

Under the circumstances every manual and every almanac offered remedies for infertility, many of them allegedly with a long history of success; for as William Sermon wrote in *The Ladies Companion, or The English Midwife* of 1671: 'the Ancients (not being ignorant of what this Sex principally desire) have left several ways for the accomplishment of the same'. Sermon's recommendations 'to make Women fruitfull' included doses of white ginger taken in a powdered form, and more imaginatively, sitting over a bath in which skeins of raw yarn had been boiled in the water and then mixed with ashes. Otherwise the infertile wife might bathe herself in water in which 'Ale-hoof, oaten and pease straw have been boiled together – then let her dry herself, and presently let her Husband do his best endeavour.'[8]

It is easy to be cynical and suggest that of all these remedies, only the advice to the husband was likely to be remotely helpful; the number and extent of such cures advocated on every side bear witness to the passionate wishes of every wife to fulfil this other part of her bounden duty. Sir John Brownlow of Belton believed in the drinking of mares' milk every morning in March and April. Rules suggested to Samuel Pepys (anxious that his wife should conceive) ranged from the drinking of sage juice – popular remedy of the time – and the 'wearing of cool Holland drawers' to the propping up of the married bed at a slant or even better 'to lie with our heads where our heels do'.[9] In spite of this, Mrs Pepys never did bear any children.

It was hardly surprising that Margaret Duchess of Newcastle, whose husband had children by his first marriage, consulted the celebrated physician Sir Theodore Mayerne when she failed to conceive after two years. His advice was sensible: 'Be in good health and then you may till your ground, otherwise it will be time lost if you enter that race frowningly.' But Margaret did not conceive. As a result she came to write with considerable acerbity about her fertile sisters – women like 'Lady S.M.' who had only been married for four weeks, but knowing herself to be with child was already proudly 'rasping wind out of her stomache … making Sickly faces … and bearing out her Body, drawing her Neck downward, and standing in a weak and faint Posture as great bellied Wives do …'[10]

Margaret Newcastle poured further contempt on the great fuss which was made about the business of childbirth itself: the making and buying of fine and costly childbed linen (although one should perhaps point out that the heiress Lady Anne Clifford used her husband's three-year-old shirts as 'clouts'). Then there was the fearful fuss over the baby, including an expensive christening – the money, she suggested, would be better spent on the child's education – swaddling clothes, baby mantles, cradles, baskets and so forth.[11] In Margaret Newcastle's general scorn for women who prided themselves on their 'great bellies', one can detect the jealous voice of one who would never be able to form the centrepiece of such a celebration herself.

The constant emphasis on the virtuous work of bearing

children – in which the mothers, as well as the fathers, preachers and advisers all concurred – casts the whole subject of contraception within marriage (never wholly clear of the shadows in any age) into a particular obscurity. The pathetic case of Mistress Augier, mother of Elizabeth Heywood, provides an extreme example of how a large family was regarded as a mark of God's favour. In 1642 Mistress Augier had been suffering from cancer of the breast for two years, enduring pangs 'so painful that she often said she would be content to have her breast ripped open for a little ease'. Under the circumstances it might seem fortunate rather than the reverse that there had been a long gap in her child-bearing; however, her husband, a Puritan minister, did not view the situation in that light. When Mistress Augier conceived once more, her husband attributed it to divine intervention. She was delivered of her child a month early, with a very long hard labour, in the course of which the midwife pronounced – correctly – that there was no hope of saving the mother's life. Mistress Augier died in terrible agonies. 'God gave her conception after almost eight years' respite,' wrote her husband after her death, 'having often put it into my heart to pray for the enlarging of my family.' He went on: 'Yet after her conception her weakness and weariness increased.'[12]

Elizabeth (Betty) Viscountess Mordaunt, who kept 'a Private Diarie', probably at the request of her spiritual adviser, also referred constantly within it to 'the Great Blessing of many Children'.[13] It was a blessing she herself certainly enjoyed, giving birth to seven sons and four daughters in under twenty years. It was, however, a tumultuous period, not only in the history of England but in her own life story and that of her husband, in which her repeated pregnancies can only have been an additional burden.

Betty Mordaunt was the only daughter and heiress of Thomas Carey, a son of the Earl of Monmouth. Besides that she was a beauty of whom it was said as a young girl:

> Betty Carey's lips and eyes
> Make all hearts their sacrifice.

John Mordaunt was a staunch support of Charles I and Charles II in turn. Clarendon paid Betty this tribute: quite apart from her physical charms, she was 'of a very loyal spirit and notable vivacity of wit and humour', sharing her husband's 'honourable dedication' to the Stuart cause.[14] Betty needed all her wit and loyalty when John Mordaunt was among three men condemned to death by the High Court of Justice in the spring of 1658, for conspiring against Oliver Cromwell in favour of Charles II. Betty was pregnant with her second child at the time, but behaved with great courage and enterprise throughout the trial; not only was she present in court, but also tried – vainly as it turned out – to bribe the members of the Court of Justice. It was however Betty who managed to get a note to her husband that while it was useless to question the court's jurisdiction (the normal Royalist reaction) the damning evidence against him was in fact comparatively slight.

For all this, Mordaunt was condemned to death. Now Betty Mordaunt paid a personal visit to the ageing Protector to plead with him for her husband's life; she remarked afterwards that the Protector 'played the gallant so well' that she believed he would have been as good as his word, and 'waited upon her the next morning' had she encouraged him. Whether Betty's pretty face, unaffected by pregnancy, and legendary lips and eyes ensnared the ageing Protector (who, contrary to the report of history, was never averse to an encounter with a pretty woman),[15] at all events John Mordaunt was the only conspirator who was reprieved. He survived to continue his intrigues on behalf of the King, being created Viscount Mordaunt of Avalon in 1659.

On her husband's tombstone, which listed his deeds of daring on behalf of the two Stuart monarchs, a gracious allusion was made to his wife: *lectissima Heroina Elizabeth Carey*. The private diary of this most excellent heroine, amid various ecstatic outpourings of a religious nature, chronicles a series of births which alone might justify the title. Betty Mordaunt wrote a prayer of thanksgiving after the birth of her son John in 1659 (the baby she had been bearing at the time her husband was condemned to death) 'for my safe deliverance from the pain and the peril of

Childbirth'. And for her daughter 'Cory', born on 29 July 1661, she recorded her gratitude for 'the blessing of a live and perfect child'. But when she miscarried twins in 1674, on her birthday, she attributed this grave loss to her own spiritual transgressions. Pregnant once more at the time of her husband's death, Betty prayed passionately: 'preserve the child within me, the time it has to stay, from every ill accident... bless my child with perfect shapes'. Little George was born safely in January 1676: Betty called upon 'my dearest Lord' [God] to be his father, 'he that was born without father, brought into the world by an afflicted mother'.[16]

It is obviously highly unlikely that women of this calibre or families like the Walkers and the Fanshawes practised any form of limitation whatsoever, given the rapid pattern of births. But was no attempt ever made to avoid the consequences of unlimited married sex, if only for the sake of the mother, condemned to what Betty Mordaunt aptly described as 'the pain and the peril' of childbirth? Or for that matter for the sake of the father and breadwinner, whose economic burden, when his numerous progeny actually survived infancy, might be well nigh intolerable during the years of their upbringing?

The subject of contraception within marriage at this date is complicated by the fact that the most effective form known (until the invention of the Pill in the present day), the sheath or condom, was not introduced to England generally until the eighteenth century. Its original purpose was prophylactic: the good news arrived in English aristocratic circles as early as the 1680s via France (where Madame de Sévigné for example wrote in praise of this hygienic measure in 1671). But Pepys, whose promiscuous life with the unofficial whores of Westminster Hall would have benefited from such a form of protection, was ignorant of it: instead he spent some anxious time calculating whether he could have been responsible for one particular pregnancy.[17]

At the same time herbal medicines which might either prevent or cure – the line between a contraceptive and an abortifacient being not always an easy one to draw – were, as they had always been, part of the folkloric knowledge of the times. Swallowing a hot mixture of spices was advocated for both contraception or abortion, as was the juice of the herb savin; hence its nickname Cover Shame – it being a 'notorious Restorative of slender shapes and tender reputations', as a pamphlet described it at the end of the seventeenth century.[18] Marjoram, thyme, parsley, lavender and 'brake' (bracken) were all proposed with the general object in view of preventing birth. Nicholas Culpepper's edition of the *College of Physicians' Directory* suggested that honeysuckle was able to 'procure barrenness, and hinder conception'. John Swan's almanacs also suggested that the juice of honeysuckle, drunk continuously by a man for thirty-seven days, would make him so that he could 'never beget any more children'. In Defoe's *Conjugal Lewdness*, early in the next century, there was advice concerning powders 'in Warm Ale'; after taking these 'she shall be out of danger'.[19]

Some of the advice on the subject might be surreptitious. It did not take much wit to appreciate that those herbs described as best avoided to prevent miscarriage, would, if administered, have exactly the opposite effect. (Women were warned, for example, that proximity to sowbread would cause abortion.) Similarly, herbs to be carefully avoided by the barren – such as rue – could be enthusiastically swallowed by those who did not wish to conceive. Violent movements during intercourse were said to inhibit conception; these same movements, if indulged, might ward off the danger.

Many of the herbal remedies were based on the sensible if slightly drastic premise that the dampening of masculine desire prevented the problem from arising in the first place: rue once again was said by the female astrologer Sara Jinner to make a man no better than a eunuch. One emetic mixture proposed consisted of radish root, agarick, and saram, boiled in barley water, to be drunk when cool.[20] Castor oil was suggested for the same purpose, as was lettuce (the purgative effects of the one and the soporific effects of the other must certainly have given them a high rate of success in extinguishing ardour).

Other measures recommended, of varying degrees of unpleasantness to the modern ear, included pessaries for the female –

rue featured here again, or ground-up bitter almonds – and a uterine clyster (what would now be called a douche) employing such herbs as camphor, castor oil and rue. The male organ might be anointed with salves of a vaguely anaesthetic nature or bathed in cold liquids, vinegar, or the juice of nightshade or henbane. For the desperate, there was always blood-letting. According to the medical theories of the time it was the special heat of the blood which was responsible for producing that superior male seed which was considered to be 'the generative faculty'. A woman was generally believed to have 'seed' too, the ovaries being the equivalent of the testicles, but just as 'her heat is lesser and weaker than his', so her 'seed' was thought to be cold and watery, in short far less important in the procreative process. (The biological role of the female in procreation was only properly understood after the invention of the microscope revealed the existence of the female 'egg' as opposed to 'seed'.)[21]

The existence of this ancient twilight world of folkloric preventives demonstrates that both contraception and abortion were underground preoccupations of the seventeenth century – at least where sexual intercourse outside marriage was concerned (not a very surprising conclusion in view of the social consequences to both parties if illicit love resulted in pregnancy). The question of whether the same preventives were taken within marriage is far more difficult to establish; clearly the same medicines were available to be swallowed, applied, or otherwise employed, by the married as by the single. The whole subject of contraception within marriage is ignored by contemporaries, even by those whose revelations are otherwise fairly intimate. The diaries of the Puritan Ralph Josselin, as their editor has remarked, leave us to guesswork on this subject.[22] For instance he records his wife's miscarriages and these do tend to coincide almost exactly with the first moment when she could have known she was pregnant (and thus used an abortifacient), but since this early stage of pregnancy would also be the likeliest time for a spontaneous miscarriage, the mystery remains unsolved.

In any case many of the above remedies have something of an air of desperation about them; even if employed they would not

have affected overmuch the child-bearing capacity of a healthy
and fertile woman having regular sexual intercourse. It seems far
more likely that those married couples who did for any reason
wish to limit their families practised coitus interruptus, a method
of birth control which, as it has been observed, it is possible for
each generation to rediscover for itself.[23] Once again, first-hand
information about the subject is hard to come by.

It has recently been suggested, albeit with caution, that the use
of this type of family limitation was gradually rising among the
middle classes as the century progressed. There are certain significant statistics: the fertility among women over thirty generally,
and the age at which women bore their last child in particular, fell
in the second half of the seventeenth century. Other researches
point to a significant gap between the birth of the penultimate
and the ultimate child.[24]

Mary Rich, Countess of Warwick provides one of the few
direct references to family limitation in her autobiography
(although she does not state the method used). The giddy young
girl who got married at fifteen to a younger son, against her
father's wishes, did not immediately ripen into the benevolent
Puritan matron at the head of her household; as has been mentioned, a spiritual conversion had to intervene. Immediately after
her marriage Mary Rich gave birth to two children in rapid succession: Elizabeth, who died as a baby, victim of two careless
nursemaids who 'tossed' her between them, and a son called
Charles after his father. She was not yet seventeen.

Twenty years later, young Charles Rich died at the age of
twenty-one. Not only was his father, now Earl of Warwick, left
without a direct heir, but the cousin who would inherit the title
by default was considered by Mary to be of a highly unsuitable
character. We have Mary's own account of the stricken couple's
passionate wish to start a new family. Although she was still only
thirty-seven, these hopes were not fulfilled, leaving Mary prey to
further remorse that she had deliberately refrained from having
further children in her youth. She gives two reasons for this
resolve: first, at the age of seventeen, one of the youthful beauties
of the court of Charles I, she feared to ruin her figure 'if she

childed so thick'; secondly, Charles Rich, as a younger son, had worried that if he had 'many to provide for, they must be poor'.[25] Certainty is impossible; but if abstinence in a young couple, who had married for that troublesome emotion, love, is ruled out, one may suppose that coitus interruptus was the method by which Mary preserved her lissom figure, and Charles Rich his modest fortune – with ultimately such disastrous results.

In 1622 a woman of twenty-six expecting her first baby, called Elizabeth Josceline, wrote how she dreaded the painfulness of 'that kind of death' during childbirth. Born Elizabeth Brooke of Norton in Cheshire, she had been brought up by her grandfather William Chaderton, Bishop of Lincoln, a friend of Coke and Lord Burghley. In 1622 she had already been married for six years. *The Mothers Legacy to her Unborn Child* was an attempt to overcome that justifiable dread which possessed so many women of the time – how would the child fare if the mother did not survive the ordeal? Elizabeth Josceline carefully garnered all the advice she would proffer her child in advance, to obviate that 'loss my little one should have, in wanting me'. It proved a popular subject: by 1625 *The Mothers Legacy* had gone through three editions, and it was reprinted unaltered in 1684.[26]

Naturally the child would have to be put out to nurse, but despite its tender age, this was to be in a house where there was no swearing or speaking 'scurrilous words' (Elizabeth Josceline wrote: 'I know I may be thought too scrupulous in this'). Later the servants were to address the child by its Christian name, without the prefix 'Master' or 'Miss', to teach it proper respect. Throughout the book, Elizabeth Josceline modestly reminded herself that she was only writing for 'a child's judgement', although at the same time she begged her 'truly loving and most dearly loved husband Taurell Josceline', to whom the book was dedicated, not to pardon its faults through fondness but to correct them.

Reading *The Mothers Legacy* today, in manuscript, still has the power to touch one, for nine days after the birth of her child

Elizabeth Josceline did undergo just 'that kind of death' she had feared. And she was wrapped in that very winding-sheet which she had already secretly bought for herself.[27] At least in bequeathing to posterity a book, she had succeeded in her declared ambition to do something more for her child than 'only to bring it forth'.

None at this time doubted that childbirth itself, whatever the desirability of founding a family, was both a painful and a dangerous ordeal. 'These are doubtless the greatest of all pains the Women naturally undergo upon Earth', wrote the midwife Jane Sharp. Margaret Duchess of Newcastle, herself of course barren, wrote that a husband who had heirs by his first wife should not complain if his second did not conceive children since 'she hazards her life by Bringing them [children] into the world'.[28]† Nor was Elizabeth Josceline alone in her apprehensions. Anne Harcourt, in her diary, confessed to her 'exorbitant fear' of labour, 'notwithstanding the former experiences of God's goodness in helping me at like times'. The jilted Anne Murray, finding happiness at last in marriage with Sir James Halkett, gave birth for the first time at the age of thirty-four. She drew up a *Mother's Instructions* before the birth of that child, and of each subsequent arrival, although in fact she lived safely on, dying in 1699 at the age of seventy-seven.[29]

Margaret Blagge, the lovely yet earnest Maid of Honour to Catherine of Braganza, John Evelyn's adored young friend, was not so lucky.[30] As a girl she had been markedly reluctant to abandon her virgin state; one of her reasons was her fear of childbirth. Evelyn hastened to reassure her: 'Little women, I told her, had little pain.' Even after marrying the young courtier Sidney Godolphin, Margaret remained full of melancholy presentiments. First she did not conceive for two years, and then when she did, she too, like Elizabeth Josceline and Anne Halkett, laid all her plans in the eventuality of her death. Enduring a very

---

†But the joint monument to the Duke and Duchess of Newcastle in Westminster Abbey still records this failure on her part, ahead of all her manifold virtues: 'Here Lyes the Loyall Duke of Newcastle And his Dutches his second wife, by whome he had noe issue…'

difficult pregnancy and 'growing bigger', her public life was gradually reduced to visits to the chapel.

Margaret Godolphin went into labour during the night of Monday, 2 September 1678; about noon on the Tuesday 'a Man Child' was born, her husband, in attendance at court at Windsor, was informed. On the Thursday the child was baptized Francis. On the Sunday Evelyn, who was at his house at Deptford, received a letter while at church from Sidney Godolphin: 'My poor wife is fallen very ill of a fever, with lightness in her head.' Evelyn's prayers were implored. But Margaret's delirium increased. Matters were made worse when the doctors hung back and refused to act except in the presence of other physicians. Evelyn then arrived, with his wife, and by his own account took charge. (Even in her delirium, he noted, his chaste young friend said 'nothing offensive'.)

But poor Margaret was now, as Evelyn wrote, 'in a manner spent'; she had already endured 'the pigeons' – a medieval remedy by which live birds were applied to the patient's feet, generally to reduce fever – and blood-letting; the latter, from a vein in the arm, was commonly believed by doctors to stop haemorrhage.[31] The momentary respite which was granted by Betty Viscountess Mordaunt's famous strengthening cordial was soon over. Erysipelas, a kind of hot red rash described by Evelyn as 'a fiery Trial', began to spread over her back, neck and arms (it was in fact produced by the acute streptococcal infection causing her 'puerperal' fever). She lasted like this in 'all the circumstances of pain and weariness' until the morning of the next day. Then her paroxysms grew worse and she died at noon on Monday, 9 September, one week after the birth of her child, being in her twenty-fifth year.

Margaret Godolphin's last letter to her husband was full of that submissive melancholy which had animated so much of her short life: 'In the first place, my dear, believe me, that of all earthly things you were and are the most dear to me ... and do not grieve too much for me, since I hope I shall be happy, being very much resigned to God's will.' In her letter to him concerning her legacies, however, she revealed that other apprehension which haunted the dying wives of the seventeenth century: if Sidney Godolphin married again, he was to 'be kind to that poor Child I leave behind, for my sake, who lov'd you so well'.[32] But Sidney Godolphin, rare among his contemporaries as we shall see in the next chapter, never married again.

Lord Falmouth, who was madly in love with his beautiful wife Mary Bagot ('His Dearest Deare'), wanted her labour to be over before he returned from the Dutch war at sea, since he could not bear to see his beloved suffer: 'I cannot endure to see you in pain or trouble.' Later he wrote: 'You are in my thoughts the first thing in the morning and last at night. 'Tis certain my Dearest Deare Child that, let your pain have been what it will, my torment in the belief of it has not been much inferior to it.' (Falmouth's daughter had in fact been born four or five days earlier, but Falmouth, killed at the Battle of Lowestoft a short while later, never saw her.)[33]

How were these harrowing ordeals and deathbeds familiar to every household, and (unlike the state of pregnancy) never glossed over in contemporary accounts, to be explained in the divine order of things? Samuel Hieron made the origin of such sufferings quite clear in his prayer to be uttered by a woman in labour: 'the smart of the punishment which thou [Lord] laidst upon me being in the loins of my grandmother Eve, for my disobedience towards thee: Thou hast greatly increased the sorrows of our sex and our bearing of children is full of pain'. The poet Edmund Waller put it another way when he threw a light-hearted curse over Lady Dorothy Sidney, who had rejected him for another: 'make her taste the first curse imposed on womankind – the pains of becoming a mother'.[34]

If woman redeemed herself from the sin of Eve by childbearing, she was none the less condemned to suffer the pains of childbirth in order to fulfil that prophecy made in Genesis: 'Unto the woman he [God] said, I will greatly multiply thy sorrow and thy conception; in sorrow thou shalt bring forth children.' This doctrine, upon which Catholics and Puritans were alike agreed, gave at least some spiritual context to the agonies of women. (It was Catholic belief that after Eve's Fall, only the Virgin Mary, being born without original sin, did not suffer the pangs of childbirth, when she gave birth to the Infant Christ.) Faced with the perpetual prospect of their wives' sufferings, there was even some relief for loving husbands in accepting the link with the sin of Eve; it alleviated a burden which was otherwise unacceptable.

The penitential element in childbirth could even be carried further. The ceremony of 'churching' had, in its Judaic origins, been intended to 'cleanse' a woman after her delivery, but by the seventeenth century it was intended quite simply as a ceremony of thanksgiving. Certain women evidently believed that Archbishop Laud, in his plans for the Anglican Church, was attempting to bring back this penitential element to the ceremony, by insisting on a handkerchief or veil being worn; with indignation, protesters compared this head-covering to the white linen sheet which had to be worn by the 'unchaste'. There are entries in the Essex and Colchester Courts for women refusing to cover their heads in this manner. In 1639 Dorothy Hazzard, wife of a Bristol parson, received women to her house for their lying-in, because they could thus avoid the more disagreeable churching ceremonies elsewhere.[35]

If the cruel pangs of labour could be blamed upon Grandmother Eve, that other affliction endured by so many mothers of the seventeenth century, the death of the child itself in infancy, could hardly be laid directly at her door. Yet such a harrowing experience, as has been seen in the case of the Walkers and Fanshawes, was an inseparable part of parenthood in the seventeenth century. It might be the death of one child, of many children, of the entire flock; it was a rare and fortunate parent who escaped this tragedy altogether.

It has been suggested in recent years, notably by Lawrence Stone in *The Family, Sex and Marriage in England 1500–1800*, that the low expectation of infant life meant that people were as a whole less attached to their children or at any rate during the child's first year of life, when its ability to survive the rigours of infant disease had not been established. He does, however, comment that the popular psychologist Richard Napier treated women disturbed by the deaths of infants; Napier's notebooks concerning his patients (who were drawn from every social class) certainly include 134 cases of disturbing grief – nearly half of which were attributed to a child's death. The vast majority of these sufferers were mothers, such as Ellen Craftes who 'took a fright and grief that a door fell upon her child and slew it. Presently head, heart and stomach ill; eyes dimmed with grief that she cannot see well.'[36]

In general one can only observe that this suggested indifference is not the attitude of those women literate or lucky enough to be able to express themselves. Since the maternal instinct of one sort or another is a universal one (if anything enhanced rather than diminished by the proximity imposed by poverty), it seems unlikely that a woman wailing without words for her baby felt the death less because she was inarticulate. As in any natural disaster, only the voice of the privileged (generally male) was heard, but everyone suffered alike.

Ralph Verney's wife Mary was delirious for two days and nights with sorrow when her baby died suddenly of convulsions; when the news of the death of her daughter Pegg reached her she felt totally unable to care for two little girls, relations of Ralph's, because to do so would simply exacerbate her own grief. Oliver Heywood, in his account of the life of his mother, described 'how great an affliction' was the death of her first-born. The poet Katherine Philips (known as the 'Matchless Orinda') wrote of the death of her baby son in 1655 in a poem entitled 'Orinda upon little Hector Philips'.

> I did but see him, and he disappeared,
> I did but pluck the Rose-bud and it fell ...[37]

In the simple pain of the sentiment she spoke for all the countless women who had also glimpsed their babies only once, and mourned in silence.

As for the slightly older children, the desperation of many contemporary comments on these deaths speaks for itself. Sir

Hugh Cholmley of Scarborough described how when one of their children, known as 'little Betty', died aged four and a half 'to the great grief of my wife and myself', he took the stricken household away on a holiday to try and recover from a sorrow unendurable amid the familiar surroundings[38] – a reaction to loss which does not alter down the ages.

A comment by Samuel Clarke, who wrote *The Lives of Sundry Eminent Persons in this Later Age*, printed the year after his death, in 1683, explains the difference in the approach to suffering of that period. There is a parallel to be drawn between the public guilt felt about the emotion of love (although love itself was undoubtedly experienced), and the guilt felt about grief over the death of a child. Clarke included among his pious ladies his own wife Katharine Overton, whom he married in 1625, when she was twenty-four. He tells us that she experienced the most terrible grief at the deaths of her children, but thought it her duty to try and overcome it.[39] Poor Lettice Falkland felt that the devil himself was tempting her because she was overcome with desolation at the death of her son Lorenzo; she began to imagine herself responsible for his death by her own transgressions – a guilt which can only have added to the natural despair of the stricken mother. Anne Digby, the cool Countess of Sunderland, provided a glimpse into the reality of contemporary suffering when she wrote to John Evelyn over the death of his beloved grandson at the age of a year: 'We are so comfortably sure that the poor innocent babies are taken out of a naughty world to be very happy, that I have often wondered at the excessive sorrow I have sometimes seen on these occasions.' She added piously: 'but … we always prefer our own satisfaction, be it never so transitory, to the most solid good for others'.[40]

Sir William Brownlow was a brother of that Sir John Brownlow of Belton who recommended mares' milk for conception; no such expedient was necessary in the case of his wife, Elizabeth Duncombe. William Brownlow kept a meticulous record of her child-bearing from 27 June 1626 when their first child Richard was born, who died in the October of that year, down to the birth of their nineteenth child twenty-two years later; a daughter who lived – unmarried – till 1726. One third of this vast progeny survived – two sons and four daughters – which on a larger scale was something like the average survival rate for upper- and middle-class families of the time, in so far as it can be estimated.[41]

At one point, between 1638 and 1646, *seven* children, born at almost exactly yearly intervals, died in a row; Thomas, Francis, Benjamin, George, James, Maria and Anne. William Brownlow's exclamations of grief as each new tragedy struck show some attempt at reconciliation to the workings of providence – 'Though my children die, the Lord liveth and they exchange but a temporal life for an eternal one' – but absolutely no diminution in grief. Little George, for example, his fifteenth child, managed to live from October 1641 to 29 July of the following year; when he died, his father wrote: 'I was at ease but Thou O God hast broken me asunder and shaken me to pieces.' That was doubtless the truth. Parents, in their heart of hearts, could not reconcile themselves to a doctrine which left the little one happier in heaven – and their arms empty.

'My dear mother, why do you mourn and weep so much for my brother Willy?' asked Alice Thornton's little daughter Naly. 'Do you not think he is gone to heaven?'

'Yes, dear heart', replied Alice Thornton, 'I believe he is gone to heaven, but your father is so afflicted for his loss, and being a son he takes it more heavily, because I have not a son to live.' At this Naly asked the logical child's question: 'Would you then have him out of heaven again?' Alice Thornton in her autobiography does not record her reply, only that she felt reproved out of 'the mouth of so young a child' for her 'immoderate sorrow'.[42]

Alice Wandesford was born at Kirklington in Yorkshire in 1627 a member of the minor gentry of the North Riding, and married William Thornton of East Newton in 1651. A woman of strong character emerges from the pages of her autobiography; she declared that her motive for writing it was to make some sense of her husband's failure in life (he ended up a bankrupt), and her own subsequent struggles to bring up her family in poverty. Memories of a golden girlhood in Ireland, when her father's cousin the Earl of Strafford was Deputy, provided a bitter contrast. Nevertheless Alice Thornton does not write bitterly, although her financial worries were compounded by her sufferings as a mother. Her sister Catherine, wife of Sir Thomas Danby, had given birth to sixteen children, of whom six were stillborn, and died as a result of a long and painful delivery at the age of thirty.

Alice hesitated for some time before accepting the suit of William Thornton through a personal wish to be single; possibly affected by the spectacle of her sister's sufferings. Conceiving shortly after marriage, she was very sick in the early stages of her first pregnancy, and the child died after half an hour. Her second child was nearly 'overlaid' by its nurse – a gruesome contemporary fate, whereby the wet-nurse fell asleep and stifled or crushed the baby. Hearing the baby 'groaning troublesomely' Alice rushed in and extricated the infant from its perilous position. As a result of this, Alice suckled the next child – 'my sweet Betty' – herself, being 'overjoyed' to do so. However, at the age of eighteen months sweet Betty died of a combination of rickets and a cough: 'When Mr Thornton and I came to pray for her, she held up those sweet eyes and hands to her dear Father in heaven, looked up and cried in her language, "Dad, dad, dad" with such vehemency as if inspired by her holy father in heaven to deliver her sweet soul into her heavenly father's hands.'[43]

Then there was the son who died because the midwife lacked skill. After this Alice, fearing that she might now be barren, went to Scarborough Spa. She did conceive a child. This was 'my dear Willy Thornton' whose death at the age of fourteen days was taken not only by his father but by Alice very hard.

In giving birth to her next child Robert, Alice suffered repeated haemorrhages, although she was able to feed him herself for two years. Expecting her eighth child, Alice nervously worried herself over their fate if she should die, and Mr Thornton married again: 'as I had been told that it would be necessary for him for his health'.[44] But it was William Thornton who died, not Alice. Despite the fact that the birth of her ninth child left her very weak, with gangrene of the breast, Alice Thornton recovered after four months spent in bed. She lived on until 1706.† Three out of her nine children survived. Little Naly was evidently a highly strung as well as a precocious child: she fell into convulsions when taken by the maids to see the show put on to celebrate the coronation of King Charles II at Richmond – soldiers, drunks, noise, and firing muskets provoked from her a series of paralysing screams. Despite this, at the age of fourteen she was 'spoken for' by the curate of Stonegrave, Thomas Comber, later a venerated Dean of Durham and Naly lived, like her mother, to a great age.

The true figures for deaths in childbirth at this time cannot be established with certainty, owing to what one scholar has called the 'exasperating rarity' of evidence in the parish registers as to why the person buried there died. One estimate gives a figure varying from 125 to 158 per 1,000 in the first half of the seventeenth century and from 118 to 147 in the second half. Research among aristocratic women has produced the statistics that 45 per cent died before the age of fifty, one quarter from the complications of childbirth; these figures do not however allow for the debilitations caused by constant parturition.[45] Many women must have died of diseases and conditions related to 'the pain and the peril', worn through by ceaseless child-bearing, who did not actually die in labour.

It was ironic, if a subtle form of social justice, that the one natural form of contraception in existence at this time was the breast-feeding of the previous baby. While lactation did not give universal protection, it certainly afforded some.[46] What was more, the general prohibition against intercourse while the woman was still feeding her baby at the breast (even if not

†This remarkable woman was buried in the nearby Church of the Holy Trinity at Stonegrave, where the Chapel of St Peter is still dedicated to her memory, a chapel which she had wished to restore; but through her husband's failure she had not sufficient funds to do so. The arms of the Thorntons and Wandesfords can be seen there combined.

universally respected) exercised its own restraint. But the great ladies, and even those much further down the social scale, such as the Lancaster grocer's wife Mrs Coward, to whom William Stout was apprenticed, did not propose to feed their own children; it being customary to pay someone else, known as a 'wet-nurse', to do the job (the word was first introduced in 1620; before that the general term 'nurse' was used).[47] So the richer women enjoyed – endured might be a better word – a higher rate of fertility than their poorer sisters, who not only nursed these wealthy cuckoo babies for money, but also suckled their own children. Both processes gave the women of the poor some kind of short respite from the eternal process of giving birth, which brought so many women of the time into mortal danger, pain and peril year after year.

In general, breast-feeding was so unusual in that section of society where the mothers could afford to pay others to perform the duty for them as always to be worthy of remark. It was the subject of comment for example when Sarah, daughter of the Quaker Margaret Fell, nursed her son herself, born when she was forty-two. Lucy Hutchinson's mother was said to love her 'above the rest of her children' just because she had suckled her. Essex Cheke, third wife of the second Earl of Manchester, had her prowess in that respect commemorated on her tombstone when she died in September 1658. She had left Lord Manchester with six sons and two daughters, seven of them suckled 'with her own breasts'. The memorial added: 'Her children shall rise up and call her blessed.' On the other hand another Essex, that Lady Essex Rich who was the beloved first wife of Daniel Finch, Earl of Nottingham, was criticized for her rashness in feeding her own child; this eccentric behaviour was thought to have contributed to the baby's death.[48]

Why did the mothers of this time refuse to feed their own children, except in rare cases? This was after all a time when the alternative of animal milk was not used except for syphilitics. Baby bottles as such were also virtually unknown, although there were drinking horns (and nipple shields also existed, made of lead, tin or silver).[49]

It was not as if the character of the wet-nurses in themselves inspired much confidence. Every domestic handbook abounded in advice on how to choose a wet-nurse; the constant reiteration that she should be healthy and full of milk shows how often the contrary was discovered to be the case. (Complexion was rated exceptionally important: red hair and freckles for example were dangerous because they betokened sour milk; a healthy 'brown' was best.) Sexual relations between the wet-nurse and her husband (or anyone else) were also considered dangerous but it is highly doubtful that such prohibitions actually brought about celibacy. Babies in general seemed to be in constant threat from 'overlaying', the fate of Alice Thornton's baby. Under the circumstances Mary Lady Verney probably made a prudent decision when she chose the wife of Ralph Rode to wet-nurse little Ralph Verney on the grounds that her own family appeared healthy: 'she [Mrs Rode] looks like a slattern but she sayeth if she takes the child she will have a mighty care of it, and truly she hath two as fine children of her own as ever I saw'.[30] Yet the circumstances in which a feeling mother would surrender a beloved baby to a woman who looked 'like a slattern' are difficult for the modern imagination to encompass.

On the one hand the importance of the bond was understood: mental and spiritual qualities also were believed to be imbibed with the wet-nurse's milk, as Oliver Heywood wrote of his wife Elizabeth that 'she being nursed and nourished at home partook of her natural parents' excellent dispositions'. The wet-nurse to two monarchs, Mrs Katharine Elliott, appealed for a grant to sell silk stockings as a reward for such intimate services, while her own daughter petitioned Charles II at the Restoration for some financial recognition of the fact that she had sucked 'at the same breast as so great a monarch'. Mrs Martha Farthing claimed a pension of £300 when her former nursling Queen Anne ascended the throne, on the grounds that she was 'the only wet-nurse to her present Majesty'. Martha Farthing had fed the Princess for fifteen months, which was slightly longer than the median age established by contemporary reports, although some medical authors recommended weaning as late as twenty-one months.[31]

On the other hand, desperate laws, like that of a foundling hospital, which declared that any nurse who had imperilled the lives of two children might not take on the nursing of a third, show how low the standards sank for all the efforts to maintain them.[52]

To explain this phenomenon, it is too simple to say that a bunch of unfeeling women, bereft of the normal maternal instinct, had mysteriously emerged at a particular moment of history. The prejudice against lactation on the part of the mother was in fact far more a matter of social usage than maternal instinct.

Breast-feeding had its theoretical advocates, particularly among the Puritans. Perkins, Gouge, Cleaver and Dod (who believed that the breast was not an erogenous zone) all recommended it as part of a good mother's duty in their Puritan publications. But for all this preaching, there is evidence that the ideal was seldom realized: it has been pointed out, for example, that William Gouge's wife only nursed seven out of her thirteen children, Gouge himself admitting that the practice could be forsworn if it proved dangerous to mother or child. It is noticeable that the midwife Jane Sharp, who had experience of the difficulties of nursing, was a good deal less positive in her advice than the male pundits.[53]

The recommendations against marital sex during the period of lactation may well have had something to do with the matter, where the feelings of the husband were concerned. The casual (masculine) point of view was exhibited by Sir William Knollys at the turn of the sixteenth century, in a letter of advice to his goddaughter Anne Fitton, Lady Newdigate. He told her that he would not like it 'that you play the nurse, if you were my wife'. He admitted that 'it argueth great love, but it breedeth much trouble to yourself'. However Anne Newdigate ignored her godfather's advice; she did breast-feed her first child and went on to suckle four more (as a result of which achievement she was considered as a possible wet-nurse to the children of Anne of Denmark and James I). In a petition as a widow, she boasted that her children were born of her own body and nursed of her own breasts ('they never suck other milk').[54]

Elizabeth Knyvet, wife of the third Earl of Lincoln, wrote a defiant plea that the mother should suckle her own child in a book called *The Countess of Lincoln's Nursery*, first printed in 1622.[55] Her motive for her crusade was the same as that of Alice Thornton, who nursed her own child after her fright with an incompetent nurse. The Countess had given birth to eighteen children herself, and at least one of her 'Babes' had died through the neglect of nurses, who had falsely pretended 'willingness, towardness, wakefulness'. In fact, in the upbringing of eighteen children, the Countess of Lincoln declared she had only encountered two careful attendants,

A foreword by Thomas Lodge contained the encouraging rhyme:

> Go then, great Book of Nursing, plead the Cause;
> Teach Highest, Lowest, all, it's God's and Nature's Laws.

The Countess swept away all the possible objections that nursing was 'troublesome ... noisome to one's clothes, makes one look old, endangers health' (making the prevailing attitudes among her contemporaries clear). Such weak women, she observed, should not have married in the first place. She also pointed out triumphantly that the period of peace while nursing provided a woman with an excellent opportunity for prayer.

As in every controversial issue in the seventeenth century, the Bible was searched for precedents. Did not Sarah – 'a great Princess' – suckle Isaac? What of Hannah? Above all, what of the Virgin Mary, suckling the Infant Christ? But in proving that breast-feeding by the mother was according to God's holy ordinance, the Countess of Lincoln played her trump card in citing the example of Eve, who must surely have suckled Cain and Abel and Seth, since no other woman existed in the world to act as a nurse on her behalf.

'We have followed Eve in Transgression', declared the Countess of Lincoln on behalf of the female sex. 'Let us follow her in obedience.' But most women of her time who had the choice, unaware of the protective value of such a practice, declined to imitate this rare piece of good behaviour on the part of Grandmother Eve.

CHAPTER FIVE

Are You Widows?

~

'Again, are you widows? You deserve much honour, if you be so indeed ... Great difference then is there betwixt those widows who live alone, and retire themselves from public concourse, and those which frequent the company of men ... In popular concourse and Court-resorts there is no place for widows.'

RICHARD BRATHWAITE, *The English Gentlewoman*, 1631

O nce widowed – the third stage of her projected life – a woman was expected to add a further virtue in the shape of fidelity to the long list of feminine virtues she already possessed, including modesty, meekness, patience and humility. The fidelity was to the memory of her deceased spouse, for the ideal widow did not seek to alter her state by marrying again. Instead, in a favourite comparison of the time, she emulated the turtle-dove by mourning her late husband in solitude; as Mary Countess of Warwick was thankful when she had married off her late husband's nieces: her worldly duties being over she could spend the rest of her life a widow devoted to God's service.[1] That at least was the theory of widowhood. The reality as we shall see was often very different.

Lettice Viscountess Falkland, on top of all her other virtues, was formally commended for being:

> A Scripture Vestal, one whose chaste desire
> Call'd it adultery not to watch one fire ...

Eschewing 'all second loves' she displayed herself until her death 'One made of ice toward Venus, and her doves'. Lady Alice Lucy, who died in 1648, was considered such an outstanding example of female virtue that Samuel Clarke chose her for one of his subjects in *The Lives of Sundry Eminent Persons in this Later Age*, published in 1683. Lady Alice began with a thoroughly submissive approach to her union with Sir Thomas Lucy of Charlecote: 'She knew that her taking of a second self, was a self-denying work; and therefore she resigned both her reason, and her will unto her Head, and Husband...' After Sir Thomas's death, she never even contemplated remarriage, for the good reason that God 'made himself her Husband, supporting her, comforting her, and enabling her prudently to manage her great Estate, and to order her numerous family'.[2]

Another 'ideal of the true mourning turtle' was Anne Lady Newdigate, she who as a widow boasted that all her children were 'nursed of my own breasts'. Petitioning in 1600 to be allowed to have the wardship of her son and his lands during his minority, Lady Newdigate hotly denied that she should ever be so 'accursed a woman [as] to marry again'. She kept her word, despite various offers for her hand, devoting her life to her children and their business interests. Her friend Lady Grey proposed a less severe attitude to remarriage – 'I must needs tell you that your too infinite care may take away that happiness which might give much content to you and yours.' Lady Newdigate's constancy was nevertheless considered heroic. Here was the reverse of the Pygmalion image: 'a fair woman' was 'turned into a marble stone'.[3]

Conversely, some very peculiar attitudes can be detected towards those widows who did take a second husband. There was an idea that marrying a widow might constitute 'bigamy', and if a widow had two spouses dead, it might even be termed 'trigamy'. John Aubrey ascribed an even more complicated view to William Harvey, the physician who discovered the circulation of the blood: 'He that marries a widow makes himself Cuckold' (that is, by the woman's dead husband). Harvey was supposed to have suggested that the children of the second marriage might even resemble the husband of the first, just as 'a good bitch', if first mated with a mongrel, would still bring forth 'curs' even after she had been mated with a dog of a better strain.[4]

The attitude of Edward Lord Herbert of Cherbury to his mother Magdalen's second marriage was positively eccentric: in his autobiography he paid a glowing tribute to her character, how 'she lived most virtuously and lovingly with her husband [his father] for many years ... brought up her children carefully and put them in good courses for making their fortune ...' At no point did he mention that in 1608 the widowed Lady Herbert had married Sir John Danvers – she being forty and he twenty years old. Danvers himself is also mentioned by name, but the relationship between the two men is not. One might well wonder what this Hamlet was endeavouring to conceal on the subject of his mother's second union, except that John Donne (who preached the funeral sermon for Lady Danvers in 1627) tells us the marriage was, in fact, a very happy one. It seems therefore that nothing more than a theoretical distaste for abandoned widowhood was at stake.[5]

This revulsion against the notion of remarriage could also take the form of sentimental surprise when it actually took place. Dorothy Countess of Sunderland was widowed at the age of twenty-five. As a girl Dorothy Sidney had been the idol of her generation, one who succeeded in her professed aim to her father, the Earl of Leicester, to be 'the perfectest good child upon earth'. For her, his Sacharissa, Edmund Waller wrote that classic lover's apostrophe:

> Go lovely Rose
> Tell her that wastes her time and me,
> That now she knows,
> When I resemble her to thee,
> How sweet and fair she seems to be.

Having rejected not only the poet (who then wishes on her that first curse of womankind, 'the pains of becoming a mother') but another aristocratic suitor for his addiction to debauched company, Dorothy Sidney made what seemed the ideal marriage to Henry Lord Spencer, later created Earl of Sunderland, a man who combined handsome looks with great taste – and great possessions. Four years later he was killed at the first Battle of Newbury (that same battle into which Lord Falkland rode looking 'very cheerful'), leaving Dorothy with a son and two daughters, but also heavily pregnant: she gave birth to a second son a fortnight later.[6]

After Lord Sunderland's death, Lord Leicester gave a classic piece of advice on the behaviour of a desolate widow to his 'dear Doll': she must cease damaging herself by her unhappiness since 'you offend him who you loved, if you hurt that person he loved'. Her children remained – 'those pledges of your mutual friendship and affection which he hath left with you' – and if she did not recover enough to take care of them, she was betraying 'their father's trust' which had been reposed in her: 'For their sake, therefore, assuage your grief...'[7] For the next ten years or so the young Dowager Countess did devote herself in approved widow's fashion to the upbringing of her family, especially her son and the management of the Spencer family estates at Althorp.

The consternation of the world when Dorothy married Robert Smythe in 1652 may seem by modern standards ludicrous. He was a Sidney family connection, a neighbour to the Leicester property at Penshurst (where Dorothy had spent her first widowhood), and although some years younger than the Countess had probably been in love with her for years. The contemporary consternation was none the less real. The Countess tactfully suggested to Dorothy Osborne that she had been swayed by pity for Smythe, although the fact that Smythe was 'a very fine gentleman' was surely at least as relevant. Even though Dorothy Osborne admitted that the Countess of Sunderland – still only in her thirties – might be growing 'weary of that constraint she put upon herself', her verdict was unforgiving: 'She has lost by it [the marriage] much of the repute she had gained by keeping herself a widow. It was then believed that wit and discretion were to be reconciled in her person that have so seldom been persuaded to meet in anybody else. But', concluded Dorothy Osborne sadly, 'we are all mortal.'[8]

This yearning for fidelity beyond the grave – the ideal of the devoted widow – makes strange reading put side by side with the nature of the society in which these men, women (and widows) lived. While there was general agreement, except by a few generous-minded or realistic spirits, that a second marriage for women was to be avoided, the facts about life in the first half of the seventeenth century give us a very different picture. Pepys, in one of the earliest entries in his diary, was much moved by a sermon he had heard on the subject of St Anne, mother of the Virgin Mary, only seven years married, who had lived to the age of eighty-four a widow. It neatly expressed the contrast between the ideal and the actual. The preacher 'did there speak largely in commendation of widowhood, and not as we do, to marry two or three wives or husbands one after another'.[9]

This was, after all, an age in which the life expectancy at birth was not much more than thirty-five years.[10] Each sex was subject to its own special threat. Women had to face the continuous peril of childbirth. Men on the other hand appear to have been more prone to disease, while the male population was also periodically decimated by war, whether at home or abroad.

Under these circumstances remarriage, far from being a distasteful aberration, was in fact a very common occurrence, it having been calculated that about a quarter of all marriages were a remarriage for either the bride or the groom. In the upper echelons of society – that is to say, those ranks where the interests of money and property were at stake in any given marriage – it has been further estimated that about 25 per cent of the population married again in the late sixteenth and seventeenth centuries, and about 5 per cent married three times. Four or even five marriages in a lifetime were as likely to be achieved then in a society with a high rate of mortality as they are today in a society with a high rate of divorce.[11]

The career of Eleanor Wortley, who married in turn Sir Henry Lee of Quarendon in Buckinghamshire, the sixth Earl of Sussex, the second Earl of Warwick, and the second Earl of Manchester, was notable more for the fact that she married a series of aged husbands than for the number of her bridegrooms. Sir Ralph

Verney (he was knighted in 1640 but made a baronet at the Restoration) actually used to refer to her in code in his letters as 'Old Men's Wife'.[12]

Lady Sussex was a woman of tempestuous character whose tribulations – as well as marriages – enlivened the existence of her friends. She also had a rather beguiling vanity. She recommended Mary Lady Verney (Mary Blacknall, the heiress, now a contented married lady) to use myrrh water for her complexion, explaining: 'I have long used it and find it very safe. 'Tis good for the head and to make one look young long. I only wet a cloth and wipe my face over, at night with it.' However, it says less for Lady Sussex's artistic sense that when Van Dyck wanted to paint her she was torn between vanity and avarice: 'I am loth to deny him, [but] truly it is money ill bestowed.' (Van Dyck got £50 for the job.) Later Ralph Verney had to intervene, in a common problem, alas, with portraiture: he prevailed upon Van Dyck at Lady Sussex's request 'to make my picture leaner, for truly it was too fat.'[13] Later, after her third marriage, Lady Sussex tried to get hold of the picture for her new husband, but perhaps deservedly, failed.

The 'Old Men's Wife' was not, however, an unloving character. As the aged Lord Sussex lay on his deathbed at his estate at Gorhambury during the Civil War, she declared: 'I will not stir from my good old Lord whatsoever becomes of me.' She assured the Verneys: 'Now I must tell you that which maybe you will hardly believe, that I heartily suffer for my good old lord who truly grows so very weak that I fear he will not hold out very long.' She then spent a considerable sum of money – £400 – on his funeral as a mark of her respect. 'Good man', she wrote of Lord Sussex after his death, 'I am confident he is happy.'[14]

Lady Sussex's third husband, Robert Earl of Warwick, was approaching sixty – a vast age by the standards of the time, when thirty was held to mark middle age. She was frank about her reasons for choosing him. 'Wanting a discreet and helpful friend...made me think of marriage', she told the Verneys, 'being unable to undergo what I found continually upon me.' The Earl of Warwick was not only 'extreme kind' as she put it, but in the view of his daughter-in-law Mary Rich one of the 'cheerfullest persons'. He was also a grandee who did not allow his religious and political Puritanism to stand in the way of the great state he kept at Warwick House in Holborn. Nine months after his death in 1658 Eleanor married another Parliamentary leader, the fifty-six-year-old Earl of Manchester, a double which won for her the sobriquet of 'the Peeress of the Protectorate'. She still, however, kept Warwick House, which had been willed to her by her third husband. It is a tribute to Eleanor's warm character that Mary Rich, by now Countess of Warwick in her turn, wept bitterly at her death in 1667. 'I was much affected for the loss of my poor mother-in-law', wrote Mary; she found it no consolation that her husband would now at last be free to use the family residence of Warwick House.[15]

By her two matches with the Earl of Warwick and the Earl of Manchester, Eleanor had entered into a remarkably complex network of relationships. At the time the situation was summed up by the saying that the Earl of Manchester, following his first wife's death had married 'Warwick's niece, Warwick's daughter and Warwick's wife':[16] that is to say his third wife, Essex Cheke, 'Warwick's niece', that philoprogenitive lady who had fed seven children at the breast, was the daughter of Warwick's sister; she was thus a first cousin of Manchester's second wife, who had been 'Warwick's daughter', Lady Anne Rich; Manchester's fourth wife was of course Warwick's widow, Eleanor. (After Eleanor's death, the ever-game Lord Manchester went on to marry for a fifth time, the widowed Countess of Carlisle, who survived him.)

The marital career of the second Earl of Warwick, straightforward compared to that of the Earl of Manchester, was not without its own incidents. His first marriage, which had taken place as long ago as 1605, was to Frances Hatton, step-daughter of that spirited Lady Hatton who was the mother of Frances Coke. His second wife was Susan Halliday, the widow of a rich London alderman; of her Mary Rich wrote: 'Because she was a citizen, she was not so much respected in the family as in my opinion she deserved to be.' Warwick's other daughter-in-law, Lady Anne Cavendish, a haughty scion of the house of

Devonshire, had been particularly unpleasant to her. Mary, however, found her 'as good as my own mother', sympathized with her ill-health, and 'when God called her away, [I did] much mourn for losing her'.[17]

Remarriage, then, was a fact of contemporary life and it was not only the great Parliamentary magnates, the leaders of their society, who indulged guiltlessly in this potentially acquisitive pastime.

That same Lord Herbert who refused to acknowledge in print the second marriage of his mother, relates in his autobiography a cold-blooded conversation with his own wife. When they had established a family of three, he called the children in front of their mother and asked her how she liked them. 'Well', she replied. In which case Herbert requested his wife to settle her estates on these children in her lifetime, because there was a strong possibility of one or other of them dying, and the survivor marrying again; he being young for a man and she 'not old for a woman' (she was thirty-one, four years older than he was). Future offspring of these hypothetical second marriages might damage the financial prospects of their existing family. Although Lady Herbert refused, on the grounds that she did not wish to find herself in the power of her own children – 'she would not draw the cradle upon her head' – her husband's premise concerning death and remarriage was not in itself surprising or shocking to her.[18]

In reality it was more often the question of the children's financial future – the children of the first marriage, that is – which bedevilled the prospect of a widow's remarriage, than the notion of her fidelity to her first husband. William Blundell quoted with approval in his diary the Latin tag of a certain widower:

> *Liberorum causa duxeram uxorem*
> *Liberorum causa rursus non duxi*

('I had married a wife for the sake of children; for the sake of my children I have not married again'). Widows too were adjured to bear in mind the consequences of a second marriage for those who had something to lose from it, such as their children. (Later the Quakers would make it a feature of their religion that proper provision should be made for the children of first marriages before a second marriage took place.) Brilliana Lady Harley summed up the two sides to the question with good sense in 1642 when she described herself as 'glad' that her cousin Catherine, widow of Oliver St John,was remarrying: 'I believe it is for her advantage; tho' in my opinion, when one has children, it is better to be a widow.'[19]

From the opposite point of view – those with something to gain from a woman's remarriage, notably her prospective second husband – no spectacle was more stirring than that of a wealthy widow. A Tally-Ho would go up when one of these creatures was sighted, followed by a pursuit which can only be compared to the contemporary chase after an heiress; except that the fox in this case was older and therefore wilier.

'If a widow happens to fall in the mean time she shall be kept in syrup for you', wrote a correspondent to Framlingham Gawdy in 1637, at the end of a list of available widows which included their incomes. Sir John Eliot, the leading spirit in the forcing of the Petition of Right upon King Charles I, a man who was imprisoned for his opposition to arbitrary power, left the question of his second marriage entirely in the hands of his friend Sir Henry Waller, who knew of a wealthy widow who had recently 'fallen', i.e. become available. Eliot made no inquiries concerning his bride's Moral character.[20]

In 1653, about the time of Dorothy Countess of Sunderland's second marriage, Dorothy Osborne went to dinner with a rich widow, middle-aged and 'never handsome', who had 'broke loose from an old miserable husband' with the avowed intention of spending all his money before she died. Whereas Sacharissa's fall from grace had shocked Dorothy, the widow's palpable state of siege thoroughly amused her. For all the widow's frank words concerning the use to which she intended to put her late husband's money, and despite her lack of physical attraction, she was, wrote Dorothy, 'courted a thousand times more than the greatest beauty in the world that had not a fortune'. They could hardly get through dinner for the disturbance caused by letters and presents pouring through the door in order to persuade the widow to change her mind.[21]

Other widows made a different use of their opportunities. Francis Kirkman described in his autobiography how his thrice-married stepmother had had a dubious past, diddling another step-son out of his estate by forging her first husband's seal on a will. But Francis Kirkman's father was hardly interested in such details. 'My father married her upon small acquaintance'; he only knew that she had a considerable estate, 'that being the chief care of most thriving citizens to inquire into that'.[22]

City widows (like Susan Halliday, the second Countess of Warwick) were a particular target, because the Custom of London concerning the disposition of a man's estate was so favourable towards his relict. Marriage to an important widow (in the commercial sense) was the basis of one of the most successful businesses built up in the City in the seventeenth century. William Wheeler was a goldsmith; a profession incidentally where there was a tradition of bright-eyed and quick-witted wives, including that famous mistress of Edward IV, Jane Shore, who displayed her 'beauty in a shop of gold'. Wheeler transferred the Cheapside shop inherited from his father to the Marygold, formerly a tavern, in Fleet Street near Temple Bar. When Wheeler died his widow Martha married one of his two apprentices, named Robert Blanchard, who then succeeded to the business. (Wheeler's daughter Elizabeth married another apprentice, Francis Child; he later inherited the business in his turn, and as Sir Francis Child, was reckoned 'the father' of the banking profession.) It was appropriate that Blanchard, who owed so much to the Widow Wheeler, should leave £200 in his will to the Goldsmiths' Company to pay £4 a year to two widows of good repute, over the age of fifty, who were less well endowed.[23]

When Sir William Craven died in 1618, his was the largest fortune known at the time from a will – at least £125,000. In turn

Lady Craven at her death was reputed by John Chamberlain to be 'the richest widow (perhaps) that ever died, of London lady'; she was said to have left an income derived from land worth £13,000 a year between her two sons. The Vyners were another remarkable City dynasty. Pepys gazed in awe at Mary, wife of Sir Robert Vyner, but for once not for her looks; it was true she was still handsome but from having been 'a very handsome woman' he reckoned her at the age of thirty-four 'now old'. No, Pepys's awe arose from the fact that Lady Vyner, a wealthy widow at the time of her marriage, was reputed to have brought her husband 'near £100,000'.[24] The prize did not however have to be on quite such a lustrous scale for the competition to be keen, as is manifested by the case of the Widow Bennett.

Elizabeth Cradock – the Widow Bennett of the story – came of a decent Staffordshire family and her father had probably been some form of mercantile agent.[25] She was still a young and attractive woman when her husband, Richard Bennett, a well-off merchant and son of a former Lord Mayor of London, died in April 1628. The widow was left with a four-year-old son, Simon, doubtless named for her husband's brother Sir Simon Bennett, who had been created a baronet the previous year. With respectable if not brilliant connections, the Widow Bennett was certainly well placed to make a sound second marriage, especially as she was the sole executrix of her husband's will, under which she received two-thirds of his estate. That was not all. She also inherited her husband's coach with its four grey coach-horses (mares and geldings), to say nothing of jewels which included chains of pearl and gold, and diamond rings. In short, the Widow Bennett was in a position to cut just that type of 'ladyfied' figure alluded to by Massinger in his satirical play *The City Madam* who wore:

> Satin on solemn days, a chain of gold,
> A velvet hood, rich borders, and sometimes
> A dainty miniver cap, a silver pin ...[26]

Only six months after her husband's death the Widow Bennett had acquired three established suitors. Like some latter-day

Paris, the widow was expected to bestow the golden apple of her fortune on one of the trio. There however the mythical comparison ends and a more homely note is struck, for, to the general amusement of society, these three suitors happened coincidentally to bear the names of Finch, Crow(e) and Raven.

Finch was undoubtedly the best of the flock. Sir Heneage Finch came of an excellent Kentish family, he had been Speaker of the House of Commons in 1626 and was now Recorder of London, and his establishments included a handsome house and garden in that countrified outpost of London called Kensington (where Kensington Palace and Kensington Gardens now lie). Crow, in the shape of Sir Sackville Crowe, was embarrassingly eager that this 'Twenty thousand pounds widow' should help him to make up that gap in the public accounts which would shortly cause him to retire from his office of Treasurer of the Navy. Raven was a doctor, and a dashing fellow – but as it proved, rather too dashing a fellow for the widow's taste.

One night Dr Raven bribed the widow's servants to let him secretly into her house. He then entered her bedroom, where the widow was sleeping, and proceeded to make passionate love to her. It was a commonly-held assumption of the time that a 'lusty widow', as the Duchess of Malfi was termed by her brother Ferdinand, must be ever on the look-out for sexual fulfilment. Ferdinand expressed the reason thus: 'You know already what man is.' Joseph Swetnam, for example, in *The arraignment of Lewd, Idle, Froward and Unconstant Women* laid it down that no widow, 'framed to the conditions of another man', could possibly 'forbear carnal act' if an opportunity came her way, since she was habitually deprived of it.[27] One can only observe that the Widow Bennett's behaviour would have proved a sad disappointment to anyone proceeding on this assumption.

Far from showing herself unable to forbear carnal act, the widow immediately sprang out of bed, and began to shriek such unamorous words as 'Thieves!' and 'Murder!' She managed to summon her venal servants, and in the course of time the dashing doctor was arrested by the parish constable. Haled before the Recorder of London the next day, the Raven found himself facing none other than the Finch. The latter having sent him into custody until the next sessions, it was some time before the unfortunate Raven, having pleaded guilty to 'ill-demeanour', was finally set free.

At this point a fourth bird joined the flock, in the shape of a recent widower called Sir Edward Dering. Much of Dering's journal of his campaign to secure the widow's hand survives; it supplies vivid details of all the necessary preparations for such an assault. Here are the Widow Bennett's servants bribed (again! it must have been a lucrative position) and supplying Sir Edward with tit-bits of encouraging gossip to spur him on. One servant would whisper 'Good news! Good news!' and Sir Edward's heart would leap. There would be a hint that 'the widow liked well his carriage and ... there was good hope', provided that Sir Edward's land was not already settled on his son by his first marriage.

Sir Edward's own efforts included the dispatch of rich presents for the widow herself, as well as her servants, and visits to the church where he might spy her – and presumably be spied. These could be quite demanding, for the good widow was a great church-goer: 'Nov 30: I was at the Old Jewry Church, and saw her, both forenoon and afternoon.' Then there were his advisers, who included the Widow Bennett's cousin Cradock, and even Sir Heneage Finch (who appeared at this point to have withdrawn from the campaign). The two men had dinner together. Others who interested themselves in Sir Edward's cause were his cousin, the Dean of Canterbury, and his late wife's mother and sister (who far from advocating any form of fidelity to his dead wife had clearly decided that Sir Edward's family would benefit generally from the supplement of the Widow Bennett's estate). When Sir Henry Wotton, the Provost of Eton, happened to meet Sir Edward in the Privy Chamber, he expressed the general interest in the pursuit by genially wishing Sir Edward 'full sail'.

Of course there was the continuing anxiety of the other suitors. Front-runners were the newly created Viscount Lumley and a Mr Butler. The latter was rejected by the widow for being 'a black blunt-nosed gentleman', but Lord Lumley also prosecuted his suit by going to the widow's church. In all of this, Sir Edward's interviews with the widow, as opposed to ecclesiastical sightings of her, were really rather disappointing, but somehow no one seems to have noticed this fact in all the excitement of rumour and counter-rumour. At one interview Sir Edward could get 'no answer of certainty, nor yet indeed any denial'. At another the widow protested that she would not marry at all, or at any rate she would make no answer to his proposal at the present time. At yet another meeting, in February, Sir Edward 'intreated of her' to grant him at least one suit: 'viz., to love herself ... viz., to choose that man with whom she might live happiest'. The widow's reply was scarcely encouraging: 'Say that you left me, and take the glory of it.'

When the dreams of the Widow Bennett – and of Sir Edward – were introduced into the proceedings as relevant evidence by her cousin Mrs Norton, another of Sir Edward's informants, they were not exactly encouraging either. The Widow Bennett dreamt that as Mrs Norton was bringing her 'a mess of milk' in bed, Sir Edward came into the room behind her, at which the Widow Bennett sprang out of bed – with that same strange lack of carnality with which she had eluded Dr Raven – and ran out of her bedroom into the parlour 'in her smock', whereupon she caught cold. Sir Edward, more prosaically, dreamt that the widow had sent him a Twelfth Night cake.

But what were these lack-lustre portents compared to the glittering prospect of her fortune? Sir Edward gloated over it: 'George Newman [her servant] says she hath suits of silver plate, one in the country and the other here, and that she hath beds of £100 the bed.'

The trouble was that the widow herself was not totally without cares in her new state. It has been mentioned that she had a small son, Simon. The wardship of this boy had been sold by the Crown to a man named Steward, according to the custom – so much resented – of the time. Throughout Sir Edward's courtship, the widow was engaged in trying to buy back the wardship of her boy into her own hands for £1,500; but having paid the amount, she then discovered that Steward himself had already sold the wardship into another's hands. Was it this problem which was causing the widow to hang back so unconscionably from matrimony?

Sir Edward, like many would-be second spouses, was well aware of the importance of little Simon in his mother's favours. He ambushed the child at his daily walk, when he was out with his nursemaid Susan and George Newman. 'Susan professed that she and all the house prayed for me, and told me the child already called me "Father"', Sir Edward reported joyfully in his journal.

Perhaps little Simon was the key to the situation. With the question of the wardship at last settled in the spring, the widow was to be found 'in a merry plight', according to her cousin Mrs Norton. The two women were drinking beer and chatting together: 'Well, Thomas,' she said to her servant, 'I must have one glass of beer more.' The widow agreed to drink a toast to Sir Edward 'as one that loved her'. And shortly afterwards in April 1629, a year after the death of her first husband, the Widow Bennett did duly marry again. She married however not patient aspirant Sir Edward, but the Finch.

It has been suggested that Sir Heneage had been advising the widow all along on the provoking matter of the wardship. The Finch may have allowed Dering's blatant courtship to conceal his own more discreet suit.[28] Be that as it may, with the marriage the dramatic story of the Widow Bennett and her suitors ends. It remains only to say that though the Finch marriage was short-lived (Sir Heneage died in December 1631 and this time the widow did not venture to remarry), it lasted long enough for the new Lady Finch to bear one daughter and conceive an even more remarkable child, born after her father's death. But the story of Anne Finch, Viscountess Conway, belongs to another chapter.

The Widow Bennett, seen through the pages of Sir Edward Dering's journal, was no pliable character on whom the masculine sex necessarily imposed: in the end she secured a distinguished second husband (of considerably higher social rank than her first) who supplied her need for 'a discreet and helpful friend', as Eleanor Lady Sussex had described her protective third husband the Earl of Warwick.

This is where the figure of the wealthy widow, that contemporary object of desire, begins to emerge as one vessel who was in practice by no means quite so weak as the rest of womankind. Widows by their very nature presented considerable problems to those pundits who postulated that obedience was the female's essential lot. If unmarried girls obeyed their fathers, and wives obeyed their husbands, whom should a widow obey? There was no clear answer to that question. Widows, indeed, could be held to be technically 'masterless', especially if their jointure or other form of inheritance was free from legal restraint.

It was a point made by a headstrong young widow, Mrs Margaret Poulteney, who was actually Ralph Verney's aunt, although only a year older than he. Enjoying a handsome jointure without encumbrances, Margaret Poulteney went and married herself secretly to a Catholic soldier named William Eure; this despite the prolonged negotiations for a conventional second marriage, made on her behalf by her family. Eure's proscribed religion, the secrecy of the event, the embarrassment felt towards Margaret Poulteney's other suitors who had been assured she was 'a free woman'; all these contributed to a feeling of collective indignation in the Verney family breast.[29]

Sir Edmund Verney hoped gloomily that 'some lucky bullet may free her of this misfortune'. Margaret Poulteney was felt to have behaved particularly badly because she had tricked Ralph's wife Mary into buying her a form of trousseau – a black taffeta waistcoat and petticoat trimmed with handsome lace – and delivering Margaret's favourite red damask petticoat and waistcoat from Claydon. Margaret used the excuse that she needed a new outfit for a christening. Instead she rushed off with her finery to meet William Eure on his way back from Scotland, where he had been serving in the King's Army.

To all these reproaches Margaret, now Mrs Eure, had an irrefutable as well as disdainful reply: 'The town makes havoc of my good name, but let them do their worst, I defy them all. None in the world can call me to account for my actions; for I am not in any one's tuition.'[30]

By the 1670s *The Ladies Calling* was trying to get round this awkward possibility by suggesting that God did not set the same value upon their being 'masterless' as some over-independent widows did: 'He [God] reckons them most miserable when they are most at liberty.'[31] This last shot was presumably mere conjecture on the part of the Anglican divine who wrote *The Ladies Calling*, the feelings of the widows themselves, which can be established with more certainty, were very different. Liberty, if accompanied by affluence, could be very sweet.

Lady Anne Twysden was a widow with two fine houses, one in London and the other at East Peckham, Kent. In her youth she had been a beauty, tall but very slender. Her own son, Sir Roger Twysden, paid this tribute to her: 'She was the handsomest woman (at least as handsome) as I ever saw', with 'skin exceeding fair' and 'light brown hair'. After forty, although she continued to look young for her age, 'fatness' was 'much trouble to her'.[32] Despite this hampering weight, ill-health generally and a lame foot where she had been dropped by her nurse as a child, Lady Anne ruled her domains with a rod of iron. Endowed with an excellent business brain, aided by a fluent epistolary style (and that female rarity, good handwriting), Lady Anne Twysden hardly accorded with the prevalent notion of woman as the helpless sex. At the time of the ship-money crisis in the 1630s, Lady Anne at one juncture had the courage to refuse to pay the tax – a development which deeply worried her son on her behalf, but which he could not affect.

Even though she was physically unable to move about the house, somehow Lady Anne, according to her son, managed to know 'every egg spent in it'. Her thriftiness was combined with a chastity, one might almost say, prudery, which prevented her from being alone with a man – even her own son when grown up – without a maid present. Thrifty and prudish as she might be, Lady Anne was also, wrote Sir Roger, 'full of motherly affection'.[33] She must have been warm-hearted, for she managed to make herself beloved to those around her, including the young gentlewomen of little fortune whom she employed as attendants (no doubt to report on the egg-spending).

One of these, the thirty-year-old Isabella Saunders, was finally selected by Lady Anne as a bride for Sir Roger, still a bachelor at the advanced age of thirty-seven. Isabella tended her mother-in-law with devotion and wept copiously at her deathbed in 1638, although after her marriage it was still Lady Anne, not the new Lady Twysden (generally termed Dame Isabella, perhaps to differentiate her), who ran Roydon Hall. Sir Roger Twysden's notebooks also leave us an exact record of the financial restraint which Lady Anne imposed upon him under the heading 'Reckonings between me and my mother'; as for example, 'The 6th July 1629 I owed her £46.12.10. pd her £20. 20 July and pd. her £40. 10 Sept and told her where she cd. have another £100 in London.'[34]

The reason that Lady Anne Twysden was able to exercise such command over every aspect of life surrounding her, including the life of her son, was simple. It was not connected with her beauty, motherly affection, or even her thriftiness. It was because Anne Twysden had been born Lady Anne Finch, another member of that large Kentish family to which Sir Heneage Finch belonged. Her mother was the heiress Elizabeth Heneage, 'a Lady of great Fortune; and having a mind suitable to it',[35] who married Sir Moyle Finch and after his death was created Viscountess Maidstone and Countess of Winchilsea in her own right as a mark of her status. Anne Finch's husband, Sir William Twysden, died in 1629. After that, as a widow with an unencumbered estate, Lady Anne Twysden was able to enjoy personally that very fortune which she had brought to her husband on marriage.

Lady Anne Clifford, like Anne Twysden, was an heiress, but on a vastly grander scale. She was born in 1590 but true happiness only came to her late in life in her role as a magnificent widow, mother and grandmother, one of whom V. Sackville-West, the editor of her autobiography, aptly wrote that she was 'born to matriarchy'. After Anne Clifford's first marriage to Richard Sackville, Earl of Dorset, in 1609, Emilia Lanier serenaded her as

> ... that sweet Lady sprung from Cliffords race,
> Of noble Bedford's blood, fair stream of Grade;
> To honourable Dorset now espous'd ...[36]

However, much of life with 'honourable Dorset' turned out to be torment for his young wife.

Her role as chatelaine of the historical Sackville palace at Knole was often invidious since Lord Dorset was openly unfaithful – even bringing his inamorata Lady Penistone – 'a dainty fine young lady' – to stay at Knole. Almost worse from Anne's point of view was the fact that Dorset refused to support her in her struggle to claim her own northern inheritance from her father's brother (since the estates had been entailed in her father's will on a child of either sex). Lord Dorset wanted to commute these rights for cash; his wife wanted to cling to the lands. Most people blamed her for her obstinacy and at one point during the row her son was removed from her care. Anne described herself in her autobiography as being 'like an owl in the desert'; while Lord Dorset went to 'Cocking, to Bowling Alleys, to Plays and Horse Races ... I stayed in the country having many times a sorrowful and heavy heart, and being condemned by most folks because I would not consent to the agreements.'[37]

Death removed Lord Dorset in 1624, but Lady Anne Clifford's second marriage, in 1630, to Philip Earl of Pembroke and Montgomery, owner of sumptuous Wilton House near Salisbury, was no happier. Notorious for his rough ways in youth, Lord Pembroke sided with Parliament in later life – possibly to secure his possessions – and was much pilloried by the Royalist pamphleteers in consequence. Fortunately – from Anne's point of view – his death in 1649 left her a widow for the second time. From now until her own demise nearly thirty years later at the age of eighty-six, she was able to enjoy not only the fruits of two rich jointures, but also those northern properties she had so much desired, released to her at last by the death of her uncle.

'The marble pillars of Knole in Kent and Wilton in Wiltshire were to me oftentimes but the gay arbours of anguish', wrote Anne of her two marriages. How different, how formidably different was the life of the Dowager Countess! Clad usually in black serge, 'her features more expressive of firmness than benignity', as a nineteenth-century local historian tactfully expressed it after studying her portraits, 'the Lady Anne', as she is still remembered in the north, gave full vent to all her tastes in a way she could never do throughout two unhappy marriages.[38] Her two surviving children being daughters, by her first marriage, they offered no impediments to her will.

These tastes included the restoration of ancient castles and chapels, part of her inheritance, on which it has been estimated that she must have spent at least £40,000. 'The Lady Anne' also took particular pleasure in raising monuments in stone: among others she was responsible for the classical monument to the poet Spenser in Westminster Abbey executed by Nicholas Stone, and a medieval type of altar tomb to her own mother which can still be seen in the Church of St Lawrence, Appleby, in Cumbria, alongside the monument which she erected to herself. John Donne had paid tribute to her conversation in youth: she was a woman who 'knew well how to discourse of all things, from pre-destination to flea-silk [a plant], a wonderful housekeeper who could still open her mouth with wisdom'. In later life the Lady Anne shared the conversational gifts which had so much impressed Donne with those poorer widows whom she had installed in a residence at Appleby in Westmorland; she made a point of dining with them once a week and talking as freely 'as with persons of the highest rank'.[39]

The Lady Anne was a great reader; as she grew old, she kept two 'well-educated females' constantly at her side to read aloud. The Psalms and the Old Testament were favourites, but she also enjoyed classical authors and had a particular love of Chaucer. When engrossed in his works, she wrote, 'a little part of his boun-teous spirit infuses itself into me'. Bounteous she certainly was, and not only in spirit. She made the giving of presents her hobby, buying books of devotion, for example, in bulk – up to fifty at a time – to give away. And she was a prodigious tipper: £3 to a man who brought her a letter from her daughter, a sum which represented something like the man's annual wage. Even if her autobiography gained a good deal from the work of certain liter-ary ghosts,[40] that in itself was a form of patronage which few women of the time other than a very rich widow could have exercised.

Even for the less privileged, widows' rights were one area where the law was by no means so unfavourable to women as it was elsewhere. For those outside the wealthier world of the marriage settlement made in advance of the ceremony, there existed the traditional widow's 'thirds', that is, a third share in the husband's estate which under common law was her due.[41] A widow's inheritance could take many different forms, some of which could enable her to make a convenient second marriage on her own terms if she so wished, while others allowed her a position of her own in commercial society.

In cases of trouble a widow's dower lands were protected if the late husband's creditors fell upon the rest of the estate. These lands could only be forfeited by the widow voluntarily. There were other perquisites: Alice Thornton, dealing with her husband's virtually bankrupted estate, was advised by her brother to cling on to her valuable 'widow-bed' instead of selling it to pay the debts. Unlike the beds left to her by her mother, which formed part of her estate – and thus part of her husband's – and so could be 'prized' away by creditors, the 'widow-bed' could not be touched.[42]

Manorial court rolls show that it was customary for a widow of a copyhold tenant to remain in occupation of his land until she remarried or died – this was called her 'widow's estate'.[43] As a new grant of a piece of copyhold land was customarily made for three lives, the widow of the first named – if she did not remarry – might survive the other two. (The fact that remarriage meant loss of the copyhold kept many widows from remarrying.) But women were also copyhold tenants in their own right in some of those manorial court rolls that have survived from the seventeenth century: thus one Henry Hellier put his wife and son's name into the copy in 1626 – a demonstration of equality. This meant that Anne Hellier could enjoy the copy after her second marriage.

Certain corporations of the period still recognized the wife's position as a business partner (even if that recognition was dwindling as the century progressed).[44] In contrast to unmarried girls who were rarely allowed to be apprenticed to the guilds, the wives of guild members could have their husbands' rights and privileges conferred upon them: as widows, they were thus often in a position to run the business, for the assistance of a journeyman still meant that the widow was in practical control. Carpenters' widows, for example, could receive apprentices. Weavers' widows were especially well treated, being able to continue to work in their own right. After the Restoration, when many similar privileges were vanishing, Charles II still upheld the rights of the weaver's widow by decree 'to use and occupy the said trade by herself'.

Widows' names appear in the contracts of the shipping trade: in 1636 Susanna Angell and her daughter Elizabeth petitioned to land fourteen barrels of powder, and another thirty-eight barrels expected to arrive in the ship *Fortune*, and either sell it or send it back to Holland, from whence it came. In *Tom of all Trades*, published in 1631, Thomas Powell recommended young men not to seek employment in the provision businesses which he termed 'the housewives' trades (as brewer, baker, cook and the like)' because the wife so often acted as her husband's business partner. Where the wife had demonstrably shared the work during the husband's lifetime, her position was often entrenched on his death. The names are known of brewers' widows, bakers' widows, and butchers' widows still plying the family trade (not all, one hopes, of the type of Elizabeth Chorlton, who was fined in the 1650s for selling 'stinking meat'). A widow could even be a vintner, if she inherited the business, an unlikely opportunity for a woman on her own account.[45]

Strongest of all was the position of the printers' widows. Membership of the Stationers' Company, which included booksellers, binders and printers, was strictly limited to twenty-two persons. Widows actually retained their freedom of the Stationers' Company not only after their husband's death, but following remarriage. In this way a printer's widow presented an eligible match for an aspirant printer, printers' businesses frequently travelling sideways in this manner, as when the widow of Francis Simson married in turn Richard Read and George Elde, carrying the vital membership of the Stationers' Company with her.[46]

These energetic women were certainly not carrying out the ideal of the widow's conduct proposed by Richard Brathwaite in *The English Gentlewoman*: 'Again, are you widows? You deserve much honour, if you be so indeed ... Great difference then is there betwixt those widows who live alone, and retire themselves from public concourse, and those which frequent the company of men. For a widow to love society ... gives speedy wings to spreading infamy ... for in such meetings she exposeth her honour to danger, which above all others she ought incomparably to tender.' What if a widow needed to plead in a law court for her inheritance, family fortunes which might 'all lie a-bleeding'? Here widows were simply reminded of the promises of Christ: 'Your Lord maketh intercession for you, rendering right judgement to the orphan and righteousness unto the widow.'[47]

The women described in this chapter would have preferred to take Christ's parable of the importunate widow as their text; which advocated a far less passive code of behaviour.

CHAPTER SIX

Poor and Atrabilious

~~~~~~~~

> '[I] could see nothing in the evidence which did per-
> suade me to think them other than poor, melancholy,
> envious, mischievous, ill-disposed, ill-dieted, atrabilious
> constitutions.'
>
> ARTHUR WILSON ON THE CHELMSFORD WITCHES, 1645

When the fifth Earl of Huntingdon succeeded to the title of his grandfather in 1604 he specifically ordered that great respect should be paid to 'my ould lady' – Dorothy Port, Dowager Countess of Huntingdon. Fifty years later a cheerful young lady, proposing to marry a peer who was on his deathbed, saw it as an undoubted advantage that she 'might be a widow in a very short time, and not be troubled long with him'.[1] But the independence of a wealthy widow, and the honour generally paid to an elderly aristocrat, found no parallels in the condition of the poor women who made up the vast majority of the widow class. The contrast between the fate of the haves and the have-nots in seventeenth-century society is alarmingly illustrated by the relative prospects of the rich and poor women in widowhood.

The very sight of a poor old woman lacking an obvious protector aroused many different primitive fears in the breast of society (nor were these fears exclusive to the male sex). To begin with, such a woman presented a social problem: where the 'masterlessness' of the wealthy widow was her opportunity for independence, the unsupported state of her poorer contemporary could all too easily mean suffering, if not actual destitution.

Recent research has dispelled the cosy notion of a society where old folk lived side by side in the same dwelling with their descendants: very few married children lived with their parents, let alone with a single surviving parent; such a household was the exception rather than the rule. At the same time the old style of welfare, based on the charity of the church or the manorial organization, had either vanished or was breaking down. A series of Tudor statutes, culminating in the Poor Law of 1601, made the succour of the weak the business of the parish, by means of compulsory rates levied on its members .[2]

There were also far more women than men at the bottom of society economically: most of the adult pensioners in the City of London were widows (however, their treatment here seems to have been benign).[3] The frequent mention of poor widows in the social projects and wills of the charitably inclined (the efforts of Lettice Viscountess Falkland and Lady Anne Clifford have been observed) makes the continuous nature of the problem clear. These and other private beneficiaries were the lucky ones. In general, the sight of a poor old woman might raise implications of possible financial responsibility in fellow members of her community – guilt never being an agreeable sensation.

Nor was the phenomenon of old age a particularly rare one, despite the short expectation of life at birth. Every village, wrote Francis Bacon in 1623, had at least one person in it over sixty; Gregory King, in his account of the English population written at the end of the century, estimated that one person in ten would be aged sixty or older.[4] The fact was that those members of society who did survive the perils of accident, disease and childbirth might live to a great age.

These figures do not refer of course peculiarly to women; nevertheless accounts of women attaining an exceptional age, even by today's standards, spatter such annals as we have. George Ballard, born in 1706, was a self-educated antiquary; his diligence at research makes his *Memoirs of Several Ladies of Great Britain who have been celebrated for their writings or skill in the learned languages, arts, and sciences*, first published in 1752, a valuable sourcebook for the previous century. He quotes among his heroines

Elizabeth Legge, who was born in 1580 and died in 1695; her two sisters lived to 100 and 112, her brothers to 109 and what must have been under the circumstances a disappointing eighty-two, respectively. Some of the early Quaker women, for all their trials, lived to an astonishing age. It has been suggested that it would be not so much the lack of aged persons as the lack of a large middle-aged group which would surprise us about the seventeenth century, in contrast to our world today.[5]

An old woman, then, as well as being an unwelcome spectacle for social reasons, was also a comparatively common one. Still further to her detriment was her actual physical appearance. Beauty, while it might be condemned by the preachers as an unstable basis for marriage, continued naturally to exercise its eternal lure; dislike of the aged physique, on the other hand, also widely inculcated, was a genuine passion of the time. It could even be justified. This was after all an age in which there was a subtle conspiracy to agree that beauty of outward form expressed an inward virtue; a view promulgated for example by Milton in *Comus* praising the appearance of The Lady – 'so dear to Heaven is saintly chastity' – or by Ford in *'Tis Pity She's a Whore*:

> So, where the body's furniture is beauty,
> The mind's must needs be virtue ...

Hic Mulier in 1620 suggested that 'good women, modest women' were 'ever young because ever virtuous'.[6] There was an obvious corollary to be drawn: physical ugliness (that common woe of the old) signified a base moral nature, if not something worse.

'The bodies of aged persons are impure', wrote William Fulbeck in his account of witchcraft in 1618; in general the breath and sight of such persons was regarded as 'being apt for contagion'.[7] The seven-year cycle after the age of sixty-two was sometimes known without much compassion as the Crooked Age. In the important seventeenth-century concept of the humours which went to make up the body, dryness and melancholy were held to be characteristic of the constitution of the aged.

The prejudices aroused by the sight of such dilapidated creatures were unquestionably worse in the case of old women than of old men. This was where many dark forces of the subconscious came into play. The ancient susceptibility of woman – the weaker vessel – to 'the devil's illusions' was the form in which these turgid fears were generally expressed in public. Woman's sexual voracity was another subject on which there was a conspiracy to agree in the seventeenth century, a period when, as has been mentioned, the potentially repetitious and thus demanding nature of the female orgasm was fully understood. As Robert Burton wrote in 1621: 'Of women's unnatural, insatiable lust, what country, what village does not complain?' We have noted that the lusty widow was a favourite concept of the times; sometimes economic necessity might become mixed up with lust. The village whore might be a widow, one such as Isott Wall of Tolland in Somerset who, according to evidence presented against her in court, boasted that 'she would open her door at any time of the night either to a married man or a young man'. Another convenient arrangement of a slightly different ilk might take place when a widow, needing a milker for her cow, paid for the work in kind.[8]

These women, evidently still in their sexual prime, were, if lusty, also ingenious in fulfilling their own needs. But what of the case of an old widowed woman, of hideous physical appearance, prone by her very sex already to the temptations of the devil? Secretly voracious, might she not be slaking her lust at some diabolical source, deprived of any other? In the writhings of the popular imagination concerning the old, all these webs – woman's weakness, her voracity, ugliness and Satan – became darkly and menacingly entangled.

The bodies of old women, twisted and gnarled by time like tree trunks, marred perhaps by protuberances and growths of different sorts including harmless warts and lumps and dangerous tumours – might the dissolving eye of fantasy not see in these ugly excrescences and bumps strange teats which the devil could suck? Was a particular wart or discoloration a mark of old age – or the witch's mark, which when pricked did not hurt?[9]

The notorious loquacity of the female – also taken for granted throughout literature, correspondence and popular report – was another characteristic where the devil's influence might be detected. Sir Thomas Overbury wrote wistfully in 1614 of *A Good Woman*: 'Her language is not copious but opposite ... She sings, but not perpetually, for she knows, silence in a woman is the most persuading oratory.' However, a great many women at the time evidently did not choose to employ silence's persuading oratory, since cases concerning the common scold, worse still a scold and brawler, and worst of all, a scold, brawler and curser, abound. A wife like that of Adam Eyre of Yorkshire: 'This morn [in June 1647] my wife began, after her old manner to brawl and revile me for criticizing her clothing and stepping on her foot and she kept on till noon', was the sort of wife every man dreaded. The words of Solomon were quoted with approval: 'It is better to dwell in the corner of the housetop than with a brawling woman.'[10]

The scold was by definition female. A woman presented to the courts for the offence and condemned faced a series of punishments: she could be fined; more picturesque and more humiliating was the practice of confining a scold in a brank or padlocked bridle; more spectacular still and on occasion more dangerous was the employment of the cucking-stool (the word was a corruption of the French *coquine* for a hussy). The occupant of the cucking-stool, otherwise known as the ducking-stool, was frequently cooled off in the village pond – whatever the season. Apparatus for the immersion of a scold was part of the social organization of the time: at Gravesend in 1636 for example, porters were paid 2s for ducking Goodwife Campion and 8d for laying up the cucking-stool afterwards. The popular almanacs of the time, containing advice by physicians as well as astrologers, all seriously defended the use of the cucking-stool; less seriously, one hopes, the cutting-out of the tongues of persistent offenders was also advocated upon occasion.[11]

Such women were Alice, wife of Thomas Crathorne, a victualler of Seasalter, Kent, who was charged in 1616 with being 'a common swearer and a brawling scould, and withal will be drunk exceedingly'. Or Isabel Richardson and Alice Worthington, 'Common Scoulds and disturbers of their neighbours' whom the jury of the manor court in Manchester directed should be confined in the 'Cucking Stool' and ducked several times in the horse pond in mid-October. Or Jane Withers of Weldon in Northamptonshire, who was sent to gaol in 1630 till she could find sureties for her next appearance at the general sessions; on her return to Weldon, the constable was ordered to 'cause her to be brought with the cuckingstool to some convenient place within the town and ... there be doused and ducked in the manner of scoulds'.[12]

It was when scolding slid into the far more serious social crime of cursing (against which Parliament even legislated in 1624) that the devil's influence was once more detected. Scolding, like other manifestations of bad temper, was frequently an end in itself, whereas curses implied a wish to injure the person concerned. It was when the devil overheard the Witch of Edmonton cursing her enemy Banks that he exclaimed joyfully: 'Now thou art Mine Own', and he prophesied concerning the churlish Banks:

> The witch of Edmonton shall see his fall,
> If she at least put credit in my power,
> And in mine only, make orisons to me,
> And none but me.[13]

It was dangerous, if you were an old woman, a beggar perhaps, of disagreeable appearance, to curse your uncharitable or unkind neighbour, or even to allow your lips and what Hannah Woolley called 'that slippery glib member the tongue' to move in some possible version of a curse. For then if your neighbour suffered a loss, grief or other form of injury, you might be suspected of having caused it ... with the aid of the devil. It would be suggested either that he had brought about the injury himself or that he had endowed you, as his partner, with the powers to do so. Thus by cursing, even muttering gibberish in a way characteristic of many harmless senile persons,[14] a friendless old woman imperilled her own safety. Her danger was even more acute if her male-dictions had some justification because she had suffered some real damage or slight at the hands of the person against whom she railed. A wealthy widow without encumbrances was a potential independent; a crone without protection was a potential witch.

Attention has been drawn to the fact that in many cases of witchcraft tried in the seventeenth century the alleged witch had a genuine grievance against the persons who declared themselves bewitched. This in turn draws attention to the fact that a poor old woman might well have no form of retaliation against the society which persecuted her, other than the hopeful practice of enchantment. One need not go as far as John Stearne, who in 1648 explained witchcraft as a female phenomenon on the grounds that women were more 'easily displeased and revenge-ful' than men, due to Satan 'prevailing with Eve'. More simply one can see that the social circumstances of many old women might well point them in that direction, out of desperation.[15]

Some form of blackmail, for example, might be exercised in order to secure an old woman a living, something otherwise diffi-cult for her to do, as emerges from the evidence at the great Lancashire witch trials of 1612–13. It was said that none could escape the fury of Elizabeth Southernes (known locally as 'Old Demdike') if her family were 'given any occasion of offence' or denied 'anything they stood need of'. John Device was supposed to have been so afraid of Anne Chattox – 'a very old, withered, spent and decrepit creature, her sight almost gone' – that he covenanted to pay her a yearly dole of meal on condition she hurt neither him nor his goods; on his deathbed he considered that he had been bewitched by her because he had left one instalment unpaid.[16]

It was a point made by Reginald Scot in his classic exposure of 1584, *Discoverie of Witchcraft*: in the case of certain old women 'their wrongs' gave them leave 'to chide and threaten' (as being void of any other way of revenge).[17] The case of the Belvoir witches indicates that not all those arraigned on charges of causing injury were innocent of the *intent* to harm — if a more rational society remains doubtful of their ability to do so.

The story begins like a fairy tale with a castle and a happy, prosperous and noble couple. (It ends like one too, with the deaths of some wicked witches.) Belvoir Castle, in Leicestershire, set augustly on a natural prominence dominating the surrounding countryside, was the seat of the powerful and ancient family of Manners, headed by the Earls of Rutland. In 1612 Francis, sixth Earl of Rutland, succeeded to the title on the death of his childless brother. Not only did the new Earl and Countess lack for nothing either of wealth or prestige, enjoying close connections with the court of King James I, but the succession was now secure, since they had two young sons, Henry Lord Roos, the heir, and Francis Manners; in addition the Earl had a daughter, Catherine Manners, by his first wife. When he succeeded to the earldom, Lord Rutland was described as one who took such honourable measures in the course of his life that he neither displaced tenants, nor discharged servants, but made strangers welcome; his wife was similarly benevolent, 'so that Beaver-Castle was a continual place of Entertainment'.[18]

Among the early objects of the benevolence of the Earl and Countess was an old woman known as Mother (Joan) Flower, and one of her daughters, Margaret. Mother Flower's poverty was relieved and she was employed as 'Char-woman' (the word, then as now, was applied to a domestic help who came in by the day) at the castle. Margaret Flower was put in charge of the 'poultry abroad and the wash-house indoors'. It cannot be said that the Flowers, mother and daughter, sound very satisfactory employees. Margaret Flower purloined provisions, and while some servants' perks were obviously tolerated, these provisions were taken out of the castle in excessive quantities. Margaret Flower also crept out of the castle, 'returning at such unreasonable hours' that mischief was suspected. This mischief was no doubt connected with the fact that Mother Flower's house was supposed to be a local bawdy-house; at any rate it was always full of 'idle and debauched company'. Here Mother Flower's other daughter, Philippa, held sway, and among other activities was 'lewdly transported with the love of one Thomas Simpson'.

As for Mother Flower, she would be described a few years later as 'a monstrous malicious woman, full of oaths, curses, and imprecations, irreligious, and for anything they [her neighbours] saw by her, a plain atheist'. The general impression left by Mother Flower was certainly gruesome: 'her very countenance was estranged, her eyes were fierce and hollow, her speech fell and envious, her demeanour strange and exotic, and her conversation sequestered'. In short, both in her appearance and in her speech, Mother Flower corresponded closely to Reginald Scot's stereotype of the breed of witch: 'commonly old, lame, bleare-eyed, pale, foul and full of wrinkles... lean and deformed, showing melancholy in their faces... doting, scolds, mad, divelish'.[19]

Furthermore Mother Flower had a pet cat called Rutterkin, and in that respect too she conformed to the stereotype of the witch. 'I come, Graymalkin... Paddock calls...', cry the witches to their familiars in the opening scene of *Macbeth* before they vanish. It is her dog Tomalin – 'My Tommy, My sweet Tom-boy!' – actually the devil in disguise, who lures the Witch of Edmonton to her destruction. The 'brindled cat' which mewed thrice, the toad of *Macbeth*, the devilish dog of Edmonton, find a hundred parallels in the witch trials of the seventeenth century, which also featured a multitude of rats, and even the occasional wasp or butterfly. During the famous case of the North Moreton witches, for example, tried at Abingdon in 1605, Agnes Pepperwell was accused of having a 'whitish mouse with a man's face called Sweat' who was a Spirit, Elizabeth Gregory had a black rat with a swine's face and a boar's tusk called Catche, and Mary Pepperwell had 'a whitish toad' called Vizett.[20]

Who knew what devilish familiar might lurk inside the humble shape of a black dog seen by the roadside or a tame white mouse on an old woman's shoulder? No domestic animal, glimpsed prowling in the shades of evening, slinking through the night, was to be totally trusted, never mind the fact that such a pet might be the natural companion – solace even – of a lonely old woman, never mind the nocturnal habits of so many such creatures, notably cats, for this was an area where common sense had taken flight before the onslaughts of fear and prejudice. So Mother Flower's pet cat Rutterkin was destined to play his part in the accusations against her.

What with Margaret Flower's light-fingeredness and her 'indecencies', and the maledictions of her mother, it was hardly surprising that the Flower family in general made themselves extremely unpopular with the household at Belvoir Castle; very soon 'nobody but the Earl's family loved them'. And then that love too faded: the Earl of Rutland turned against Mother Flower 'and used not that Freedom nor familiar conferences with her as usual'. When a certain Peake wronged Mother Flower, the Earl of Rutland, hitherto her patron, paid no attention to the injustice, which was thus not remedied.

As for the Countess, she too became disillusioned with Margaret Flower for her neglect of her duties, so that to the pleased derision of the neighbours, Margaret Flower found herself ejected from her comfortable billet at the castle. The Countess of Rutland seems to have behaved with financial generosity over the dismissal, giving Margaret Flower 40s (as much if not more than a year's pay), a bolster, and a mattress of wool. Nevertheless the feelings of Mother Flower and her family towards the Earl and Countess of Rutland now turned to 'Hate and Malice'.[21]

For all this, when in 1613 the heir to Belvoir, Henry Lord Roos, sickened and died of a disease for which the doctors could find neither cure nor explanation, witchcraft was not suspected. It was only when the second boy Francis, now succeeded to his brother's courtesy title of Lord Roos, sickened, and the girl Catherine Manners also went into some form of decline, that doctors and desperate family alike, interested neighbours and dependants, looked round for some explanation outside the natural world as to why this tragedy should be threatening the house of Rutland.

By an unfortunate coincidence – from the point of view of the Flower family – there was at this juncture a witch trial in progress at the nearby Leicestershire Assizes, at which three women who knew the Flowers, Anne Baker, Joan Willimot and Ellen Green, were being accused. Familiars played their part in this drama. Anne Baker revealed that Joan Willimot had given her two spirits in the likeness of a kitten, which went with deceptive innocence under the name of 'Puss', and a mole called 'Hiffe'. Both animals had leapt on her shoulder and immediately sucked at her ears (sucking was an acknowledged attribute of familiars). Anne Baker bestowed the kitten upon a baker who had struck her and the mole on one Anne Dawse who had termed her 'witch, whore, jade'. Within a fortnight both the baker and Anne Dawse were dead.[22]

Intensive examination of the three women also produced a number of weird accusations against Mother Flower concerning the vengeance she had vowed to take on the Earl of Rutland. Later the Flower daughters provided further details of the affair. Possibly in their case some form of physical torture was used,[23] but generally speaking where suspected witches were concerned, relentless questioning by the authorities, combined with the other harsh deprivations associated with imprisonment, produced confessions readily enough. Mother Flower was by this time, as we shall see, beyond human aid or punishment, but the story of her vengeance, as pieced together from the various confessions, went as follows.[24]

After Margaret Flower's dismissal the devil had seen an excellent opportunity to use the family as 'Instruments to enlarge his kingdom'. He therefore offered them whatever they might want, accommodatingly suggesting that he should attend them in the guise of a dog or cat or rat, in order to allay suspicion. 'Abominable kisses' and 'an odious sacrifice of blood' sealed this unpleasant compact. Although the Flowers did take the opportunity thereafter to produce the occasional 'Tempest' for the ruin of the crops, it was of course personal vengeance against the Earl of Rutland which chiefly preoccupied them.

Joan Willimot, herself a widow, like Mother Flower, testified to the latter's boast that though she could not have her will of the Earl of Rutland 'she had spied my lord's son and stricken him to the earth with a white spirit'. Spitting on some earth and working it with her fingers, she announced herself well satisfied that 'though she could not hurt the Lord himself, yet she had sped his son'. Margaret Flower supplied further details as to how her mother had carried all this out. Mother Flower had asked her daughter to procure a glove belonging to the young Lord Roos, and Margaret had duly picked one up which she found lying 'on the Rushes in the Nursery'. Mother Flower then first used the glove to stroke her cat Rutterkin, then dipped the glove in hot water, 'pricked it often' and within a week, lo and behold Henry Lord Roos was 'tormented'.

The glove of Francis Lord Roos was discovered by Margaret Flower on a dung-hill; she brought it to her mother where it received similar treatment of immersion in hot water and rubbing on the belly of Rutterkin. However in the case of Francis, because the boy, although sickly, was still alive in 1619, it was stated that Mother Flower had merely threatened him 'a Mischief' and had predicted (inaccurately as it turned out) that he would mend again.

A piece of handkerchief belonging to Lady Catherine Manners was similarly applied to the belly of Rutterkin, at which point the cat was ordered to 'fly and go'. According to Margaret Flower, Rutterkin merely replied with the word 'Mew' and did not either fly or go; however, this refusal was somehow interpreted as evidence that even her familiar did not have power over a witch like Mother Flower. The lewd Philippa Flower confirmed her sister's confession concerning the glove and its treatment; ultimately her mother had buried it 'wishing the owner might never thrive'. Philippa also contributed that her mother frequently cursed both the Earl and Countess of Rutland, boiling 'feathers and blood together, using devilish speeches and strange gestures'.

We do not have to accept the wilder statements of Margaret and Philippa Flower in order to suppose that Mother Flower had not only threatened to be revenged on the Earl of Rutland, but had actually indulged in some form of witchcraft to do so. Nor was her successful form of vengeance intended to be kept secret. Anne Baker had been told three years earlier by 'two wives of

Belvoir' concerning the death of Lord Roos that a glove had been buried and as it 'rotted and wasted, so did the liver of the lord'. Writing towards the end of the eighteenth century, when descendants of the deponents were still living, John Nichols in his *History and Antiquities of the County of Leicester* wrote that there was 'no doubt of their intentional guilt ... In short they believed themselves to be witches.'[25] For a malevolent old woman, ranged as she saw it against the powerful Rutland family interest, witchcraft represented not so much one possible form of revenge as the only possible form. The coincidental (as we must believe) sickenings and deaths of the Manners children represented therefore at once Mother Flower's triumph and her downfall.

After the Leicestershire accusations against the Flowers had been heard, the family were fetched by the Justices of the Peace, who bound them over to appear at the Assizes at Lincoln. Margaret and Philippa reached Lincoln, but Mother Flower died suddenly *en route* and was buried at Ancaster. Even the manner of her death was appropriate to one whose 'whole course of life gave grave suspicion that she was a notorious witch'. It was remembered that Mother Flower had predicted that she would be 'neither hanged nor burnt'. This time her prediction was certainly successful although there is no evidence that she had additionally foreseen the precise manner of her death. This came about as Mother Flower was eating a piece of bread and butter. She called on the morsel to choke her if she was guilty of being a witch. She was and it did.[26]

The Flower sisters were less fortunate. A series of Tudor statutes against witchcraft had culminated in the toughest one of all at the beginning of the new reign. By the Act of 1604 it was no longer necessary to have actually caused the death of a person by the use of witchcraft, the mere practice of it if proved was sufficient to ensure guilt. This law, which was not repealed until 1736, also made any form of consultation with or feeding of an evil spirit a felony; so much for Rutterkin and his kind, the kitten called Puss, the mole called Hiffe and so forth and so on, an endless stream of evil spirits masquerading as domestic animals who were undeniably being harboured by their mistresses. By this standard, Philippa Flower too, like her mother, was probably guilty of practising witchcraft – in her case to cause Thomas Simpson to love her; Margaret by her own account had supplied the fatal gloves belonging to Lord Rutland's sons.

Margaret's confessions in general sounded that pathetic note of hysterical delusion which marks so much of the evidence at the witch trials.[27] She admitted that she had two familiar spirits 'sucking on her', one white, the other black and spotted. The white spirit sucked under her left breast, and its black-spotted fellow 'within inward parts of her secrets'; they had agreed to carry out all her wishes in return for the promise of her soul. While Margaret was in gaol at Lincoln, four other devils also appeared to her, one of whom had a black head like an ape; unfortunately Margaret could not recall anything about their encounter except that she had been angry that the devil had not been 'plainer' in the manner of his speaking. The other three took the forms of Rutterkin, 'little Robin' and another spirit.

Philippa Flower too bore witness to the existence of a white rat sucking at her own left breast – in fact a spirit – for three or four years, to which she had promised her soul if it would cause Thomas Simpson to love her. And Philippa confirmed that Rutterkin, now recognized for what he was, a devil in disguise, had persistently bitten and sucked at her sister's neck over the years.

In March 1619 the two daughters of Mother Flower were executed at Lincoln 'to the terror of all beholders'. The Earl of Rutland, hearing them cry out against the devil 'for deluding them' and now breaking his promise of assistance 'when they stood most in need of his Help', no longer felt any difficulty in believing in their 'Wickedness and horrible Contracts'.[28] A year later when their sickly son Francis died in his turn, the Earl and Countess, now left without male heirs, must have felt themselves still further convinced that justice had been done.

We can follow the rest of the sad story in the Rutland family accounts. In 1619 £20 had been given to Mr Jephson for prosecuting the witches at Lincoln, and another £20 had been spent on 'my Lord's journey to the Assizes'. With the death of Francis in March 1620 £26 was the total sum incurred for breaking the ground for his burial, and payments to the chanter, the Dean, choristers, vergers, grave-makers, as well as eight dozen torches and sufficient frankincense. The coffin itself cost 10s. In July payments were noted relating to a journey by 'my lady' to take the waters at Tunbridge Wells. She went 'for Barrenness', the waters there being celebrated for relieving that unhappy condition.[29] The cure did not work. It turned out to be one of Mother Flower's less successful predictions that after a long while the Earl and Countess 'should have more children'. No more children were in fact born to the stricken Rutlands.

This absence of male heirs did, however, have the unlooked-for effect of improving the fortunes of the Earl's daughter by his first wife, Lady Catherine Manners. About the time the Flower sisters were being put to death at Lincoln, Lady Catherine, already an heiress from her own mother's property, had found herself courted by the most glittering figure of the age, George Villiers, Duke of Buckingham. It has been suggested that Buckingham sought Catherine as much for the satisfaction of her Manners connection – the Villiers had once been minor gentry in the area dominated by the Manners family – as for her money;[30] 'that puir fool Kate', as she was dubbed by King James I, was certainly not pretty.

At first the match hung fire; despite her love for Buckingham, Catherine, who was a Catholic, declined to change her religion, while 'the mother Countesses', that is the Countess of Rutland and Buckingham's baleful mother, the former Lady Compton, now created Countess of Buckingham in her own right, quarrelled. But the death of Francis transformed Catherine from a considerable into a magnificent heiress; Buckingham was now far more likely to receive the vast dowry he was said to be asking for 'the sister' – £20,000 ready money and land worth £4,000 a year, the latter figure to be doubled if Lord Roos died.[31] At last in May 1620 Buckingham succeeded in marrying the 'puir fool', who bestowed upon him not only her heart but a fortune hugely augmented by her brothers' deaths.

The transformation of the daughter of the Earl of Rutland into the Duchess of Buckingham, wife of the King's splendid favourite, cannot have been what Mother Flower intended to bring about with her spells and curses.

'[I] could see nothing in the evidence which did persuade me to think them other than poor, melancholy, envious, mischievous, ill-disposed, ill-dieted, atrabilious [that is, black-biled] constitutions' – so wrote the historian Arthur Wilson charitably, and doubtlessly accurately, of the Chelmsford witches at their trial in 1645.[32] For if Mother Flower had a genuine grudge against the Earl of Rutland and tried to practise some kind of vengeance, there were many old women throughout the seventeenth century who suffered simply because they corresponded to the stereotype of the witch.

In many ways it was a circular argument. Whatever the present disagreements about the precise nature of seventeenth-century witchcraft, it is at least common ground that the vast majority of witches actually tried were both female and old (with widows at a special risk).[33] Contemporaries were well aware of the fact. King James I put the proportion of females to males at 20 to 1 and Alexander Roberts put it at 100 to 1. In his pamphlet of 1648, John Stearne, a close associate of the witch-hunter Matthew Hopkins, wrote that it was 'evident' that of witches in general 'there be commonly more women than men … especially of the hurting witches'. Reginald Scot had connected witchcraft with the menopause, a phenomenon peculiar to the female, when women suffered delusions because of 'the stopping of their monthly melancholic flux'. Witches were also believed for the most part to live 'in most base esteem and beggary', a supposition also borne out by the figures available.[34] Thus was the stereotype constructed in both literature and public opinion.

This meant that while some younger women and a few men were certainly tried for or suspected of practising witchcraft, they were considered as individuals; the species to which they belonged was not of itself under suspicion. (Pregnancy incidentally saved a woman from being hanged, at least for the time being; a woman who was not pregnant would sometimes plead so in order to save herself – a claim which would be investigated by the local midwives.) But because the agreed characteristics of a witch were those of an old woman, any old woman might be suspected of being a witch owing to characteristics over which she had no control. Another witness to the witch-hunting forays which produced the Chelmsford trials wrote that suspicion fell on 'every old woman with a wrinkled face, a furred brow, a hairy lip, a squint eye, a squeaking voice, or a scolding tongue, a skull cap on her head, a spindle in her hand, a Dog or Cat by her side.'[35]

The Bideford witches – three crazed old women who were put to death in the West Country in 1682 – provide tragic examples of persons who were probably guilty of little except advancing age, destitution and wandering wits. Temperance Lloyd, a widow, Susanna Edwards, a widow, and Mary Trembles, a single woman, were tried at the Devon Summer Sessions in front of Sir Francis North, the Lord Chief Justice, and Sir Thomas Raymond. North described them later: they were, he wrote, 'the most old, decrepid [sic] despicable, miserable creatures that ever he saw. A painter would have chosen them out of the whole country for figures of that kind to have drawn by.' They were in fact damned by their own confessions, which as North pointed out, exceeded even the testimonies brought against them, which of themselves were 'very full and fanciful'.[36]

Certainly there was much which was 'fanciful' about the evidence produced against the three women.[37] Temperance Lloyd was subjected to a crude physical examination. This was a routine procedure for a suspected witch, in order to discover either the devil's mark – which could be pricked without pain – or some form of teat – which could suckle a familiar (described as 'a common token to know all witches by'). Mrs Anne Wakeley, wife of a Bideford husband, headed the body of women who found in Temperance Lloyd's 'secret parts' two teats 'hanging right together like unto a piece of flesh that a child had sucked. And that each of the teats was about an inch in length.' Temperance

Lloyd herself confessed that a 'Black man' sometimes in the shape of a magpie, had sucked at them. The devil had also helped her to disguise herself as a 'grey or braget' (honey-coloured) cat, in order to deposit a child's puppet in the chamber of one Grace Thomas to whom she wished to do harm.

Anne Wakeley testified that while nursing Grace Thomas, 'something in the shape of a magpie' had come into her chamber. Grace Thomas contributed that Temperance Lloyd had fallen on her knees and wept in Bideford High Street allegedly for joy at seeing her, Grace, 'so strong again'; however, that night clearly as a direct result of the encounter, Grace Thomas had been overcome by agonizing pricking pains from head to foot. Significantly, in her opinion, Grace Thomas recovered once Temperance Lloyd had been hauled off to prison.

The old woman further testified that she had disguised herself 'in the form of a red pig' to bewitch one Lydia Burman who had given evidence against her in another trial (Temperance was however acquitted on this particular charge). Some of Temperance's revelations cast a pathetic light on the nature of her daily round. The devil, she said on the eve of her death, had appeared to her while she was fetching some brooms: 'This poor woman has a great burthen', he exclaimed, offering to ease her of it. But Temperance refused the devil's offer: 'I said The Lord had enabled me to carry it so far, and I hope I shall be able to carry it further.' Sometimes she revealed an understandable sense of grievance: 'I sold apples, and the child took an apple from me, and the mother took the apple from the child; for the which I was very angry.' But, added Temperance piteously, the child itself died of smallpox, not witchcraft.

Another routine test of a witch was to compel her to recite the Lord's Prayer or the Creed; a test incidentally that a confused and illiterate old woman was all too likely to fail. Failures of memory, stumblings or mumblings indicated the devil at work. Old Temperance recited both the Lord's Prayer and the Creed most imperfectly.

As for Susanna Edwards, she recounted how she had met the devil about two years ago 'in the Parsonage Close' in the shape of a fine gentleman 'apparelled in black'. Hoping to get some money from him, Susanna curtseyed. The devil, discovering from her what he was apparently not sufficiently omniscient to know, that Susanna was very poor, promised her that she would not want for meat, drink or clothes in future if she placed herself in his power; after this encounter, the devil – 'something in the shape of a little boy' – sucked at her breast. Then it was Mary Trembles's turn: she confessed that she had been persuaded by Susanna Edwards to follow her into mischief. She had then had carnal knowledge with the devil in the shape of a lion: he had sucked her 'and caused her to cry out with pain'.

In the end Susanna Edwards was convicted of bewitching one Grace, wife of John Barnes, and Mary Trembles of bewitching a mariner's wife called Dorcas Coleman, whose violent internal pains her doctor had been quick to ascribe to witchcraft. Both these women incidentally were alive and healthy at the time of the trial, so the witchcraft had evidently done little permanent damage. The reason Susanna and Mary gave for 'tormenting' Grace Barnes was a significant one: it was to punish her for having refused them 'meat and tobacco' when they begged for it. Like Temperance's fury with the child and its mother who robbed her of payment of her apple, these admissions were evidence of the kind of low-level village grudge which must have existed in multitudes. It was when a child died, a woman rolled in agony and the slighted person corresponded to the black-biled – 'atrabilious'– stereotype of a witch, that the hue and cry of prejudice frequently followed.

A pamphlet printed shortly after the deaths of the three old women (which accused them amongst other things of sneezing a woman to death and causing a boy out at sea to fall to his doom from the main mast of his ship) gives the following account of the execution scene.[38]

Old Temperance Lloyd went on her last journey from the prison quite unconcerned, 'eating all the way'. She does not even seem to have comprehended the danger she was in. Mary Trembles, on the other hand, 'lay down' and had to be tied on to the back of a horse before she could be moved.

Just before the hangman did his work, the Rev. Mr Hann, a local clergyman, subjected the three women to one last cross-questioning on the subject of their diabolical past. Mary Trembles protested her innocence. While admitting that she had seen the devil once (although no longer quite sure of his shape – 'looking, I think, like a lion') she denied what had been sworn at the Grand Inquest, that she had 'a teat in her privy parts', and denied too that she had had carnal knowledge of the devil.

In so far as Temperance Lloyd had any understanding of what was happening to her, she seems to have made a last ditch attempt to blame Susanna Edwards:

MR HANN: 'You say you never hurt ships nor boats: did you ever ride over an arm of the sea on a cow?'
TEMPERANCE LLOYD: 'No, no, Master, 'twas she' (meaning Susanna).

At this Susanna burst out in her turn that Temperance 'lied'. And so after a prayer by the Rev. Mr Hann, Susanna Edwards suggested to Mary Trembles that they should sing part of the Fortieth Psalm (which ends, appropriately enough, 'But I am poor and needy; yet the Lord thinketh upon me: thou art my help and my deliverer; make no tarrying, O my God'). As Susanna Edwards mounted the ladder, she said: 'The Lord Jesus speed me; though my sins be as red as scarlet, the Lord Jesus can make them as white as snow; The Lord help my soul.' In the words of the pamphlet, 'Then was executed.'

Mary Trembles went to her death with similar piety: 'Lord Jesus receive my soul; Lord Jesus speed me.' Then Mary too 'was executed'.

This left old Temperance Lloyd, whom the sheriff described to her face as 'the woman that has debauched the other two'.

SHERIFF: 'Did you ever lie with the devil?'
TEMPERANCE: 'No.'
And later:
SHERIFF: 'Did the devil never promise you anything?'

TEMPERANCE: 'No.'

SHERIFF: 'Then you have served a very bad Master, who gave you nothing. Well, consider you are just departing this world; do you believe there is a God?'

TEMPERANCE: 'Yes.'

SHERIFF: 'Do you believe in Jesus Christ?'

TEMPERANCE: 'Yes; and I pray Jesus Christ to pardon all my sins.'

'And so was executed.'

It is quite possible, as was stated by a later pamphlet, that the judge actually tried to get Susanna, Mary and Temperance off: 'these three poor old women [as he supposed] were weary of their lives and that he thought it proper for them to be carried to the Parish from whence they came, and that the Parish should be charged with their Maintenance; for he thought their oppressing Poverty had constrained them to wish for Death'. But in another version, the judge, while referring to the harmless effects of 'melancholy or delusion', regretted that mercy could not be shown to the old women in the present state of the Law: 'we cannot reprieve them without appearing to deny the very being of witches'.[38]

Not all old women witches who practised some form of primitive magic suffered as cruelly as the Bideford witches. The mysterious nature of 'black' witchcraft, as it was regarded in the seventeenth century, is underlined by the fact that 'white magic' co-existed with it, as indeed forms of 'white magic' had always been practised since ancient times (and are, in various forms from fortune-telling to herbal healing, still practised today). 'Cunning folk', who unlike witches were often male, existed in abundance: in *The Anatomy of Melancholy*, Robert Burton wrote that there were 'Cunning men, Wizards and white-witches ... in every village'. Their protection was quite simply that they were believed to do good. Thus a 'cunning woman', one with certain curative arts at her disposal from which black magic was specifically excluded, might pursue an active and even lucrative career, provided she kept herself carefully free from the taint of witchcraft. Sir Ralph Verney's son and heir Edmund, generally know as 'Mun', had a 'distracted' wife called Mary. It was decided to send for a cunning woman called Old Judith.[40]

First of all Mun Verney asked Old Judith to assure him that she did not 'use any manner of Charms, Sorceries, or Magic whatsoever'. Old Judith hastily gave 'devout assurances' to the contrary. She was then permitted to carry out her experiment. This was to take a hare's head – 'Jack Hare' – and wrap it in a cloth; she then bound the wrapped hare's head round the patient's own head for three days and three nights. When the hare's head was finally removed, it was inserted into the patient's pillow, amid the feathers, to lie there 'so long as they live'. The idea of the cure was that there was a 'sympathetical Virtue' in a 'melancholy Hare's Brain' which would 'draw away all Melancholy out of that hare-brained people' (i.e. the mad).

The cure did not work. As Mun Verney wrote: 'It would be very pretty if so slight a thing could cure.' Poor mad Mary Verney never fully recovered her wits. All the same, Old Judith suffered no ill consequences for her efforts, while Mun Verney in his slightly sceptical attitude to the whole affair represented a kind of tolerance which not only co-existed with harsh prejudice but also grew as the century progressed.

Among rational people, it had always seemed strange that the devil should choose the 'poor and atrabilious' and invest them with such colossal powers. As the newspaper *The Moderate Intelligencer* put it in 1645, it was 'a great wonder' that devils should be conversant with 'silly old women that know not their right hand from their left'. In 1641 Henry Oxinden of Barham, father of the headstrong Peg, wrote with marked good sense about the case of one Goodwife Gilnot, who was accused by a man called Brake of having lost his sheep. Oxinden pointed out that he too had frequently lost sheep – without going to the trouble of thinking himself bewitched.[41]

As for Goodwife Gilnot, who was accused of having a teat upon her upper body – actually a small wart – 'Believe it', he wrote, 'there is none so familiar with her as to receive any sustenance from thence'. He went on: 'Such deep root hath the fables of witchcraft taken hold in the heart of this and other silly men ... they will not with patience endure the hand of and correction of God ...' It was being suggested 'that certain creatures here on earth, called witches, be the authors of men's miseries, as though themselves were innocents and had deserved no such punishments ...' Henry Oxinden concluded: 'Moreover I cannot see how any rational man can persuade himself that a simple woman should do such things as these.'

The progress in scepticism on the subject has been summed up by Christopher Hill in these terms: 'In 1600 most respectable people believed in witches ... by 1700 this was no longer true.'[42] The last execution of a witch occurred at Exeter in 1685, three years after the deaths of the three 'decrepid' Bideford women: Jane Wenham, the last person to be condemned (in 1712) was reprieved. Yet as late as 1704 *The Athenian Oracle*, a magazine for answering popular queries whose view on life was otherwise quite enlightened, when asked whether it was permissible to kill a witch to preserve oneself, answered: as to those 'wretched and malicious Creatures ... we should make no scruple to strike or stab them'.[43]

But these old women, wretched and malicious as they often were, might have framed on their own behalf the bitter question posed by the Witch of Edmonton:

> Cause I am poor, deform'd, ignorant
> And like a bow buckled and bent together ...
> Must I for that be made a common sink
> For all the filth and rubbish of Men's tongues
> To fall and run into?[44]

CHAPTER SEVEN

Unlearned Virgins

～

…But think you, Helen,
If you should tender your supposed aid,
He would receive it?…
A poor unlearned virgin…

COUNTESS OF ROUSILLON TO HELENA,
All's Well That Ends Well

'Thou mayest perhaps think I have lost my labour': thus Elizabeth Josceline to her husband in 1622 on the prospect of her giving birth to a daughter. The best way to palliate the blow would be to think of those biblical exemplars, Elizabeth, Esther, and chaste Susanna. Betty Viscountess Mordaunt was equally frank on her own account: 'If it be thy blessed will, let it be a boy' – this was her fervent prayer when she was once more pregnant in 1665, although she already had six sons. And when a seventh boy was indeed safely born, Betty Mordaunt apostrophized the Almighty in verse:

To all the rest, thou hast this added more
The blessing of a son, to increase my store.

Anne, wife of the Royalist commander Sir Simon Harcourt, shared the primitive feelings of her husband who wrote back to her from the campaign in Ireland: 'with God's blessing bring me another lusty boy'. After his death Anne Harcourt married the Parliamentary general Sir William Waller, a widower with sons. Her diary, kept like that of Betty Mordaunt for spiritual reasons, is a long record of public and private trials and her own 'transgressions'. Throughout, whenever pregnant, she pleads for the safe birth of a living child with all its parts and limbs – 'and a son'.[1]

The experience of Agnes Sim, a servant of East Brent in Somerset who had become pregnant by her master, was on a cruder level. She 'asked him [her master] who should father the child. He said he would, if it was a boy, but if it was a maid, she should lack a father for it.' (Servants did sometimes undertake the responsibility of providing their sonless masters with male heirs; the sex of the child being, it was believed, determined by the female.)[2] Neverless Agnes Sim discovered for herself what Betty Mordaunt and Anne Harcourt expressed so eloquently in their spiritual diaries, that primitive desire for a boy which in a sense disadvantaged the girls of this period even before their birth.

Cary Verney was one of the five sisters of Ralph Verney and as a child had been the 'she-darling' of her father Sir Edmund. Married at fifteen, but with the settlement never completed owing to the difficulty of wartime conditions, Cary found herself at the age of eighteen a pregnant widow, when her husband Captain Gardiner was killed in 1645. Then, 'My sister was brought to bed of a girl to all our griefs', wrote Ralph Verney. Having provided no male heir, with no proper marriage settlement, even her own jointure in peril, poor Cary was grudged her very food at the Gardiner home at Cuddesdon; finally she fled back to her own family. Cary Verney did enjoy an exceptionally happy second marriage to John Stewkeley of Hampshire; but it was no wonder, as one of the jolly, gambling, gossiping ladies of the Restoration court, that she regretted hearing the news that her nephew John Verney's wife (already the mother of a son) had given birth to a daughter: 'for I find our sex is not much valued in our age'.[3]

One of the primary reasons why the average female was 'not much valued', as Cary Verney lightly but aptly expressed it, was that she was not much educated – in comparison, that is, with the average male, her brother as it might be, that child who had fulfilled his parents' primitive expectations by being born of the favoured sex.

Even women despised other women for their silliness. Margaret Duchess of Newcastle was sharp enough to see the reason for this foolishness: in 1655 in *The Worlds Olio* she wrote that 'in Nature we have as clear an understanding as Men, if we were bred in Schools to mature our Brains'. Nevertheless in practice she found the tittle-tattle of women intolerable.[4] Conversely, even those women who did for a number of individual reasons receive a proper education might well be scorned for their attainments. In principle, society rewarded the learned woman with disapproval or at best suspicion.

Anne Lady Newdigate, that devoted mother, unconsciously summed up the contemporary attitude to the education of the sexes when she wrote in her will, dated 1610: 'that my boys may be brought up in good learning and both they and my daughters to be bred up in virtuous and godly life'. Elizabeth Josceline, laying down instructions in *The Mothers Legacy to her Unborn Child* for the education of that hypothetical daughter for whose arrival she had apologized in advance, hoped she would be taught 'The Bible, housewifery, writing and good work'. (She herself, incidentally, had been highly educated by her grandfather, learning both languages and history in the enlightened tradition of the late sixteenth century.) Elizabeth Josceline added: 'other learning a woman needs not, though I admire it in those whom God hath blest with discretion yet I desire it not much in my own, having seen that sometimes women have greater portions of learning than wisdom'. And if her husband himself wanted to have 'a learned daughter'? At least: 'my dear ... I pray God give her a wise and a religious heart'.[5]

Where a highly educated woman did escape censure, it was generally for some extraneous reason which might be exceptional piety, of the sort which Elizabeth Josceline hoped would redeem her own 'learned daughter'. Or it might, in a more worldly fashion, be due to her high position in society. In private Dorothy Osborne poked fun at Margaret Duchess of Newcastle, who admittedly did cut a fairly weird figure in society, at any rate where her costume was concerned. In 1653, Dorothy was 'satisfied that there are many soberer people in Bedlam', and she wrote that the Duchess's friends were 'much to blame to let her go abroad'.[6] In public, however, Margaret Newcastle's rank (that of a very rich Duchess, wife of a Royalist grandee who had been Governor to Charles II as a boy) obtained for her some handsome tributes from academics at both universities.

The Duchess used to present favoured colleges with her own works. Expressions of gratitude were published after her death in a special volume: *Letters and Poems In Honour of the Incomparable Princess Margaret, Dutchess of Newcastle*. A letter from the Master and Fellows of St John's College, Cambridge, sets the tone: 'In your Poesy we praise that Life and native Verdure, every way Confident with its self, Castilian like, it stands not still, nor boils over, but with a gentle stream doth touch our Ears and slide into our Minds. In your Philosophy we praise that lightsome and piercing acuteness, nothing constrained, nothing obscure; you render all things clear and genuine ...' However, Trinity College, in wondering aloud 'how it came to pass that Eloquence, Poetry, Philosophy, things otherwise most different, should without the help of a Tutor, without the Midwifery of a University, at length, agree in a Woman' showed that the Duchess was very much the high-born exception to the general rule.[7]

It was not a rule which showed signs of lapsing as the century progressed. On the contrary, the prejudice against education for girls – and its dreaded end-product, the learned woman – had derived fresh impetus from the presence of a male sovereign after 1603. It had always been rather tactless to attack the learned woman with too much zest so long as that paragon of female erudition Queen Elizabeth occupied the throne. As the poet Anne Bradstreet wrote in memory of 'our dread Virago' forty years after her death:

> Let such as say our Sex is void of Reason,
> Know 'tis a Slander now, but once was Treason.

Not only were men freed from the inhibition of the 'dread Virago's' intellectual example by her death, but that male sovereign, James I, had himself a scant opinion of the female intelligence. Perhaps the frivolity of his Queen, Anne of Denmark, had something to answer for; at any rate when it was suggested that his daughter, another Elizabeth, should learn Latin, the King replied that 'To make women learned and foxes tame had the same effect: to make them more cunning.' And he forbade it.[8]

Such sentiments would have come as a marked surprise to his English royal relations of yore: those Tudor princesses of the Renaissance, not only Queen Elizabeth herself who could translate Latin into Greek, and the famously erudite Lady Jane Grey, but Queen Mary Tudor, celebrated at the time for her knowledge of science and mathematics. For that matter James's mother Mary Queen of Scots, whose intellectual attainments have been overshadowed by her dramatic life story was, as a princess, automatically instructed in the classics. We know from the English Ambassador to Scotland that she used to read Livy regularly for pleasure after dinner, with George Buchanan.[9]

In the sixteenth century Sir Thomas More had written: 'I do not see why learning...may not equally agree with both sexes.' At the end of Queen Elizabeth's reign a classical education was a mark of elegance in the circle round Mary Countess of Pembroke: William Wotton, in his *Reflections on Ancient and Modern Learning*, wrote of that period: 'It was so very modish, that the fair sex seemed to believe that Greek and Latin added to their Charms: and Plato and Aristotle untranslated, were frequent Ornaments of their Closets.' Such a tradition lingered on at a place like Little Gidding. Here the many daughters of the house, in the tranquil religious retreat founded by the Anglican theologian Nicholas Ferrar in the 1620s, were carefully educated in Latin, as well as arithmetic, writing and music (and such practical matters as book-binding). But it was in the seventeenth century that George Herbert was able to list among well-known proverbs: 'Beware of a young wench, a prophetess and a Latin woman.'[10] While women themselves were often contributing a note of ritual apology whenever they felt they had stepped outside the modest mental boundaries which circumscribed their sex.

Lady Elizabeth Hastings, carefully educated by her 'Vigilant Mother' Lucy Countess of Huntingdon to know French, Latin and Italian, was advised by her on marriage merely 'to make herself fit conversation for her husband'. As a result, Lady Elizabeth showed herself so modest – that favourite epithet again – throughout her short married life with Sir James Langham that he never had 'all those inconveniences which some have fancied, so necessarily accompany a Learned Wife'. She died still young in 1664. This model existence on the part of one who might otherwise have caused Sir James a great deal of trouble with her accomplishments, was summed up in a quatrain:

> That Skill in Scripture, and in Tongues she got,
> Made her a living Bible Polyglot.
> These did not puff her up, she did descend
> To the kind offices of Wife and Friend.[11]

It was not that women did not read the books where they had the ability or the opportunity to do so. In 1647 we find Adam Eyre of Yorkshire spending 1s 8d on a book at a fair at Wakefield for his scold of a wife – presumably to palliate her bad temper on his return. There was, as might be expected, a heavy bias towards what Lettice Falkland's biographer called 'good authors'. Mary Countess of Warwick's tastes ran to the works of Jeremy Taylor, Foxe's *Martyrs*, and Baxter's *Crucifying of the World by the Cross of Christ* (which she described as her favourite book) as well as the poetry of George Herbert – who often features in ladies' reading at this time. But Lady Anne Clifford read Turkish history as well as Chaucer, and had Ovid's *Metamorphoses* read aloud to her by her cousin Maria. Lady Cholmley, wife of Sir Hugh, the Governor of Scarborough Castle during the Civil War, was 'addicted to read and well versed in history'.[12]

Nevertheless an atmosphere of excuse was apt to prevail when a female achieved anything out of the ordinary of a literary nature. Mrs Dorothy Leigh, author of *The Mothers Blessing*, which had reached its seventh edition by 1621, dedicated it to her three sons (she was a widow). Writing, she admitted in this dedication, was 'a thing unusually among us' since women generally used words to exhort. The book itself contained a lot of advice on the sort of wives her boys should marry, and the need to exhibit patience towards them subsequently: 'Bear with the woman,' she pleaded, 'as with the weaker vessel.'[13]

It was not a coincidence that one of the few Englishwomen in the first half of the seventeenth century who believed, without apology, in the need to educate girls properly was a Catholic nun: Mary Ward.

The disappearance of the convents at the time of the Reformation had deprived English girls not only of convenient local places of learning, but also of a pool of women teachers in the shape of the nuns themselves. Indeed, when the convent of Godstow near Oxford was being disbanded, a petition for its preservation (unsuccessful) was mounted on the grounds that 'most of the gentlewomen of the county were sent there to be bred'.[14]

At home in England the position of the woman teacher had not recovered from the collapse of the nunneries. (Again, it was no coincidence that the Anglican Little Gidding, derided by opponents of its high church sympathies as a 'Protestant nunnery', also placed a value on female education.) Many of the daughters of the English Catholic families however continued to be sent abroad to convents in the Low Countries to receive their education. These girls – Knatchbulls, Gages, Vavasours, Blundells – embarked on journeys of much danger and difficulty, defying the authorities to reach their goal abroad.[15]

It was their parents' intention in sending them that they should be preserved in the ancient faith. A Petition of the House of Commons of 1621, which asked for all children of Catholics to be recalled from abroad and given Protestant teachers at home, also had in mind re-educating such children religiously. But these girls who wended their way to the Low Countries, often remaining there as nuns, also found a kind of independence unknown to their sisters still at home – paradoxically in view of the black reputation of such convents back home in Protestant England.

Mary Ward's obsession with women's education (which has been shared by most people through history who have wished to improve the female lot in a permanent fashion) had as its ultimate objective the reconversion of her native England to Catholicism. But as a woman of remarkable independence of judgement, Mary Ward was quick to see that women in religious orders could not carry out their proper part in this apostolate, if they were not correctly prepared for it. As she told Pope Paul V, when she pleaded with him to be allowed to found an order of 'English Virgins': 'the education of girls is congruous to our times'. Nor was this education intended to fit girls solely for the religious life. Mary Ward's memorandum to the Pope on the subject of the 'English Virgins' described their aim as being to instruct young girls in 'piety, Christian morals and the liberal arts' so that they could 'profitably embrace either the secular or the religious life'.[16]

Mary Ward was born in Yorkshire near Ripon in 1585: her baptismal name was Joan (she took Mary at her confirmation).[17] She came of a prominent recusant family, related to half the other Catholics in England: two of her Wright uncles were involved in the Gunpowder Plot and her father was one of the many Catholic gentlemen arrested on suspicion immediately afterwards. On Mary herself the influence of her grandmother, with whom she lived for five years, was probably even more powerful since Mrs Wright was famous for being 'a great prayer'. As a young girl, Mary became engaged to a member of the Redshaw family, but on his premature death, despite her 'extreme beauty' which attracted new suitors, she abandoned all thoughts of marriage. Instead she joined the Poor Clares at St Omer.

It was at this point that Mary encountered a completely new world from that of the hunted recusant Catholics in which she had been brought up. Women as a whole, and particularly women of rank – whether in religious orders or not – led much freer lives in the Low Countries. This was something on which travellers commented, including the fact that women here participated equally in conversation and argument with men. At the same time the generally passive or secluded role of women within the Catholic Church itself had begun to be questioned in certain quarters after the Council of Trent. The spirit of the Counter-Reformation, incarnated by the career of the great Spanish nun, St Teresa of Avila, suggested that women could achieve much not merely by prayer and contemplation but by direct participation in the worldly work of the Church. As Mary Ward was to put it later, women were proposing 'to follow a mixed kind of life, such as Christ and his Blessed Mother lived on earth'.[18]

At Gravelines Mary Ward attempted to found a Poor Clare convent for Englishwomen out of her own resources, and later she did found a boarding-school for English girls at St Omer, where she was aided by five English friends, including her sister Barbara. On one occasion at St Omer the nuns' confessor made an unwise observation, ascribing their diminishing religious fervour to the weakness of their sex. Mary Ward strongly rebutted him. Was their failure 'because we are women? No, but because we are imperfect women. There is no such difference between men and women', she went on, 'that women may not do great things! ...' As for the Catholic religion, 'It is not *veritas hominis*, verity of men, nor verity of women, but *veritas Domini*' – the truth of God. Mary went on to quote the example of the (female) saints: 'And I hope in God it will be seen that women in time will do much.'[19]

Certainly Mary Ward herself fulfilled her own prophecy that women in time would 'do much'. Her life story was one marked by unusual reverses and dangers even by the standards of the seventeenth century; she was also dogged by ill-health. None of this stood in the way of her determination to prove that the education of girls was 'congruous' to the times in which she lived.

As time went on, an increasing number of English girls were sent abroad to be taught under the auspices of Mary Ward and her friends. This had the double effect of increasing Mary Ward's contacts with the English Catholic world she had left behind via these young ladies, and also necessitating journeys to England itself to seek out new pupils, or in certain instances annuities to pay for their board and tuition.

The account of these travels, made by Mary Ward between 1608 and 1618, makes exciting reading: a sort of *Westward Ho!* in reverse. London at that period was a honeycomb round which government informers buzzed, seeking to rout out secret Catholics. The 'English Virgins' came to be nicknamed the Apostolicae Viragines or the Galloping Girls by their pursuers. The technique of Mary Ward and her friends was to come in plain clothes, as it were, and blandly to hold open house, as though there was nothing to hide. Then they pursued their mission under the noses of the Government and its spies. But the 'plain clothes' were in fact deliberately splendid garments such as ladies of quality would have worn if they had *not* been nuns. We have a description of Mary's sister Barbara 'in a bright taffeta gown' with a starched yellow ruff 'à la mode' and richly embroidered petticoats.[20] When Mary Ward herself was hauled to the Guildhall to answer for her missionary work, she abandoned concealment and carried a rosary in her hand in defiance of the law – and her own safety. In the court she denounced the magistrate for blasphemy, and recited the litanies of the Blessed Virgin Mary in her coach on her way to prison.

It would be nice to be able to record that Mary Ward, allowed to vanish beyond the seas once more, was warmly received on the Continent. Unfortunately, for all her energies and perseverance in the cause of female education there, she was destined to arouse quite as much – and in a sense more – damaging hostility abroad. Here her enemies lay within her own Church. 'Runaway nun!', 'Visionary!', and worst of all, 'False Prophetess!' had shouted the townspeople of Gravelines. The spirit of the Counter-Reformation, where women were concerned, had its ardent supporters and also its furious detractors. While the immediate reaction of Pope Paul V to Mary's idea of a new Institute of women following 'a mixed kind of life' in the world had been favourable, and his successor Gregory XV received her kindly in 1621, the atmosphere in Rome soon changed for the worse.

It was Mary's intention to place her Institute under a superior general directly dependent on the Pope (on the model of the Jesuits). That was an unpopular notion with the Catholic Church as a whole, and in particular the bishops. But her conviction that women could 'do much' was equally unpopular with that section of the Catholic Church which remained convinced that women *could* do much – at home or in a secluded convent. Exaggeration is always a skilful weapon of attack. Mary Ward was accused of wishing women to rival men in the ministry, that is to say, usurp their functions as preachers; Mary Ward had in fact deliberately made the point that women could not and should not preach or administer the sacraments, and wives should also be subject to their husbands.[21] Yet the unfair charge succeeded in its aim.

Mary Ward's convents and schools, founded as far apart as Liège and Cologne, Vienna and Prague, Rome and Naples, flourished. But opposition to the new Institute intensified until in 1631 a decree was issued by Pope Urban VIII dissolving it; its members were only allowed to continue their ordinary work of religious education if they took purely private vows.†

Mary Ward herself was imprisoned in Germany, in a tiny airless filthy cell at the orders of the Church (but not the Pope – who had her released when he heard the news). Subsequently she lived quietly in Rome, and in 1639 she returned to England.

Here, the patronage of the Catholic Queen Henrietta Maria seemed to promise her the opportunity of continuing her work of female education. There were 'common schools for girls in London' to be founded, and young women needed to be taught Latin; unlike King James I, Mary Ward was a fervent believer in the importance of Latin studies for girls. Or perhaps it would be accurate to say that Mary Ward approved of such studies for exactly the same reason as King James disapproved of them: she thought it important that women should become 'more cunning' – in the service of God. As Mary Ward wrote of a young nun in

---

†It was not until 1703 that Mary Ward's congregation received papal approval, and not until 1877 that the then Pope officially described Mary Ward as its foundress. Finally, in 1951, Pius XII described Mary Ward, with St Vincent de Paul, as the outstanding pioneer of the lay apostolate of women. Today Mary Ward's Institute of the Blessed Virgin Mary, a mainly teaching foundation, spreads across five continents.

her care: 'let Kate perfect her Latin with all possible care, without loss of health.' She added: 'no talent is so much to be regarded in them [young nuns] as the Latin tongue'.[22]

The outbreak of the Civil War and the flight of the English royal family from London put an end to Mary Ward's new London apostolate. She went north to her native Yorkshire, and died in 1645, having lived through the siege of York. Most of her adulthood she had suffered torments probably from stones, and the last twenty years of her life she was in such pain that she could not lie down, but had to sleep in a rocking-chair. Yet in her last hours, with characteristic spirit, she insisted on the sisters round her singing to stop their tears, and managed to sing with them. Her last recorded words were firmly practical: 'It matters not the who, but the what.'[23]

In general, with her independence and her gallantry, as well as her excellent sense of humour in the most trying circumstances, Mary herself stands for the best kind of English spinster. 'From my palace', she headed a letter written in her filthy German cell. The Elector of Bavaria, in her private code, was known as 'Billingsgate', a slang term of the time for bad language. 'When she travelleth she is extraordinarily jovial', complained one of her contemporaries, who was shocked by her apparent lightheartedness. But Mary Ward had her answer: 'Mirth at this time is next to godliness', she observed of one particular tight corner. When she did travel – crossing the Alps four times, frequently in winter and through snow – Mary Ward retained a kind of splendid English curiosity which sent her sightseeing in Prague and buying silks in Venice. She was notably fond of 'a fine view', yet shocked the fashionable Romans by proceeding on foot all the way to Perugia, wearing old clothes and leading a sick sister on her own donkey.

Above all education, and the need for education in women if they were to perform God's work, aroused her fervour. 'She was a great enemy of ignorance', wrote a contemporary.[24]

In general, if an English girl, regardless of rank, did receive a good education, it was very much a matter of individual luck. Alice Heywood, Oliver Heywood's saintly mother, made herself responsible for sending the children of her neighbourhood to

school as a work of charity, buying the 'poor ignorant sottish creatures' books. A maidservant might become an accomplished
reader if she happened to fall into the employment of a benevolent mistress, such as Elizabeth Walker or Mary Countess of
Warwick, both of whom saw it as their evangelical duty to instruct
their maids to read (so that they could at least read the Bible and
Psalms). A forlorn creature came to Elizabeth Walker's door, who
only knew her name was Mary Bun, 'almost eat up with scabs and
vermin, with scarce rags to cover her, and as ignorant of God and
Christ as if she had been born and bred in Lapland or Japan'.
Elizabeth Walker decided to save her not only by stripping her,
washing her and curing her of 'The Itch', but also by teaching her
to read, so that finally a rich farmer took Mary Bun as his apprentice. The formidable Lady Anne Clifford also delighted in giving
her maids 'such a book as they had not before'.[25]

As a result intelligent and forceful maids often feature prominently in the life stories of their mistresses: as 'Honest Dafeny'
Lightfoote, Alice Thornton's maid inherited from her mother,
who both could and did write and became as a result the main-
stay of the beleaguered Thornton household after Mr Thornton's
death as a bankrupt. 'God hath sent me a friend after my own
heart', wrote Alice Thornton. Bess, maid to Sir Ralph and Lady
Verney, who accompanied them into exile in France at the time
of the Commonwealth, learnt French easily.[26]

A good Free School or benevolent patronage or both might
account for sudden unexpectedly high figures of local literacy. A
recent study by David Cressy quotes women as a whole (they are
not analysed by class) as displaying the same high level of illiteracy as labourers and husbandmen; a figure of 90 per cent illiteracy amongst women is given for London – the most favourable
area – in 1600, declining in 1640 quite sharply to around 80 per
cent; in East Anglia at the same period female illiteracy is given as
nearly 100 per cent.[27] The accounts of the Russell family headed
by the Earls of Bedford at Woburn Abbey in Bedfordshire, over
a considerable period during the seventeenth century show that
the skills among the maids varied. One year, out of seven or eight
maids there would be two or three who could write well, another

year none (whereas amongst the male footmen there would always be two or three who could write well). One housekeeper, Ann Upton, wrote well; her predecessor could not write at all. Apart from contact with the Russell family themselves, some of these literate servants had probably been educated at the local Free School founded by the second Earl of Bedford.[28]

Where a girl of the upper classes was concerned, it was a happy accident if she came from a large family of brothers spread out over a number of years; she might then enjoy the services of their tutor, who would not automatically vanish when the eldest boy went away to school or university. In this way the disparity between the education offered to brother and sister might be somewhat lessened. The Ladies Diana and Margaret Russell were the daughters of William, fifth Earl of Bedford, he who married Anne Carr, worthy daughter of the unworthy Frances Somerset, for love. The education of these little girls, like the literacy of the maids, can also be traced in the accounts for Woburn Abbey.[29]

Anne Countess of Bedford, like Betty Mordaunt, was the proud mother of seven sons, as well as four daughters. As a result, for a number of years Diana and Margaret were taught by their brothers' tutor, the Rev. John Thornton, a remarkable pedagogue and a man of formidable intellect who came straight to the services of the Russell family from Cambridge in 1646. The influence of this dissenting divine on the character of the girls' brother William Lord Russell (the celebrated Whig martyr of the reign of Charles II) is a matter for the history books; but for the Russell girls, especially Lady Diana, who was Mr Thornton's favourite, a rare opportunity occurred for instruction.

Mr Thornton believed in the new principles of education introduced by Comenius, which amongst other things supplemented teaching by pictures. One entry in the accounts reads:

Pictus Orbis Comenii for Mr Robert	2s
The Assemblies Pieces in Latin for Mr Robert	2s 4d
Small Catechisms at several times for them and for Lady Diana	2s 6d
Paper and Quills for them all for these five years	3s 6d

It will be seen that even under Mr Thornton's care Lady Diana did not learn Latin (something which would have grieved Mary Ward). However, Lady Diana did receive the best Bible: an edition in 'fair minion print' costing 12s 6d where the other children's Bibles cost 3s 6d.

Ultimately the gorgeous brothers departed – for Westminster, for university, for the Grand Tour – and when the last of them was gone, it was time for the Ladies Russell to be given over to the dancing master, music teacher and French master who would give them that education deemed in principle suitable for young ladies of their station. Lady Diana grew from the beguiling little girl painted by Lely with another sister Anne (who died of eating poisonous berries at the age of five) into a woman of resolute character. She married twice: first at the age of fifteen, being left a childless widow a year later, and secondly to Lord Alington of Wymondley. Lady Diana maintained however a lifelong friendship and correspondence with Mr Thornton. In later life Lely's charming child came to believe sternly in total abstinence from food as a cure-all for sickness. 'If he would come down to me, I should quickly cure him by fasting', she wrote of one troubled member of the family.[30]

Outside the aristocracy both the educationalist Basua Makin and the scholar Elizabeth Elstob benefited from early association with gifted brothers. Basua Makin was born in 1612, the daughter of the rector of Southwick in Sussex, and the sister of the astonishing scholar John Pell – at the age of twenty he was reputed to know Hebrew, Greek, Latin, Arabic, Italian, French and both High and Low Dutch. Influenced by his example, Basua herself by the age of nine was said in some measure to understand Latin, Greek, Hebrew, French and Italian; we shall consider the conclusions she drew for female education as a whole from this exceptional upbringing in a subsequent chapter. At the end of the century Elizabeth Elstob, the pioneer of Old English studies, was able to work in Oxford because she had accompanied thither her brother William, who was at the university. The antiquary George Ballard, who knew the Elstobs at Oxford and included Elizabeth among his celebrated ladies, was another with an erudite sister who at the age of fourteen had 'an extraordinary genius for Coins' and had made a collection of them.[31]

It was no wonder that the sisters, watching the world through their brothers' eyes, often developed passionate attachments to these young gods who could roam freely, while they were kept confined at home. Ann Oglander, daughter of another happy marriage, that of Sir John and Lady Oglander, described by her father as '*Très belle* Ann'— the most beautiful of all the family – was in despair when her brother George left for Caen on the Grand Tour. Her sorrow was premonitory, for he died abroad shortly afterwards.[32]

As a child Anne Viscountess Conway, daughter of the Widow Bennett by her carefully selected second husband Sir Heneage Finch, worshipped her step-brother John Finch, who was five years older – all the more so because her father had died before her birth. Little Anne hung around at home and in the gardens of Kensington House, plagued with sick headaches. Her family put her frequent maladies down to too much reading, unsuitable to her sex.[33] Given the intellectual achievements which marked the adult life of Anne Conway despite this handicap, it is more likely that a proper education (her step-brothers went to Westminster and Christ Church or Eton and Balliol) would have helped rather than hindered her health.

The most celebrated example of a sister's devotion to a brother was that of Katherine Viscountess Ranelagh for Robert Boyle, the famous physicist and chemist who arrived at the eponymous Boyle's Law (which stated that the pressure and volume of a gas were inversely proportional). Bishop Burnet proclaimed after her death that 'Sister Ranelagh', otherwise known as 'the incomparable Lady Ranelagh', had cut 'the greatest figure in all these revolutions of these kingdoms, for above fifty years, of any woman of her age'.[34] It was significant that this one woman whose learning merited universal respect not censure was not only well-born and pious but chose to exercise her powerful influence privately rather than through the writing and publication of books, spending the last forty years of her life caring devotedly for her brilliant brother. In her decency, her active kindness – she was both hospitable and charitable – and above all in her acceptance of the self-abnegatory nature of female intelligence, Sister Ranelagh incarnated the masculine ideal of a good woman. Her learning therefore, far from being a disturbing quality, became an added grace. As a result she had the distinction, perhaps a slightly dubious one, of being the one woman of whom Milton actually approved.

Katherine Boyle was born in 1614, one of the vast brood of children of Richard Earl of Cork. Four sons and four daughters survived the original family of fifteen; others besides Robert Boyle were talented. Mary Rich (née Boyle), Countess of Warwick, was Katherine's younger sister; Roger Boyle, Lord Broghill, later Earl of Orrery, author of the play *Mustapha*, was a writer as well as a soldier. 'Precious sister Kate', married at fourteen to an Irish nobleman, the second Viscount Ranelagh, quickly displayed that mixture of liveliness and godliness which would later captivate Commonwealth London. 'The sweetest face I ever saw' and 'the best company in which to be merry' – those were some of the compliments she attracted as a young married woman in Dublin.[35]

Her own arranged marriage was unhappy: unlike wilful Mary she had not made a choice for love. The best thing that could be said about Lord Ranelagh, remarked a contemporary, was that he seldom came sober to bed. But 'that excellent sister of mine', as Mary Warwick called Katherine, showed no signs of envying Mary's superior happiness. On the contrary, it was Sister Ranelagh alone in the family who forgave Mary instantly for her imprudent love match; it was Sister Ranelagh alone who visited Mary when she was laid low with smallpox; it was Sister Ranelagh who enabled Mary to bear the long strain of her husband's protracted deathbed, the agonies of gout producing little serenity of temperament in the dying man. Mary's verdict on Sister Ranelagh was as 'the most useful and the best friend, for soul and body, that ever any person I think had'.[36]

Separated from her unsatisfactory Irish husband, Sister Ranelagh came to make her life in England instead; her house in Pall Mall, Westminster, now became a home-from-home for her brother Robert Boyle at Oxford. Katherine was already acquainted with John Milton: in the late 1640s she dispatched her nephews to be educated by him at the Barbican. It was when Milton moved to Petty France, becoming Sister Ranelagh's close neighbour, that the friendship properly ripened; Milton describing her as standing to him 'in the place of all kith and kin'. At this point Lady Ranelagh's son Richard Jones was also sent to Milton, probably to read Greek and Latin with him.[37]

In London Sister Ranelagh, gifted with a memory, according to Mary Warwick, 'that will hear a sermon and go home and pen it after dinner verbatim' took lessons in Hebrew from 'a Scotch teacher'. He later dedicated his *Gate to the Holy Tongue* to her, congratulating Lady Ranelagh on her 'proficiency' in the language considering the short time she had learnt it and 'amidst so many abstractions as she was surrounded with'. However, at the end of Robert Boyle's life (when he was living with his sister) we are told that weak sight forced him to give up reading the Scriptures in Hebrew 'since he had none about him that could read it to him', so perhaps the 'abstractions' of Sister Ranelagh's busy life had proved more formidable than her teacher supposed. On firmer ground, Sister Ranelagh expressed herself as well satisfied with the new Experimental Philosophy which her brother and others were trying to institute, believing it would help mankind to understand 'this great frame of the invisible world', and thus the power of Almighty God. And it was her suitably bountiful task to distribute gratis all the 'noble Medicines' which Robert Boyle compounded in his laboratory in her house.[38]

A priggish note creeps into some of Sister Ranelagh's later letters; or perhaps too many years of acting as the fountainhead of good advice to a wide circle, with Roger Lord Broghill as well as Robert Boyle hanging on her judgements, had corrupted her. Sometime in about 1658 Robert repeated to his sister a compliment paid to her by the poet Edmund Waller, whom Boyle had visited at Hall Barn, near Beaconsfield. But Sister Ranelagh was no Sacharissa. She responded: 'I know his calling as a poet gives him licence to say as great things as he can, without intending they should signify any more than that he said them or to have any higher end than to make him admired by those whose admirations are so volatile as to be raised by a sound of words...' That category did not include Sister Ranelagh. Why should Waller, so eloquent 'upon things that so little deserved them... be so unwilling to apply that faculty to those subjects that were truly excellent?' she wrote. For this reason she returned 'his great professions' with a 'plain hearty wish' that he should employ them 'for the time to come' upon higher topics than herself.[39]

So much for Waller's compliments. Was this the same woman who had once been 'the best company in which to be merry'? One is not altogether surprised to learn that one of Sister Ranelagh's three daughters, perhaps finding the high moral tone unendurable, ran off with a footman. 'Niece Jones', as Mary Warwick and Robert Boyle described her, did not however gain much happiness from this plunge into passion. Robert Boyle, referring to his six nieces in his will, left property to Niece Jones, now Mrs Melster, and the daughter of the *mésalliance* Catherine Melster, the latter's portion to be held till she was twenty-one 'because of her peculiar circumstances'.[40]

Lady Ranelagh's experiences as a mother were in general disheartening. Her son Richard Jones, the third Viscount Ranelagh, was a spendthrift who succeeded in being expelled from the House of Commons (although his reputation rests more pleasantly with posterity, since he built Chelsea House and laid out Ranelagh Gardens). Her favourite daughter – 'a good person' according to Mary Warwick – died unmarried in 1672; another married daughter died young.[41]

It was as the beloved hostess to Robert Boyle, the centre of a distinguished and learned circle hanging on her good sense and judgements, that Lady Ranelagh enjoyed her true happiness. As late as 1687, when she was well over seventy, Sister Ranelagh was advising John Locke's friend Damaris Lady Masham on how to cure melancholy, acting as 'her physician' in this cause, as Lady Masham told Locke. When Sister Ranelagh died at the age of eighty-seven in December 1691, Robert Boyle, her companion of forty years, only survived her by a week; it was popularly believed that he had died of grief. The brilliant brother and his 'dearest sister and constantly obliging friend' as he had termed her in his will, were buried together in the chancel of St Martin-in-the-Fields.[42]

If the fraternal association was a fortunate chance, the advantage of a supportive parent at this period, where female education was concerned, can hardly be overestimated. Elizabeth Walker, for example, took particular care to teach her daughters to read. The modest yet learned Lady Elizabeth Hastings was described as being educated in 'a School or rather Academy' – in short, by 'her Vigilant Mother' Lucy Countess of Huntingdon.[43] It is notable how many of that slender band of female writers on whose auto-biographical works we depend pay tribute to a mother who actively encouraged them to learn.

The mother of Anne Murray, Lady Halkett, was governess to the younger children of King Charles I, but did not neglect her own family: she 'paid masters for teaching my sister and me to write, speak French, play on the lute and virginals, and dance, and kept a gentlewoman to teach us all kinds of needlework'. The mother herself oversaw her daughters' Bible reading: five a.m. in the summer and six a.m. in the winter. Ann Lady Fanshawe's mother saw to it she was offered 'all the advantages that time afforded, both for working all sorts of fine works with my needle, and learning French, singing, lute, the virginals, and dancing'. Alice Thornton's mother had her taught to read the Bible and the Psalms, also writing, singing and dancing, playing the harpsi-chord and the lute, and everything else thought fit for a lady.[44]

The ultimate advantage, however, for a daughter, was to be born of an erudite father, one who for whatever motive – possi-bly seeking a son-substitute – set out to provide her with a 'mas-culine' education. When Helena, the heroine of *All's Well That Ends Well*, offered to cure the King of France of his fistula, the Countess of Rousillon suggested with alarm that her aid was hardly likely to be accepted – that of a 'poor unlearned virgin' – where so many celebrated doctors had failed; Helena, however, armed with her father's 'prescriptions of rare and prov'd effects' went on to cure the King, and win the hand of her desired Bertram.[45] There were a few Helenas in the seventeenth century, although their contemporaries tended to react with the same alarm as the Countess of Rousillon at the idea of such accomplishments in 'a poor unlearned virgin'.

Like Katherine Ranelagh, Lucy Hutchinson had 'a great memory' as a girl and put it to the same pious use: 'I was carried to sermons', she tells us and, 'while I was very young could remember and repeat them so exactly, and being caress'd, the love of praise tickled me and made me attend more heedfully'. Lucy Hutchinson, born in 1620, the daughter of the Royalist Sir Allen Apsley, is one of the most attractive of the gallery of seventeenth-century women.[46] Although she sprang into print in order to write a justificatory memoir of the husband she adored, Colonel John Hutchinson, Governor of Nottingham Castle and judge at the trial of Charles I, it is the witty, independent, ever courageous character of Lucy which animates the text, rather than that of the Puritan John Hutchinson.

In Lucy's case she began life well with a mother who actually did want a daughter after bearing three sons. Lucy was also delicate, and received special care (including breast-feeding) from her mother, who feared she would not live. Furthermore, Lady Apsley began to dream of having an 'eminent' daughter when she found that Lucy could read perfectly by the age of four. Being given a Frenchwoman as a 'dry-nurse' as soon as she was weaned, Lucy was also bilingual in French and English at an early age.

At this point her mother lost confidence and began to worry that so much study would ruin Lucy's health. It was Lucy's father who had her taught Latin. Thus encouraged, Lucy began to outstrip in her progress her three brothers who were at school, despite the fact that her father's chaplain, who acted as her tutor, was in her own words 'a pitiful dull fellow'. Lucy became an avid reader: 'every moment I could steal from my play I would employ in any book I could find'; at the same time her mother took to having her daughter's own books locked up, to preserve her health. Her mother also worried at Lucy's lack of progress in dancing, and at the lute and harpsichord, and 'for my needle', wrote Lucy, 'I absolutely hated it'.

In an autobiographical fragment,[47] Lucy confesses that she was disliked by the other children for her solemnity, and her tendency to give little knowledgeable lectures. She was not however a prig, and passion always had a high priority. The maids fortunately were more appreciative of Lucy's lectures, as a result of which she was delighted to find herself their confidante in their love affairs. It was to Lucy's great satisfaction that her learning, far from depriving her of a husband as was generally prognosticated, actually won her the love of John Hutchinson. Idly, he spied some Latin books lying on the shelves at Lucy's parents' when she was away in the country; hearing they belonged to a mere girl, he became curious about this unusual character and asked a series of questions about her. The other girls, thinking to belittle her, told Hutchinson 'how reserv'd and studious she was, and other things which they esteem'd no advantage'.

They had mistaken their man: thus was ignited a lifelong love, John Hutchinson and Lucy being married in 1638, when she was eighteen. Many years later, after Hutchinson had died in the prison to which his allegedly treasonable activities had brought him (only Lucy's energies in tackling her Royalist relations saved him from death), she summed up her feeling for her husband as follows: 'So, as his shadow, she [Lucy] waited on him everywhere, till he was taken into that region of light which admits of none, and then she vanished into nothing.'[48] It was a romance stirred not by a pair of gloves, a favour or a fan, but by a shelf of books in the Latin language.

Although one should perhaps add that Lucy Hutchinson, like that other clever woman Margaret Newcastle, never evinced a very high opinion of the rest of her sex: doubtless the behaviour of her early companions rankled. The influence of Queen Henrietta Maria, for example, she thought to be disastrous: it was an 'unhappy kingdom' where the hands which were made only for 'distaffs' affected 'the management of sceptres'. And Lucy praised Queen Elizabeth for acceding to her male counsellors.[49]

We have dealt with the exceptions, the products of fortunate chance. What happened to those who were not singled out in this way?

No one was very interested in the formal education of the daughters of the poor for the obvious reason that reading and writing were not likely to be skills which would enable them to support themselves in later life. Where provisions had to be made by the authorities, as in the case of foundlings, emphasis was very much on the practical – knitting rather than reading or writing. A Free School was endowed at Great Marlow in Buckinghamshire in 1626 to teach twenty-four girls to knit, spin and make bean-lace – twenty-four boys, however, were to be taught to read. The well-known school for the 'Red Maids' of Bristol – daughters of 'decayed' (poverty-stricken) or dead freemen, so called after their uniform of red cloaks – had been intended by its founder to teach the girls either reading or plain needlework; the latter accomplishment, so much more economically useful, soon swallowed up the former.[50]

The quality of public education offered to girls also went downhill from the late sixteenth century onwards, as the practice by which a few girls had attended the grammar schools, if not to an advanced age, ceased. In 1594 for example Banbury Grammar School forbade the inclusion of girls above the age of nine, or when they could read English. Where girls did attend the grammar schools in the seventeenth century – their presence attested by girls' names in the margins of school books – this was where the curricula of the schools in question were not limited to a strict grammar course; girls were not permitted to take the ordinary public grammar course (with its heavy grounding in Latin).[51]

Richard Mulcaster was the first headmaster of Merchant Taylors' School, and subsequently High Master of St Paul's until his resignation in 1608 (he died in 1611). As an educationalist he was liberal compared to most of his contemporaries, believing in the value of such 'extras' as music, theatricals and physical training. He also viewed the education of girls with approval, generally advocating it in *Positions ... for the training up of Children*, first published in 1581 and dedicated to Elizabeth – 'a Virgin and a Learned Queen'. Yet it is significant that to this champion (by the standards of the time) the education of girls was only as 'an accessory by the way' to the upbringing of youths.[12]

In no way therefore did Mulcaster approach the position of Mary Ward, who believed that there was nothing to stop women one day, like men, doing 'great things'. On the contrary, he qualified his general approval for female education in a number of important respects. First, he proposed that girls had a 'natural weakness'; using this to explain the awkward fact that they often 'ripened' intellectually earlier than boys. Since girls' brains were not so much 'charged' as those of boys, explained Mulcaster, 'therefore like empty casks they make the greater noise'.

Second, Mulcaster was careful only to 'allow them [girls] learning … with respect to their ends'. What were these ends? 'I meddle not with needles nor yet with housewifery,' wrote Mulcaster, 'though I think it and know it to be a principal commendation in a woman to govern and direct her household … because I deal only with such things as be incident to their learning.' Since these girls were to be in the future 'the principal pillars in the upholding of households' it was useful for them to learn to read; moreover reading was needful for the study of religion. But Mulcaster saw no point in the admission of girls to the public grammar schools or the universities.

There were a rising number of girls' boarding-schools, particularly in the environs of London (we have noted how the heiress Sara Cox was snatched from Mrs Winch's school at Hackney in 1637). To these the prosperous middle classes began to send their daughters; at the school of Mr and Mrs Robert Perwick, also in Hackney, which flourished from 1637 to 1660, there were as many as 100 girls at a time. Other such schools have been traced at Westerham in Kent, Manchester (where there were two), Oxford, Exeter (two) and in Leicester.[13]

The first public school actually recorded was the Ladies' Hall at Deptford in Kent; here in 1617 the 'young gentlewomen', fetchingly attired in loose green garments covered in silver and carnation lace, their shoulders bare, their arms half naked, their hair 'dishevelled' (but artistically so), wearing green pumps and gloves, were presented to Queen Anne, wife of James I. They bestowed on her examples of their needlework. The Queen was then hailed in delightfully zeugmatic terms;

> Then bright Goddess, with thy sweet smile grace all
> Our nymphs, occasion, and our Ladies Hall.[54]

This emphasis on needlework and graciousness was characteristic. In 1647 Unton Lady Dering summed up what was expected for Peg and Elizabeth Oxinden, aged twelve and eleven, at Mr Beven's finishing school at Ashford: 'And besides the qualities of music both for the virginals and singing (if they have voices) and writing (and to cast account which will be useful to them hereafter) he will be careful also that their behaviour be modest...' In these boarding-schools, as in the homes of Anne Halkett, Ann Fanshawe and Alice Thornton, it was the education 'fit for her quality' in Alice Thornton's phrase, that is, 'lady's' quality, which was being provided, rather than the sort of learning which Sir Thomas More had had in mind in the previous century when he wrote that a wife should be 'learned if possible, or at least capable of being so'.[55]

Some practical accomplishments were of course taught – a form of shorthand for example (not so much for secretarial purposes as suitable for taking notes on 'good' reading), enough arithmetic for household accounts as Lady Dering suggested, legible handwriting, even tolerable orthography was considered desirable – although any girl who actually succeeded in these achievements would find herself way ahead of most of her female contemporaries.† At the same time all this was a world away from the kind of heavy grounding in Latin which was being automatically given to the girls' brothers at the grammar schools: Latin being the key not only to entrance to the universities, but to all forms of serious scholarship at the time, as well as science and

---

†The editors of the Verney letters and Oxinden papers comment on the 'evident decline' in female education and 'lack of advance' in female literacy respectively in the seventeenth century as compared to the sixteenth.[56]

medicine (something Mary Ward had appreciated in her emphasis on the subject to her young nuns).

As the boys' grammar schools themselves improved with the progress of the century, the rift between male and female education grew into a chasm. Scholarship was not the only loss. By the Restoration, classical knowledge was a prerequisite of the cultivated gentleman. It was left to the playwright Aphra Behn to mourn on behalf of her sex:

> The God-like Virgil, and great Homer's verse
> Like divine mysteries are concealed from us.[57]

Dainty French was however thought to be a desirable female accomplishment at court and elsewhere. An early seventeenth-century French grammar was written to enable women to 'parlee [sic] out their part with men'. The arrival of a French Queen – Henrietta Maria – in 1625 continued the trend. The influx of French Protestant (Huguenot) refugees into London resulted in the establishment of a few French schools, and provided a number of French teachers. French maids and French nurses were to be found in fashionable households. Later French romances began to flood into England and were read avidly, sometimes in the original: Brilliana Lady Harley, ordering a book from her son at Oxford, in 1638, asked for it in French: 'for I would rather read that tongue than English'.[58]

Humphrey Moseley, a leading bookseller, published a translation of Mademoiselle de Scudéry's novel *Artamenes or The Grand Cyrus* 'now Englished by F.C., Gent' in 1653; he dedicated it to Lady Anne Lucas on the grounds that she was known to have a perfect command of French (thus presumably not needing the services of F.C., Gent). Moseley added: 'Were it a Discourse of the most profound Learning that Humane Nature is capable of, and written in Greek or Hebrew, I would make its Dedication to your Noble Lord...'[59]

That was the difference.

In 1650 the Eure girls, Ralph Verney's cousins, children of his aunt Margaret Poulteney's romantic second marriage to William

Eure, were taught 'what is fit for them, as the reading of the French tongue and to sing and to dance and to write and to play of the guitar'. In contrast, when Sir Ralph heard that his god-daughter Nancy Denton, child of his friend and kinsman the learned Dr Denton, was going to be taught the classics, he read first the doctor, and then Nancy a lecture. 'Let not your girl learn Latin', he pronounced to the former, condemning shorthand too for good measure. 'The difficulty of the first may keep her from that vice, for so I must esteem it in a woman; but the easiness of the other [i.e. shorthand] may be a prejudice to her; for the pride of taking sermon notes, hath made multitudes of women most unfortunate.'[60]

Nancy, a girl of spirit, wrote back to her godfather that her cousins might out-reach her in their French, but she would out-strip them by learning 'ebri grek and laten'(let us hope that knowledge of Hebrew, Greek and Latin improved Nancy's spelling in English). Sir Ralph however refused to concede; in a further letter he condemned such unfeminine attainments once again: 'Good sweet heart be not so covetous; believe me a Bible (with the Common Prayer) and a good plain catechism in your Mother Tongue being well read and practised, is well worth all the rest and much more suitable to your sex; I know your Father thinks this false doctrine, but be confident your husband will be of my opinion.'[61]

Sir Ralph did put his seal of approval upon learning French. He offered to start a French library for Nancy on his next visit to Paris, since matters suitable for women's perusal were often written in that language; he included in that category not only romances, plays, poetry, but also all manner of subjects suitable to good housewifery such as recipes and gardening hints. In French could also be read profitably the stories of 'illustrious (*not learned*)' women from the past, wrote Sir Ralph firmly.[62] The dis-tinction between the two was not one which would have been appreciated by that 'dread Virago', Queen Elizabeth I. Yet Sir Ralph was no fierce male brute: he was on the contrary a good husband, a loving and considerate brother to his five orphaned sisters, a caring father to his daughters. He was merely expressing the philosophy of his times; while Nancy Denton, the daughter of an enlightened father with a particular interest in female education, represented one of the fortunate exceptions.[63]

CHAPTER EIGHT

Living under Obedience

'Teach her to live under obedience, and whilst she is ummarried, if she would learn anything, let her ask you, and afterwards her husband, *At Home*.'

SIR RALPH VERNEY TO DR DENTON

Susanna Perwick, daughter of those Perwicks who kept a fashionable girls' school at Hackney, was one of the few Englishwomen of this time – the age following the death of Queen Elizabeth – to be glorified under the title of virgin. Susanna, an exceptionally talented musician if her biographer John Batchiler is to be believed, died in 1661 at the age of twenty-four. Batchiler called his work *The Virgin's Pattern: in the Exemplary Life and lamented Death of Mrs Susanna Perwick*[1] ('Mrs' was the title then applied to respectable unmarried females, 'Miss' except in the case of very young girls being reserved for the other sort). Her musical talents were early encouraged, since the Perwicks' school staff included such luminaries as Simon Ives, the collaborator of Henry Lawes, as singing-master, and Edward Coleman the song-writer. Batchiler mentions that first Thomas Flood, then William Gregory, taught Susanna; others would gladly have taken their place, such as Albertus Bryne, the composer and 'famously velvet-fingered Organist' of St Paul's Cathedral. Susanna's proficiency at the violin quickly attracted favourable attention and she was also skilled at composing extemporary variations on a given theme; in addition she played the lute and harpsichord, sang, and studied books on harmony.

It was no wonder that ambassadors and other foreign visitors attended the Hackney school as the fame of this paragon spread, lured further by her sweet face, and her conversation – which, unlike that of most women, was 'rather sententious than garrulous'. According to Batchiler, Susanna had other skills beyond music: calligraphy, accountancy and cookery.

Alas, at the age of twenty-four Susanna caught a violent fever from sleeping in damp linen on a visit to London from Hackney. When she realized she was dying, she bequeathed her belongings in the neat orderly fashion which had characterized her whole short life: her books went to the young gentlewomen of the school, with the dying wish that they would not read other 'vain books' or waste time dressing-up. Then in the course of her protracted deathbed, Susanna herself gave 'small silent groans', in between her 'smiling slumbers', while her family wept loudly around her. At her funeral, attended by the whole school, Susanna's velvet-clad hearse was carried by six white-clad maidservants; while the pupils who had known her best, dressed in black, with white scarves and gloves, held up the mourning sheet. She was buried in the Hackney church, in the same grave as Mrs Anne Carew, a schoolfriend, 'a fine costly garland of gumwork' being placed on the coffin. Susanna's epitaph made her ultimate destination clear:

> Here Beauties, Odours, Musicks Lie
> To shew that such rare things can die ...
> From Heav'n she came with Melodies
> And back again to Heav'n she flies.[2]

And it was highly satisfying to an age which particularly enjoyed the significance of a good anagram that the letters of Susanna(h) Perwick's name could, with a little pious cheating, produce the words: AH! I SEE (C) HEAV'N'S PURE SUN.'†

Although the title of his work, *The Virgin's Pattern*, celebrated

---

†In the first half of the seventeenth century, about forty books concerning anagrams were printed in Latin alone; a preoccupation compared by one scholar to the modern love of palmistry.[3]

Susanna's unmarried state, Batchiler was careful to make it clear that she had by no means rejected altogether that 'blessed knot' of matrimony which was the lot of dutiful (Protestant) womankind. Admittedly after the early death of her fiancé, Susanna had dismissed various other proposed bridegrooms as wanting in spiritual riches; but Batchiler announced that Susanna had made another 'secret choice' before her death, and died in the arms of the man concerned.[4] It was a significant assurance in a work much closer to hagiography than biography; readers could feel confident that the conventional virgin's pattern of the seventeenth century – which was in fact to eschew virginity and marry – had finally been followed.

Yet Susanna Perwick's character, as it can be discerned beneath the veil of Batchiler's melancholy ecstasies, has something distinctly austere and as we should now say, nun-like about it; certainly her persistent rejection of her suitors, even if allayed by a deathbed change of heart, does not indicate any great enthusiasm for the matrimonial state. Like the Catholic Mary Ward, who suffered a similar loss, Susanna Perwick regarded the death of her betrothed as a significant affliction from God. For Susanna there followed a form of spiritual 'conversion'; Mary Ward decided to devote her life to God and took the veil. The option of the convent was of course not open to the Protestant girl; indeed Susanna remained very much opposed to the 'Romish' religion, which she considered to be positively 'anti-Christian'.[5] Susanna was compelled to construct her own life of retirement within the confines of her parents' busy boarding-school.

Susanna also resembled Mary Ward in that she had the gift of beauty: Batchiler refers to the contrast of her brilliant complexion – 'red and white, Mixed curiously gave great delight' – with her 'black, jetty, starry' eyes. And for once the frontispiece to *The Virgin's Pattern* does actually show a pretty face, although there is a hint of firmness as well as humour in the curved mouth, above the legend: 'Here's all that's left.' Nevertheless, after the death of her betrothed Susanna adopted a deliberately plain, neat garb, abhorring the black spots and patches which were just becoming the rage of fashionable London; not only for her own use, but also making her mother confiscate them from the giddy young ladies at the boarding-school. At least Susanna showed enough sympathy with adolescent frailty to wear the jewellery she would otherwise have eschewed in order to please the girls. Batchiler also eulogized her bosom – 'Her pair of round crown'd rising hills' – but these rising hills were, after Susanna's conversion, sternly covered with a whisk or handkerchief, contrary to the usual custom of the time.

It was easy for Susanna to refuse to attend public revels where there would be dancing; it was more difficult to find peace at home for prayer and meditation, with 100 girls, to say nothing of the servants, perpetually 'going up and down'. So Susanna, like so many of her serious-minded contemporaries such as Mary Warwick and Dorothy Osborne, turned to the garden and there would read her Bible for an hour or so, secure from interruption (she had read the whole of the New Testament twice in the year of her death). For Susanna too, like Elizabeth Walker, there was the period of early morning prayer which would leave her red-eyed; before supper she would regularly meditate on death. Even if complimented on her music in later years, Susanna was liable to reply – rather off-puttingly – that music was as nothing compared to the joys of heaven.[6]

Throughout the seventeenth century it was customary for stout English Protestants to condemn the Catholic convents with horror as barbarous concomitants of the 'Romish' religion. Yet one cannot help noticing how much easier it was for a Catholic young woman, a Mary Ward for instance, to construct a life of serious purpose on her own terms, than it was for a Susanna Perwick.

'Convenient storage for their [the Catholics'] withered daughters' was how Milton dismissed the convents. Lettice Countess of Leicester was struck with horror when 'a Popish orphan' named Mary Gunter, whom she had taken into her household, persisted in wanting to go 'beyond the seas, to become a nun' on the grounds that this was 'the surest and most likely way to go to Heaven... the nearest way'. There was however nothing withered about Mary Pontz, an associate of Mary Ward. She was an acknowledged beauty who was on the point of marriage when Mary Ward's mission captured her spirit; she sent her cavalier a bizarre form of dismissal in the shape of her own portrait in which one half of the face had been eaten by worms![7] For Protestant girls who experienced these or similar urges there was little outlet; and Milton's derisive comment omitted to state that for the withered daughters of Protestants – those who had probably been allowed to wither on the bough unmarried because they lacked dowries – there was no convenient refuge at all.

Some Protestant women, who thought for themselves, could see that it was by no means fair to condemn the Catholic nunneries wholesale. Margaret Duchess of Newcastle, for example, with her usual gift for stating the truth, however uncomfortable, thought it better for a girl to be 'walled up' in 'a monastery' than unhappily married. Margaret Godolphin, herself so earnest, so reserved, so worried by the implications of matrimony, went further. She was impressed by the convents she visited in France: 'Their Nunneries seem to be holy Institutions,' she reflected. 'If they are abused, 'tis not their (the nuns') fault; what is not perverted? Marriage itself is become a snare.' Earlier she had wished that there might be some kind of similar Protestant refuge to which she might fly and eschew the claims of the world.[8]

It was a desire echoed by the youthful Anne Murray, at the end of her unhappy love affair with Mr Thomas Howard.[9] As a girl without a fortune (her portion was ensnared in a legal tangle), Anne was aware that her marriage to Howard would not be permitted by his parents, and she honourably refused the young man's passionate request for a secret ceremony. Despite this evidence of rectitude, even Anne's own mother poured fury on her daughter for her behaviour, on the grounds that it was financially necessary for Howard to marry a rich citizen's daughter. She made Anne promise not to see her lover again. Anne kept her promise to the extent of saying goodbye to Howard blindfold, when he was packed off by his own relations to France. Even so, the disgust of the mother was so great, that she refused to speak to Anne except in anger for fourteen months.

It was at this point that Anne inquired privately from her cousin Sir Patrick Drummond, who was Conservator (consul) in Holland, whether there was not some Protestant nunnery there, consistent with her religious principles, because if so she would retreat thither immediately. But Sir Patrick addressed his answer to the angry mother, leaving Anne to explain herself: 'for since I found nothing would please her that I could do, I resolved to go where I could most please myself, which was in a solitary retired life'. A further blow was in store for Anne when Howard returned from France and married another lady, having cut Anne publicly: 'Is this the man for whom I have suffered so much?' she cried, falling on her bed. Her unfeeling mother laughed. It was no wonder that Anne secretly approved when her maid Miriam, as it will be remembered, called down a curse of barrenness upon Howard's bride.

Gibbon pointed to the plight of the runaway slaves under the universal government of the Roman Empire: nowhere to flee for the victims of injustice, for whom the world thus became 'a safe and dreary prison'. English girls who could not or would not marry were similarly without refuge. In contrast the remarkable longevity of many of the so-called 'withered daughters' who made the adventurous journey to the Continent to become Catholic nuns is also worthy of note. Two abbesses of Rouen, for example, died at over ninety; one of whom, Mother Francisca Clifton, had completed seventy-five years in religion. This longevity argues a life of purpose very different from that which faced many of their sisters at home – and of course freed in addition from 'the pain and the peril' of childbearing which brought so many of these other young women to an early death. Spiritual considerations quite apart, there was something to be said for the point of view of that 'Popish orphan' Mary Gunter (she was in fact not allowed to become a nun and died in England, still young, in 1633).[10] A life of chosen virginity, led in an ordered, secure and educated society, was certainly not the worst fate which could overtake a young woman in the seventeenth century.

In seventeenth-century England, neither legally nor psychologically was there a proper place for the unmarried female or 'maid' – the term generally in use in 1600 – except on her way to marriage. Psychologically, it was hard to look on a young woman as a heroine. The Blessed Virgin Mary was no longer the official pattern of English womanhood as she had been before the Reformation, no longer praised in nightly Ave Marias, daily or weekly masses as a chaste and sinless female. On the Catholic Continent, the position of respect she enjoyed was emphasized in the seventeenth century by the institution of a number of new Marian feasts in the church calendar.[11] Candles glimmered before the multitudinous wide-eyed depictions of the Virgin, painted by Murillo in honour of the growing cult of the Immaculate Conception. In England, the whole subject of the Virgin Mary was complicated by the fact that Marian devotion in any form – 'Mariolatry' – was regarded as High church or Laudian, liable to lead directly to Rome.

There was justice in this contention. Anthony Stafford, for example, who wrote a book entitled *The Femall Glory* in 1635, in which he attempted to rescue the Virgin Mary as a figure to be admired and emulated – she was not to be considered 'a mere woman' – was a follower of Laud, as was his patroness, the learned Lady Theophila Coke, to whom he dedicated the book. Stafford described Mary's marriage to Joseph as being intended merely to 'serve as a bar to the importunity of other Suitors ... so she might the more freely enjoy the inconceivable pleasure she took in her vowed Virginity'. As for the conception of Jesus: 'most blessed Virgin ... let thy Modesty rest secure; for the Operation of God, and not of man is here required'.[12]

This kind of heady talk was anathema to the Puritans, to whom the Blessed Virgin Mary was no more than 'Mall [a nickname for Mary], God's Maid'.[13] So Protestant womanhood was left with Grandmother Eve alone – that fearful guilty ancestress – to represent them. There was no chaste heroine in their pantheon: Grandmother Eve being very much a wife and mother, in her own guilty way, as all women in the seventeenth century were supposed to be.

Legally, the position of the 'feme sole' was equally ignored: her legal rights were assumed to be swallowed up in those of her nearest male protector. This does not overlook the fact that young women of the labouring class (that is, the vast majority of the population) worked to support themselves by one method or another from an early age;[14] it was from the 'spinsters', for example, a considerable number of young women working at home, that the modern legal term for the unmarried female was derived during the seventeenth century. Certain professions such as that of dairymaid or milkmaid had a tradition of independence, based on the adventurous expeditions to market which such 'maids' carried out in the course of their work, a freedom of movement not enjoyed by their sisters at home in the village.

The bold girls admired by Pepys at Westminster in the May Day parade of 1667, garlands round their milk-pails, 'dancing with a fiddler before them' as they collected tips from customers, came of a long tradition of such independent lasses; they were probably from farms nearby (Westminster then being on the edge of a rural area) and on their way to the Maypole in the Strand. Dairymaids were also amongst the highest paid of women workers: in 1647 a dairymaid who brought a cow to Hatfield so that the Lord Cranborne of the day could drink its milk was given a 2s tip – at a time when women agricultural labourers were lucky to get 4d a day.[15] Nevertheless an unmarried milkmaid, even if she enjoyed some practical freedom, was still legally in the care of her father, like any other young woman, and on marriage passed into that of her husband.

The point has been well made that it was only at marriage that men entered fully into the society into which they had been born;[16] that was also true of women, who in taking up their destined place as wives, were filling that place most convenient for the rest of society – which was male. The concept of an unmarried female, beyond a certain age and not demonstrably in the care of a male, tended to bring about a kind of bewilderment at best.

'Are you a maid, or widow, or a wife?' asked a Suffolk magistrate of Sister Dorothea, an English Catholic nun and follower of

Mary Ward, when she was brought before him in 1622.[17] At the time of her arrest, Sister Dorothea was posing as the kinswoman of Lady Timperley of Hintlesham Hall, near Ipswich; from this vantage point she had taught local children of 'the vulgar sort' their Pater, Ave, Creed and Commandments, but she had also done a great deal of good work among the sick and the poor, which had made her popular in the neighbourhood and somewhat inhibited the magistrate in his treatment of her.

'I am a maid,' was the answer of Sister Dorothea.

'So much the better,' the magistrate exclaimed with relief, feeling that the problem was now virtually solved, 'for then I hope a good husband will persuade you to change your religion.' In vain Sister Dorothea protested that she had no intention of changing her state; the magistrate, taking his stand on the fact that the nun had performed much service to the poor – 'to give you your due' – and armed with the comforting thought that her religious eccentricity could not be of long duration, dismissed her. It was a point of view robustly expressed by Sir Ralph Verney, echoing the words of St Paul (a favourite source where he was concerned) to the Corinthians. He remonstrated on the subject of Nancy Denton, that ambitious scholar, to her father: 'Dr Denton, teach her to live under obedience, and whilst she is unmarried, if she would learn anything, let her ask you, and afterwards her husband, *At Home*.'[18]

Obedience was thus the watchword.

One version of it was the obedience practised by the numerous serving-maids living in other people's houses as part of their 'family' – the significant term used for the household. The role of the serving-maid, as opposed to that of the free unmarried female, was a conventional one, fully understood by society. For one thing it was widely fulfilled: it has been suggested that between one quarter and a third of all households of the period contained servants, in view of the fact that the lowly as well as the mighty entertained them.[19]

Marriage – especially to another servant – did not necessarily bring this kind of obedience to an end in any case since, as has been pointed out, girls outside the moneyed or landed class married quite late.[20] Not only in the great social edifices such as Woburn Abbey but in the little country dwellings were maids to be found – often the daughters of friends, leaving their own family to practise obedience (and work for their keep) in the 'family' of another, not necessarily removed further up the social scale.

Domestic service in the seventeenth century was not only a common fate, it was also not a bad way of life and the horror stories of later times – the Victorian era, for example – should be dismissed from the imagination as anachronistic. The intimacy denoted by the use of the word family had considerable advantages: food was shared, and where plentiful, it was plentiful for maid as well as master (or mistress). Indeed, the free regular provision of food, and often clothing as well, placed the domestic in a privileged position not only compared to those many unfortunates at the very bottom of society, who seldom had either, but also to their social equals, day-labourers.

Moreover, such provision places the apparently low annual wage of about £2 a year given to maidservants in perspective. The board wages for food for the maids at Belton House, Grantham, seat of Sir John Brownlow, when the family went away to London were 6s a week; in a 1688 inventory of the fine new palace designed for the Brownlow family by Wren, all the rooms including the servants' rooms had feather-beds, besides three blankets and a quilt. The maids' rooms at Woburn Abbey had pictures on their walls.[21]

Servants featured prominently in wills, where quite large sums would be bequeathed; if these legatees were mainly older women, married or widowed, nevertheless such legacies betokened the care and affection lavished in general upon their maids by those women they served. Mary Countess of Warwick left £80 to Martha Upsheer, a chambermaid, £70 to Anne Coleman, another old servant, and £40 to 'my ancient servant Mary Taverner', formerly her housemaid. Mary Warwick's executors were instructed to use the money to purchase annuities for these women. Dame

Margaret Verney, wife of Sir Edmund and mother of Sir Ralph, mentioned all the women servants at Claydon when she made her will (and incidentally they were all still there in service when she died ten years later).[22]

As long as the concept of the domestic as part of the 'family', held by most people at the beginning of the seventeenth century, lingered, so the scale of the maids' existence remained in proportion to the people they served. In the 1680s Mary Woodforde, wife of a Prebendary at Winchester Cathedral, wrote of the marriage of her servant Ann: 'She lived with us thirteen years and a half.'[23] The idea of a maid as an inferior creature, entitled therefore to a far inferior standard of life, came later.

With so many domestic servants to consider, it was natural that the topic of their treatment should come under common discussion. Inordinate severity was generally frowned upon; the Puritan handbooks pointed to it as morally wrong. Winefrid, sister of William Blundell of Lancashire, busy engaging a servant at 15s a quarter for a lady of rank in London who wanted a Lancashire servant, had time to reflect that 'some sweet encouragement', not perpetual severity, was the way to treat servants. In 1688 Lord Halifax took pains to tell his daughter that as a newly-married mistress of a household of servants she must not abuse her position: 'The Inequality which is between you, must not make you forget that Nature maketh no such distinction.'[24]

What then were they like? What of Nell Duck, Mary Hearne and Mary Croast, maids and cook-maid to Dame Isabella Twysden? What of Betty Bushin, Lydia Long the laundry-maid, and 'Alice-about-the-house', all in service to the Earl of Bedford at Woburn Abbey?[25] In many cases the lives of these maids come to us merely in tantalizing glimpses, like the rustle of a petticoat or the turn of an ankle, in the incidental references of accounts of their employers.

In 1614 at Chartley Manor in Staffordshire, seat of the Earl of Essex, three maids fell into the moat as they were doing the laundry. Two were saved by long poles, but one continued to drown. The Earl of Essex stood on the bank as the girl struggled, crying in some excitement: 'Now she sinks! Now she's gone!'

until another bystander, Arthur Wilson (who tells the tale), plunged in and saved her. Thereafter the delighted Earl received Wilson 'in his private chamber' and made him his gentleman-in-waiting – which equally delighted Wilson. Of the bedraggled laundry-maid nothing more is heard.[26]

From the Woburn Abbey accounts, it is possible to know details such as the fact that they were often given clothes as presents, or part-presents ('To Abigail, towards a nightgown. £1 10s 0d'). The Woburn maids also took – or were given – a great deal of medicine, and they were constantly bled for hysteria.[27] About the emotions or even events which might have prompted the hysteria, it is far more difficult to know.

The fact, referred to by Lord Halifax, that nature made 'no such distinction' was sometimes wryly underlined by the sexual connections formed between master, or master's son, and maid; another side-effect of household intimacy. The opinion of the time held this to be a two-way hazard. Francis Kirkman, in his autobiography, confessed that he had a dread of being caught by a maid in marriage if he 'toyed' with one; for she might then try to prove he had already married her. It was considered to be a sign of madness in the son of Lord Grey of Wark, destined to marry the Earl of Northumberland's daughter, that he fell in love with his mother's chambermaid, or at any rate the experience was blamed for causing his 'weak brain' to 'turn over';[28] yet madness was not necessarily the explanation for such a socially unsuitable infatuation, propinquity being a more likely cause.

Another story told by Kirkman is probably more typical of the kind of blackmail which prevailed in which dismissal or worse was threatened if the maid proved obdurate. A certain married couple could never agree on a maid, for the master would not accept a plain nor the mistress a pretty one (a dispute no doubt as old as domestic service itself). In the end the master compromised by accepting a girl who was 'liquorish' hoping 'to have a lick at her honeypot'. When the 'liquorish' girl was duly discovered broaching her master's cask of Canary wine in the cellar, she had to submit to his advances under threat of imprisonment for theft in Bridewell.[29]

Fear of unemployment followed by destitution was surely enough to account for Alice Thornton's story of the goings-on in the *louche* household over which the Earl of Sussex and his 'most odious' Countess presided. Alice Thornton recounted with shocked surprise that when the Earl ordered six of the house-maids to dance naked, only one 'modest chaste maid', said she would not do it, and when 'pressed' by the Countess, immediately left her service. On the other hand Robert Hooke's maid Nell, who slept with him three times a month for no extra money in the 1670s, as he records in his diary, presumably found the bargain worth while (at £4 a year, and more for sewing, she was already well paid).³⁰ In her own way Nell was living under obedience.

But some fell through the net and some did not care to be confined by it. Jane Martindale was an independent-minded Lancashire girl who in 1625 revolted against the narrow life pre-scribed for a yeoman's daughter. (We happen to know her brief story because her brother Adam, the Nonconformist minister, wrote his autobiography.)³¹ Jane, in her brother's words, had 'her father's spirit and her mother's beauty'. She objected for instance to the restrictions imposed on the dress of women of her class – freeholders' daughters customarily wore 'felts' (a covering garment) over petticoats and waistcoats with handkerchiefs round their necks, and white cloths covering a coif on their heads. ''Tis true the finest sort of them wore gold or silver lace upon their waistcoats, good silk laces (and store of them) about their petticoats,' wrote Martindale. 'But the proudest of them (below the gentry) durst not have offered to wear an hood, or a scarf … not so much as a gown till her wedding-day.'

1625 was a year in which one of the major outbreaks of plague had taken place in London; as a result a number of refugees from its devastation had reached Lancashire. When the time came for them to return, Jane Martindale decided to go with them, leaving her home village of Prescot, and seek the more adventurous life of the big city; she hoped to get a place serving 'a lady' since she was 'ingenious with her needle'. Jane's parents pleaded with her, pointing out that she wanted for nothing at home, while the

London atmosphere might well prove dangerous to one who was not very hardy, having been brought up in the pure air of Lancashire. If Jane wanted to get married, her father told her that he could afford that luxury for her too – being able to provide a dowry.

Jane persisted. She took a little money from her family to get established in London and off she went. Perhaps her plan to serve 'a lady' with her ingenious needle might have worked – a form, naturally, of domestic service, but the life of serving 'a lady' in London offered opportunities for advancement unknown to a yeoman's daughter in Lancashire. Unfortunately she herself caught the plague and the plan had to be abandoned. Even so, her spirit was not altogether extinguished; she sent for a goose-pie from her family, in order that she might make merry with her friends, and they duly sent one, encased in 'twig-work' all the way from Lancashire. Jane added that some money for drink would also be appreciated, that 'the goose might swim', without cost to herself. But the carrier took three weeks to deliver pie and money; in the meantime Jane was in such dire poverty that she contemplated selling her own hair; 'which was very lovely', wrote her brother, 'both for length and colour'.

Ironically it was 'this blessed knot' of matrimony which rescued Jane in the nick of time; not the independent life she had envisaged. One of the young men who had travelled back to London with her had fallen in love with the beautiful Jane. He now married her, and the newly-wedded pair set up to run an inn called the George and Half Moon, just outside Temple Bar, which divided the City of London and Westminster. Jane's parents assisted her to furnish the inn, and sent country produce down from Lancashire.

Jane's city life then ran smoothly until the spring of 1632 when her mother became seriously ill. Jane bought 'an excellent swift mare' and rode home to Lancashire; too late – her mother was dead on her arrival. At this point Jane and her husband decided to sell the London inn and set up again at Warrington, to be closer to her remaining family. During one of her journeys between London and Lancashire to arrange all this, Jane stopped off at an inn to have a drink, where some children were suffering from smallpox. She caught the disease and died, being buried at Prescot in August 1632, beside her mother.

Several of the little 'chapbooks' as they were later known, popular fiction sold by pedlars for 2d a story, centred upon strong-minded – and strong-bodied – heroines. *Long Meg of Westminster*, which first appeared in 1582, is a notable example,[32] Long Meg being an Amazonian Lancashire lass who comes to London on a carrier's cart at the age of eighteen, like Jane Martindale seeking a place in service. But although Long Meg takes to touring London at night, dressed in men's clothing and beating men in fair fight, she ends by marrying a soldier, just as Jane Martindale had in the end married. To please her readers, most of whom were, of course, male, Long Meg vows to be a submissive wife: 'It behoveth me to be Obedient to you, and, never shall it be said, though I Cudgel a Knave that Long Meg shall be her Husband's Master.'

Only the real-life heroine Mary Frith, subject of Middleton and Dekker's comedy *The Roaring Girl*, never succumbed to the economic necessity or social ideal of obedience. But then Moll Cutpurse, as she was known, did not succumb to the law either. 'She could not endure the sedentary life of sewing or stitching, a sampler was as grievous to her as a winding-sheet.' Dressed as a man, sword and all, she was first of all notorious as 'a bully, pick-purse, fortune teller, receiver and forger'. Later she became what it would be appropriate to term a successful highwayperson. Building up a gang of thieves, she used her house in Fleet Street as a centre for her operations, give or take a spell in Newgate. On Sundays this female Robin Hood would visit the gaols and feed the prisoners out of her haul. Moll Cutpurse, untroubled by obedience, lived to the ripe old age of seventy-five, and was buried in 1659 after an Anglican service at St Bride's.[33]

Moll Cutpurse was the exception, as is demonstrated by the popular wonder accorded to her – several books were written about her as well as Dekker's play, and her biography *The Life and*

Death of Mistress Mary Frith appeared in 1662. Living under obedience, as most women did, married or unmarried, they might be as garrulous as they pleased – so the satirists averred – at home, but their voices were unlikely to be heard in the public forum. The undesirable talkativeness of the female sex in the domestic circle was axiomatic; the desirability of its silence outside was equally taken for granted. Yet even before the Civil War, certain individual women, whether wilful, eccentric or just plain deluded, had already discovered a way in which the female voice might be raised without immediate masculine control.

Women were of course forbidden to preach in the churches – on the direct authority of mighty St Paul himself. But when a woman started to 'prophesy' as did a pedlar called Jane Hawkins at St Ives near Huntingdon in 1629, the matter was somewhat more complicated. 'This rhyming preacheress', as she was later described, made a strong local impression.[34] For by claiming direct inspiration from God – and expressing this inspiration in trances, descriptions of visions and other 'prophecies' – a woman made it that much more difficult for her voice to be extinguished; there would always be those around her, credulous or sympathetic, who believed that this extinction was suppressing the direct message of God. If the politics of Church and State were introduced, the matter became more complicated still. At the same time the dreaded implication of witchcraft, ever present for a woman who refused to conform, was avoided if the language was sufficiently religious in its expression to suggest possession by the Almighty, rather than some more sinister power.

Jane Hawkins, 'having fallen into a rapture or ecstasy', foretold on the one hand such disagreeable eventualities for the Anglican Church as the downfall of the bishops; on the other hand she magnified' the ministry of the local vicar, the Rev. Mr Tokey. When her prophetic rhyming continued for three days and nights, it was perhaps hardly surprising that the 200 people who listened to her included Mr Tokey, his curate, and another 'scholar' who sat at the feet of Jane Hawkins's bed, rapidly copying out the verses – amounting to some thousands – which were emitted from the entranced woman. The plan was to make a fair copy of the verses later 'with intent to print them'. At which point however, the Bishop, less enthusiastic at having his downfall predicted than Mr Tokey at having his ministry magnified, had the verses seized.

When Mr Tokey refused to abandon the claims of his spiritual patroness to be a true visionary, he was suspended, while his curate was 'put quite away'; the Justices of the Peace were given a warrant by the Bishop to look after Jane Hawkins herself and ensure that the neighbours did not visit her. Reports said that the local people were deserting their 'rhyming preacheress'; soon they were said to 'cry out against her'. Finally the unfortunate vicar made a written acknowledgement that Jane was an impostor, and that he himself had been guilty of indiscretion.

It is noticeable that the Bishop's attitude to Jane Hawkins was from the first one of suspicion on the grounds of her sex. Here was 'a witty crafty baggage', who was deliberately stepping out of her low station in life to make trouble for the rest of the world; he was disgusted that she would not 'confess' to having written verses before, or to having written them of her own accord now. To the end he referred to 'this imposture' of the woman at St Ives; it was not within his cognizance that someone of Jane Hawkins's ilk could have genuinely believed in the strength of her own visions.

Yet there had been a brief moment of glory when Jane Hawkins, a 'poor woman (and she but a pedlar)' as she was contemptuously described, lay on a bed surrounded by 200 local people, led by the vicar, who hung on her words with bated breath, and even had them copied down for widespread publication. The point has been made by Keith Thomas that in an age when women were unable to attend grammar schools, let alone attend university, and of course unable to preach, the self-styled role of prophetess enabled a woman frustrated of any normal means of self-expression to make her voice at least heard.[35]

A far more notorious 'rhyming preacheress' – because of her high station in life – was the woman born Eleanor Audeley, daughter of the Earl of Castlehaven, and wife in succession to Sir John Davies, Attorney-General for Ireland, and Sir Archibald

Douglas. By her first marriage Lady Eleanor Davies (the name by which she is generally known) bore a daughter Lucy, whose life was early affected by her mother's eccentricities. In 1623 at the age of ten Lucy was married off by her father (without a licence) to Ferdinando Lord Hastings, who succeeded his father as sixth Earl of Huntingdon in 1643; the hasty ceremony was probably intended to save Lucy from her mother's drastic influence. Sir John Davies's death meant that the young couple went to live together much earlier than had been anticipated.[36] Life in the wake of a scandalous parent had its predictable effect on Lady Huntingdon: an intellectual, Lucy also had a strong regard for the conventions. It was she who had prepared her own clever daughter Elizabeth Hastings so well for marriage that her husband never suffered 'all those inconveniences' generally believed to accompany a learned wife (see p. 149).

'Inconveniences' certainly surrounded the career of Lady Eleanor Davies.[37] In 1625, when she was in her mid-thirties, according to her own account she received a revelation while lying in bed at home at Englefield Manor: 'nineteen and a half years to the Judgement and you as the Meek Virgin'. Sir John Davies died the next year, but since Lady Eleanor – who shared the contemporary preoccupation with anagrams – made of her husband's name DAVIS IUDAS, she can hardly have regretted his demise. Sir John's particular betrayal was described by Lady Eleanor: it was her first book which 'was sacrificed by my first husband's hand, thrown into the fire'. Lady Eleanor responded with her own weapons, giving Sir John details of his 'doom', telling him 'within three years to expect the mortal blow'. To hammer the point in, she wore black – 'my mourning garment' – from that time forward.

There had been other troubles in the marriage: Lady Eleanor's son by Sir John, known as Jack, was an idiot. There is a great deal that is touching about the mother's attitude to her son's deformity, including the conviction (in 1617) that if Jack 'were now put into the hands of some skilful man ... [he] might be brought to speak'. Lady Eleanor went on: 'for he is wonderfully mended in his understanding of late ... he understands anything that is spoken to him without making any signs, so as it is certain he hath his hearing… then the defect must be in his tongue'.[38] But in the event poor Jack was drowned, leaving Lucy Davies, incidentally, as heiress to an important fortune.

To the outside world, however, Lady Eleanor was clearly marked down as a trouble-maker, even before she turned her attention, fatally, to matters of Church and State. In 1622, for example, a certain man called Brooke reproached her for abuse (not recorded) of his wife and innocent child. Brooke declared that Lady Eleanor had by her behaviour abandoned all 'goodness and modesty', being not only mad and ugly, but also blinded with pride in her own birth; in retaliation he threatened on the one hand to 'scratch a mince-pie' out of her; on the other hand he wished Lady Eleanor, as being the most horrible curse in his power, to remain exactly what she was.[39]

Lady Eleanor's second marriage to Sir Archibald Douglas was by her own account not much more successful than her first. It took place only three months after Sir John Davies's death 'contrary to a solemn Vow', and soon there was a recurrence of both the old trouble – 'he likewise burning my book' – and the old revenge. For Sir Archibald 'escaped not scotfree', being bereft of his senses while at Communion and 'instead of speech made a noise like a Brute Creature'.[40] In later life (he lived until 1644) Sir Archibald believed he saw angels, and became, like his wife, preoccupied with anagrams.

REVEALE O DANIEL! This, the transformation of her maiden name, if spelt ELEANOR AUDLIE, was the crucial anagram in Lady Eleanor's own opinion (how very different was this strident call from that meek cry – AH, I SEE HEAV'N'S PURE SUN – composed by her admirers out of the name of Susanna Perwick). Altogether this self-styled Daniel was responsible for twenty-eight tracts of a prophetic nature, which have been described in modern times as 'an almost unintelligible mixture of religion, politics and prophecy'.[41] Unfortunately for Lady Eleanor, in her own time they were not altogether unintelligible, and unfortunately too, she had the occasional Cassandra's knack of prophesying accurately some rather unlikely and extremely unpleasant event.

The first prediction which brought Lady Eleanor real notoriety was that of the impending assassination of the Duke of Buckingham, made in June 1628, with the rider that the Duke's 'time was not till August'. When Buckingham was duly struck down by John Felton on the twenty-third of that month, Lady Eleanor's stock as a prophetess was understandably high amongst the common people of London, who elevated her as 'a cunning woman'. (However, lest Lady Eleanor be credited too firmly with supernatural powers, it has been suggested that her prophecy was common knowledge that summer and Felton may actually have timed his blow to fit in with it.)[42]

Lady Eleanor's successful prophecies concerning the pregnancies of Queen Henrietta Maria, if less ostentatious, probably had more effect in gaining her a reputation as a seer in high places – and thus leading in the end to her downfall. It was the inevitable way of royal life that soon after Henrietta Maria arrived in England in June 1625 as a bride, her possible pregnancy should be the subject of speculation. When two years later there was still no sign of an heir to the throne, it was also inevitable that the Queen (and those around her) should be concerned about her possible infertility. According to the story, it was on All Saints' Day, 1 November 1627, that the Queen paused as she was leaving the evening service and asked Lady Eleanor when she would be with child. Lady Eleanor replied that the Queen's first child would be christened and buried all in one day. And in May 1629 the Queen's firstborn, a Prince named Charles James, did die more or less as Lady Eleanor had predicted. In response to a further emissary from the court, a Mr Kirk, Lady Eleanor struck lucky again by predicting that the Queen's next baby would be another boy, but an exceptionally strong child – as the future Charles II, born in May 1630, proved to be. The King was irritated by Lady Eleanor's influence over his wife but Mr Kirk among others spread the lady's fame.

Three years later the lady's 'prophesyings', which she had printed at Amsterdam (where she needed no licence) under the legend 'Reveale O Daniel', were of a more extravagant nature. Now it was a question of the 'doom' of Charles I; referring to the

King as 'Belshazzar' and describing her vision of a Beast ascended out of the Bottomless Pit, having seven heads to signify the seven past years of the King's rule, Lady Eleanor foretold the final execution of the King. In addition Laud, newly appointed Archbishop of Canterbury, was picturesquely evoked as 'horned like the lamb, hearted like a Wolf.'[43]

The King's annoyance was pardonable. This kind of prophecy was in theory a grave offence (even to cast the monarch's horoscope without authorization was treason). Lady Eleanor was summoned to the court of High Commission on 24 October 1633, and there committed for 'compiling and publishing certain fanatic and scandalous pamphlets'. At least two of the judges thought that Lady Eleanor should acknowledge her offence at St Paul's Cross, while the Bishop of Rochester suggested Bedlam – the madhouse. In the end Lady Eleanor was fined £3,000 and sentenced to imprisonment in the Gatehouse. Her books however did not get off so lightly, being burnt publicly: 'this is the third day their dead bodies throwed in loose sheets of paper lie in the streets of the great city', she wrote in anguish.[44]

Even more humiliating to her spirit was her actual experience in court. Efforts were made to convince Lady Eleanor of the meaninglessness of her prophecies, and in particular of her precious anagrams. To illustrate the point, some had the happy thought of pointing out that DAME ELEANOR DAVIS could be transformed into NEVER SO MAD A LADIE, 'which happy fancy brought that grave Court in to such a laughter, and the poor woman into such a confusion' that Lady Eleanor herself never alluded to this particular incident subsequently.[45] It is an ironic scene in retrospect: the august body of judges, from whom the future was happily hidden, attempting in vain to convince the distracted woman that anyone who predicted the execution of Charles I must necessarily have their wits a-wandering.

The fine was probably not paid, but Lady Eleanor remained in the Gatehouse despite her daughter Lucy Countess of Huntingdon's petitioning for her release. Lucy was careful to admit that her mother had been confined 'by just censure', but she asked that she might have some free air, 'for womanhood' some female of her own to attend her, and perhaps a clergyman as well.[46]

In 1635 Lady Eleanor was released from her London prison and went to live in the cathedral town of Lichfield in Staffordshire. Here she found no peace. Flouting the conventions, she freely used those seats reserved for the wives of the bishop and the canons within the cathedral; worse still she sat herself down on the episcopal throne, and declaring that she was both 'Bishop and Metropolitan', sprinkled a mixture of tar and water on the cathedral hangings.

This time there was no escaping 'Bedlam's loathsome Prison' even for the mother of the Countess of Huntingdon. Here sightseers would come to gape at Lady Eleanor (and other inmates). Nor was Lady Eleanor's prophetic voice silent. Particular alarm was caused when she predicted a fire within Bedlam, and fires duly occurred – although the fire risks were so great, that was hardly a surprising occurrence. Finally, after a spell in the Tower, Lady Eleanor was released into the care of her daughter and son-in-law in 1640.

The prophesying – and the violent treatment – continued. In 1646 Lady Eleanor was sent to another London prison called the Compter and incarcerated in a black cell by the Keeper, an experience she described graphically: 'Not long after (she all unready, etc.) between two of them carried down thence, instantly shut and bolted was into the Dungeon-Hole, Hell's Epitomy, in the dark out of call or cry, searching first her Coats pockets: Frustrate that way, with the Key took away the Candle, there left in their Pest-house on the wet floor to take up her lodging.' Fortunately, so that Lady Eleanor could examine her cell all night long till dawn: 'the Heavens without intermission flashed out Lightnings, as Noonday'.[47]†

It seems unfair that for all her charitable treatment of her own 'dear mother' Lucy Countess of Huntingdon was the victim of a series of tragedies as a mother herself. Her first three sons all died; the fourth, Theophilus, who eventually became Earl of

† In 1932 the editor of *Dougle Fooleries* compared Lady Eleanor Davies's 'obscurity of meaning and ... freedom from syntax' to that of James Joyce or Gertrude Stein.[48]

Huntingdon, was not born until 1650, when the Earl and Countess of Huntingdon had been married for over a quarter of a century. *Sion's Lamentation*, a powerful piece – and for once politically innocent – was written for the funeral of one of these boys, Henry Lord Hastings, in 1649, by the prophetic grandmother. Lady Eleanor described the eerie emptiness of the streets through which the funeral train passed. As when Joshua made the sun and moon stand still at his command at Gibeon, the Lord harkening to his request, so the cortège 'saw not the face of Coach, Cart or Car, which passed by, either that met us, or stood in our way'.[49]

But by this date the whole world, not only the world of the distracted Lady Eleanor, was turning upside down – never so mad a lady till the present, perhaps, but other prophetesses were coming forward to rival her. Lady Eleanor, like these other frustrated women living in theoretical obedience, who poured their bizarre imaginings into prophecies, looked to the new order in the shape of Oliver Cromwell. We shall meet Lady Eleanor again in 1648, presenting a copy of the notorious 1633 prophecies to the great man himself.

For war was coming, a time when many women, not only the strange and wilful, would lead lives of chaos and disruption; a time of war, when the great mass of women who simply expected to exist, as their foremothers had done, rejoicing in the cyclical happinesses, enduring the private sorrows of domestic life, living under obedience, would not be able to do so. War, the great challenger, was coming to them all.

PART TWO

With the War — Stronger Grown

To most 'tis known
The weaker vessels are the stronger grown.
The vine which on the pole still lean'd his arms
Must now bear up and save the pole from harms.

JAMES STRONG, *Joanereidos: or, Feminine Valour Eminently
discovered in Westerne Women,* 1645

CHAPTER NINE

Courage above her Sex

〜

'My dear wife endured much hardship … and though by
nature, according to her sex, timorous, yet in greatest
danger would not be daunted, but shewed a courage
even above her sex.'

SIR HUGH CHOLMLEY,
GOVERNOR OF SCARBOROUGH CASTLE

At the beginning of the wars, which lasted on English soil
from August 1642 until September 1651, when Cromwell
finally routed the young Charles II at Worcester, it was
taken for granted that woman, the weaker vessel, lacked not only
the martial spirit but also courage itself.

After the wars the theory of woman's timidity continued to be
preached: in 1653 Margaret Duchess of Newcastle's first published work contained *An Epistle to Souldiers*, preface to a long
poem describing the battle between Courage and Prudence
before the Fortress of Hope. The Duchess was careful to explain
that 'these Armies I mention, were rais'd in my brain, fought in
my fancy, and registered in my closet'. Anything else – from a
woman – would be ludicrous. 'Great Heroicks!' she addressed
the male sex, 'you may justly laugh at me, if I went about to
censure, instruct or advise in the valiant Art, and Discipline of
War … according to the constitution of my Sex, I am as fearful
as a Hare, for I shall start at the noise of a Potgun, and shut my
eyes at the sight of a Bloody Sword, and run away at the least
Alarm.'[1]

Reality in the previous decade had been very different. The
Civil Wars threw up a considerable number of 'Great Heroicks'

of the theoretically weaker sex: women of the calibre of the Countess of Portland who at Carisbrooke Castle 'behaved like a Roman matron' and rather than surrender 'declared she herself would fire the first cannon'. Or there was the lioness Lady Mary Winter, wife of the Royalist commander Sir John, who declined to give up Lidney House, near Gloucester, to the Parliamentary commander Colonel Massey with some well-turned words on the subject of her absent husband's 'unalterable allegiance to his king and sovereign'. Thus Massey's 'hopes were disappointed by the resolution of a female'.[2]

Of these the most celebrated were the valiant ladies on both sides who in the absence of their husbands found themselves withstanding the enemy's siege. Less celebrated, but in quite as much danger, were the ordinary women also involved in the siege, maidservants and so forth; these too threw themselves into the fray. So that far from being fearful as hares, women showed themselves capable, on many different levels, of gallantry at least equal to that of their menfolk; and if they were indeed inherently timorous, then it could be argued that their courage was correspondingly even greater.

This seemingly contradictory heroism of the weaker vessel was easily explained on the surface: an individual woman such as Brilliana Lady Harley was said to have exhibited 'a Masculine Bravery' or displayed that 'constancy and courage above her sex' which her memorial tablet ascribed to the valiant Lady Bankes of Corfe Castle.[3]

Elizabeth Twysden, Lady Cholmley, married Sir Hugh Cholmley of Yorkshire, later Royalist Governor of Scarborough Castle. Throughout the siege of the castle, following the Parliamentary victory of Marston Moor, she stayed resolutely at her husband's side; as he wrote later, she 'would not forsake me for any danger', although her daughters sailed for Holland and her sons were away in London. When the besieging commander Sir John Meldrum threatened total massacre, Lady Cholmley begged her husband not to consider her own safety; throughout the defence Lady Cholmley led the nursing of the wounded and numerous sick (scurvy soon broke out) with the aid of her maids.

Sir Hugh Cholmley's tribute to his wife's gallantry stands for many: 'My dear wife endured much hardship, and yet with little show of trouble; and though by nature, according to her sex, timorous, yet in greatest danger would not be daunted, but showed a courage even above her sex.'[4]

Yet the conventional refusal to impute courage to the female sex as a whole (while granting it tenderly to individual members) did not survive the wars quite unaltered despite Margaret Newcastle's ostentatiously modest words. Indeed, one can detect a certain masculine desperation in the repeated claims that the heroines of the wars acted out their martial role with the greatest reluctance. As we shall see, not a few of the 'Great [female] Heroicks' accepted their unusual destiny with zest; nor did this enthusiasm escape notice at the time, especially when it reflected derogatorily on the lady's husband.

'Three women ruined the Kingdom: Eve, the Queen and the Countess of Derby': this comment from a Parliamentary source, by associating Charlotte de la Trémoille, Countess of Derby with Grandmother Eve and the hated Catholic Henrietta Maria, paid tribute to her pre-eminence as a Royalist heroine. But there were also sneers at her husband, James Stanley, seventh Earl of Derby: it was said that of the two she had proved herself the better soldier, or more crudely, that she had stolen 'the Earl's breeches'.[5]

Certainly the Countess was bred to be a heroine: in an age when royal women were among the few allowed to revel in public attention, she was by birth close to being a princess. A French Huguenot, daughter of the Duc de Thouars, she was a granddaughter of William the Silent (of Orange) by his Bourbon wife. Through her marriage to the Earl of Derby, himself connected to the English royal line, she had enjoyed the full richness of English court life before the war; and since the Earl of Derby was the greatest magnate of the north-west, there she found herself a queen by his side: mighty Lathom House being generally considered 'the only Court' in the north.[6] The habit of command then came naturally to her. (And it may also be noted that she was seven years her husband's senior.)

Early in 1643 the fall of the Royalist stronghold of Warrington in Lancashire brought neighbouring Lathom House to the attention of Parliament. At this point the Earl of Derby was in the Isle of Man (also part of his estates) at the request of the Queen, while the Countess, a woman in her early forties, remained at Lathom House with two of her seven children, the Ladies Mary and Katherine Stanley. The aim of Sir Thomas Fairfax, the Parliamentary General, was to secure the surrender of Lathom House without bloodshed; to this end on 28 February he sent an official summons to the Countess by the hand of a Captain Markland.

At this point the formal rules governing a seventeenth-century siege become relevant (and indeed remain so through all the sieges, major or minor, which will be discussed in the ensuing chapter). These rules, which could have barbarous consequences for civilians plunged involuntarily into a siege, were nevertheless framed for the preservation rather than the destruction of life.

In short: after the besieging commander had issued an official summons to the defenders of a stronghold to surrender, a choice had to be made. If the defenders promptly surrendered, then the civilians – mainly women and children – within the stronghold were generally allowed to depart peacefully, leaving the soldiers within the stronghold to negotiate the details of the surrender, including the surrender of their arms. Before he captured Bridgwater, in July 1645, Sir Thomas Fairfax was said to have shown particular 'pity and commiseration' for these non-combatants by sending them a free offer of quarter before his troops began to fire. 'Upon which there came out a whole regiment of women and children.'[7]

If, on the other hand, there was no surrender, then according to the rules of war, the besieged civilians were equally at risk with the military when and if the stronghold was taken by force; there need be no quarter given. (It was under these rules, incidentally, complying with contemporary procedure, if outraging the instincts of humanity, that Cromwell at Drogheda and Wexford in 1649 permitted the slaughter of civilians as well as soldiers, because neither fortified town, after repeated summonses, agreed to surrender.) At Sherborne, shortly after the successful siege of Bridgwater, Fairfax 'according to his wonted nobleness' sent a messenger to the commander, Sir Lewis Dyve, that 'if he pleased to send out his lady, or any other women, he would give way to it'. Sir Lewis, while expressing himself grateful for the favour, gave no very positive answer, and Lady Dyve remained within the stronghold. It was not until the 'storm' of Sherborne had begun that a white flag was hung out; this was too late to stop the sack, in the course of which the soldiers acquired a great deal of booty and everyone (except Lady Dyve) was 'stripped'. Lady Dyve was lucky since by this point there was no theoretical guarantee of her safety. At Grafton House, near Stony Stratford, on Christmas Eve 1643, all the women of the house were 'stripped to their naked skins' by the troops of Major-General Skippon, after the fortress surrendered.[8]

It may be asked what justification there could be for this ritual; the answer lies in the nature of siege warfare at that time. Without such a proviso it was greatly to the advantage of the defenders, if they had sufficient food and water, to hold out as long as possible, or at least until these supplies had been used up; after all they were warmly sheltered, and the possibility of rescue from outside remained. Meanwhile the besiegers were leading a far less agreeable existence, enduring the rigours of exposure, which led quickly to disease; the prospect of attack from the rear, in the shape of rescuing forces, only increased as time passed. Under these circumstances, some grim inducement had to be offered to the defenders to obey the summons: hence the harsh rules of siege war. Given these conditions the 'Welsh howlings' of the women who wanted to urge surrender upon their husbands at the siege of Oswestry (a walled town about to be blown up) were perfectly comprehensible.[9]

Lathom House in the 1640s was a massive and ancient fortress. The walls were six feet thick; a moat, eight yards across and six feet deep, surrounded them; after that came a strong palisade. Nine towers dominated the walls, each containing six pieces of ordnance or mounted guns; mightiest of all was the Eagle Tower, over which flew the proud motto *Sans Changer*.

There was an excellent water supply. Even the terrain favoured the defence, for the ground rose up round Lathom House like another natural fortification.

The Countess of Derby's answer to Captain Markland's summons was not outright defiance. Instead she played for time, while subtly reminding both the Captain and his superior of her own renowned social status. It was after all only six months since the outbreak of this 'war without an enemy', as the Parliamentarian Sir William Waller called it in a letter to a Royalist friend: the pre-war standards of courtesy and respect towards a great lady still prevailed. Not only did the Countess request further time to consider the summons, but she firmly declined to emerge from her fortress in order to 'treat' with the enemy; in the first of a series of magnificent communications she observed that 'notwithstanding her present condition, she remembered both her Lord's honour and her own birth, conceiving it more knightly that Sir Thomas Fairfax should wait upon her, than she upon him'.[10]

Various other summonses were equally rebuffed in the same high style. The Countess's final answer was as follows: 'That though a woman and a stranger divorced from her friends, and robbed of her state, she was ready to receive their utmost violence, trusting in God both for her protection and deliverance.'[11]

Apart from the protection of God, the Countess also had a considerable garrison of soldiers, under a Captain Farmer, and the men from the Derby estate, the keepers, fowlers and suchlike who, being by profession skilled marksmen, manned the towers. Nevertheless the bombardment which ensued, including 'flaming granadoes' (grenades) as well as the pounding of a great mortar, was severe and left its impact on the besieged: several women had their hands scorched. A contemporary diary of the siege pays tribute to the courage of Mary and Katherine Stanley, 'for piety and sweetness truly the children of so princely a mother'. Having inherited the Countess's spirit as well, 'the little ladies had stomack to digest canon', although 'the stoutest soldiers had no hearts for granadoes'.[12]

The Countess remained staunch. The pinnacles and turrets of

Lathom House began to crumble to the pounding of the mortar, a culverin and a demi-culverin, but still she continued to refuse in ringing terms that safe-conduct for herself and her daughters which would have implied surrender. It was, she declared, 'more noble to preserve her liberty by arms than to buy peace with slavery'. As for negotiations: "tis dangerous treating when the sword is in the enemy's hand'. Although the diary of the siege refers to the indignities the Countess and her daughters had to suffer, listening to the language and affronts of the besieging soldiery, the cowardice of her neighbours presented a more practical problem. One petition suggested that the Countess would do well to surrender – for the future of the surrounding countryside. The Countess of Derby made short work of it. There is no evidence that the more forceful comments of the Parliamentary preachers on her character, couched in biblical terms – the Scarlet Woman, the Whore of Babylon and so forth – made any impact on her spirit either.

The besiegers attempted to drain off the castle water supply, where the spring rose on the hill. But the real danger was presented by the great mortar loaded with stones thirteen inches across, eighty pounds in weight, daily, relentlessly pounding them to pieces. The successful sally of the defenders out of the gates to capture the mortar and drag it inside was therefore a triumph of the desperate – except that the Countess would not admit to being desperate. Instead she commanded a public thanksgiving.

It was not the least of her pleasures to discover that the commanding officer of the besiegers, Colonel Rigby, had summoned his neighbours to watch Lathom House either yield or be burnt. They were thus present to witness his humiliation. Lady Derby gave him instead 'a very scurvy satisfying answer, so that his friends came opportunely to comfort him' (instead of rejoicing with him). Her enemy was 'sick of Shame and dishonour, to be routed by a lady and a handful of men'.

Three months later it was the arrival of Prince Rupert at the head of a considerable force which relieved Lathom House. The Prince conveyed twenty-two of the enemy's colours to the great lady who had held fast. Although the actual military manoeuvres were conducted by Captain Farmer, it is evident that without a woman of the lofty courage – one might add the aristocratic arrogance – of the Countess of Derby, Lathom House would have fallen to the enemy almost immediately. As it was, when it did surrender in December 1645, the Countess was far away on the Isle of Man. After the Restoration, her daughter Katherine, who retained vivid childish memories of the siege, would take to task a historian who suggested that the Countess had been present at, and thus connected with, this final débâcle. Thomas Dugdale, in his widely read 1660 *Continuation* of Sir Richard Baker's 1637 *Chronicle*, perpetuated this error, based on two false Parliamentary reports. Katherine, now Marchioness of Dorchester, joined with Lucy Countess of Huntingdon and her son (anxious to refute the rather more substantiated charge that Lady Eleanor Davies had foretold the death of Buckingham). As a result, Dugdale, while retaining the error, inserted a slightly equivocal compliment to the Countess in the 1665 edition: 'in her defending of that place' (Lathom House) the Countess 'had manifested a more than Feminine Magnanimity' – that is, greatness of spirit. It was not until 1674 that the error concerning the 1645 surrender was eliminated and the Countess's role in the original victory enlarged.[13]

The 'Heroick Countess' herself lived until 1664, surviving not only the wars but the tragedy of her husband's execution at the orders of Parliament for his part in the Worcester campaign (she tried, despite the objections of the inhabitants, to surrender the Isle of Man in return for his life). As an old lady she would tell stories of the wars to her Lancashire neighbour William Blundell, which he found difficult to understand on account of her French accent: 'a defect' in 'my lady's English'. To the end she was something of a tartar: where the Quakers were concerned, for example, 'she shut out all pity and tenderness' when they were imprisoned for non-payment of tithes.[14]

The Countess, so confident in her birth, and the utter rightness of all her opinions, would have appreciated Dugdale's equivocal compliment to her 'more than Feminine Magnanimity'.

From the point of view of the enemy, a high-born heroine in charge of a siege represented a double hazard. Most obviously, her combination of gallantry and authority would fuel the chivalrous defenders to greater efforts; secondly, the hoped-for effect of an official summons upon the defenders' nerves might be largely nullified by the presence of such a feminine figurehead, No one had any particular desire to kill, maim or wound her or her family: hence the constant pleading requests to the Countess of Derby to accept a safe-conduct. When the husband himself conducted the defence, his wife's presence at the siege was still embarrassing to the attackers, as in the case of the Marchioness of Winchester, another brave woman whose refusal to quit inhibited her opponents.

The siege of Basing House, magnificent dwelling of the great Catholic magnate John, fifth Marquess of Winchester, which lasted from August 1643 until October 1645, was one of the most famous and protracted of the war.[15] When finally captured, Basing House was found to number amongst its contents not only riches and pictures and art works and furnishing – but also the engraver Wenceslaus Hollar and Inigo Jones himself (who was carried out naked, wrapped in a blanket). A passionate supporter of the King's cause, Lord Winchester was said to have '*Aimez Loyauté*' engraved on every window of Basing House.

Honora Marchioness of Winchester was, as Clarendon wrote later, 'a lady of great honour and alliance', being the daughter of the Earl of St Albans and Clanricarde, and the granddaughter of Queen Elizabeth's Machiavellian statesman, Sir Francis Walsingham.[16] From the point of view of Parliament, however, it was more important that she was half-sister to their own general, the Earl of Essex (to whom one of the besiegers, Colonel Hammond, was also related). Here was the problem of a civil war in a nutshell. The Parliamentary besiegers were understandably anxious to have such a lady safely removed from Basing House.

So Sir William Waller duly invited the Marchioness to lead out her own children (she was the mother of seven), and all the other women and children in the house, during a parley. He used exceptionally courteous terms, 'excusing the rudeness of his disorderly guns'. The Marchioness's answer was, like that of the Countess of Derby to Sir Thomas Fairfax, superbly scornful: 'she thanked God that she was not in that condition to accept of fair quarter at Sir William Waller's hands, being resolved to run the same fortune as her Lord, knowing that there was a just and all-seeing Judge above, who she hoped would have an especial hand in this business'. From this august judge, she added, Sir William Waller could 'pretend no commission'.

Then the Marchioness and her ladies set to with a will, casting bullets from lead hastily stripped from the roofs and turrets of the house. During a lull in the siege she also visited Oxford (where the King was) and solicited diligently for help for her husband.

By the autumn of 1645 time had run out for Basing House, and its courageous defenders of both sexes. It was now the one remaining Royalist garrison guarding the south-west, and as such received the attentions of Oliver Cromwell himself, since the victory of Naseby that summer the hero of the Parliamentary forces. During the final bombardment, one of Cromwell's shells 'brake in' to the Marchioness's lodgings, killing a waiting-woman and a chambermaid (demonstrating how perilous might be the fate of such innocent anonymous females caught up in these great events).

What happened to the Marchioness? Accounts vary. Either she escaped from Basing House before the final stage of the siege on 8 October, or she was captured and subsequently exchanged for another prominent (male) prisoner. Either way her name was specifically mentioned in the Articles of Surrender, as were those of other chatelaines. (At the surrender of Bletchingdon House to Cromwell in April 1645, the eighth Article read; 'That the lady of the House [Mrs Windebank] shall enjoy her goods as before ...')[17] Thus was war in its own strange way bringing the names of women to the fore. While the Marchioness of Winchester survived to bring comforts to her sick husband imprisoned in the Tower of London, Basing House was 'slighted', or razed to the ground, at the orders of Parliament and its gorgeous contents looted.

Where the Countess of Derby and the Marchioness of Winchester were already illustrious figures before the war, through the panoply of their high lineage, 'prudent and valiant' Lady Bankes, defender of Corfe Castle, made her own name by the sheer courageous obstinacy of her resistance; and like Lady Derby, she gave every impression of enjoying her role, for all its perils. Mary Bankes came of a good if not a brilliant family, being the daughter of Ralph Hawtrey of Ruislip; her husband Sir John Bankes, described as 'a grave and learned man in the profession of law',[18] had prosecuted John Hampden as Attorney-General, and later became Chief Justice of the Court of Common Pleas.

The law had proved lucrative. It will be recalled that in 1617, at the time of the disastrous marriage of Frances Coke to Buckingham's brother, Corfe Castle was part of the rich settlement Frances was expected to receive from her mother Lady Hatton; the failure of Lady Hatton to part with it resulted in the King creating the bridegroom Viscount Purbeck as a consolation (see p. 19). So Corfe Castle remained in the possession of Lady Hatton. About 1634, Sir John Bankes bought it from her.

Mercurius Rusticus, the Royalist newspaper, would call Corfe Castle 'one of the impregnable forts of the kingdom'. Its peculiar site close by the Dorset coast, on top of a steep hill which lay in 'the fracture' of another hill, guarding the only route inland, had ensured 'Corph' a place in history since Saxon times; it possessed its own kind of grim female tradition, for hereabouts had been the *domus* of Queen Elfrida and here her step-son King Edward the Martyr had been murdered, according to later allegations, at her instigation, that her own son Ethelred might succeed. The present massive structure, with its walls ten feet thick, was complete by the reign of Henry II. Later Henry VII had repaired Corfe Castle for his own mother, the Countess of Richmond.[19]

Lady Bankes retired to Corfe Castle on the eve of the Civil War, leaving her husband to follow the political fortunes of the King, first in London, later at Oxford. We have some picture of how she lived there.[20] There were suites of gilded green leather, and blue damask hangings, a silk quilted carpet for the withdrawing-room, a rich ebony cabinet with gilded fixtures, fine tapestries in the gallery and another tapestry in 'my lady's bedroom' with a white dimity bed and hangings. In the large windows were embroidered satin cushions, and other cushions of crimson velvet. Everywhere there was crimson velvet – chairs and stools as well as cushions were covered in it – together with rich carpets from Turkey and Persia.

For all the splendour of Lady Bankes's circumstances, supported by her husband's earnings as a lawyer, it was perhaps a pity that the previous owner, Lady Hatton, being, as a contemporary account put it, 'one (you may imagine) rather of Venus than Mars his company', had sold the 'chiefest guns' out of the castle. When it became obvious that a Parliamentary siege was imminent, Lady Bankes found herself armed with maidservants a-plenty, but as a garrison had a mere five soldiers. She was however not only 'a virtuous' but 'a prudent lady'; in her portrait she shows an extremely determined face to the world, with her strong long chin, her well-chiselled nose, firm lips and fine brave eyes – and she clutches the keys of Corfe Castle in her hand. Lady Bankes had no intention of having these keys snatched from her, not by stealth and not by surprise.[21]

Lady Bankes's prudence was displayed in a number of ways: for example in acquiring a great store of provisions. Aware of the Parliamentary sympathies of the town, she also kept the castle gates securely locked: for example on May Day when the Mayor and 'barons' of Corfe had the right to course a stag on her domains. When some troops of horse from Dorchester thought of surprising her, Lady Bankes 'very wisely and like herself' called in a guard, although the commanders of the troops denied that any harm was intended. She bore the foul language used by the common soldiers outside the castle with stoicism – as the Countess of Derby endured the indignities and affronts of her own besiegers.

When the local Parliamentary Committee at Poole demanded the four small pieces of ordnance left inside the castle, Lady Bankes's prudence led her, like Lady Derby, to play for time, instead of indulging in the outright defiance for which she was not yet prepared. There was a great deal of questioning of the seamen's warrants, and finally when the guns were placed on their carriages, Lady Bankes had them taken off; the seamen were beaten off by the five men of the garrison assisted by the 'maid-servants at their Lady's command' to 'the small thunder' of guns. Lady Bankes secured an additional and far more substantial garrison of over fifty men from the Royalist commander Prince Maurice, brother of Prince Rupert. This was headed by a Captain Lawrence.

Despite the installation of these soldiers, her neighbours (like those of Lady Derby) did not match Lady Bankes in their stomach for a fight: 'presently their wives came to the castle, there they weep and wring their hands and with clamorous oratory persuade their husbands to come home and not by saving others to expose their own houses to spoil and ruin'. In the end Lady Bankes did let the great guns go – and that was prudent too, because it gave her a respite in which she could revictual the castle; it also gave Parliament the false impression that the prizing of Corfe would present no problem.

In fact Lady Bankes absolutely refused to surrender the castle at her enemies' summons; and when she was informed that no quarter could now be expected for the women and children inside the castle, according to the rules of war, took that threat with equanimity too.

The first siege of Corfe began on 23 June 1643. The castle had to stand an assault of 500 or 600 men, armed with a demi-cannon, a culverin and two sakers (small forms of cannon). In order to approach the walls in safety, the besiegers constructed two engines, known as the Sow and the Boar: however the marksmen found their legs entangled in these structures and abandoned them. The besiegers, headed by Sir Walter Erle, were also able to fire at Corfe with great impunity from the neighbouring church. According to the Royalists, Sir Walter conducted the entire siege wearing a bearskin coat for fear of musket-shot, and since it was summer and since he additionally crept about on all fours to avoid stray bullets he must have presented a bizarre spectacle.

As with the siege of Lathom House, there were sallies; food, not a mortar, was the object here – in the course of one of them, the defenders captured eight cows and a bull. The final assault came on a misty morning and the besiegers divided themselves into two parts to attack the upper and lower wards of the castle. By this time their numbers had been swelled by a rabble of sailors, dispatched by the Parliamentary Admiral the Earl of Warwick (Mary Rich's father-in-law) who brought with them the dreaded fiery granadoes and also scaling ladders. These bellicose fellows were fortified with alcohol to make them 'pot-valiant' (£1 12s 0d features in the accounts for 'a firkin of hot waters')[22] and assured that Corfe Castle would provide rich booty. Among their number were former felons, released from the prisons (the brands on their limbs were visible), but the courage of these 'silly wretches' gradually diminished in view of the fierce nature of the defence. The watchword for the attack was to be 'Old Wat', an allusion to their commander Sir Walter Erle; but 'Old Wat' was also the hunter's traditional nickname for a timorous hare which would not leave the cover of the bushes, a coincidence which the defenders at least thought highly appropriate.

Lady Bankes herself – 'to her eternal honour be it spoken'[23] – defended the upper ward of the castle, with her daughters, her women and five soldiers. This motley but determined force heaved stones and hot embers over the battlements so successfully that the soldiers were prevented from scaling their ladders.

Finally the strength of the assault wavered and gave way: hearing a report that the King's forces were coming, the besiegers 'ran away crying'. Corfe had been saved, as *Mercurius Rusticus* reported, by a combination of 'the fears of Old Sir Wat' and 'the loyalty and resolution of this honourable Lady'.

For some time after that Lady Bankes lived unmolested. Sir John Bankes (still absent from her side) died in December 1644. It was not until 1645, in the collapse of the Royalist side following Naseby, when other isolated centres of resistance such as Basing House and Lathom House were also captured, that Lady Bankes found herself once again besieged. In December Sir Thomas Fairfax sent a regiment of horse and two of foot to take Corfe. Even so, Lady Bankes was still stoutly holding out in

February of the following year. It also seems that the final surrender of the castle was in fact due to treachery, although the long blockade must have contributed to it.[24]

One of her officers, a Lieutenant-Colonel Pitman who had served in Ireland under the Earl of Inchiquin, was by now 'weary of the king's service'. Proposing to fetch reinforcements from Somerset, he left the castle and contacted the enemy's commander on the pretext of arranging an exchange for his brother, then a Parliamentary prisoner. 'Under this colour' between 50 and 100 men were introduced into the castle disguised as supporters, many of whom knew its lay-out extremely well. So Corfe Castle fell at last, the prey to Colonel Pitman's Trojan horse.

Lady Bankes and her children were allowed to depart in safety. The gallant lady lived on until 1661; her son Sir Ralph Bankes enjoyed a long political career as well as enriching Dorset by building the noble house of Kingston Lacey. It was typical of Lady Bankes's resolve that her son actually got married on the day of her death – because she had concealed her pangs so successfully. She was buried at her native Ruislip where a tablet in the church still records that she 'had the honour to have borne with a constancy and courage above her sex, a noble proportion of the late Calamities'.

Corfe Castle, and its luxurious contents, fared less well than Lady Bankes and her reputation. Like Basing House, it was 'slighted'.† As for the trunkfuls of Bankes belongings carted away so joyfully by the besiegers during the sack of the castle, those would take Lady Bankes's descendants many years to recover after the Restoration. A broker named Stone in the Barbican in the City of London seems to have bought £1,000 worth of goods, including some tapestry hangings which he sold 'to a fine lord'. As for Sir Walter Erle – 'Old Wat', that timorous hare – in 1661 he was to be found writing to Ralph Bankes in the following

---

†In 1774 John Hutchins wrote of Corfe Castle in his *History of Dorset*, 'The vast fragments of the King's Tower, the round towers, leaning as if ready to fall, the broken walls and vast pieces of them tumbled down into the vale below, form such a scene of havock and desolation as strike every curious spectator with horror and concern.'[25] The curious spectator today will find the scene scarcely changed.

terms concerning the missing building materials of Corfe, in which injured innocence and innocent surprise were oddly mixed: 'And when the spoil was made, and the materials were carried away, I never gave any direction by letter or otherwise for bringing any part of it to my house, nor knew any such thing done more than the child unborn, until a good while after, coming down into the country, I found some part thereof among other things remaining of the ruine of my own house, laid by for future use.'[26]

Compared to such an iron character as Lady Bankes, Brilliana Lady Harley, who conducted the defence of Brampton Bryan Castle near Hereford, presents an altogether gentler image. Indeed, with her touching modesty of character combined with her strong sense of duty towards her absent husband's interests and property (which inspired her to a defiant course she would not otherwise have contemplated), Brilliana Lady Harley is really the seventeenth-century masculine ideal of a wartime heroine. She played her martial role with genuine reluctance but play it she did, most honourably, and to the death. And then there was that other aspect of her militarism, which might be termed the chivalry factor. Brilliana Lady Harley, whose husband Sir Robert supported Parliament, had Royalist relations herself, and as we shall see, her very sex made King Charles I notably reluctant to press against her, where he would have moved mercilessly against a male commander. At the same time, Parliamentarian propaganda waxed indignant against the Royalist besiegers: 'those capon-faced cowards who have unmanned themselves in offering violence to so noble a lady'.[27]

Brilliana Conway was born in 1600; her unusual Christian name reflected the fact that her father was Lieutenant-Governor of the Netherlands town of Brill at the time of her birth. In 1623 she married, as his third wife, Sir Robert Harley; a marriage, as has been mentioned (see p.65), which was characterized by tenderness from its inception. Thereafter her life appeared to be punctuated by childbirth, for she bore her husband seven children between 1624 and 1634 (her predecessor, Sir Robert's second wife, had borne *nine*). However, Brilliana's letters which have survived show her to have been a woman of education as well as piety: she knew not only French but also Latin.[28]

Brilliana's maternal affections were concentrated on her son Ned, to whom, when at Oxford University, she directed a stream of rather touching advice. She sent Ned liquorice for his cold, 'eye water' for sore eyes, recommended beer 'boiled with liquorice' first thing in the morning for the kidneys. She would also have sent him a cold pie, except for two things: first, his father had assured her that Ned did not want it and second, and more cogently, Mrs Pierson (wife of the rector at Brampton) told Brilliana that when *her* son was at Oxford, she too sent him such things, until 'he prayed her that she would not'. A little purse of money – 'if only so he will think of her'– was presumably a more welcome present.[29]

An occasional flash of spirit does however remind one that Brilliana, for all her douce maternal femininity, had another side to her nature. Ned's letters have not survived, but we can imagine the one which provoked this retort, in a postscript: 'Dear Ned, My age is no secret; tho my brother Bray is something mistaken in it.'[30]

All this while Sir Robert Harley, who was one of the MPs for Herefordshire, was busy with parliamentary affairs in London. In his absence his business became somewhat neglected; it is noteworthy that Brilliana made no attempt to gather the reins into her own hands at this juncture. She contented herself with sending him veal pies and pairs of shoes from the country. Sharing her husband's Puritan sympathies, in many respects Brilliana found the year 1642 highly exciting: 'It is the Lords great work that is now a-framing,' she wrote to Ned in May. Yet she agonized over her growing responsibilities: 'what is done in your father's estate pleased him not, so that I wish myself with all my heart, at London, and then your father might be a witness of what is spent'. The plumbers who were mending the house, for example, were charging 5s a day! (although Brilliana thought the cost worth it). In July Brilliana the good housewife sent off the Harley silver plate to London for safe keeping in a trunk marked as containing cake. On 19 July, barely a month before the outbreak of the war, Brilliana also wrote off desperately for instructions as to how to guard Brampton Bryan; she was particularly concerned about treachery within and without since so many of her neighbours in Royalist Herefordshire favoured the King's cause. One 'roguish boy' working at the castle was sent up to London with a letter to get rid of him, lest he join the other side and betray them.[31]

Still Brilliana did not want Ned to come down and protect her; that would endanger him. And still she refused to budge from the castle. 'If I go away,' she told her son, 'I shall leave all that your father has, to the prey of our enemies; which they would be glad of.' As for the danger of her present position, defending Brampton Bryan: 'I cannot make a better use of my life.'[32]

In December 1642 came the expected stern demand from the Royalist Governor of Hereford that Lady Harley should hand over Brampton Bryan to the King's cause. As the Royalist gentry all about her assembled their levies, confident that with Sir Robert Harley at Westminster the stronghold would soon be theirs, Lady Harley told Ned: 'They [her neighbours] are in a mighty violence against me.'[33]

Yet Lady Harley's public defiance, as her letters to Ned reveal, covered an inner turmoil. Was she really right to hold out? What was Sir Robert's desire? 'I will be willing to do what he would have me do,' confided poor Brilliana to Ned. 'I never was in such sorrows.' Her tenants now found an excellent excuse for not paying their rents; money and food were short. By January 1643 the fowlers were forbidden to bring her game, her young horses had been commandeered and her servants dared not go into the town. 'Now they say they will starve me out of my house,' she wrote in February, when her cattle were driven away. The alternative was to dismiss her garrison, but that would be to invite plunder by all the local rogues: 'If I leave Brampton, all will be ruined.'[34]

In March Lady Harley received a summons but declined to hand over the castle. In June, still not yet officially beset, she burst out in a letter: 'O! my dear Ned – that I could but see you … you are both a Joseph and a Benjamin to me.' On 26 July 1643 the siege began in earnest, at about two o'clock in the afternoon, with the arrival of two or three troops of horse, who proceeded to stop all passage between the castle and the outside world. Then 200 or 300 foot arrived; a total of 700 faced the beleaguered garrison. In the evening a trumpeter, according to custom, officially summoned the 'honourable and valiant Lady Harley' to surrender the castle, in the name of the High Sheriff of the City of Hereford, and others. The summons was politely worded: the Royalist troops and their commander Sir William Vavasour wished to prevent 'further inconvenience' to her.[35]

Lady Harley's reply was more dramatic. 'I dare not, I cannot, I must not believe', she exclaimed at the sight of Sir William drawing up his forces before the house. What of the King's many solemn promises on the subject of liberty? 'I have the law of nature, of reason, and of the land on my side.' At this, Sir William, although still polite, showed himself more menacing. He referred to his wish to keep from Lady Harley 'all insolencies that the liberty of soldiers, provoked to it by your obstinacies, may throw you upon'. However, he went on: 'if you remain still wilful, what you may suffer is brought upon you by yourself, I having by this timely notice discharged those respects due to your sex and honour'. It was left to Brilliana to conclude this fruitless exchange with the protest that there was no 'drop of disloyal blood' in her body.[36]

The next day, 27 July, some small shot was exchanged; the Royalists plundered Lady Harley's sheep and cattle, and more dangerously invested the town and church – from the latter they were well placed to bombard Brampton Bryan. How much Lady Harley's bold words to Sir William belied her own fears is demonstrated by her letter of 30 July: she believed her state of misery was without parallel. That 'One of my condition, who have my husband from me and so wanting comfort should be besieged, and so my life, and the lives of my little children, sought after!' Yet, the next day, when Sir William offered her a protective guard for the house, and the guarantee of safety for herself and her family if they would lay down their arms, Brilliana firmly declined on the grounds that this would be betraying her trust to her dear husband who had confided his home and children to her care. Lady Harley ended pointedly: 'I do not know that it is his pleasure that I should entertain soldiers in his house.'[37]

So the ordnance began to play upon the walls of the house; 'their loud music' was heard daily, including on the Sabbath, which further shocked Lady Harley. The fact that no one within this 'close house' became sick during these 'dog-days' of August was regarded by her as the workings of providence. However, a few days later Lady Coleburn lost an eye as a result of the bombardment and another woman, Mrs Wright, wife of the doctor, was injured. Fortunately news of a Parliamentary victory by Sir William Brereton was smuggled into the castle; this made up for the fact that shots fired from the church steeple had broken some precious Venetian glasses. It is interesting to note that the language of the soldiery – abuse shouted up at the castle inhabitants for being 'Essex bastards, Waller's bastards, Harleys bastards, besides rogues and thieves' – was, as at the Royalist strongholds Lathom House and Corfe Castle, regarded as being a major part of the ordeal. Great earthworks had been thrown up by the besiegers in the gardens and walks of the castle, which 'lay so near us that their [the Royalist troops'] rotten language infected the air; they were so completely inhuman, that out of their own mouths, and the mouths of their guns, came nothing else but poisoned words and poisoned bullets'.[38]

For all this, for all Sir William Vavasour's original announcement that nothing more was due to Lady Harley's 'sex and honour', the siege of Brampton Bryan had by the third week of August reached a stalemate; just because its defence was being conducted by one of the weaker vessels – and a respected one at that. The Royalists hesitated to press. The lady refused to surrender. On 24 August Sir John Scudamore was allowed into the castle by means of a rope ladder, a drum having announced a parley; he presented a letter from King Charles I to Brilliana Lady Harley.

The King declared himself 'very desirous' to believe that what had happened at Brampton had been due rather to Lady Harley's being seduced by evil counsel, than 'out of your ill-affection to us'. He was still willing to avoid 'effusion of blood' and he was 'unwilling that our forces – in respect of your sex and condition – should take such course for forcing or firing of the same as they must otherwise take'. Lady Harley read the letter, but refused to receive Sir John personally. Perhaps it was just as well, for Sir John observed later that he would have told her squarely not only of the King's victories (which made her defiance absurd) but also of other members of her sex in London, crying out in multitudes against the House of Commons: women 'who cry out for their slain and imprisoned husbands; divers women killed by the soldiers in this tumult, yet unappeased'.[39] The implication concerning Lady Harley's own unfeminine conduct was clear.

Brilliana replied to the King in comparatively humble terms: she reminded him that the castle was hers 'by the law of the land', but if he did require it of her, at least let him permit her, with her family, to pass somewhere where they would not perish. According to Lord Falkland (husband of Lettice) the King was much moved by this, 'so far [as] to reflect with pity upon the sex and condition of the petitioner'; he suggested that Brilliana should stay at Brampton Bryan, under the protection of a Royalist garrison, until she found new accommodation. However, the only answer Brilliana actually received was a letter from Sir William Vavasour, offering once again a free pass, and a convoy for the lady and her servants to march safely away. At this stage of a siege this offer was in theory a concession. Brilliana was not appeased; especially as Sir William's letter was followed in the evening by a sharp letter from Sir John Scudamore demanding the instant surrender of castle and arms.[40]

Buoyed up by secret intelligence that the Parliamentary forces were approaching, Brilliana prevaricated. She also protested when the Royalists moved their gun carriages during this period of cessation of arms, and shot at them to teach them a lesson; when the Cavaliers stole her bells; 'we sent some of his Majesty's good subjects to old Nick for their sacrilege'.

And relief was in sight. When Fairfax reached Gloucester,

'these bloody villains' were obliged to depart, leaving Brilliana to instigate a service of public thanksgiving for the deliverance of 'our poor family' from the 'malignants of seven counties'. There were public tributes also to the courage of her who 'commanded in chief, I may truly say, with such a masculine bravery, both for religion, resolution, wisdom and warlike policy, that her equal I never saw'.

So the fame of Brilliana Lady Harley spread throughout the kingdom; even her enemies greeted her story 'with admiration and applause'. And it was said that those who had proceeded against her – a mere woman, albeit a brave one – were jeered at in the opposing King's Army.[41]

What should she do now? Should she leave Brampton Bryan or remain? Brilliana confided her worries to Ned on 24 September, being already confident that Ned – by now in the Army himself – would thoroughly disapprove of 'all plundering unmercifulness'. By October the forces of the King were once again menacing the safety of Brampton Bryan. And there was another ominous development. Brilliana had never been strong; throughout the previous siege her health had been progressively weakening. In a letter of 9 October, Brilliana revealed that she had taken 'a great cold'. It was 'an ill time to be sick in' she told Ned ruefully, adding that her last wish was to see him: 'for you are the comfort of your B.H., yr. most affect. mother'.[42]

Her wish was not granted. Later the same month Brilliana had 'an apoplexy and defluxion of the lungs' and lay for three days in extremity. Still her temper remained resolute: she 'looked death in the face without dread'. On the fourth day she died, leaving behind 'the saddest garrison in the three kingdoms, having lost their head and governess'. Once her commands had 'carried us into the cannon's mouth', as a grief-stricken eye-witness, Captain Priamus Davies, wrote; now her death was saluted not with the thunder of guns but with 'volleys of sighs and tears'.[43]

Brampton Bryan did not long survive the loss of its 'head and governess': hideous tales of the fate of the defenders of Hopton Castle nearby scarcely encouraged the civilians left within Brampton Bryan, under Dr Wright, to proceed with their defiance now that the chivalrous protection due to Brilliana's 'sex and honour' could no longer be expected from the King's Army. So Brampton Bryan, early in 1644, surrendered.

Prince Rupert – a legend to his opponents for his savagery – was said to have ordered its inhabitants to be put to the sword, but Sir William Vavasour, more of a gentleman, refused. In the event, as the Puritan defenders of Brampton Bryan were carried away to captivity at Ludlow they 'baited us like bears', wrote Captain Davies, 'and demanded where our God was'.[44] But worse did not befall. And Brilliana's bereft children, baby Tom, and Ned's 'sweet little sisters' Dorothy and Margaret, aged eleven and thirteen respectively, were well treated by the Governor of Ludlow Castle and also by the Royalist Sir John Scudamore – who was, incidentally, their kinsman.†

The castle itself was of course 'utterly ruined'. Sir Robert Harley estimated that he had lost nearly £13,000 worth of goods, for all his wife's frenzied wish to protect his property. At least the legend of Brilliana's heroism survived: 'That noble Lady and Phoenix of Women died in peace,' declared the minister at her husband's funeral, 'though surrounded with drums and noise of war, yet she took her leave in peace. The sword had no force against her.'[45]

From time to time, relating the exploits of the 'Great Heroick' ladies, contemporaries commended in passing the activities of their female acolytes: Lady Cholmley's maids who nursed the sick at Scarborough, Lady Bankes's chambermaids defending the upper ward of Corfe Castle, the Marchioness of Winchester's maidservants who turned lead into bullets at Basing House ... Where the women of the people were concerned, their Amazonian deeds in their own defence, if they attracted public notice, were certainly officially applauded.

†Ned's subsequent distinguished career – as Sir Edward Harley – eschewing the extremism of both Roundheads and Royalists, and sitting for Parliament throughout the reign of Charles II. would have heartened his adoring mother. It was his son and Brilliana's grandson, another Robert Harley, who was that celebrated Tory politician of the reign of Queen Anne.

After the siege of Gloucester in 1644, the town clerk John Dorney collected various pamphlet accounts of its defence. One referred to the 'cheerful readiness of young and old of both sexes ... to labour in the further fortification of our city' as being admirable to observe. The young women who ventured forth to gather fuel were specifically commended: 'Nay, our maids and others wrought daily without the [earth] works in the little mead, in fetching in turf, in the very face of our enemy.' The fortifications of the City of London were thrown up with the assistance of a number of women, not all as socially prominent as the Lady Mayoress armed with her own entrenching tool. This democratic spirit was celebrated by Samuel Butler in *Hudibras*, describing how women

> From Ladies down to oyster wenches
> Labour'd like pioneers in trenches.[46]

During the siege of Bristol by Prince Rupert, one Mary Smith valiantly took out provisions to the men on the out-works, and helped construct the fortifications. Joan Batten and Dorothy Hazzard helped to stop up the Frome Gate; and about 200 women were said to have gone to the Parliamentary commander Colonel Fiennes and offered to place themselves in the mouth of the cannon to ward off the shot. Women in Nottingham patrolled the streets, keeping a look-out for fires. During the siege of Nantwich in Cheshire, women were employed to put out the 'terrible fire' in the brush-wood ricks in a back-yard and saved Dorfold House.[47]

The most renowned of these group-heroines were the women of Lyme, on the Dorset coast, who in 1643 successfully helped to repel the attacks of the Royalists under Prince Maurice. Their fame was spread in a long poem by a local man named James Strong, the son of a tailor at Chardstock, who after being educated at Wadham College, Oxford, held livings at Bettiscombe and then Ilminster. *Joanereidos*, printed in 1645, declared its subject to be: 'Feminine Valour Eminently discovered in Westerne Women';

> To most 'tis known
> The weaker vessels are the stronger grown.
> The vine which on the pole still lean'd his arms
> Must now bear up and save the pole from harms.

Joanereidos was to be much satirized in later years:

> Which I should most admire, I know not yet
> The womens valour, or the Poets wit.
> He made the verses, and they threw the stones …
> O happy stones which those fair fingers gripped![48]

Even at the time it was not altogether clear that the masculine pole relished the principle of the female vine's assistance – even if he enjoyed it in practice. (Never mind the fact that these intrepid women were already well equipped to defend themselves by the lives of physical endeavour they led at home or in the fields – war was different.) An uneasy impression that women were 'stronger grown' was one of the many disquieting feelings produced in the masculine breast by the course of the Civil Wars in England.

Camden in *Britannia* described Lyme as 'a little town situate upon a steep hill … which scarcely may challenge the name of a Port or Haven town, though it be frequented by fishermen' being 'sufficiently defended from the force of winds with rocks and high trees'. And then there was its Cobb, a long spit of stone cutting off the harbour from the open seas. In 1643 Prince Maurice paid his own kind of tribute to the town which managed to frustrate his advance by referring to it as 'the little vile fishing village of Lyme'.[49] The fact was that Lyme (the Regis came later, ironically enough for the town's loyalty in aiding the escape of Charles II after Worcester) held off Prince Maurice against all expectations; and contemporaries were agreed that this was owing to the exceptional enthusiasm of the defence.

On their arrival in the area in April, the Royalists had described the capture of Lyme as 'breakfast work … they would not dine till they had taken it'.[50] Thomas Bullen captured

Stidecombe House, three miles from Lyme, and on 20 April Prince Maurice took some nearby dwellings. Weeks later 'little vile … Lyme' still held off the invader, although cut off from the interior by the Prince's forces.

The defenders consisted of some 1,100 men on day and night duty; but they were far from being well-equipped – they had not, for example, sufficient shoes and stockings to go round. Nevertheless their ferocity in their own defence was so great, and so many of the besiegers were slaughtered, that at one point their water supply was coloured rusty brown with blood. Some of the more affluent ladies inside Lyme when the blockade began were taken off – 'to the ease of the town' – in the Parliamentary ships of Lord Warwick, lying off the coast. It was left to the rest to suffer their casualties with the men. Following the bombardment, fire arrows were shot into the town, setting alight twenty houses. One maid lost her hand while carrying a pail to put out the conflagration, and another lost both her arms. A woman was killed while drying clothes on the strand near the Cobb-gate.[51]

This was suffering in the pursuit of ordinary domestic duty. The women of the town also filled the soldiers' bandoliers as they fought, which meant they shared the dangers equally with the men. They acted as look-outs, especially at night, work commemorated by Strong as follows:

> Alas! who now keeps Lime? poor female cattell
> Who wake all night, labour all day in Battle
> And by their seasonable noise discover
> Our Foes, when they the works are climbing over.

(The satirists later compared these faithful women to the geese who saved the Capitol:

> Geese, as a man may call them, who do hiss,
> Against the opposers of our Country's bliss.)[52]

In fact the women of Lyme threw stones with the best of the

defenders; and with the best of the defenders it seems they too cursed the besiegers.

Finally, on 14 June the siege was raised and the Royalists departed. Then it was the women of the town, 400 of them, who fell upon Prince Maurice's earthworks and fortifications, and with spades, shovels and mattocks, levelled them. As a result of their efforts in 'throwing down ditches', the fortifications which had threatened them were removed in a week.[33]

Three years later, Parliament, by now in control, ordered £200 a week to be set aside for the relief of the wounded of Lyme, and of the widows and children. This the Puritan John Vicars, in his history *Gods Arke*, described as 'a good piece of State-Charity'. And Vicars gives us too the reaction of that unfortunate maid who lost her hand in the fire. When asked how she would now earn her livelihood, she is said to have replied: 'Truly, I am glad with all my heart that I had a hand to lose for Jesu Christ, for whose Cause I am as willing and ready to lose not only my other hand but my life also.'[34]

Vicars described this as 'A sweet and most Saint-like speech indeed', and perhaps it was. Or perhaps the tone, far from being one of sweet submission, was one of belligerence, new belligerence.

CHAPTER TEN

His Comrade

~~~~

Her Husband was a Souldier, and to the wars did go,
And she would be his Comrade, the truth of all is so.
'The Gallant She-Souldier', 1655

'In my poor judgement these times can bring no good end to them', wrote Sir Ralph Verney's aunt, Margaret (Poulteney) Eure on the eve of the war: 'all that women can do is to pray for better, for sure it is an ill time with them of all creatures, for they are exposed to all villainies'. Three years later, when the first phase of the hostilities was ending, a pamphlet entitled *The Scourge of Civil War and the Blessing of Peace* seemed to indicate that Margaret Eure's gloomy prophecy had been fulfilled: war was said to have enforced the mother to behold the ravishment of her own daughter, and made the sister mingle her tears with her brother's blood; on a more mundane level, it was said to bring 'A Famine of Bread, Virtue scarce and nothing public but disorder'.[1]

The helplessness of the female in wartime – falling on her knees in prayer for want of anything better to do to protect herself – was another article of conventional belief like her lack of courage; her passive suffering was colourfully, even gleefully, described by both sides in the usual propagandist style.

In fact the women who lived through the period of the Civil Wars were far from passive. Fund-raising was one activity: women brought their jewellery to the Guildhall to aid the Parliamentary cause. In London, Canterbury, Coventry and

Norwich, women formed committees to raise funds for troops of horse for Parliament. These were known in consequence as Virgin or Maiden Troops: Cromwell took the Norwich Maiden Troop into his own regiment in August 1643; 'I thank God for stirring up the youth (your men and maids) to cast in their mite', he wrote.[2]

Then as spies or 'intelligencers', or simple emissaries, women had a mobility often denied to the other sex. Lady Byron, for example, was able to escape from the siege of Chester in December 1645 and ask the King (then at Oxford) for assistance. An unknown 'poor woman' at Portsmouth acted as an agent between Charles I and Henrietta Maria at the beginning of the war. The handsome red-haired Jane Whorwood played a more sustained part in the efforts to free the King from his various places of detention and imprisonment. As such she earned the praise of Anthony à Wood for being 'the most loyal person to King Charles I in his miseries, as any woman in England'.[3] Indeed Jane Whorwood's various attempts to come to the King's assistance, by their very nature, could hardly have been undertaken by a member of the opposite sex.

At the beginning of the war Jane Whorwood was twenty-seven years old. Red hair was generally censured in the seventeenth century (traditionally it was a witch's colour; it was also to be avoided in a wet-nurse for fear of sour milk) but Jane Whorwood was generally held to be 'well-languaged', 'tall' and 'well-fashioned' – even if she did have pock marks on her face. She had strong, even intimate Royalist connections: her father had been Surveyor of the Stables to King James, and her step-father, James Maxwell, was one of the Grooms of the Bedchamber to Charles I. In 1634 Jane had married Brome Whorwood, eldest son of Sir Thomas Whorwood of Holton in Oxfordshire, and had given birth to a son (also red-headed, according to Anthony à Wood) the next year.[4]

In 1647, when King Charles I was held at Holdenby in Northamptonshire by orders of the English Parliament, Jane Whorwood, 'bold' as well as handsome, visited him in order to convey funds which had probably originated with her step-father. She was seized and searched, but released; later a letter in cipher was found behind the hangings where she had stood in the King's chamber.[5]

From Holdenby, the King was conveyed to Hampton Court, having been transferred into the power of the English Army from that of Parliament. Here again Jane Whorwood visited him, bringing money. She also took an enthusiastic interest in the possibility of the King's escape from the Army's 'protection', consulting the celebrated astrologer William Lilly as to his best destination. From Lilly came the suggestion of Essex, where he was 'certain he might continue undiscovered'. Unfortunately the King had already fled 'in the night-time westward'.[6] (In view of the disastrous consequences of the King's choice, Carisbrooke Castle on the Isle of Wight, one should not perhaps scoff at the workings of astrology.)

To Carisbrooke too came the faithful Jane Whorwood after more consultations with Lilly. Here the King found himself far more securely incarcerated under the control of the Puritan Colonel Hammond; at the same time the need for liberty in order to resume the royal juggling act between Army, Parliament and Scots was yet more urgent. Neither Jane Whorwood – nor anyone else – secured the King's escape; but Jane kept up a barrage of attempts, including an effort to get him secretly on to a ship 'to waft him to Holland'. On the advice of Lilly, she purchased aqua fortis, or nitric acid, to weaken the bars on the royal windows, so that they might be pulled from their sockets. Most of that was spilt on the way to the Isle of Wight; but at least Jane got as far as the King's stool-room with a file also procured by the astrologer. Throughout the autumn of 1648 Jane Whorwood conveyed messages to and from the King at Carisbrooke and according to Lilly, also advised him of the most favourable astrological hour to receive the Scottish Commissioners. 'I cannot be more confident of any', wrote Charles I. Since Colonel Hammond was warned of the intentions of this 'well-languaged' gentlewoman, it must have been her sex which protected her and allowed her the immunity of these frequent – if in the end unavailing – journeys.[7]

The disadvantage of Jane's sex lay in the fact that sooner or later she was accused of being the King's mistress. There is no evidence to support such a suggestion, which in any case would have been quite outside the King's character: Charles I was blamelessly uxorious. That however was the penalty Jane Whorwood paid for being an active helper to her sovereign – and at the same time a woman. Afterwards Anthony à Wood innocently increased the rumours by stating the King had bestowed a casket of 'precious jewels' upon Jane Whorwood – in fact they went to Lady Wheeler, the King's laundress. What was true was that Jane Whorwood ran forward to greet the King as he went to his execution[8] – but then that was in her 'bold' and loyal nature.

The romantic efforts of Jane Whorwood achieved in the end little. The partnership of Anne Murray, later Lady Halkett, and her lover Colonel Bampfylde, achieved in one respect much. For in 1648 this couple secured the rescue of James Duke of York from Parliamentary captivity in London. The what-might-have-beens of history are notoriously beguiling; all that can be said with certainty about the incident is that Charles I was extremely anxious his second son should not remain in Parliament's grip as a potential pawn. Beyond that one can only speculate what might have happened if James, next in line to the throne after the Prince of Wales, had lingered in London, a possible titular king in place of his father and brother.

When we last heard of Anne Murray, she had just been slighted by her reluctant lover Thomas Howard, and pined in consequence for some (Protestant) convent to which she could flee (see p. 177). This was in 1644. Thereafter matters still did not mend for portionless Anne, since she fell victim to the charms of the dashing Colonel Bampfylde, a man who was certainly a Royalist agent, and later probably a double-agent as well.

The two-facedness of Colonel Bampfylde extended to his emotional life: a married man, he pretended that his wife was 'dead and buried' in order to overpower the scrupulous Anne. Wartime conditions made that kind of deception easier. Besides, the inventive Colonel gave as a reason for keeping this 'death' secret the fact that his wife's fortune would otherwise be sequestered by Parliament. It seems all too likely that the Colonel did overpower Anne's moral objections to his sexual advances by this stratagem. The truth was eventually discovered – the wife still lived – and Anne, telling the tale in her memoirs, without exactly admitting to her seduction, does react with the utter horror and mortification of one who has sacrificed her principles for a fantasy.[9]

In 1648 all this pain lay ahead. Anne had begun assisting Colonel Bampfylde in his operations since either early this year or late the preceding one. When Charles I indicated to Bampfylde his extreme anxiety that the fourteen-year-old James should be spirited away from St James's Palace, it was to Anne that Bampfylde turned for a vital part in the plan.[10] The choice was approved in advance by Charles I, for Anne's mother had been governess to James's sister, the Princess Elizabeth, and her brother William Murray was in attendance on the King himself. It was also assumed that Anne as a young woman, like Jane Whorwood, would enjoy a kind of freedom of action certainly not granted to a known loyalist such as the Colonel.

So to Anne was entrusted the task of securing a suit of women's clothes in which the young Duke might make his escape. First she got the Colonel to take a ribbon with him to St James's Palace in order to mark 'the bigness of the Duke's waist' and 'his length'. Armed with this, Anne went to her tailor and inquired how much mohair would be needed to make a petticoat and waistcoat for 'a young gentlewoman' with these measurements.

There was a long silence. Then the tailor replied that he had made 'many gowns and suits but he had never made any to such a person in his life'. Privately Anne thought that the tailor was certainly right. However, his actual meaning was to do with the strange measurements which confronted him: 'he had never seen any woman of so low a stature have so big a waist'. Fortunately the tailor was more baffled than suspicious; he forthwith made a garment of mixed light and dark mohair, with a scarlet under-petticoat.

Now it was up to the young Duke. James, with some perspicacity, instituted a series of games of hide-and-seek in St

James's Palace, so that his guardians should become accustomed to his absences. He also secured the keys to the gardens by a trick and had his pet dog locked up lest it should follow him. In this manner he managed to take advantage of his 'hiding' during a game to reach the Privy Garden and so the outside, where Colonel Bampfylde awaited him with the first stage of his disguise: a cloak and a periwig. They travelled first by coach and then by water from Westminster Bridge.

Anne's turn came next. With her faithful maid Miriam she was to await the arrival of the Colonel and his protégé at the house of a surgeon named Low near the next bridge down river from London Bridge. The Colonel's instructions were to remain till ten o'clock at night; after that, if he did not come that meant the plot had been discovered, and the women must save themselves as quickly as possible. As it was, ten o'clock came and went without the Colonel's arrival. But still Anne refused to flee.

Her confidence was rewarded. After a while 'a great noise' was heard; Anne imagined that the soldiers were coming to take her. In fact the first sight which met her eyes was the person of the young Duke himself, in those days, as the Grande Mademoiselle of France assures us, 'extremely good-looking and well made' (the saturnine looks of the future Charles II were considered much less appealing).[11]

'Quickly, quickly, dress me,' called the boy. So Anne did as the Duke commanded, finding him 'very pretty' in his woman's clothes. She also provided James with some food, including a Woodstreet cake, which she had procured because she knew he loved them. So the Duke, now outwardly a young lady if a somewhat oddly shaped one, departed for Gravesend in a barge 'with four oars'. And Anne and Miriam set off in a coach, helter-skelter, for the safety of her brother's home. At that moment all was confident action. The disillusionment concerning the Colonel's marital duplicity lay ahead.

If women were not passive, true it is that they suffered in the period of the wars (and so of course did the men). There was the most obvious suffering of all caused by the loss of the loved ones, bringing with it that grief which is the handmaiden of wars throughout history. Margaret Eure (for all her meek words a lady of some spirit, as her choice of the Catholic William Eure for her second husband had indicated – see p. 113) certainly found no 'good end' in the war. The 'lucky bullet', which her brother-in-law Sir Edmund Verney had once angrily hoped would free the headstrong young woman from the 'misfortune' of her second marriage to a Papist, found its mark. Colonel William Eure was killed in 1644. Margaret's romantic love for him had never faded: far from being relieved, she described herself as having suffered 'the greatest misfortune that could ever happen to me in this world ... the Death of the gallantest man that ever I knew in my Life'.[12]

Grief struck equally at both sexes, but women were more likely to experience those pangs of divided loyalty peculiar to civil wars, brought about by marrying from one political allegiance into another. Thus Mary Rich, daughter-in-law of the Puritan Admiral of the Fleet, the Earl of Warwick, was also the sister-in-law of the Royalist Commander Lord Goring. She was alone at the Rich seat in Essex, Leighs Priory, when Goring arrived to help himself to the Warwick armaments stored in the house. Goring, blithely believing that Mary would favour her own family rather than that of her husband, sent a message to say that he would first take dinner with her, and then commandeer the arms. Mary did serve dinner – but thereafter did her level best to save the store from Royalist depredation.[13]

The agonies of a Royalist mother whose son joined the side of Parliament are affectingly recorded in the letters of Susan Countess of Denbigh.[14] 'Su' Denbigh was the sister of the magnificent Duke of Buckingham, favourite in turn of James and Charles I; she had thus been raised in intimate contact with the court, with kings and for that matter queens – she was now a lady-in-waiting to Henrietta Maria, and when the French Queen left for Holland to raise money and troops, Su Denbigh went with her. A friend and patron of the poet Crashaw, it was to Lady

Denbigh that Crashaw recommended the Catholic Communion in the lines:

> What Heaven-entreated heart is this,
> Stands trembling at the gate of bliss?[13]

And she did subsequently convert to the Catholic Church.

William Earl of Denbigh, who had been Master of the Robes to James I, was equally a staunch Royalist. He was over sixty but he stood forth for the King at Edgehill; to the pain and humiliation of the mother her eldest son Basil Lord Feilding appeared on the opposite side of the battlefield for Parliament.

Clearly Basil Lord Feilding had the gift of inspiring affection (remember the adoration of his third wife, exclaiming 'Dear! how thy Betty loves thee!'– see p. 65). For Lady Denbigh loved while she agonized. 'I suffer [more] for the ways you take ...' she wrote 'than ever I did to bring you into this world.' And again: 'Let my pen beg that which, if I were with you, I would do upon my knees with tears.' Or: 'I do long to hear my dear son Feilding speak once again to me in the duty he owes to his Master and dread sovereign [Charles I], the master of your poor afflicted mother, banished from the sight of you I do so dearly love.'

The Earl of Denbigh was severely wounded in the head by 'swords and poll-axes' at Birmingham, under Prince Rupert, in 1643; Lord Feilding visited him under a flag of truce – but by the time he arrived, his father was dead. Now let Lord Feilding give her 'the comfort of that son I do so dearly love', wrote Lady Denbigh from Holland from the depths of her grief. 'Leave those that murdered your father,' she pleaded, 'for what can it be called but so? ... there was no mercy to his grey hairs but wounds and shots, a horror to me to think of.' Before, her son had been merely in error; now his adherence to Parliament was 'hideous and monstrous'. Nevertheless Basil Lord Feilding remained true to Parliament; and Susan Countess of Denbigh remained true to the service of the Stuarts. She died in exile in Paris in 1652 without having seen her beloved son again.

Then there were the ordeals of the women who found themselves in the mindless path of the war. If divided loyalties were the painful prerogative of those somewhere near the political centre of things, it was aggravated distress which threatened those lower down the social scale. One Alice Stonier of Leek in Staffordshire was one member of this dejected flotsam, bobbing about between armies, countries and peoples – a lucky one as it turned out, since the righteous justices and churchwardens of Staffordshire eventually came to her rescue. Alice Stonier had been taken over to Ireland by her husband, an unsuccessful drover; there they had been robbed, their house burned, themselves driven out and stripped naked except for a ragged woollen cloak by the somewhat inhospitable native Irish population. The Stoniers slept in the fields at night till they reached Dublin; at which point Thomas was 'pressed' (conscripted) to be a soldier, and almost immediately killed. Because Alice and her five children represented Protestant victims of Irish Catholic aggression (a popular English concept at the time) the Stonier family were shipped back to Staffordshire, where Alice was granted 8d a week and her three eldest children were placed 'in good service'.[16]

Others were not so lucky. It has been pointed out that natural phenomena, common throughout the seventeenth century, such as harvest failure, disease and fire, had a far more disastrous effect on the lives of common people than the wars themselves.[17] Plague pointed its finger and periodically decimated the population; a woman's lot, in an age when effective birth control did not exist, comprised the ceaseless bearing of children, and the perils thereof, wars or no wars. Nevertheless civil strife in one version or another ploughed up the soil of England for nearly ten years. In addition English soldiers, both Cavalier and Roundhead, fought and continued to fight in Ireland; Cromwell installed an English Army of occupation in Scotland after the victory of Dunbar which remained there till the Restoration; under the Commonwealth English soldiers and sailors were involved in military action against the Dutch, the French and the Spanish, including an expedition to the distant West Indies. Women's lives could hardly go unaffected by these hazardous peregrinations on the part of their menfolk.

Alice Coles of Poole had the awkward problem of explaining how she had conceived a child during her husband's absence serving in the Army in Ireland; accused at the quarter sessions, she claimed, with some, verve, that he had paid her a miraculous visit! Another West Country wife was propositioned by an enterprising gentleman after her husband likewise had been away serving in Ireland for some time on the grounds that 'her husband used the company and lay with women in Ireland and had the carnal knowledge of their bodies and he would wish her to do the like with men here in England'.[18]

These were mere hiccups compared to the financial sufferings often experienced by the widows and families of soldiers, and the dependants of the maimed, as the numerous petitions for their relief make clear. Towards the end of the century Gregory King would cite the families of soldiers and seamen among the three groups of the perpetually insolvent.[19]

Of course social disruption could affect every class, and it would be insensitive to suppose otherwise. The death of the Royalist Sir Edmund Verney in 1642, bearing the King's standard at Edgehill, left his five unmarried daughters breathing in a climate of genteel despair, their portions sequestered along with the rest of the estates. Sue, Pen, Peg, Molly and Betty Verney huddled together at Claydon; to be joined by a sixth unhappy sister in the shape of the widowed Cary Gardiner and her pathetic little daughter – for Cary had been so contemptuously treated by her dead husband's family that she preferred to take refuge at Claydon (see p. 145). So the girls spent their time with little prospect of a glorious match, quarrelling peevishly amongst themselves in an attempt to keep up vanished standards. 'I did speak to Peg as her maid might serve both her and Pen, but she will not it be so by any means', wrote a relative. 'I told her now their father and mother was dead, they should be a helper one to the other … but all would not do [so].'[20] Without a man to protect them, the girls felt threatened by lawless soldiers on both sides while the King was at Oxford, since Claydon lay roughly on the borders of Royalist and Parliamentary territories.

Sir Ralph Verney's relations, the Denton family of Hillesden, suffered the capture of their house by the forces of Parliament. Sir Ralph wrote feelingly of 'the ruin of sweet Hillesden and the distresses that happened to my aunt and sisters'. Yet here it should be noted that the Dentons displayed a certain emotional resilience not granted to the Verneys. Susan Denton, walking in her distress over the fields to nearby Claydon, somehow captured the heart of one Jeremiah Abercromby, a member of the attacking force and himself a Covenanter. His love being returned, the unlikely pair got married. 'I think few of her friends like it,' wrote her brother gloomily, 'but if she hath not him, she will never have any, it is gone so far.' Alas, the next year the bridegroom was killed in a raiding party.[21]

More natural perhaps was the romance of Susan's sister Margaret Denton and Colonel Smith, the defender of Hillesden, who was taken to the Tower of London together with the Dentons, when Hillesden fell. There in the Tower a courtship took place which resulted also in a marriage. Margaret's aunt, Mrs Elisabeth Isham, wrote: 'I think it will be a happy match if these ill times doth not hinder it.' Although many thought it 'a bold venture' to wed a prisoner, Mrs Isham reflected: 'if these times hold, I think there will be none men left for women'. Finally the gallant Colonel escaped, abetted by the Denton women, who after a further confinement of eight days as a punishment, were themselves released.[22]

For all the disturbances endured by the Verneys and the Dentons, the fate of those lower down in society who found themselves robbed not only of their natural protector but also of an actual livelihood in the absence of their man, was undoubtedly worse; as in all periods of distress, those at the bottom of society's pile found themselves more woebegone than ever. The absence of the male – James Strong's 'pole' to whose authority the female 'vine' was supposed to cling – was a serious economic loss. Letters have survived from two wives of militia men. The latter were members of the so-called trained bands, not professional soldiers but supposed, since the time of Queen Elizabeth, to come to the aid of their county or city in a time of crisis. In 1642 these recruits were generally raw and frequently reluctant; it is noticeable that the two women share a pathetic sense of grievance against their husbands for subjecting them to an experience which they are convinced could somehow have been avoided.

In September 1643 Susan Owen, wife of John Owen serving under Lieutenant-Colonel West in the Blue Regiment, advanced a number of arguments as to why he should return to her side. First, she was pregnant and in danger of suffering a miscarriage. Second, the neighbours were mocking her for his departure: 'you did it on purpose to show your hatred of me'. Third – the most poignant plea – 'Why can everyone come [home] except you?'[23]

The letter of another Susan, wife of Robert Rodway, was addressed to her husband, a militia man in the Westminster Liberty Regiment; known as the Red Regiment (like the Blue) from the colour of its flag, it was one of those involved in the early unsuccessful assault on Basing House in 1643. Susan Rodway's letter was entrusted to 'Robert Lewington, the Hampshire carrier', but intercepted on its way by the Royalists and published as it stood in their newspaper *Mercurius Aulicus*:

Most dear and loving husband, my king love. I remember me unto you, hoping that you are in good health, as I am at the writing hereof. My little Willie have been sick this fortnight. I pray you to come home, if you can come safely. I do marvel that I cannot hear from you as well as other neighbours do. I do desire to hear from you as soon as you can. I pray you to send me word when you do think you shall return. You do not consider I am a lone woman; I thought you would never leave me thus long together, so I rest ever praying for your safest return

> Your loving wife
> Susan Rodway

Ever praying for you till death I depart. To my very loving

husband, Robert Rodway, a trained soldier in the Red Regiment, under the command of Captain Warren. Deliver this with speed I pray you. [24]†

But Captain Warren had led the 'forlorn hope' of the Red Regiment in one of the fiercest assaults on Basing House. Robert Rodway was probably already dead by the time Susan wrote her poignant letter. [25]

The absence of the male 'pole' was the central hazard. This is not to say that episodes of violence, ravishings, assaults and the like, did not take place on the part of the soldiery when discipline broke down; but then such episodes happened to unprotected women throughout the seventeenth century. However, few of the truly gloating propaganda stories, *pace The Scourge of Civil War and the Blessing of Peace*, bear up to close examination.

For instance, the report by the Roundhead Colonel Edward Massey and Major John Bridges of the mayhem, including rapine and robbery, created by the Northern Horse of the Royalist Sir Marmaduke Langdale was certainly wildly exaggerated. The Northern Horse, about 1,500 strong, were to a great extent officers: 'This march of theirs was accompanied with many unheard-of cruelties. They robbed all the country people of their goods and took away their cattle. They ravished the women and bound men neck and heels together, and ravished their daughters in their sight. One woman they ravished who was within a week of her time ... etc. etc.' On the other hand it is substantiated that two Royalist soldiers, charged by their own side in Coventry with ravishing women, were stripped and given a public lashing. [26]

The xenophobic cruelty meted out to an old Irishwoman left behind by the Royalist forces after the unsuccessful siege of Lyme was the true type of atrocity which women had to fear in

---

†Susan Rodway's letter as printed is a good example of the spelling of a literate woman of the time: 'My little Willie have bene sick this forknight. I pray you to come whome, ife youe cane cum saffly. I doo marfull that I cannot heere from you ass well other naybores do. I do desiere to heere from you as soone as youe cane. I pray youe to send me word when youe doo thenke youe shalt returne. You doe not consider I ame a lone woemane; I thought you woald never leve me thuse long togeder, so I rest evere praying for your savese returne.'

wartime. Unknown, unwanted, unprotected, the old woman stumbled into Lyme itself, not realizing that the troops to whom she had attached herself for some reason long ago forgotten, now never to be recorded, had departed. She was seized by the victorious defenders. Accounts as to the exact nature of her treatment vary; although all agree that it ended in a hideous death. First the old woman was robbed of her money – 20s or 40s. Then according to one version she was 'slashed' and her dead body thrown into the sea, from whence it was eventually cast up to lie 'till consumed' on the coast between Lyme and Charmouth. In another version the viragos of Lyme – heroines as they might be to their own side – pounced upon the stranger and incarcerated her in a hogshead full of nails, and then as in some frightful fairy tale, rolled her into the sea.[27]

How then was a woman to cope, she whose husband (or protector) had gone to the wars? It is clear that a great many women, out of a mixture of motives – commercial enterprise, loneliness, starvation or sheer love of adventure – went along too. The armies of the Civil Wars, and the various armies of occupation later, were attended by hordes of female camp-followers. Many of these adopted male clothing, more from convenience than caprice, which of course makes the numbers of this protean band hard to assess. All that can be said with certainty is that now in skirts, now in breeches, now as bawds, now as 'horse-boys', now as virtuous – and determined – wives, an amorphous mass of women went raggle-taggle along with those troops who comprised, for one reason or another, their means of livelihood.

Whores served the Army as – given the opportunity – they would have served the same men in civilian life; but here was a greater concentration of custom. One prostitute who had followed the King's camp from London was 'taken by the soldiers, and first led about the city [Coventry] then set in the pillory, after in the cage, then ducked in a river, and at last banished the city'. Others received a warmer welcome. 'There they had their whores with them', wrote Bulstrode Whitelocke of the sacking of his house, Fawley Court; and the troops subsequently quartered there by the Royalist Sir John Byron included some women who for convenience's sake 'counterfeited' their sex.[28]

On 13 July 1643 King Charles I issued a proclamation in which the general licentiousness, profanity, drunkenness and whore-mongering of the Army was roundly castigated. Moreover the cunning adoption of male dress by females made it especially difficult to curtail the latter activity. These were the orders to be published at the head of every regiment: 'because the confounding of Habits appertaining to both Sexes and the promiscuous use of them is a thing which Nature and Religion forbid and our Soul abhors, and yet the prostitute Impudency of some women ... have (which we cannot think on but with Just Indignation) thus conversed in our Army; therefore let no Woman presume to Counterfeit her Sex by wearing mans apparell under pain of the Severest punishment which Law and our displeasure shall inflict'.[29]

But there is no reason to suppose that King Charles I, for all his 'Just Indignation', any more than his predecessor King Canute, was successful in turning back this particular tide.

Wives as well as whores proceeded to 'counterfeit' their sex and adopt soldiers' attire. Sometimes they did so purely in order to follow their man. It was often better to be a man's comrade, however rough the going, than to be left as a charge on the parish at home, with all that entailed; a soldier's pay, a soldier's keep was at least a form of sustenance. Then there were the types of a seventeenth-century Fidelio. Sometimes, with despairing devotion, a wife or mistress or betrothed would set out to search for her beloved, vanished into the maw of the armed services; in this case male dress was not so much an economic convenience as a necessity – lest the unguarded female be thought to be displaying that 'prostitute Impudency' which had shocked King Charles I.

The 'Gallant She-Souldiers' saluted in contemporary song probably sprang from a mixture of these categories; once again their true numbers will never be known (the object of the exercise being after all anonymity rather than publicity). A newspaper of July 1642 told of a girl who disguised herself as a soldier to stay near her lover in the Earl of Lindsay's regiment, but was later detected. And when Shelford, near Nottingham, was taken by Major-General Poyntz of the New Model Army in November 1645, one of the Royalist prisoners there was said to be a woman corporal.[30] Jane Ingleby, who is said to have fought at Marston Moor in the cavalry, and being wounded, escaped on horseback to her home, was probably a Yorkshire yeoman's daughter.[31]

Eight years after the Restoration a play by the popular comic actor John Lacy called *The Old Troop* celebrated both types of camp-follower, the promiscuous whore and the faithful mistress. Lacy himself, who specialized in funny accents, played Monsieur Raggou the French cook; the character of Dol Troop was a prostitute, hailed by Raggou in the following terms: 'Begar, Madam Dol, you be de great whore de Babylon.' Dol's widespread generosity – if such it can be termed since she had saved about £400 out of her earnings – led her to remark when she discovered herself to be pregnant: 'I cannot say I am with child, but with children; for here has been all nations, and all languages to boot.' On the other hand Dol's tenderest feelings were reserved for the handsome young cornet's boy – who was of course a girl in disguise. Biddy had joined the Army for love and, unlike Dol, maintained her virtue throughout the play. It is legitimate to assume that Lacy, who began his career as a lieutenant of cavalry, had not only known Dols, but Biddys too.[32]

Dol Troop saw her pregnancy as a means of mulcting the entire regiment of payment. ('I mean to lay this great belly to every man that has but touched my apron strings.') But where the genuine she-soldiers were concerned, it was pregnancy which very often provided the means of detection. The popular ballad of 1655, 'The Gallant She-Souldier', described the real-life adventures of a woman who successfully masqueraded in the Army as 'Mr Clarke':[33]

> Her Husband was a Souldier, and to the wars did go,
> And she would be his Comrade, the truth of all is so.
> She put on Man's Apparel, and bore him company,
> As many in the Army for truth can testify.

No lewd camp-follower she: 'Mr Clarke' was not only 'upright and just' but 'Modest still'. However, for all this vaunted modesty, 'Mr Clarke' was just as good as any man at firing a musket or beating a drum, until the untoward appearance of 'a pretty little son' upset her disguise. She also took part in many soldiers' recreations such as wrestling, leaping, cudgels and cuffing, drinking and taking tobacco with the best of them.

Indeed when 'Mr Clarke's' commander commented on his soldier's surprising girth: 'Tom, why do you grow so fat?', the she-soldier answered cunningly: ''Tis strong beer and tobacco which is the cause of that.' Finally, when 'Mr Clarke' was in labour, concealment was no longer possible. The she-soldier now became concerned to stress her own virtue: as for the baby: ''Twas by her honest Husband, she could not be beguil'd.' At the end of the ballad, those interested to see 'the young Souldier and his mother' were asked to repair to the sign of the Blacksmith's Arms, in East Smithfield near Tower Hill. 'Mr Clarke', one notes, was still the name to ask for.

The moral drawn from the tale of 'Mr Clarke' was of a praise-worthy fidelity, not always exhibited by the weaker vessel:

> I wish in heart and mind
> That Women to their Husbands were everyone so kind,
> As she was to her Sweet-heart, her love to him was so
> That she forsook all others, along with him to go.

Another conclusion can however be drawn from this and other ballads on the subject, such as 'The Famous Woman Drummer', whose heroine's devotion and courage, dressed in man's apparel at her husband's side, is similarly stressed:

> They have been both in Ireland, in Spain and famous France, sir,
> And lustily she beat her Drum, her honour to advance, sir,
> Whilst Cannons roar'd, and bullets fly, as thick as hail from sky, sir;
> She never feared her foreign Foes, when her Comrade was
>
> > nigh, sir.[34]

This conclusion, supported by cases of she-soldiers outside the realms of ballad, concerns female physical strength and endurance.

Most women could obviously manage pistols, and a sword would not have presented great problems (in any case soldiers' weapons tended to be sorry blades, not particularly long or heavy). A halberd, a cross between a spear and an axe, would also have been easy to manage. Muskets were weightier, with barrels officially four feet in length, reduced to three in the course of the Civil War, and had heavy – one and a half ounce – bullets. The arquebus, reduced from three to two and a half feet during the war, and the carbine which armed the light cavalryman would have been less of a burden. But what of the pike? Its proper length was eighteen feet, later reduced to sixteen; and although in practice often cut a good deal shorter by the soldiers on active service, one still might suppose it presented a challenge to the physique of the weaker vessel. But it is clear that women managed pikes too. The protagonist of 'The Female Warrior', for example, 'was at push of Pike some say, As good as ever struck'. The 'Famous Woman Drummer' was also said to have been adept with the pike, as well as the musket.[35]

It was traditional among the English to suppose that it was the women-folk of their Celtic neighbours who possessed a relentless ferocity. The Irishwomen in particular, attached to the Royalist armies, had a bad name (perhaps that contributed to the violence of the attack on the old Irishwoman found wandering about Lyme, although unconscious prejudice against her age and sex may also have had something to do with it). Irishwomen at the siege of Nantwich were said to have been armed with knives half an ell long – nearly two feet. After their capture it was recommended they should all be killed or thrown into the sea; it was Fairfax who had them exchanged for Roundhead prisoners instead.[36]

The Scots were thought to have included females among their forces when they marched towards Newcastle in 1644, to swell their numbers 'and their women (good Ladies) stood with blew-caps among the men' wrote the newspaper *Mercurius Aulicus*.

When King Charles I moved against the Scots in 1639, the militancy of the Calvinist Lady Ann Cunningham – 'a notable Virago' – struck terror not only into the hearts of the English, but also into that of her own son, the Marquess of Hamilton, who did not share her religious convictions. At Berwick on 5 June, she rode with a case of pistols at her saddle, and her 'dags' (daggers) at her girdle, at the head of her troop of horse. All her attendant women had been obliged to become expert marksmen; the Marquess aroused her special ire. She threatened to shoot him personally if he came ashore with the King, and to that end, either with magic craft or with an aristocrat's due in mind, was said to have carried golden bullets with her.[37]

The truth was different: the Celts did not have the monopoly of Amazons. Any woman, desperate or convinced enough, English as well as Scottish or Irish, might find it in herself to play the 'Virago'. Commitment and necessity brought physical strength. (As indeed women have throughout history, in modern as well as ancient times, performed military service with success when circumstances demanded it.) Besides, whatever the mystique of feminine weakness, and even fragility, enjoyed by the ladies of the middle and upper classes, the women of the English labouring class were in their ordinary peacetime lives indulging automatically in feats of manual strength: a great scythe wielded all day at harvest-time was not such a bad preparation for 'push of Pike'.

It hardly needs stressing that at a time of sparse hygiene dress itself and concealment presented little problem: short hair (which was easily achieved) vanished in any case from the Roundhead philosophy shortly after the start of the war; the thick buff cassock coat and breeches of the average soldier was at once disguise and protection. Many must have acted as did Christian Davies, born in 1667, who, going in search of her soldier husband towards the end of the century, adopted the simple expedient of cutting her hair and donning his clothes 'having had the precaution to quilt the Waistcoat, to preserve my Breasts from hurt which were not large enough to betray my Sex'.

In her autobiography (sometimes ascribed to Defoe), *The Life and Adventures of Mrs Christian Davies, commonly call'd Mother Ross ... Taken from her own mouth when a Pensioner of Chelsea Hospital*, Christian Davies describes herself as one who as a girl had always enjoyed 'manly Employments, such as handling a rake, flail, pitchfork, and riding horses bareback'.[38] Such a one was perhaps the authenticated she-soldier Anne Dymoke, 'a young person' who turned up in the military garrison stronghold of Ayr, in 1657, during the occupation of Scotland by the Cromwellian Army. Anne described herself as the daughter to one John Dymoke of Keale, near Bullingbrooke Castle in Lincolnshire. The Dymokes, of which the main branch lived at Scrivelsby, were a distinguished family, headed by the King's Champion, who as Cavaliers had ruined themselves in the royal cause. But this was back in the bad old days of the Civil Wars; in any case there is no record of Anne in the main branch of the family, so perhaps either John or his daughter Anne was illegitimate. As it is, her adventures demonstrate that the ballads scarcely exaggerated in their dramatic descriptions of the she-soldier's life.[39]

Anne Dymoke's father and mother being both dead, she went to live with her aunt. Here she fell in love with one John Evison (or Ivison), like herself of Lincolnshire origin, but who had served in the Army in London. Her affection was returned. Unfortunately her friends would not hear of the match, and without their approval, Anne saw no way of 'accomplishing her end' – which was to throw in her lot with that of John Evison – 'but by putting herself into man's habit'. This she did in May 1655, and so attired went to London with her lover.

In London, however, John Evison proved to have no means of supporting her, so the couple decided to enter service together, describing themselves as two brothers, 'this maid still keeping in man's apparel'. As 'Stephan' Evison, Anne Dymoke lived at the house of a coachman in Chick Lane called Taylor for two years, while John Evison lived in Islington. John and 'Stephan' Evison then took a sea voyage. Tragically, in the course of this voyage, 'the said John was cast away', that is, washed overboard and presumed drowned. It was in this manner that the bereft Anne, 'keeping still her man's habit', arrived at Carlisle.

What was she to do, a young woman, friendless and alone in a strange city? The course Anne Dymoke adopted was to enlist as a soldier under a Major Tolhurst, using this time the name of her dead lover John Evison. And it was in this manner that she ended up at Ayr, where as Colonel Roger Sawrey was careful to make clear in reporting the incident: 'I can perceive nothing but modesty in her carriage since she has been with us.' Nor was Anne Dymoke any less keen to distinguish herself from Dol Troop and her ilk. In the garrison at Ayr she 'never was known to any, which she declares very solemnly to be all the way of her progress in her disguise'.

There was one particular woman's skill which in wartime made her man's valuable comrade, and that was nursing. The weaker vessel, just because her weakness also comprised softness, tenderness and compassion, was held to be a natural nurse (as man, the stronger vessel, was supposed to be a natural soldier). Sir Ralph Verney spoke as roundly on the subject of nursing to his son John as he had done on the subject of education to Dr Denton, only this time he found for women. ''Tis not a man's employment,' he declared of nursing, 'but woman's work, and they both understand it and can perform it much better than any Man can do.'[40]

There was a practical side to this as well. Before the war most nursing had been done at home, and as we have seen, housewives from great to humble regarded the provision of homegrown medical remedies as part of their essential duty. The wartime nursing of the wives among the body of camp-followers was in one sense merely an extension of this role; just as Lady Cholmley, the chatelaine of Scarborough Castle, nursed the sick during its siege, a task she would have performed, if on a lesser scale, in peacetime.

The field arrangements for nursing during the hostilities were on both sides also extremely sketchy. Commanders might rage –

King Charles I might inveigh – against the peripheral nuisance of the camp-followers, but in this case at least, the value of their services was unarguable. General Venables's ill-fated expedition to the West Indies under the Protectorate was generally censured – rightly – for its lack of preparation. But when the General was also criticized for allowing some of the soldiers to be accompanied by their wives, he struck back with some justice, referring to 'the necessity of having that sex with an army to attend upon and help the sick and wounded, which men are unfit for'. Had even more women gone, he protested, 'I suppose that many had not perished as they did for want of care and attendance.'[41]

There were no movable hospitals during the campaigns, and a far from abundant supply of surgeons and physicians. There was also very little proper organization to get the wounded away from the field of battle afterwards to what hospitals did exist. Left too often where they had fallen, soldiers of both sides were fortunate to enjoy the natural nursing instincts and skills of some local woman. After Edgehill, for example, one Hester Whyte petitioned for reimbursement because she had taken charge of wounded Parliamentary soldiers 'in great misery by reason of their wounds' for three months and had laid out her own money to supply their wants.[42]

Royalist prisoners who were taken to Nottingham Castle and encountered Lucy Hutchinson were particularly fortunate. Lucy Hutchinson, 'having some excellent balsams and plasters in her closet', was busy attending to the wounds of her own side, and with the assistance of a gentleman that had some skill, she managed to dress all their wounds: 'whereof some were dangerous, being all shots, with such good success that they were all well cured in convenient time'. At this point the Governor's wife noticed three Royalist prisoners, 'sorely cut' and bleeding, being carried down to the castle's prison, known as the Lion's Den. Despite the protest of a Roundhead captain that these men were 'the enemies of God', the high-principled Lucy insisted on doing 'what she thought was her duty in humanity to them, as fellow creatures, not as enemies'.[43]

Another remarkable character in this respect was Elizabeth

Alkin, otherwise known as 'Parliament Joan'. Elizabeth Alkin first came to prominence at Portsmouth when war broke out, and in the general chaos took it upon herself to take back the wounded to be cared for in London; for which humanitarian service she was paid £15 16s 8d. Later she went to Harwich, where she cleansed the bodies of the wounded, cut their hair and had their clothes mended. Like some earlier Florence Nightingale she demanded 'more hammacoes [hammocks], candles, wood etc.' for the needs of the sick; she also spent her own money: 'I cannot see them in want if I have it.' As a result of these further efforts, she was paid a further £15 by the Committee of Sequestrations in October 1647 (out of confiscated Royalist property) and granted a house for life. The later career of Parliament Joan, by now a 'fat woman ... about fifty', was as a spy or intelligencer for the Government, ferreting out illegal Royalist newspapers, and later still as a polemical journalist; but as a nurse it should be recorded that with Lucy Hutchinson, she saw it as her duty to tend the sick of all nations, treating Dutch prisoners equally with the English wounded.[44]

In the hospitals themselves, once again the pre-eminence of the softer sex in nursing was taken for granted. Amongst women, widows of soldiers were considered to be the best nurses of all; however, economic factors were probably at work here as well as the theory of compassion. For nursing wages were conspicuously low (including those of the Matron). For instance the joint salaries of thirteen nursing Sisters at the Savoy Hospital for sick and wounded soldiers, established in 1644, came to £52 a year. These wages being lower fan those offered to the better-class domestic servant, it was not surprising that few women who had a choice expressed a preference for nursing.[45] The soldiers' widows, generally speaking in a depressed class, might be expected to have no choice.

As it was, women's traditional faults, as well as their virtues of mercy and tenderness, were not ignored in the rules made for nurses in hospitals. 'Scolding, brawling or chiding' were sternly forbidden. And those nurses who carried comradeship to the point of marrying soldiers within the hospital were thrown out.[46]

Colonel Bampfylde's erstwhile comrade, Anne Murray, put her practical abilities to good use nursing the injured and sick in Scotland. Her further adventures had led her here at the period when King Charles II, now allied with the Covenanters, was expected to land. In between there had been yet another humiliating interlude with a family at Nantwich Castle: the lady of the house suspected Anne of designs on her husband, designs which the husband in turn showed every sign of harbouring towards Anne; yet the poor girl had no money to leave. After the Royalist defeat at Dunbar in 1650, Anne was amongst those who tried to succour the wounded Scottish soldiers. She, like Lucy Hutchinson, had her own special balsam and plasters, which in this case she had brought with her from England. She treated at least sixty one day and twenty the next, some of them stinking with maggots and gangrene.

For the next two years Anne remained at Kinross, helping the sick. In later life as Lady Halkett her love of physics and surgery made 'things of her preparing' very popular; certainly she had scope enough in Scotland during the war and post-war years. It is good to record that her flight to Scotland resulted at last in that suitable marriage which Anne Murray had surely long deserved. She was by now a governess in the household of Sir James Halkett, her employer being a widower. As Anne observed demurely in her memoirs: 'It is so usual where single persons are often together to have people conclude a design for marriage, that it was no wonder if many made the same upon Sir James and me.'[47] Yet even now, because the matter of her portion was still unresolved, Anne hesitated. What was more, while matters were hanging fire, the duplicitous if fascinating Colonel Bampfylde made yet another appearance, with more tall tales about his wife, asking Anne soulfully whether she was yet married to Sir James Halkett.

'I am,' said Anne stoutly aloud, adding 'not' under her breath.[48]

Then at last, with a simple appearance in front of the Justice in Commonwealth style (who called for a glass of sack to drink their health) and a subsequent religious ceremony in front of the Minister, at the age of thirty-three Anne achieved the long-sought state of matrimony...

CHAPTER ELEVEN

A Soliciting Temper

~

'Certainly it would not do amiss if she [Lady Verney]
can bring her spirit to a soliciting temper, and can tell
how to use the juice of an onion sometimes to soften
hard hearts.'

SIR ROGER BURGOYNE'S ADVICE
TO SIR RALPH VERNEY, 1646

'In these late Times', wrote Basua Makin after the Restoration,
not only did women defend their homes and 'play the soldier
with Prudence and Valour' but they also 'appeared before
Committees, and pleaded their own Causes, like men'. The
necessity for women to make public appearances in their own
interests was one of the most surprising developments of the
wartime period. 'The customs of England' were changed as well
as the laws, as Margaret Duchess of Newcastle expressed it, with
women 'running about' and acting as 'pleaders, attorneys, petitioners and the like'.[1]

What began as a necessity would later be regarded as an
opportunity. A decade or so later, Basua Makin was advancing
this type of wartime activity as evidence of the female's fitness
for that education generally denied to her. Yet ironically enough,
women's influential role as 'solicitors' actually developed out of
their own supposed weakness.

The sequestration or confiscation of Royalist estates (and
rents) had its origin in the Parliamentary side's desperate need for
money in the early stages of the war, lacking resources to acquire
supplies and pay troops. On 27 March 1643, Parliament passed
an ordinance which sequestrated the estates of all those giving

assistance to the King; in practical terms, the property of such a 'delinquent' was to be sequestered by a committee of that county in which it was situated. In October of the same year, the lands and houses of those Members of Parliament who had absented themselves, or those who had neglected to pay Parliamentary taxation were ordered to be let, so that the rent might serve as a security for loans for Parliament.[2]

Women, however, were not delinquents, or if they were, it was a rare state, more likely to be connected with their Catholicism than their Royalism. Of the Kentish delinquents listed for example only 5 per cent were female, and of those who did feature, about 93 per cent were Catholic recusants; the tiny category of women sequestered in their own right, widows and spinsters, were accused of such offences as selling goods to Royalist garrisons.[3]

Women were not delinquents because of their own dependent legal status: there their dependency worked to their advantage. Technically, because all her rights at law were swallowed up in his, a woman's husband was also responsible for her crimes. Conversely his delinquency could not be laid at her door; there could be no guilt by association. This principle however had the awkward effect of leaving the weaker vessel not responsible for the crimes of the stronger, yet enduring all the same their practical consequences. So, the Parliamentary ordinance being framed to raise money rather than to impose suffering, delinquents' families had to be given some kind of protection from the complete destitution which would otherwise have been their lot following the sequestration.

For this reason, another ordinance was passed in August 1643 which set aside a special sum, not to exceed one fifth of the sequestered income of the delinquent, for the benefit of his wife and children. It was the right to this 'fifth', if she pleaded for it personally before the committee concerned at the Goldsmiths' Hall in the City of London, which gave to the wife – the woman – a new and special importance in that society where her public silence had previously been rated an eminent virtue. A Royalist ballad saluted the change:

> The gentry are sequestered all;
> Our wives you find at Goldsmith Hall
> For there they meet with the devil and all.[4]

At the same time the jointures of wives and the settlements of heiresses were not supposed to be sequestered along with their husband's own property, no matter how masterful a 'malignant' (as the Parliamentarians termed their adversaries) he had proved himself to be. It is a commentary on the postulated legal innocence of the weaker vessel that Lady Bankes complained bitterly – and with perfect justification – over the sequestration of her jointure along with the rest of her husband's assets after the fall of Corfe Castle. Yet, as we have seen, no one could have shown a finer sense of the need to assist the King than the woman who held the upper ward of the Castle and poured stones and hot embers on the heads of the invaders.

As Protector, Oliver Cromwell harkened to the plea of Lady Ormonde, heiress of the Irish Desmond estates, but also wife to the Marquess of Ormonde, the arch-Royalist leader, and as such condemned to poverty-stricken exile. A lady, he decided, should not 'want bread' for the bad luck of having 'a delinquent lord'; he ordered the Desmond inheritance to be restored to her. Indeed Cromwell, then the single dominant force in Britain, had 'a very general fame' for helping the weak, as Lady Ormonde pointed out hopefully in a letter from Caen; in most cases where he had made a personal intervention, the weak consisted of women, whom he regarded as innocent victims of their husbands' or fathers' wrongdoings.[5]

Of course the figure of the suppliant female being granted mercy by an all-powerful male was as old as history – or monarchy – itself. Cromwell as Protector was merely carrying on the tradition of the clement sovereign. As King James I passed graciously through his new dominion of England, to take up royal residence after the death of Queen Elizabeth, he presented an excellent opportunity for suppliance on the part of those whose relatives had offended under the previous regime. At Doncaster, a widow named Muriel Lyttelton flung herself at his feet and begged that the forfeited estates of her late husband might be returned, that she might somehow be able to raise and care for her children.

Muriel Lyttelton's husband, a Catholic, had been convicted of high treason under Elizabeth for his part in the Essex conspiracy and died in prison. As a result of Muriel Lyttelton's plea, the estates were returned and in the first year of James's reign, the act of attainder reversed. A careful businesswoman (she had some of the steely prudence of her father, the Lord Chancellor Sir Thomas Bromley), Mrs Lyttelton then tended her children's inheritance so well that she eliminated all debts. It was with some justice that an eighteenth-century history of Worcestershire wrote of this importunate widow that she 'may be called the second founder of the [Lyttelton] family'. Sir Edward Digby was another Catholic executed for conspiracy. His widow, Mary Lady Digby, twenty-four years old at his death, did so well with her suits and begging letters that in 1608 she was able to reclaim his forfeited properties for her sons; as a result of her perseverance, Sir Kenelm Digby inherited £3,000 a year.[6]

In the rising drama of the King's powers versus his subjects' rights in the 1630s, some of the most vivid incidents occurred when the Star Chamber sentenced men to physical punishments for the sake of the words they had spoken, written or printed. Wives played their convenient role here in appealing for mercy.

Henry Burton was a Puritan minister, denounced to the Star Chamber for preaching 'seditious sermons' at the same time as William Prynne was accused for his work *Histriomastix*; like Prynne, Burton was sentenced to have both his ears cut off while confined to the public pillory, and after that to be imprisoned for life. Sarah Burton was not allowed to visit him while he lay in prison in London, his wounds healing; but when he was deemed recovered and dispatched to a new prison in Lancaster, she followed him in a coach. On 7 November 1640, after he was transported to Guernsey, Sarah Burton petitioned to the House of Commons (now feeling its mettle against the practices of the Star Chamber) to allow him to return. Her language was carefully modest: 'as she knows not how to manage so weighty a business' she asked the House of Commons to take 'her distressed condition' into their serious consideration. On 10 November Burton was released. The language of John Bastwick's wife, asking at the same time to visit him in the Scilly Isles (he had been convicted of a scandalous libel under Archbishop Laud) because she could not provide for the children, was remarkably similar: 'your petitioner being a woman [is] no way able to follow nor manage so great and weighty a cause'.[7] Bastwick was released in December.

In January 1644, the Houses of Parliament at Westminster (as opposed to the King's Parliament at Oxford, a body whose validity they did not recognize) offered pardon to all Royalists who would submit before a certain date; the condition was that they should compound for their delinquency by payment of a sum, to be assessed, towards the public relief. After October 1645 when the capture of Bristol meant that the whole of England (with the exception, as we have seen, of a few fortresses) was at Parliament's mercy, this offer was renewed and extended.

The theoretical procedure was as follows: 'delinquents' who wanted to free themselves from sequestration by this method had to present themselves at the Committee for Compounding which sat at the Goldsmiths' Hall in the City of London, in Gresham Street near the Guildhall. The delinquent took an oath before the Committee binding himself not to bear arms against Parliament, and another (religious) oath, that of the Covenant. He then had to declare the full value of his estate, any mis-statement making him liable to a heavy fine. Rates of payment varied: MPs might lose half their estates, lesser delinquents only a sixth.[8]

In practice these negotiations were very often bedevilled by local jealousies – not forgetting that the original sequestration was carried out by the Committee of that county where the estates lay – as well as the separate but hideous complications attendant upon all bureaucracies, but particularly newly instituted ones. Some Royalist husbands were in prison – how were they to arrive at accurate figures concerning an estate and its rents? Others were in exile, not wishing to return until the principle of the compounding had been securely established. This was where the 'innocent' wives, already having the right to their 'fifth', might well be in a better position than the husbands to arrange for the compounding or obtain the vital certificate of sequestration from the local county Committee.

Above all, women had a mobility denied to the male; even if the word mobility has an ironic ring applied to persons who were often sick, often pregnant, often some combination of the two, yet finding themselves undertaking journeys which involved considerable physical hardship even for the healthy.

All this was nothing compared to women's peculiar fitness to play the suppliant role. As the imprisoned Thomas Knyvett wrote to his wife in 1644: 'I think it will be fit for thee to come up and Appear in the business, for Women solicitors are observed to have better Audience than masculine malignants.'[9] It was in keeping with the contemporary estimate of the so-called weaker sex that any member of it could entreat most plangently without being accused of more than fulfilling her own feminine nature. This implicit social approval of 'Women solicitors' was the reverse side of that attitude which found excessive martial courage in wartime disquieting because it was considered masculine.

Lady Cholmley, she who had shown 'a courage above her sex' in her husband's estimation during the siege of Scarborough Castle, remained firmly in Yorkshire after its surrender.[10] Sir Hugh Cholmley was allowed to sail away to the Continent by the besieging commander Sir Mathew Boynton; Lady Cholmley however declined a pass to go abroad. It was important to establish that the Cholmley house at Whitby was hers, in order to avoid its sequestration with the rest of her husband's property.

Lady Cholmley's instinctive fear that in this case possession was nine if not ten points of this law was certainly right: the Roundhead Captain at Whitby refused to leave the house, despite Lady Cholmley's authority. Homeless, Lady Cholmley was obliged to take lodgings in Malton, with her young daughters, and wait on events. Fortunately for her – if not the Captain – plague broke out in Whitby, and one of the Captain's servants died; the Captain promptly fled. Seeing her opportunity, and unlike the Captain, careless of her own safety (although she left her daughters at Malton), Lady Cholmley then undertook a remarkable journey from Malton to Whitby, in the depths of winter. She was now in her late forties, but she went on foot 'over the bleak and snowy moorland' of North Yorkshire, a distance of some twenty miles as the crow flies, and rising to nearly a thousand feet. Attended by only one manservant and one maid, she took possession of her house again.

The plague vanished, the Captain tried to return. Lady Cholmley declined to be ousted. Finally, with the help of her brother-in-law, she secured officially that 'fifth' of Sir Hugh Cholmley's estate which was her legal right; the following February her son William Cholmley (upon whom the manor of Whitby had in fact been settled by his father) arrived to look after it. So at last Lady Cholmley was able to go to her husband abroad; at Rouen in March 1647 joyfully she re-encountered her son, another Hugh, whom she had not seen for five years.

A period of Cholmley family peace – albeit in exile – followed. However, in February 1649, shortly after the execution of Charles I had put an end to one set of Royalist hopes, it was Lady Cholmley who returned to England and arranged, with the help of some Yorkshire friends, composition of favourable terms for her husband's estate. Once the first instalment had been paid, Sir Hugh himself was able to come back in June 1649. After a period of helping William at Whitby, Lady Cholmley returned to her native south (she had been born Elizabeth Twysden, daughter of the grand Lady Anne Twysden, of East Peckham in Kent) and spent the rest of her days with Sir Hugh, mainly at her brother's home of Roydon Hall. She died in 1655. As a tribute to her fidelity Sir Hugh Cholmley, who died two years later, elected to be buried with his wife in the south, rather than with his own forebears in Yorkshire.

Lady Cholmley's sister-in-law Isabella was another indomitable helpmate. We last heard of Isabella, the model daughter-in-law to Lady Anne Twysden, nursing the older woman with devotion through her last illness, having been picked by Lady Anne from amongst her gentlewomen, at the somewhat advanced age of thirty, as a bride for her son Sir Roger Twysden, the antiquary and MP (see p. 114). Sir Roger was a politician of independent mind: he had been sure that the demand for ship money had been wrong because the King had not acted in Parliament. But in the spring of 1642 he was one of the so-called Kentish Petitioners who protested to Parliament, amongst other things, on behalf of episcopal government and against religious 'heresy' in any form, a gesture which was extremely ill-received by the Puritan element in the House of Commons. According to Sir Roger, it was however owing to the private malice of his Kentish rivals Sir John Sedley and Sir Anthony Weldon that he was then imprisoned.[11]

Dame Isabella Twysden was now a woman of thirty-seven, her physique already wearied by child-bearing.[12] Nevertheless on hearing the ill news concerning Sir Roger she sent her babies to an aunt at West Mall and set off for London. It was not until Sir Roger was freed on bail that she returned to Roydon Hall with him. In the April of the following year, Roydon Hall was ransacked by soldiers. Sir Roger, having no wish to stand by while the extremists fought each other, tried to set out for a self-imposed exile in France with his son William; he was stopped. On 17 May 1643 the order was given for the sequestration of his estate, and Sir Roger himself was immured in the Compter Prison in Southwark.

It was now the melancholy duty of Dame Isabella to appeal to the county Committee – that of Kent – for that fifth which was her due for maintenance. But at this point the Kent Committee demanded that Sir Roger had first to acknowledge his own delinquency and thus by implication the justice of the sequestration, otherwise she would get nothing at all. This message, which was in effect an attempt to get Sir Roger to throw in his lot with Parliament, was duly passed on by Dame Isabella. Sir Roger refused to make the acknowledgement.

At this the Kent Committee set to and not only had Sir Roger's coppice woods felled – which if the sequestration order was accepted, was their right – but also certain trees which Sir

Roger considered to be his standing timber. Sir Roger was convinced – no doubt with justice – that his old enemy Sir Anthony Weldon as Chairman of the Kent Committee was responsible; so that he in his turn decided to petition the central Committee of the Lords and Commons for Sequestrations, which sat at Westminster. For his emissary Dame Isabella, who was ill at the time, this involved daily journeys between Westminster and the Compter prison.

In late February 1644 Sir Roger was allowed to leave the Compter for a less formal confinement in Lambeth Palace, in the rooms of the former chaplain to the Archbishop of Canterbury. Moreover Dame Isabella was permitted to share with him the three rooms and a study, the latter 'a fair chamber with a chimney' in which Sir Roger was able to write and copy, following his antiquarian bent. The Westminster Committee also decided at last that the Kent Committee was not justified in their behaviour. However when Dame Isabella returned to Kent with this news, the local Committee merely greeted her with a yet more violent denunciation of her husband.

Sir Roger's petition was heard by the Westminster Committee in August: bitterly hostile witnesses from Kent testified against him, and Dame Isabella, with her counsel, was not allowed to remain in the room while judgment was reached. It was hardly surprising that the decision went against Sir Roger. Dame Isabella was privately informed of the reason: that 'for one man's sake', it would not do to disoblige the entire county of Kent. At least the Westminster Committee made an order to the Kent Committee at the beginning of September that they 'do allow the said lady a fifth part of her husband's estate'; a recommendation was added that Dame Isabella should be allowed the mansion house and the lands adjoining.

Dame Isabella's health was worse; she was also, in her fortieth year, in the early stages of pregnancy (altogether she bore six children between her early thirties and late forties). Nevertheless she battled down to Kent, and presented the order. All that happened was that the Kent Committee, under the hated Sir Anthony Weldon, refused outright to give her the lease, and furthermore put off granting her her fifth, on the pretext of requiring certain rentals from her – as Dame Isabella pointed out, they were in a better position than she was to supply these rentals, since they had confiscated the land concerned. So that it was back to Westminster, to the Committee of the Lords and Commons, and to Sir Roger; but the members of the Westminster Committee, saying frankly they had done all they could, ended by recommending her to return to Kent.

On 2 November the Committee of Kent treated Dame Isabella courteously. However, she was told now that she could not receive her fifth until she had supplied those vital details of the estate, which, it will be remembered, it was the duty of the owner of a sequestered property to provide. This was all very well in theory, but in practice was a prodigious labour since the estate had already been sequestered for eighteen months, with its master in prison, unable to keep a record of rents. Dame Isabella was undeterred. She set about visiting all the tenants herself and constructing a proper return. In this manner she was able to go back to the Committee of Kent on 2 December although it was not until 18 December that the certificate was finally made out. Ten days later the Committee of Kent allowed Dame Isabella one fifth of the rents and profits of the estate, and an allowance from the receipts of the rents since Michaelmas (which in fact constituted another piece of meanness, since most people were allowed a fifth of the total rents received since sequestration). But Dame Isabella was not to be permitted to occupy Roydon Hall; and the felling of the timber went on.

It was the latter injustice which caused Sir Roger, fretting impotently in his London confinement, particular pain. Once again it was the task of Dame Isabella to petition the Westminster Committee: '... the woods adjoining to the said house, being as she conceived in her fifth part, were then in felling...' Westminster did give out an order for this to stop; although privately once again they confessed that they could do little more to help her against the Committee of Kent.

At this point Dame Isabella started to keep a diary, which lasted for the next six years;[13] this document, besides charting the political rigours of the life of a 'Woman solicitor', gives small intimate glimpses of that domestic existence from which 'soliciting' distracted her. Thus are chronicled the coming and going of nurses, or matters such as the 'breeching' of young Roger Twysden at the age of six: this was a miniature nursery ceremony of the time, when the boy child officially deserted the 'skirts' of his sisters for masculine attire; on this occasion Roger's mother noted regretfully that although he was six years old, he was 'very little of growth'.

The return to Kent with the new order, on 8 February 1645, was recorded as follows (her own spelling): 'I came to Peckham great with child, and ride all the way a hors back, and I thank God no hurt.' Dame Isabella must have been in fact eight months pregnant, for her son Charles was born at the beginning of March; she rode pillion behind the loyal tenant George Stone, with whom the children had been boarded. At the beginning of the sequestration, her husband had kept a man for her but now he could no longer afford to do so. Her endurance was however fruitless, for the Committee of Kent simply nullified the Westminster order. Thereafter Dame Isabella's health took a long time to recover from the twin ordeal of childbirth and the journey. It was not until the end of May that she was well enough to return to London.

The fortunes of Sir Roger Twysden too mended slowly. In February 1646 he was allowed to leave his confinement for his London lodgings; in August 1647 he was further permitted to return to East Peckham, except that troops billeted there arrived the following week. In May 1649 Sir Roger was finally allowed to compound, at a rate of a tenth of his estate: and by this time 'a thousand oaks' had been felled. Dame Isabella reflected painfully in her diary how great her husband's sufferings had been; and all for that one 'Kentish' petition to Parliament before the outbreak of war. Even then their lives were not immune from brutal interruption: in April 1651 troopers burst into Roydon Hall at four o'clock in the morning. They took Sir Roger away, with his brother-in-law Sir Hugh Cholmley, to nearby Leeds Castle, in order to search 'as they said, for arms, and letters'. Dame Isabella commented: 'For no cause, I thank Christ.' Sir Roger Twysden was released, but Sir Hugh Cholmley, a more suspect figure, as the former Governor of Scarborough Castle and a returned exile, was kept shut up until June.

Dame Isabella gave birth to her last child, Charles, in 1655. The scene at her deathbed, two years later, is passionately described in his manuscript notebooks by Sir Roger. When the end was clearly near, she rallied briefly at three o'clock in the morning; although speechless she could still respond: 'When I kissed her which was the last I ever did whilst she lived, she gave me many kisses together so as I told her "here is the old Kisses still". She smiled as though she knew what she did use to do.' After her death Sir Roger kissed Dame Isabella again – one last time.[14]

In his notebooks Sir Roger praised his wife without stint – for her wisdom in her solicitations to the Committees: 'with what magnanimity she went through these miserable times', and for her courage later in facing death. A witness at Dame Isabella's deathbed was so impressed by this fortitude that she told her – a significant comment – 'she feared she was not a woman!' But Sir Roger was well aware of the cost to Dame Isabella of combining the two roles of wife and solicitor. For him she had submitted to the 'loathsomeness' of prisons; for him she had undertaken, heavily pregnant, 'great journeys in Kent', saying all the while she would endure more, 'much more for my sake'. 'She was the saver of my estate,' wrote Sir Roger, 'never man had a better wife, never children a better mother.'[15]

The pilgrimage of Mary Lady Verney to get the sequestration lifted from the estates of her husband, Sir Ralph, was arguably even more arduous than those of Dame Isabella since the Verney household had actually settled in France. Separation from her beloved spouse added a further distressing element to Mary Verney's story.

The marriage between the undergraduate Ralph Verney and the child heiress Mary Blacknall, described in the first chapter of this book (see p. 24 ff.), had proved one of remarkable happiness. As we have seen, Ralph had completed with 'the sweetness of a kiss' what had been begun under more mercenary auspices. Mary was Ralph's 'Budd', his 'Mischiefe' and he was 'her dearest Rogue'. Of course Mary's – and Ralph's – life had contained its share of that endemic seventeenth-century sorrow, the death of a child. Mary's first child, a daughter, was born and died in 1632 when she was only sixteen; another daughter died at birth the following year; the year after was born Anna Maria, who died just before she was four. However their next three children all survived: Edmund, born in 1636, Pegg, born in 1638, and Jack, born in November 1640.

Ralph, who was knighted in 1640, sat in both Short and Long Parliaments as MP for Aylesbury. Unlike his father Sir Edmund, killed at Edgehill bearing the King's standard, he was not a passionate Royalist, but he was a devout Anglican. This was an unhappy combination of views for any Member of the House of Commons to hold (we have seen the trouble it brought to Sir Roger Twysden) and in 1643 Sir Ralph Verney adopted that solution which Sir Roger Twysden had also sought – voluntary exile. By doing so, he certainly avoided taking the oath of the Covenant; but as an absent MP he also placed himself in that category of non-combatants whose estates were none the less liable to sequestration.

At Claydon remained Sir Ralph's pathetic unmarried sisters, together with the baby Jack, the 'saucy child', who was not yet three, so that Mary against her will was persuaded it would be safer to leave him; the real truth was that his aunts could not bear to let him go. To France went Mary, Ralph, seven-year-old Edmund and five-year-old Pegg. The ordinance for the sequestration of Claydon was duly dated 1644; Sir Ralph being named as a delinquent, and his tenants warned that rents in future should be handed over to the county Committee at Aylesbury. (Although it seems it was not totally carried through until September 1646.)[16]

It is the lot of the exile to be plagued by aggravating domestic detail, quite apart from the central fact of displacement, and the

Verneys were no exception to this rule. They did have with them that bright maid from Claydon, Bess, who managed to learn French with ease, and a superior attendant, Mary's gentlewoman, Luce Sheppard; but in general French servants were violent and cheated them while 'no English maid will be content with our diet and way of living'. It was a question of good red meat. The Verneys had no money to keep up great state: 'Of late, I roast but one night a week for suppers, which were strange in an English maid's opinion.' As a matter of fact, Luce and Bess, although loyalty kept them at Mary's side, did not care for her economical substitutes – un-English 'potages' and 'legumes' – either.[17]

Sir Ralph showed himself more accommodating by approving of French wine (although it is significant that when he had an opportunity to send for some 'dear old English sack' from Claydon, he did so). At least Mary could continue to make that good bread for which she was famous, and she had brought with her a portable oven for roasting apples. Meanwhile their friends at home took advantage of the Verneys' residence at the centre of things in one sense of the word, by sending for details of the latest Paris fashions. An English correspondent was to be found inquiring for some costly new-fangled aids to beauty: 'little brushes for making clean of the teeth, most covered with silver and some few with gold and silver twist', together with some little boxes to keep them in.[18]

The decision that Mary should return to England to get the sequestration lifted was, however painful for her husband, a natural one under the circumstances. Dr Denton, father and educator of Nancy, confirmed the increasing value of female solicitation in August 1646 in a blunt message to Sir Ralph: 'women were never so useful as now, and though you should be my agent and solicitor of all the men I know … yet I am confident if you were here, you would do as our sages do, instruct your wife, and leave her to act it with committees'. He went on: 'Their sex entitles them to many privileges, and we find the comfort of them now more than ever.' Earlier in the same year another friend, Sir Roger Burgoyne, had given precise advice as to how Mary should behave if she did venture across the Channel. This was no place for emulating the staunch ways of the male sex. On the contrary: 'it would not do amiss if she [Mary] can bring her spirit to a soliciting temper and can tell how to use the juice of an onion sometimes to soften hard hearts'.[19]

To this Sir Ralph had replied at the time, 'I know it is not hard for a wife to dissemble, but there is like to be no need of that; for where necessities are so great the juice of an onion will be useless.' Certainly by the time Mary arrived in London, in late 1646, she scarcely needed an onion to provoke her tears. Everyone in the capital seemed cheerful, she told Ralph, 'yet I never had so sad a time in all my life'.[20] Bess stayed in France to look after Edmund and Pegg; Luce Sheppard accompanied Mary. The sea journey was delayed because of bad weather and high seas. When they arrived, Mary had to look for lodgings; for two rooms up two flights of stairs she was charged the exorbitant sum of 12s a week, fire, candles, washing and 'diet' were all extras. Mary was also pregnant (since her baby was born the following June, she must have known of her condition when she left France). Both maid and Mary fell ill.

Sir Ralph and Mary had arranged a code between them. This was the point at which their friend Eleanor Lady Sussex, newly married to that powerful Puritan grandee the Earl of Warwick and thus expected to play a crucially helpful role in the negotiations, was nicknamed 'Old Men's Wife' (see p.103). The other code names were equally appropriate: sequestration was 'Chaine', the sequestrators 'Chainors', the Covenant was 'Phisick', money was 'Lead', and Newcastle was 'Coals'. Armed with this, Mary hoped to deal with the mountain of debts left behind by her father-in-law Sir Edmund Verney, and secure, like Dame Isabella Twysden, that vital certificate of sequestration from the Committee of the county in which Claydon lay – in this case Buckinghamshire. She then intended to petition the Committee of both Houses at Westminster 'after we have made all the friends that we possibly can', to get the sequestration lifted.[21]

If that failed, then there was nothing for it but the dreaded Goldsmiths' Hall. For all their praiseworthy endeavours, the experience of the Goldsmiths was much dreaded by the women petitioners (which made their courage that much the greater). The jaunty Royalist ballad quoted earlier referred to wives encountering there 'the devil and all'. We have Margaret Duchess of Newcastle's description of her own experience when she appeared on the arm of her brother (her husband being abroad) to plead for her due allowance; on receiving 'an absolute refusal' before she had even begun to speak, she whispered to her brother to take her out of such an 'ungentlemanly place' and left in silence.[22]

Thereafter Margaret was inclined to deride women who had done better, and expressed herself as indignant at reports that she had in fact pleaded before this and that committee. Women were chatterboxes — this was one of her favourite themes — and life at the Goldsmiths' Hall encouraged them in this regrettable tendency: 'if our sex would but well consider and rationally ponder, they will perceive and find that it is neither words nor place that can advance them but worth and merit'. But this was writing with hindsight ten years later, and perhaps with a little mortified pride. In fact a woman like Mary Verney by words — her own solicitation — and place — a London 'exile' far from her husband's side — stood to achieve a great deal more than by 'worth and merit' in France. Nevertheless she was human enough to dread the prospect of the Goldsmiths' Hall: 'where we must expect nothing but cruelty, and the paying of more Lead [money] than I fear we can possibly make'.[23]

Under the circumstances it was peculiarly distressing to find that 'Old Men's Wife', Eleanor Lady Warwick, was not prepared to exert that favourable influence with the new regime on which the Verneys had counted. 'I told her many times that it was friends which did all', Mary reported back to Ralph with indignation; and she proposed to sell the valuable watch which she had brought with her with the idea of rewarding Lady Warwick for her intervention. How differently the Verneys themselves had behaved to Eleanor, then Lady Sussex! They had even lent her the famous black Verney mourning bed with all its doleful trappings to mark one of her earlier widowhoods. This bed, used amongst others by Ralph's aunt Margaret Eure at the death of her husband William in battle, was accustomed to travel about England like an enormous raven, croaking its melancholy message. Now the new Lady Warwick, no longer having any such gloomy need, dispatched the raven back to its owners; but she made the Verneys pay for the carriage, which as Mary observed was 'not so handsomely done'. It is true that Lady Warwick subsequently explained to Mary that her life with her new husband was not quite the bed of roses that she had expected at her marriage: she lived in Lord Warwick's house 'like a stranger' and had to pay two thirds of her estate for her keep, receiving in return from her husband merely a diamond ring, no proper jointure. At the time, about the best thing which Lady Warwick did was to send round a pheasant and two bottles of wine when Mary and her maid were ill.[24]

The course of events for Mary Verney before the Committee of the two Houses in London followed the same dreary pattern of delay and frustration as it had for Isabella Twysden, and like Dame Isabella, Mary was tormented by a Committee in Buckinghamshire whom she described as 'very malicious and extremely insolent'.[25] 'The villains in the county might have given me a certificate if they had pleased', she told her husband, 'without putting me to this trouble.' When Mary visited Lady Warwick, her husband, the powerful Earl, sat 'like a clown' and said nothing. He did promise to turn up on Mary's behalf at the vital Committee but then failed to do so. It was not until April that Mary secured the all-important certificate giving the cause of the sequestration: 'it is for nothing but absence' she told Ralph – because Ralph Verney as an MP, had vanished abroad.

By now Mary's pregnancy was far advanced; the prospect of childbirth alone in London further appalled her: 'to lie [in] without thee, is a greater affliction than I fear I shall be able to bear', she told Ralph. Already the Verneys had argued by post over the baby's name, Mary wanting Ralph if it was a boy, but Sir Ralph choosing Richard. They both agreed on Mary for a girl (the three little daughters who had died young or at birth when Mary was still in her teens had all been called some variant of Mary). Mary also had orders from Ralph to get a minister to the house to christen the baby as soon as possible in the old way; for this type of christening, together with godparents, had vanished under the new dispensation: the father was merely supposed to bring the child to the church 'and answer for it'. Mary complained: 'Truly one lives like a heathen here.' She found it impossible to find a decent service to attend in a London church.

On 3 June the child was born; it was a boy and Mary did call it Ralph. In France nine-year-old Pegg expressed herself dissatisfied because she had wanted a sister. But Ralph was thrilled to see Mary's own handwriting as a postscript to Dr Denton's letter breaking the news. 'I have borne you a lusty boy.' He fussed over her health: knowing that Mary being delivered would now try and get down to Claydon to sort out matters there, he begged her to go by coach, regardless of the cost; or if she insisted on going on horseback to save money, at least to lodge somewhere on the way. (Later when Mary visited 'Aunt Eure' in Leicestershire she reported the ordeal of 'a cruel trotting horse' because the coach was too expensive.) It was true that Mary was far from well: the 'lusty boy' was in fact quite weak, and Mary suffered from pains in the head.

Furthermore her journey to Claydon brought her small comfort, apart from the wonderful reunion with little Jack, whom she had not seen for four years. He trotted round after her as she made the inventories, enchanting her with his funny sayings and little songs: 'he is a very ready witted child and is very good company', she told Ralph, 'he is always with me from the first hour that I came'. Alas, Jack was also suffering from crooked legs due to rickets: a fate of many seventeenth-century children, however grand the nursery, including King Charles I. Jack also stammered and had been totally spoilt by his aunts. 'He would very fain go into France with his father', Mary told Ralph, and this time Mary was determined to take him with her.

Claydon itself was however in a disastrous state: the linen worn out, the feather-beds eaten by rats and the fire-irons corroded by rust. The soldiers quartered there had committed a series of crimes liable to grieve the heart of a careful housewife, such as ruining the cloth on the musk-coloured stools. Far worse than any of this was the death of baby Ralph from convulsions. Mary was delirious with sorrow for two days and two nights. It was fortunate that she did not then know that her daughter Pegg had died too about the same time in France; it was when the news finally reached her that Mary turned away in agony from those two other little girls, Peg and Mall, the children of 'Aunt Eure' and for the time being could not bring herself to care for them.

It was not until January 1648 that the Committee of both Houses at Westminster lifted the sequestration – and it seems that the Warwicks did in the end play some kind of helpful role, 'My dearest Rogue, it joys my heart to think how soon I shall be with thee', Mary wrote to Ralph in March, and she hoped to bring Jack safely to him. They were finally reunited in April.

The tenderness – and the teasing – of their married life was resumed. When Sir Pickering Newton, taking his wife abroad, asked Mary's advice as 'an old housekeeper in France' Sir Ralph reported that his wife was cross. 'Had you called her an old woman, she would never have forgiven you such an injury. You know a woman can never be old (at least not willingly, nor in her own opinion); did you dread her displeasure but half so much as I do, believe me you would run post hither to make your peace.'[26]

But Mary never did live to be old, neither in her own opinion nor in anyone else's.

She died at the age of thirty-four. The cause was consumption; but her condition must have been aggravated by her sufferings during that eighteen-month period of privation and worry in London. Sir Ralph's own calendar of his letters to Dr Denton in London (a list, combined with extracts, giving both Continental and English dating) relates the progress of his anguish:

15/5 May 1650. I write Dr [Denton] word I received his letter, but could write of no business, Wife being so ill.

22/12 May 1650. Oh my … my deare dear.

29/19 May 1650. Friday the 20/10 May (at three in the morning) Was the Fatal day and hour. The disease a consumption … I shall not need to relate with what a Religious and cheerful joy and courage this now happy and most glorious saint, left this unhappy and most wicked world … I entreat you presently to pay one Mr Preswell (a silk man in Paternoster Row) about forty shillings, which he said she owed for something taken up there, though she could never call it to her remembrance.[27]

Mary's body was taken in its coffin for burial in England. Sir Ralph wrote: 'every puff of wind that tosses it at sea shakes me at land'. 'Ah Doctor, Doctor,' he wrote, 'her company made every place a paradise unto me.'

Later Sir Ralph wondered what sins he could have committed to deserve such punishments: the loss of two out of his three eldest children, his brother, his father and mother, and now his wife 'who was not only willing to suffer for and with me here, but by her most exemplary goodness and patience both helped and taught me to support my otherwise almost insupportable Burden. But, alas,' he concluded, 'what shall I now do!'[28]

What Sir Ralph Verney did not do was marry again. Luce Sheppard and Bess cared for the children. Unusually for his time – and responsibilities – Sir Ralph remained for the rest of his long life a widower. He died in 1696, nearly half a century after Mary, still faithful to the memory of his 'dear, discreet and most incomparable wife'. As with others who have tasted the matchless joy of a happy union, Sir Ralph worried over Christ's words of the New Testament concerning a marriageless Heaven. In the end he worked out his own form of faith: 'And although … in the Resurrection none marry nor are given in Marriage, yet I hope (without being censured for curiosity) I may piously believe, that we who ever from our very childhoods lived in so much peace, and christian concord here on Earth, shall also in our Elder years for the full completing of our Joys, at least be known to one another in Heaven.'[29]

It was this thought which comforted him during those terrible moments when he was 'almost swallowed up' by sorrow.

CHAPTER TWELVE

Sharing in the Commonwealth

'Since we are assured of our creation in the image of God, and of an interest in Christ equal unto men, as also of a proportionate share in the freedom of this Commonwealth ...'

PREAMBLE, *The Petition of Women*, APRIL 1649

During the Civil Wars and after, it was axiomatic that women were enjoying a new kind of freedom and strength, just as it was conventional in many quarters to deplore the fact. On the one hand biblical women who had assumed some kind of active role, such as Esther, Deborah and Jael, became popular images of liberty, without such images being attached to any precise notion of rights. On the other hand the idea of a Parliament composed of ladies was generally mocked: in January 1642 some 400 women presented a petition to the House of Lords on the subject of the decay of trade and their general distress:

'Away with these women,' cried the Duke of Lennox, adding sarcastically, 'We were best to have a Parliament of women.'[1]

This notion also provided a convenient metaphor for satirists to use to attack other targets. The republican politician and pamphleteer Henry Neville wrote two pamphlets in 1647, *The Ladies Parliament* and *The Ladies, a Second Time, Assembled*, and another in 1650, *The Commonwealth of Ladies*, aimed at the *louche* morals of the Cavalier aristocrats in a series of *double entendres* in which the inherently absurd notion of such an assembly was taken for granted – as well as woman's natural venality.[2]

The 'Rattel-head Ladies' were stated to have assembled at 'Kattes' in Covent Garden – the notorious Oxford Kate's, a hostelry already half-way to being a bawdy-house. The beautiful and dissolute Lady Isabella Thynne resolved 'That no Roundhead dare to come into any of their Quarters.' Ladies Montagu and Craven were thanked for favours to Cavaliers beyond the seas. A complaint was officially registered against Sir Henry Blunt, who was said to prefer the favours of common women to those of 'Ladies of Honour'; other members of the Parliament discussed 'the common enemy', their husbands. And in attendance, to help with the ladies' 'pressing affairs', were Doctors Hinton and Chamberlen – who were in fact fashionable obstetricians.

The Commonwealth of Ladies began: 'There was a time in England, when men wore the breeches ... which brought many grievances and oppressions upon the weaker vessels; for they were constrained to converse only with their homes and closets, and now and then with the Gentleman-usher, or the Footman (when they could catch him) for variety ...' Now they have 'voted themselves the Supreme Authority both at home and abroad'. Lubricious details of their use of this new freedom followed.

Nor was this kind of gibing limited to Cavalier targets. The wives of the Army leaders were regularly and gleefully subjected to the scurrilous charge that they had 'usurped the general's baton' – as it was said of Sir William Waller's first wife, who was accused of being 'ambitious of the popular favour' and 'predominant' over her husband. Later Mrs Venables, wife of the commander of the disastrous West Indian expedition, would be arraigned in very similar language as one who had caused her husband to 'lower his topsail to a petticoat'.[3] Not much could be made along these lines of Oliver Cromwell's wife, a homebody if ever there was one (sneers at the economical housekeeping of 'Protectress Joan', as she was nicknamed, came closer to their target). But Fairfax's spirited wife Anne, daughter of Lord Vere of Tilbury, was regularly known to pamphleteers as 'Queen Fairfax' (as Elizabeth Lilburne was known as 'Queen Besse'). It was suggested that his wife's unfeminine ambition was causing Sir Thomas Fairfax to aim at the throne. 'Tell me not of gowns or lace nor such toys!', Queen Fairfax was supposed to have exclaimed to 'Madam Cromwell' in 1647, 'Tell me of crowns, sceptres, kingdoms, royal robes; and if my Tom but recovers and thrives in his enterprise I shall not say pish to be Queen of England.' When Fairfax later withdrew from the trial of the King, and in effect from the Parliamentary cause, it was once again conjectured – with more plausibility – that his wife had influenced him.[4]

Some of this freedom was genuine enough, even if it had only developed through the breakdown of traditional social organization either during or after the war. A member of the older generation like Clarendon deplored the fact that 'the young women' at this date 'conversed without circumspection or modesty'; that, perhaps, was only to be expected. Yet lack of chaperonage and in many cases lack of parents or at least fathers had led to the breeding of a rootless and thus independent generation. The Eure girls Peg and Mall, daughters of Ralph Verney's 'Aunt Eure' (whose father had been killed in 1644) dealt very saucily with efforts to marry them off in the 1650s. Peg broke off one alliance and announced that she would marry no one with living parents who might order her about! Her forthright words on the subject would surely have made Sir Edmund Verney turn in his grave: 'Sir, I am to lead my life with them [her possible in-laws] ... and know so well my own temper that I fear I shall never be happy with them.' She added that if dragged to the church, she would say no to her bridegroom at the altar. As for Mall, she turned down her cousin, Sir Ralph's son and heir Edmund, on the extraordinary grounds that she found him personally repulsive; although 'Mun' professed himself madly in love with her.[5]

This was the kind of behaviour to which Margaret Duchess of Newcastle drew attention in 1650 when she discussed women 'affecting a Masculinacy ... practising the behaviour (but not the spirits) of men'. Margaret Newcastle did not hesitate to ascribe this new confidence and boldness, or even impudence, as women began 'to Swagger, to Swear, to Game, to Drink, to Revell, to make Factions' to the evil effects of the recent conflict. Civil wars were, she wrote, 'the greatest storms that shipwreck honest Education', and especially for women, that are 'Self-admirers'.[6]

Unfortunately this new liberty enjoyed by women in the Civil War and Commonwealth period was frequently associated with two phenomena dreaded by sober citizens of whatever politics. The first of these was sexual licence. Certain extreme religious sects were accused of preaching sexual licence although such scandals were often the product more of rumour and prurient imagination than of knowledge. One hundred members of the Family of Love (a sect founded in Münster in the sixteenth century) were said to be living in Bagshot, in a broadsheet of 1641; the feast of Priapus being celebrated among their calendar of saints. The Familists *did* have their marriages arranged for them by elders, hence rumours spread that they practised sexual communism. And because the Anabaptists practised 'dipping' as a form of baptism, and sometimes 'dipped' at night, they were accused of public nudity and thus immorality.[7]

Not all the accusations were the product of misunderstanding or ill will. Some of the women among those sectaries known as the Ranters were unbalanced and hysterical. James Naylor was not a Ranter – he condemned them – but an extreme form of early Quaker who was at one point tried for blasphemy. Some of the women surrounding him were very wild in their behaviour, such as a couple known merely as Mildred and Judy, or Martha Simmonds, in whom 'an exceedingly filthy spirit … got up; more filthy than any yet departed …' None of this was reassuring to those who feared excess in women in the first place.[8]

Ironically enough the few instances where free love was publicly advocated benefited in practice the male rather than the female. A Wiltshire rector named Thomas Webbe believed that he had rights to all women: 'there is no heaven but women, nor no hell save marriage' was the motto. Abiezar Coppe, a scholar of Oxford University, claimed that property was theft and pride worse than adultery: 'I can kiss and hug ladies and love my neighbour's wife as myself without sin.' One Laurence Clarkson preached that to the pure all things were pure, moving from place to place lying with 'maids' until he founded a little group in London called 'My One Flesh', a cooperative of willing maids; Clarkson justified himself by the example of Solomon. After returning to his wife in the country, Clarkson proceeded to travel England with another woman, a Mrs Star, until arrested by the Privy Council in 1650 for preaching the doctrine of free love.[9] Yet by seventeenth-century standards such incidents were as much to the discredit of the female sex as to that of the male sex, if not more so.

The second dreaded phenomenon was that of the 'Amazonian' all-female mob. This fear was not totally without reasonable basis: hopeful praise of female modesty and gentleness notwithstanding, such a force had a long history. To go back no further than the beginning of the century, women had led a successful revolt in 1603 at Market Deeping in Lincolnshire, against the draining of Deeping Fen, which threatened their own livelihoods. About 200 women had emerged from Langton and Baston 'and did cast down a great deal of the captain's ditch on the north side of the fen, threatening further to burn his houses, drown his servants, and if they had himself, to cut off his head and set it upon a stake'. It was only the intervention of 'a gentlewoman' who happened to be passing which dissuaded the women from their violent course, otherwise they would have done the captain, Thomas Lovell, 'some great mischief'. Thirty-four years later the women of the Fens had lost none of their vigour in defence of the lands on which their cattle grazed, when threatened with enclosure, and were among those who resisted the work of the 'overseers' at Holme Fen with scythes and pitchforks. Again in 1641, the crowd which broke into an enclosed fen at Buckden consisted mainly of women aided by boys.[10]

In Wiltshire in the 1630s the enclosure of Braydon Forest was resisted with what the Privy Council described as 'riotous insolencies ... committed in the night season by persons unknown, armed with Muskets'; when the principal actors were arrested, women's names featured as well as men's. At York in May 1642, women destroyed an enclosure and went to prison for their pains; like the she-soldiers, these particular viragos enjoyed tobacco and ale 'to make themselves merry when they had done their feats of activity'. Nor did the capital lack its own viragos: after the flight of the five members of Parliament in January 1642, King Charles I unwisely came to the City of London, hoping to secure their arrest at the instigation of the Lord Mayor. He failed (the members were not there) but after his departure certain citizens' wives fell on to the Lord Mayor, pulled his chain from his neck, and at one point looked like pulling him and the Recorder of the City of London to pieces.[11]

A tract, *The Women's Sharpe Revenge*, which appeared in 1640, under the pseudonymous authorship of 'Mary Tattle-well and Joane Hit-him-home, Spinsters', was probably the work of middle-class women – tradeswomen for example. Here grievances were aired, many about education, which have a familiar sound to modern ears: if women were taught singing and dancing it was 'the better to please and content their [men's] licentious appetites'. Daughters in general were 'set only to Needle, to prick our fingers: or else to the Wheel to spin a fair thread for our undoings'. It was the policy of all parents in any case to subdue their daughters 'and to make us men's mere vassals, even unto all posterity'. Marriage was the be-all and end-all of the female existence: 'What poor woman is ever taught that she should have a higher Design than to get her a Husband?' At the same time it was claimed that the female character was infinitely preferable to that of the male, being for example far more chaste – the Virgin Mary, not Grandmother Eve, was cited here.[12]

When war broke out, however, these outwardly genteel preoccupations were swallowed up in the general disturbance. Those primitive cries of female protest which did make themselves heard tended to be on the basic subjects of food, money – and peace. All this had a raucous sound to frightened ears of both sexes (it was not only the men who shrank back in disgust or terror or both from the image of the Amazon). Certain groups of strong women who had long enjoyed the protection and even the encouragement of society now appeared to assume a more menacing aspect in these troubled times.

Of these the fishwives of Billingsgate market provided a strik-
ing – and strident – example. Women had been connected with
the sale of fish in London as far back as medieval times, if not
further, since an act of Edward III allowed the 'continuance' of
itinerant fish-women called 'billesteres' (the poor who sold their
fish in the street, first crying up their wares).[13] These women were
not however permitted to keep stalls 'nor make a stay in the
streets'; they were also enjoined to buy their fish from free fishmongers. A similar liberty was granted to a category described as
including both 'Persons and women' who came from 'the
uplands' with fish, 'caught by them or their servants, in the
waters of the Thames or other running streams'.

In the latter years of the seventeenth century, the fishwives'
trade became depressed in the face of the activities of salesmen
who cut out these middlewomen and sold Thames fish directly
on commission. To try and remedy this, in 1699 the Government
ordered that Billingsgate be kept as an open market daily, and
'not permitting the fisherwomen and others to buy the said fish
of the said fishermen, so that the fishermen were obliged to sell
their fish to the fishmongers at exorbitant rates' was explicitly
condemned.

However, in the early part of the century the fishwives flourished. In 1632 Donald Lupton gave a jovial picture of them in his
Characters of London:[14] 'these crying, wandering and travelling creatures carry their shops on their heads', he wrote, their storehouse
being Billingsgate or the foot of London Bridge and their habita-
tion Turn-again Lane. As well as all sorts of fish, their tiny shops
– 'some two yards compass' – would hold 'herbs or roots,
strawberries, apples or plums, cucumbers and such like' and
sometimes even nuts, oranges and lemons.

Going on their rounds, they would first of all set up 'a good
cry', hoping to sell the contents of their basket for 5s; 'they are
merriest when all their ware is gone', he reported. Then they
would 'meet in mirth, singing, dancing, and the middle as a
Parenthesis, they use scolding'. If a particular fishwife was
missing of an evening in a drinking house, it was suspected that
she had had a bad return, or paid off some old debts, or gone

bankrupt. If anyone 'drank out' their whole stock, the remedy was simple: 'it's but pawning a petticoat in Long Lane or themselves in Turnbull Street to set up again'. In short the fishwives were 'creatures soon up and soon down'.

Lupton's reference to the fishwives' 'scolding' in the midst of all their merry singing and dancing was significant. The fishwives' language was notorious. By the Restoration, the term 'fishwife' had become synonymous with one who swore (as 'Billingsgate' was already used to denote foul language); in the early eighteenth century 'a Billingsgate' was defined as 'a scolding, impudent slut', Addison making a whimsical reference to 'debates which frequently arise among ladies of British fishery'. During the Civil War period, James Strong, author of *Joanereidos*, stressed this aspect of their charms, saluting:

> ... ye warlike bands
> That march towards Billingsgate with eager hands,
> And tongues more loud than bellowing Drums, to scale
> Oyster or Herring ships, when they strike sail ...

Those not sharing Strong's admiration for women who had 'stronger grown' were on the contrary much alarmed by the appearance of the stalwart and loud-mouthed fishwives among the women who petitioned the House of Commons. As Samuel Butler wrote in *Hudibras*:

> The oyster women had locked their fish up,
> And trudged away to cry 'No bishop'.[15]

The fact that the women's tongues probably were louder than 'bellowing Drums' did not add to the cogency of their case; on the contrary it confirmed that disgust for and fear of a scolding woman mentioned in connection with witches, and associated at a primitive level in society's consciousness with female activists.

The great women's peace petition of August 1643 – Parliament having recently rejected proposals which many had hoped would lead to the end of the war – was variously described.[16] The women arrived wearing white silk ribbons in their hats 'to cry for Peace, which was to the women a pleasing thing'. Numbers as large as 6,000 were mentioned although one contemporary report spoke more plausibly of 200 or 300 'oyster wives', who with other 'dirty and tattered sluts' arrived at the House of Commons and threatened to use violence to those there 'as were Enemies to Peace'. Another report referred to 'Whores, Bawds, Oyster-women, Kitchen-stuffe women, Beggar women and the very scum of the scum of the Suburbs, besides abundance of Irish women' (here were a number of prejudices neatly combined). Other reports spoke more simply of citizens' wives with their babies at the breast. Ironically enough, this was the peace-seeking mob – 'divers women killed by the soldiers in this tumult, yet unappeased' – which the Royalist Sir John Scudamore mentioned approvingly to Brilliana Lady Harley as an implied reproach to her unfeminine conduct in prolonging the siege of Brampton Bryan Castle (see p.217). In London their violence had appalled both Houses of Parliament.

First of all the women forced their way into the yard at Westminster, beating the sentinels about and yelling at each dignitary who passed on his way to the House of Lords: 'We will have Peace presently, and our King'. Other women bewailed the loss of their husbands slain in the war. Sir Simonds D'Ewes, he who had, as we shall see, put an effective end to the voting of the women freeholders in Suffolk, displayed some cunning by declaring himself all for peace. In this manner he was able to pass through the mob easily, even receiving some 'benedictions'. Others were less wily and thus less fortunate. Violence continued to be shown; ministers and soldiers, especially those with short hair (still at this date considered a mark of a Roundhead), had it pulled. The women's especial venom was reserved for those MPs such as Pym who had received them favourably over earlier petitions in 1642, and promised them that their distress would be alleviated.

By the afternoon, despite the efforts of a trained band, the women had blockaded the House for two hours. When the militia men shot powder at them the women howled scornfully that it was 'nothing but powder' and hurled brickbats in reply. Another howl went up to produce 'the Traitors that are against peace, that we may tear them in pieces. Give up Pym in the first place', cried the women. A troop of soldiers was ordered up but the women simply tore their colours out of their hats and assaulted them in turn. Provoked, the soldiers began to use the flat of their swords: one woman was said to have been killed and another lost her nose. At last someone – it was not clear who – sent for a troop of horse, Waller's Horse, known derisively as 'Waller's Dogs', who cudgelled the petitioners with their canes. The women fled but before they could escape the pursuing horse further casualties were suffered, estimates of which varied from one or two to 100; and there were injured women as well.

Many of the women were sent to Bridewell, including 'a most deformed Medusa or Hecuba, with an old rusty blade by her side', whose hands had to be tied behind her back with 'Match' (the long fuse used for lighting the soldiers' muskets).

There were persistent rumours that this outburst, and other similar outbursts by women, were not in fact genuine if over-violent expressions of the misery caused by the war, but something far more menacing: highly organized demonstrations on behalf of the other side – in this case the Royalists. It was suggested that the Royalist Earl of Holland had egged on the campaign and even provided the white silk for the favours. As a rider to this, it was often suggested that any particularly virulent body of protesting women had contained men within its ranks, dressed up as women; Jenny Geddes, for example, the Scotswoman who hurled her stool at the preacher in St Giles' Cathedral in 1637, was alleged to have been an apprentice in disguise.[17]

It was of course impossible to disprove these propagandist allegations afterwards – which is why they were so effective. The mere possibility that a female mob might constitute an instrument to be wielded by the enemy, and even include the enemy itself concealed within, made yet more sinister a spectacle already disquieting enough to the male eye. It was not considered relevant that most of those women decked in white silk favours were probably sincere when they raised their voices and cried for peace – sweet peace 'which is to women a pleasing thing'. For if peace was pleasing to women (and to many men also) the sound of women's voices raised in tumult calling for it was not.

Woodcuts of the time show plenty of women present in the crowd of spectators which watched the execution of King Charles I on 30 January 1649, anticipating the *tricoteuses* of the French Revolution by 150 years. This was the type of 'Virago' from whom her contemporaries shrank back.

Hindsight – but only hindsight – has shown the importance of female suffrage in the elevation of women's condition; this importance was certainly not appreciated in the seventeenth century.

On 'an extreme windy day' in October 1640 the Parliamentary elections for the borough of Eye in Suffolk were being held according to the contemporary custom, in public – in 'Mr Hambies's field'. Some women, widows, arrived, to be 'sworn', as it happened on behalf of the two Presbyterian candidates, Sir Philip Parker and his uncle Sir Nathaniel Barnardiston. When the two knights were duly elected there were accusations of cheating from their opponents, amongst which was registered the fact that women had been allowed to be 'sworn'. At which point everyone, not least the knights concerned, made haste to point out that the women had not got very far in their endeavour, owing to the prompt conduct of the High Sheriff of Suffolk, Sir Simonds D'Ewes.

At first, it is true, the women did have their votes taken owing to the ignorance of the clerks concerned, but when D'Ewes heard what was going on, 'Mr Sheriff would have us take no women's oaths'. Both the knights requested the women's votes to be removed from the total, and when the High Sheriff 'cast up the Books, he cast out the women of the general sum'. Sir Simonds D'Ewes was quite clear in his own mind as to the reason for his behaviour: 'conceiving it a matter very unworthy of any gentleman, and most dishonourable in such an election to make use of their [women's] voices, although they might in law have been allowed'.[18]

It was significant that the women in Hambies's field in 1640 were widows; once again, the widow, by her very status outside conventional male authority, occupied a position of potential strength. This was in any case a time of franchisal doubt concerning who could or could not vote (in those elections which were disputed and where public voting actually took place; undisputed nominations to Parliament were arranged behind the scenes).[19] It is important to realize therefore that these widows were not acting as agitators but freeholders.

It was the association of the vote with material wealth – the 'permanent fixed interest' in the country – which had enabled some women freeholders in the past to use their 'voice' in Parliamentary elections. It was in this sense that Sir Simonds D'Ewes at Eye admitted with some disgust that the Suffolk women's 'voices' might 'in law' have been allowed. In the remote medieval past, those Catholic abbesses who were early patterns of powerful womanhood had named representatives. Under Elizabeth there had been two cases of borough-owners, who happened to be women, returning Members of Parliament. More recently, in the reign of James I, a judge pronounced in the case of Coates v. Lyle that a 'feme sole', if a freeholder, could vote; in the cases of Catherine v. Surrey and Holt v. Lyle, the same judgment was given, although it was added that on marriage the right passed to the lady's husband. In 1628 Sir Henry Slingsby endeavoured – but in vain – to use the votes of widowed burgage holders in Knaresborough in Yorkshire.[20]

For all this, the little episode at Eye was not the harbinger of numerous occasions at which female freeholders attempted to be sworn; despite the fact that the Members elected were Presbyterians and that the Parliament concerned was that famous innovatory body which would be known as the Long Parliament. The incident in Mr Hambies's field on a windy day in 1640 was not a prologue but an epilogue to the subject of female suffrage. In 1644 the *Institutes* of Sir Edward Coke were published without challenge, in which it was laid down that 'Multitudes are bound by Acts of Parliament which are not parties to [the] election'. In this silent subject herd were to be included males under twenty-one, 'all they that have no freehold...and all women having freehold or no freehold'.[21]

It was true that at another Yorkshire election, that of Richmond in 1678, widows were explicitly disallowed in advance – 'it being against common right' – although they could assign their votes to others; but this was less an indication of potential female rights than of the vague nature of the English electoral roll at the time.[22] It was more significant that throughout a period of unparalleled radicalism – and radical debate – in English history, when so many revolutionary political ideas were discussed that to contemporaries it must have seemed that Pandora's Box had been opened, the serious question of giving a vote to Pandora herself was never even mooted.

At the Army's Putney debates in the autumn of 1647, the Levellers among their number put forward startling demands for the extension of the suffrage in their document *The Agreement of the People*, based on the premise that the consent of the governed was needed for government: a man could rule over other individuals 'no further than by free consent, or agreement, by giving up their power to each other, for their better being'. The Army's high command, including Oliver Cromwell and Henry Ireton, found this whole concept of a franchise based on rights rather than property both dangerous and appalling. But this was *manhood* suffrage which was being discussed, and those Levellers who did raise the question of universal suffrage at Putney, envisaged it in terms of adult males. Disconcerting as it may be to the modern inquirer, even male 'servants' were to be excluded from the new franchise of the Levellers if they were not householders, since roughly speaking household franchise was what was required. It was not even thought worth mentioning that women, whose legal rights were so obviously swallowed up in those of their husbands, were excluded.[23]

Henry Ireton's answer came down firmly on the side of that freehold qualification for voting which had been the founding notion of Parliament since its earliest days in the time of Edward I (and was incidentally to remain so for the next two centuries). No one had a right to choose those 'that shall determine what laws we shall be ruled by here', he declared, who did not have 'a permanent fixed interest in this Kingdom', by which Ireton meant the possession of freehold property, or some other form of freehold such as an office or benefice (a fellowship at an Oxford or Cambridge college entitled the holder to vote at county elections).

In the late 1640s even the extreme opinions of the Levellers did not lead them to challenge the concept of a woman's legal subordination to her husband. One scholar has written that no plea for female franchise was put forward in the Civil War period so far as he can discover.[24] Towards the end of the century, Locke omitted women from natural equality, and James Tyrrell, one of Locke's associates, observed: 'There never was any government where all the promiscuous rabble of women and children had votes, as not being capable of it, yet it does not for all that prove that all legal civil government does not owe its origin to the consent of the people.' It was a contrast on which Mary Astell, the educationalist, would reflect bitterly at the beginning of the next century: 'how much soever Arbitrary Power may be dislik'd on a Throne, not Milton ... nor any of the Advocates of Resistance, would cry up Liberty to poor Female Slaves or plead for the lawfulness of Resisting a Private Tyranny'.[25]

The very few possible exceptions to this rule only serve to emphasize the monolithic nature of male supremacy at the time, at least in the political sphere, for none of them bore fruit. The short-lived Diggers' movement, whose members, extreme radicals, believed that land should be held in common, did result in some revolutionary suggestions on the subject of marriage from its leader Gerrard Winstanley. Article 56 of Winstanley's 'Laws for a Free Commonwealth' proposed that: 'Every man and woman shall have the free liberty to marry whom they love, if they can obtain the love and liking of that party whom they would marry, and neither birth nor portion' should hinder the match. The reason given was: 'for we are all of one blood, mankind, and for portion, the Common Storehouses are every man and maid's portion, as free to one as to another'.[26] Here was indeed a revolutionary suggestion; as we have seen, the disposal of the young in marriage for reasons other than affection was a cornerstone of society, without which the building could be expected in the minds of contemporaries to collapse. Marriage itself, in the same free style, was to take the form of a simple verbal declaration in front of witnesses.

Further Digger clauses on the subject of rape and the begetting of illegitimate children by men were even more startling. If a man lay with a woman forcibly and she cried out (as testified by two witnesses) he was to be put to death while the woman went free: 'it is robbery of a woman's bodily freedom'. If a man lay with a maid and she conceived, he was to marry her.

With the extinction of the Diggers' movement vanished Winstanley's revolutionary notions on marriage. Their effect on society as a whole had in any case been insubstantial; except to link radicalism still further with the upsetting of the natural order as regards the family. It was significant that the governmental – Puritan – legislation concerning sexual relationships between man and woman was of a very different order. The harsh new Act of 1650 made adultery a capital crime; however, the man could escape execution by pleading that he did not know the woman was married (a convenient loophole). The woman on the other hand could in theory only avoid execution if her husband had been absent more than three years. It seems that only one woman, Ursula Powell, brought before the Middlesex Quarter Sessions, was actually put to death under the law (and there is even some doubt about her fate); this was because juries refused to convict, or dealt out lesser penalties of imprisonment or whipping.[27] Nevertheless the principle of the greater guilt of the female was explicitly stated, in marked contrast to Winstanley's vision of justice.

In 1646, the year before the Putney debates, in *The Freemans Freedome Vindicated*, John Lilburne, the Leveller leader and theoretician, did at least include women in his doctrine of consent. He wrote that of 'every particular individual man and woman ... by nature all equal and alike in power, dignity, authority, and majesty' none had by nature any authority over any except by 'donation, that is to say, by mutual agreement or consent'. It has been proposed by one of his biographers that inclusion of women in the franchise was at least 'consonant with Lilburne's actions';[28] nevertheless he did not in fact postulate such an inclusion.

The early history of the Levellers was however marked by the courage of their 'lusty lasses', as *Mercurius Pragmaticus* described them. Not all of these lasses were as young as such a cheerful description implied. Katherine Hadley was an old spinster who tended John Lilburne in the Fleet prison in 1639, where he had been incarcerated the previous year for printing and circulating unlicensed books, having been first fined, whipped and pilloried. She was subsequently accused of distributing Lilburne's pamphlet *A Cry for Justice* at the Whitsun holiday to some apprentices, and another Lilburnian appeal to both apprentices and clothworkers. Arrested without a warrant, she was consigned by the Lord Mayor of London to the Poultry Compter prison in the City, where she withstood seven months of harsh conditions. When she petitioned for liberty, Katherine Hadley was transferred to Bridewell on 1 October – still without trial or even examination. Here, to her chagrin and suffering, she was placed, as she put it, among 'the common sluts, whose society is a hell upon earth to me, that fears the Lord'. She was not set free until December 1640, in that newly liberal climate which also led to the release of Burton and Bastwick. Thanks to Lilburne, Katherine Hadley received £10 in compensation for what she had endured.[29]

Mary Overton, the wife of the pamphleteer Richard Overton, who under the name of Martin Marpriest attacked the Westminster Assembly of Divines mercilessly, was another woman who suffered for a principle with fortitude. At the time of the Long Parliament, Overton published attacks on the position of the bishops anonymously; later he moved on to theological matters and it was when he described, still anonymously, the doctrine of immortality – 'the present going of the soul into heaven or hell' – as 'a fiction' that his work incurred the displeasure of the House of Commons, who ordered the licensing committee to inquire into its author, printer and publisher. In August

1646 Overton was arrested for printing some of John Lilburne's pamphlets and taken to Newgate.

Mary Overton's petition for her husband's release would later refer with indignation to the fact that he had 'constantly adhered to the Parliament'. She described his incarceration in Newgate as 'the high violation of the fundamental Laws of this Land, the utter subversion of the Common Liberties of the people and of your Petitioner's husband's native Right and Inheritance in particular', quoting a list of protests starting with that of Magna Carta and going right forward to the Petition of Right in 1628.

She also described the traumatic moment of the arrest (she was sick in bed, having recently given birth), when the officers of the law broke open and ransacked their house, followed by another visit at which the officers were sent again 'to enter, search, ransack and rifle your Petitioner's house, her trunks, chests, etc. to rob, steal, plunder and bear away her goods, which were her then present livelihood for her imprisoned husband, her self, and three small children, her brother and sister'.[30]

In January 1647 Mary Overton herself was arrested, together with her brother Thomas Johnson, when they were discovered stitching the sheets of a seditious pamphlet written by her husband with the assistance of Lilburne, *Regal Tyranny Discovered.*[31] She was taken before the Bar of the House of Lords, but here she stalwartly refused to answer any questions or to take any oath against herself or her husband. At which point she was herself committed to prison. What was more she was literally dragged there 'on two cudgels ... headlong upon the stones through all the dirt and mire of the streets' with her six-months-old baby in her arms, and incidentally once more pregnant. As if this was not enough, the officers of the law abused her all the way, 'with the scandalous, infamous names of wicked Whore, Strumpet etc.'. Finally she was thrown into the 'most reproachful gaol' of Bridewell, that 'hell upon earth' to decent women as Katherine Hadley had described it, where of course Mary Overton joined the company of all the genuine whores and strumpets (and lost the child she was carrying).

In Mary Overton's petition to the House of Commons of late

March, she begged for a speedy sentence. If wrong had been done, then she was prepared to face execution; if not she should be granted her freedom; but arbitrary imprisonment at the orders of the House of Lords was utterly intolerable. Despite these cogent arguments, she was not released until July. And Richard Overton, issuing a number of broadsheets against his arbitrary imprisonment, continued to be associated both in and out of gaol with the Levellers.

Of all the Levellers' wives, Elizabeth Lilburne, born Elizabeth Dewell, excites at once the most sympathy for her sufferings and the most admiration for her endurance; these feelings being not unmixed with pity for the fate of anyone married to John Lilburne. (In general the story of Elizabeth Lilburne recalls that definition of a saint as one that is married to a martyr.) The kind of freedom which Elizabeth Lilburne shared with her husband was short-lived if it existed at all; the best tribute to her character being those words of Lilburne's in 1646 from *The Freemans Freedome Vindicated*, quoted earlier, in which man and woman were declared equal alike in dignity and authority; these sentiments – so much in advance of Lilburne's time – it must be plausible to ascribe to her husband's intimate knowledge of one splendid woman. His later treatment of her is not so edifying.

John Lilburne was about twenty-four when in 1638 he was sentenced by the Star Chamber. It has been suggested that Elizabeth Dewell, like Katherine Hadley, may have been among the women who visited him after his whipping. She certainly comforted him in the Fleet prison. Lilburne was released at the beginning of the Long Parliament and took to brewing. After his marriage, Lilburne described Elizabeth as 'an object dear in my affections several years before from me she knew anything of it'. At least these early days must have been a sweet period, for John could write later: 'I confess I partly know it by experience that divers months after marriage are most commonly a time of dotage.'[32]

At the beginning of the Civil War, Lilburne joined the

Parliamentary Army and fought at Edgehill; Elizabeth was probably present too, quartered with the other women at Kineton, along with those baggage trains which the dreaded 'Prince Robber' Rupert plundered. John Lilburne was subsequently captured at Brentford, and having been tried for high treason for bearing arms against the King, was shut up in Oxford Castle in danger of execution. From there he smuggled out a letter to his wife; whereupon she, although pregnant, set out for the Royalist headquarters, which she reached after 'so many sad and difficult accidents to a woman in her condition, as would force tears from the hardest heart'. Lilburne's liberty was secured by exchange: he wrote later that by her 'wisdom, patience, diligence' Elizabeth had saved his life.[33]

On his release Lilburne's thirst for agitation proved to be in no way quenched by his ordeal. Elizabeth had secured him a government position at £1,000 a year; to her 'extraordinary grief' he rejected utterly the possibility of an easier life: he 'must rather fight for 8d a day'. It was true that Lilburne had an astonishingly quarrelsome nature, as well as passionate political convictions. He left the Army in the spring of 1645, refusing to take the oath of the Covenant. His contentiousness as much as his conscience soon led to further periods of imprisonment, this time at the orders of Parliament. Elizabeth, pregnant again, lived with him in Newgate prison in the autumn of 1645 until he was released in October; it was peculiarly painful to discover that when the Stationers' Company's agents had ransacked their house in Half-Moon Alley for seditious writings, they had also stolen the childbed linen which was carefully stored there (much as the Overtons had been robbed).

During a further period of more severe imprisonment in the summer of 1646, Elizabeth occupied herself in active campaigning on her husband's behalf. It was Elizabeth who undertook the presentation of John's defence in a letter to the Keeper of Newgate prison which was later printed with a characteristic challenge: 'as a free Commoner of England, I do here at your open Barre protest…'.[34] On 10 July, Lilburne was committed to the Tower of London and not even allowed to receive food at his wife's hands. With about twenty other women, Elizabeth visited the House of Commons in September to present Lilburne's petition for justice, headed 'For J. Lilburne from his wife and many women', and she continued to protest at being barred from his side. Day after day this devoted body appeared at Westminster until a Committee of the House was appointed to hear Lilburne's case and Elizabeth was permitted to join him.

In February 1647 Elizabeth herself was arrested while at her husband's side for dispersing his writings. Unlike Mary Overton she did not remain silent: in court she gave vent to a furious outburst on the subject of 'a company of unjust and unrighteous Judges'. In this instance it was the quick-tempered John who demanded that what she had said should be overlooked: the court should 'pass by what in the bitterness of her heart being a woman she had said'. It was a perfect example of the weak but protected role of the female at law: Lilburne secured Elizabeth's discharge on the grounds that he, as her husband, must be held responsible for what had happened.[35]

Elizabeth Lilburne remained free to haunt the Army headquarters at St Albans and Kingston, petitioning for her husband's release and carrying messages to Leveller meeting places. But when Lilburne was offered bail in the autumn, his address to his family expressed the classic position of the man of conscience: 'Shall I for love of them, sin against my soul…?'[36]

Elizabeth even had an opportunity to protect her husband physically. In January 1648 Lilburne was brought before the Bar of the House of Commons to answer further charges; in the lobby the soldiers turned on 'Freeborn John' with their musket butts until Elizabeth flung herself in the way. Lilburne was subsequently taken to the Tower, from which he was released in August. The great Leveller petition of 11 September is thought to have been largely his work. It was signed by 'Thousands of well-affected, dwelling in and about London'; in it the demands of *The Agreement of the People* were repeated, together with a demand for the abolition of the 'negative voices' of the King and the House of Lords.[37]

By the end of 1648, however, Lilburne had become

disillusioned with the Army and its leaders, including Cromwell, seeing in its control of Parliament after Pride's Purge merely another face of tyranny. In the New Year, although he approved of the execution of the King in principle, he thought that an ordinary jury of the people should try him, following the establishment of a republic, rather than a High Court of Justice.

At the beginning of 1649 therefore, thanks to John Lilburne's temporary withdrawal from public affairs, a short period of domestic peace was enjoyed by Elizabeth and her family, now including three children, two of whom had been born while John was in prison (Tower was the unusual if appropriate name chosen for the youngest). But by the spring Lilburne, as the voice of the Levellers, had abandoned domesticity for strife once more. Once again Lilburne was demanding liberty of conscience, attacking the new Government. Once again he was clapped into prison. Once again it was necessary to petition for his release.

The presentation of *The Humble Petition of divers well-affected Women inhabiting the City of London, Westminster, the Borough of Southwark, Hamblets and places adjacent* to the House of Commons in April 1649, and the events surrounding it, represented the high point of political female activity at this period; just as the ardent demonstration at the funeral of the executed Leveller soldier Robert Lockyer was the most overt instance of public Leveller sympathies. The coffin was decorated with sprigs of rosemary dipped in blood. The long column of mourners adorned with black and sea-green ribbons – sea-green was the adopted colour of the Leveller cause – was brought up by a body of women at the rear, sea-green and black ribbons mingled at their breast.

The women petitioners for the release of Lilburne, Overton and the others, first tackled the House of Commons on 23 April, when they were simply told that the House was too busy to receive them. The next day the Sergeant at Arms dismissed them with the words that the matter was one 'of a higher concernment' than they understood. Besides the House had already given an answer to 'their husbands'; therefore 'you are desired to go home, and look after your own business, and meddle with your housekeeping'. Some angry repartee followed this condescending dismissal, in which the women gave as good as they got. One unwise Member attempted to say that 'it was not for women to Petition, they might stay at home and wash the dishes' only to be told smartly: 'Sir, we have scarce any dishes left us to wash, and those we have are not sure to keep.' Another MP ventured the milder observation that it was strange for women to petition; 'It was strange that you cut off the King's head', was the answer, 'yet I suppose you will justify it.'[38]

On 25 April twenty women were at last admitted to the lobby of the House of Commons bearing a petition, although the attendant soldiers threw squibs at them, and cocked their pistols. The women, with equal determination if not equal violence, grabbed Cromwell's cloak and began to lecture him on their grievances.

'What will you have?' cried Cromwell in answer to their tirade. 'Those rights and freedoms of the Nation, that you promised us ...' was the ominous reply. Whatever the public indignation of these furies, *The Petition of Women* was a considered document; it is likely that Lilburne had a strong hand in its production.[39] It called on all women who approved it to 'subscribe' (that is, sign or mark) and then deliver their signatures to women who would be 'appointed in every Ward and Division to receive the same'. Apart from the release of the Leveller leaders, grievances for which redress was sought included high taxes, lack of work, and arbitrary government in general.

The most interesting passage came in *The Petition of Women*'s preamble when the issue of women taking such an apparently unnatural step as to petition was squarely faced. There was a token reference to the 'weak hands' of women; but this was followed by the counter claim that 'God had wrought many deliverances for several stations from age to age by the weak hand of women' as they knew for their own 'encouragement and example'. Deborah and Jael were quoted in this context, as were the 'British' women who delivered the land from the Danes, and more recently the Scotswomen who fought against 'episcopal tyranny'. As for the charge that it was not the custom for women to address themselves publicly to the House of Commons, the Preamble began with the bold words: 'Since we are assured of our creation in the image of God, and of an interest in Christ equal unto men, as also of a proportionate share in the freedom of this Commonwealth...'

Was there perhaps, as has been suggested, an implicit demand here for a share in the franchise as well as the freedom? If implicit, it was once again not explicit. Two more petitions on behalf of Lilburne were presented at the beginning of May by 'bonny Besses in sea-green dresses' as *Mercurius Pragmaticus* picturesquely termed them. There were satirical mentions of 'my brave Viragoes, the Ladyes-errants of the Sea-green order... so lately fluttering like flocks of wild Geese about the Parliament ears, for the liberty of their champion Jack and his confederates'.[40] Then the brutal quelling of the Burford mutiny in the middle of the month led to the collapse of the Leveller cause as a political force.

Petitioning on the part of Leveller women did not, however, fade away altogether. In October 1651 women were included in a Leveller petition that debtors should be released from prison to work off their debts (a favourite Leveller proposal and one of the many in which they were excitingly in advance of their times). In June 1653, a body of women, including the 'clamorous' Katherine Chidley, presented still further petitions for the release of John Lilburne, enduring yet another spell of imprisonment.

In July Katherine Chidley got into the pulpit at Somerset House and along with another sectary – a young man – 'preached to the people very much in Lilburne's behalf'. In the same month about a dozen women, headed by Katherine, presented a petition to Parliament on behalf of Lilburne, said to have been 'subscribed by above six thousand of that sex'.[41] This was that Little Parliament (sometimes known as the Barebones Parliament after one of its members, Praisegod Barebones, an Anabaptist leather-merchant) which was created following Cromwell's purge of the Rump Parliament of April 1653; it was disbanded when he became Protector in the following December.

The Leveller women 'boldly knocked at the door, and the House taking notice that they were there, sent out Praisegod Barebones to dissuade them from their enterprise, but he could not prevail; and they persisting in their disturbance, another Member came out and told them, the House could not take cognizance of their petition, they being women, and many of them Wives, so that the law took no notice of them'. The women issued a reasonable challenge to the notion of total female dependency based on wifehood by replying that 'they were not all wives, and therefore pressed for the receiving their petition'. The rest of the conversation was not quite on this high level. If their petition was refused, the women went on, the Members of Parliament 'should know that they [the women] had husbands and friends', who 'wore Swords to defend the liberty of the people etc.'. The members should 'look to themselves, and not to persecute that man of God [Lilburne] lest they were also destroyed, as the late King, Bishops, Parliament and all others that ever opposed him, who were all fallen before him'.[42]

But Lilburne was not released.

The story of Elizabeth Lilburne continued on more poignant if less dramatic lines as the petitioning woman of the 1640s gave way to the despairing – but still soliciting – wife of the 1650s; having much in common with Dame Isabella Twysden and Mary Lady Verney, despite the difference in their husbands' politics. To retrace our steps in John Lilburne's story: at the end of the Burford mutiny, he was still held in prison in the Tower of London. Elizabeth Lilburne therefore was still holding together the little household in London as well as she might in her husband's absence. At this point the family received 'a melancholy visitation' in the shape of smallpox; hardly an uncommon seventeenth-century occurrence, but the consequences in this particular case were heart-rending. Both of Elizabeth's sons died – 'the greater part of his earthly delight in this world', as John Lilburne would later describe them.[43] Elizabeth herself and her daughter hovered on the brink of death. Under these circumstances Lilburne was at least allowed to visit them from prison. Finally in November 1649 he was released.

It is understandable that the stricken Elizabeth now hoped

that her husband would make his peace with the new Commonwealth and settle with what remained of his little household. (Another son, John, was born in October 1650.) She hoped in vain. As a result of a vendetta against Sir Arthur Haselrig, Lilburne was banished for life by an Act of Parliament in January 1652, and a huge fine was imposed. While he was in exile, Elizabeth found herself in great hardship, having to sell or pawn most of her household goods; she also suffered a miscarriage, and her other children were ill. Under the circumstances, she refused to send him papers which she believed would merely lead to more fruitless troubles. Lilburne referred to her letters as 'new paper skirmishes ... filled with womanish passion and anger'.[44] Outsiders may find it easier to comprehend the element of despair which was now creeping into her dealings with her intractable husband.

All the same, by May 1653 Elizabeth had scraped together enough money to visit John at Bruges; Lilburne had expected her to bring a pass for England from the newly installed Protector Cromwell. He was furious it was refused. Relations between husband and wife were evidently cool: in a letter to the Protector Lilburne blamed Cromwell for the fact: 'Your late barbarous tyrannical dealing with me hath exposed her to so much folly and lowness of spirit in my eyes, in some of her late childish actions, as hath in some measure, produced an alienation of affection in me to her ...' He referred ominously to 'that tenderness of affection that I owe to her whom I formerly entirely loved as my own life'.[45] Lilburne sent Elizabeth to England once more for the pass and awaited her return at Calais. On hearing the news of a second refusal, he returned to England anyway, whereupon he was arrested, imprisoned once more in June 1653 and finally tried in July.

This was the celebrated trial which had the people roaring in chorus:

> And what, shall then honest John Lilburne die!
> Three score thousand will know the reason why!

John Lilburne did not die; in effect he was acquitted; but the Government declined to release him (provoking those petitions on the part of the Leveller women to which reference has already been made). By July 1655 he was in prison on the island of Guernsey. Elizabeth, her soliciting temper unabated by her privations – and John's recriminations – petitioned Cromwell that he should be released: 'Our grievous afflictions have obtained no remission!' she wrote. 'I beg you take away all provocation from his impatient spirit, weared out with long and sore afflictions. I durst engage my life that he will not disturb the state.' John's own poor health lent plausibility to Elizabeth's last statement: it was probably she who got Fleetwood, Cromwell's brother-in-law and colleague, to persuade the Protector of Lilburne's newly pacifist frame of mind.[46]

When Lilburne reached Dover Castle, Elizabeth was living at the house of a friend who kept an inn at Guildhall; after years without a proper home life, or even a proper income, she had fallen into a state of depression, indicated by the fact that her newest baby, Benomy, had been a year old when she had had him baptized.[47] In London she received another startling piece of news concerning her husband's spiritual odyssey. He had now become a Quaker.

It was one thing for John to require Elizabeth to send him Quaker books down from London. But the language in which he hoped for Elizabeth's own conversion was scarcely such as to bring comfort to the weary homeless woman. He spoke of self-denial: 'even to a final denial of father, kindred, friends, my sweet and beloved (by me) babes'. Above all her conversion would enable her 'to go cheerfully and willingly along hand in hand' with her husband. Such a step, he wrote, 'abundantly would render thee more amiable, lovely and pleasant in mine eyes although thou wert then clothed in rags…' Elizabeth had just escaped death by drowning in the Thames – John's sympathy with her plight was cursory. The fact that Elizabeth and the children *were* to all intents and purposes clothed in rags, John Lilburne treated with equal shortness. He wrote: 'I am also sorry that thou art so straitly put to it for money, but to live upon God by faith in the depth of straights, is the lively condition of a Christian: O that thy spirit could attain to it!'[48]

When the couple did meet again in November 1655, they had a bitter quarrel; yet even now, for the higher purpose of marital union, it was Elizabeth who agreed to a reconciliation on John's terms. By August 1657 John Lilburne, although nominally still a prisoner, was allowed to rent a house at Eltham in Kent; moreover Elizabeth was pregnant again (she underwent a total of ten pregnancies, five of her babies, including the boy named Tower, dying young). The house was for the *accouchement*, 'that I might be near my friends at my lying-in'. She duly gave birth. Then Cromwell, hearing of Lilburne's freedom, and being prepared to grant him an allowance but not to have him at large, called for his return. It was too late. John Lilburne was now 'sick and weak'.[49] On 29 August 1657, at the age of forty-three, he was dead.

Elizabeth was now in a state verging on destitution, with three children to care for, including a new-born baby. Her grief was not allayed by the Quaker funeral which followed. All that was left for her to do was to petition the all-powerful Cromwell, who, whatever his treatment of the dissident John, had as we have seen a merited reputation for helping distressed women. Cromwell responded with an order for the payment of the arrears due to Elizabeth, and a continuation of the 40s a week allowance granted to Lilburne. Unfortunately this was not to be the end of Elizabeth's 'piercing sorrows'. By the time Richard Cromwell succeeded his father as Protector, she was still petitioning to have Parliament repeal that Act of 1652 which had sentenced John to a colossal fine: 'Your late father professed very great tenderness to me', she wrote desperately to Richard.[50] The 1652 Act was finally repealed in February 1659.

This, little enough, was the material reward secured by Elizabeth Lilburne: in return for a small allowance (still being paid in March 1660) she surrendered John Lilburne's papers. If Lilburne himself would not have approved,[51] who can blame the exhausted widow, who had, as she told Richard Cromwell, endured 'seventeen years' sorrows' and longed for 'a little rest and comfort among my fatherless children'. A more equitable award lay in the earlier judgement of Lilburne himself. Dispatching a petition to Cromwell by her hand, he wrote: 'This I have sent by the gravest, wisest, fittest messenger I could think of.' He added, in this at least a conventional product of the seventeenth century, 'and, though a Feminine, yet of a gallant and truly masculine spirit'.[12]

CHAPTER THIRTEEN

When Women Preach

~~~~~~

When women preach and cobblers pray
The fiends in hell make holiday.
'Lucifer's Lackey or The Devil's New Creation', 1641

'Let your women keep silence in the churches: for it is not permitted unto them to speak'; it was this verse from St Paul's First Epistle to the Corinthians which was at the root of the accepted condemnation of female preaching (and participation in church government) at the beginning of the seventeenth century. To conventional Christian ears, the mighty voice of the Apostle still thundered down the centuries with undiminished vigour and there seemed little distinction to be drawn between St Paul's admonition to the inhabitants of Achaea in the first century AD, and the will of God 1,600 years later.

For women, as a whole, there had to be a more private – and one might add less voluble – way of influencing their contemporaries; or as the epitaph of the pious and charitable Lettice Viscountess Falkland phrased it:

> And now, though Paul forbids her Sex to preach,
> Yet may her Life instruct, and her Death teach.

Richard Brathwaite, in *The English Gentlewoman* of 1631, that mine of advice on the conduct of the modest female, took the argument one stage further. Just as 'discourse of State-matters' would not become her, it was equally unsuitable 'to dispute of high points of Divinity': since women were forbidden to be speakers in church it was not right that they should discuss theological matters in private either.[1]

By October 1650 when Sir Ralph Verney was having his brush with Dr Denton (and Nancy) on the subject of a girl's rightful education, all this had changed. 'Had St Paul lived in our Times', wrote Sir Ralph gloomily, 'I am confident he would have fixed a Shame upon women for writing (as well as for their speaking) in the Church.'[2] Preaching among the women sectaries was a phenomenon of the English scene from the 1640s onwards; the shame that St Paul would or would not have felt being a subject of hot debate not only amongst outsiders hostile to the sects, but also within their ranks.

Women probably first began to preach in Holland in the 1630s in the Baptist churches, whose congregations had always included a large number of their sex. (There were said to be more women than men in the large body of English separatists who went to Holland in 1558; thereafter on the Continent women had held numerous church offices and taken some part in lay preaching.) In the New World – Massachusetts – women were known to have preached by 1636. In England in the 1640s women preached weekly at the General Baptist Church in Bell Alley, off Coleman Street, in the City of London. Anne Hempstall was described as preaching to 'bibbing Gossips' in her house in Holborn and Mary Bilbrowe, wife of a bricklayer of St Giles-in-the-Fields, preached in her parlour, although the pulpit, which was made of brick, was so high that only her tippet could be seen. As early as 1641 a tract, *The Discovery of Women Preachers*, referred to their existence in Kent, Cambridge and Salisbury.[3]

Women were notable among the Brownists, those enthusiasts who led a tumultuous existence on the wing of the so-called Independent Church. (The name derived from one of their spokesmen, Robert Browne.) It was fear of these Independent sectaries which had led in March 1642 to the drawing-up of the Kentish petition, with Sir Roger Twysden as one of its leaders –

that move to save the nation from 'heresy, schism, prophane-ness, libertinism, anabaptism, atheism' which had led to all the subsequent troubles of the Twysden family (see p.256). Later the division between Independents and Presbyterians would give way to a new type of alignment: because Brownists could not accept any form of central authority in religious matters, they now found themselves opposed to many of their previous Independent colleagues, as well as the Presbyterians.

The style of such pioneers could hardly be expected to be self-effacing. In London Mrs Attoway, 'Mistress of all the She preachers in Coleman Street', who was capable of preaching for well over an hour, seems to have run off with another woman's husband and in addition secured contributions to finance a journey to Jerusalem, a project which unlike her elopement remained largely in her imagination. Some of these women displayed undeniably an 'eerie spirit'; others were less 'eerie' than 'brazen-faced'.[4] The trouble was that the kind of woman who possessed the audacity to challenge the ruling of St Paul was not likely to combine it with that feminine modesty which would win society's respect for the cause of the woman preacher.

On the contrary, all the old gibes concerning woman's talkativeness – 'the natural volubility of their tongues' – proved useful yet again in the conflict over the 'preacheresses'. Prejudice could cause a woman preaching to be condemned first as 'a prater' or 'prattler', so by implication as a scold, and lastly even as some kind of witch – remembering the connection in the popular mind between scolding and cursing. Additionally, her 'Bible-thumping' could be held to demonstrate the perils of any form of education, however rudimentary, for women since they were clearly not capable of making good use of it.[5]

By 1645 the moderate Puritans were criticizing the Brownists for allowing women to take part in church government and to preach. Prynne attacked this implication of Independency, and in 1646 John Vicars, in *The Schismatick Sifted: Or, A Picture of Independents Freshly and Fairly Washt over Again*, deplored the fact that not only 'saucy boys, bold botching taylors' but also 'bold impudent huswives' were taking it upon themselves 'to prate an hour or more'. The principal attack was that mounted by Thomas Edwards in the same year in *Gangraena*, deploring the fact that these 'whirligigg spirits' of the Brownists included smiths, tailors, shoemakers, pedlars, and worst of all women who were giving 'constant lectures'. He thought this to be against not only the light of Scripture but that of nature.[6]

On 14 January 1646 aldermen and common councillors of the City of London delivered a petition to the House of Commons concerning the multitude of religious schisms in the City which they wanted eliminated. They claimed that in one parish there were 'eleven private congregations and conventicles who deserted the parish churches and have tradesmen and women preachers'. As a result, later that month several women preachers were committed to custody and others were brought before the Committee of Examinations of the House of Commons. Then in December 1646 the House resolved that no person should expound the Scriptures unless he be ordained in 'this or some other Reformed Church'.[7]

With due respect to St Paul, why did the question of women preaching arouse such extreme apprehension? A popular rhyme of 1641 entitled 'Lucifer's Lackey or The Devil's New Creation' ran:

> When women preach and cobblers pray
> The fiends in hell make holiday.

At the bottom, it was woman's demand for freedom of conscience rather than for freedom to 'prate' which caused concern. The crude mockery of 'Lucifer's Lackey' masked a real dread that a woman who placed conscience above husband and family might consider herself outside the former's control. The question as to whether a woman sectary had the right to leave a husband who was 'unsanctified' was never officially settled, though much discussed in the early 1650s. But the fact that some women sectaries such as Mrs Attoway did cast out or abandon 'unsanctified' husbands in the 1640s did nothing to relieve such fears.[8]

For this reason those women who were not 'eerie spirits' –

and thus were in control of what they said – generally took care to emphasize their own weakness in advance of their message. This self-deprecation might be expected to win the sympathy of a masculine audience, or at very least avoid arousing its hostility. Elizabeth Warren, a pamphleteer, declared herself fully conscious of her own 'mental and sex-deficiency' in her preface to *The Old and Good Way vindicated* of 1645, which bewailed the troubles of the times and defended a certain persecuted clergyman. In *Spiritual Thrift* she even went so far as to acknowledge that 'we of the weaker sex, have hereditary evil from our grandmother Eve'. Claiming for herself in general a 'silent Modesty', she defended her action in having her sentiments printed, aware that she might be accused of having deserted both this silence and this modesty.[9] As we shall see, even the redoubtable Katherine Chidley was not above pleading the weakness of her sex on occasions when it seemed politic.

Katherine Chidley lived in Soper Lane, off Coleman Street, a centre of Brownist activity, where St Pancras was one of the most famous of the Independent churches. Her son Samuel Chidley was also a leading sectary and later one of the treasurers of the Leveller party, hence Katherine Chidley's prominence among the women who had tried to secure John Lilburne's release. In the eighteenth century Ballard described Katherine Chidley as fighting as violently as Penthesilea, the Amazonian Queen, for the cause of Independency. The language in which she was described in her own time was less romantic if equally evocative. Thomas Edwards, a fanatical Presbyterian supporter, called her 'a brazen-faced audacious old woman', both 'talkative and clamorous', qualities as undesirable in a woman as they were in a witch.[10]

There is no reason to doubt the essential features of Edwards's picture (although it may be pointed out that the language of Edwards's attacks on the Independents certainly far exceeded in virulence anything the most 'clamorous' old woman could achieve). With Samuel, Katherine Chidley journeyed through England in 1641, and founded 'a small gathered church' at Bury St Edmunds where eight adults signed the Brownists' covenant. That took persistence and presumably a certain stridency too. In 1641 also Katherine Chidley wrote *The Justification of the Independent Churches of Christ*, to combat Thomas Edwards's attack upon Independency.[11] It was a sharply worded document. When Edwards argued that Independency would breed divisions within families, setting husband and wife against each other, Katherine Chidley countered that there had been a division in the first family, but that had been caused by Satan, not by toleration.

She wrote: 'Next you will say: "Oh! How will this take away that power and authority which God hath given to Husbands, Fathers and Mothers, over wives, children and servants."' To this Katherine Chidley answered that St Paul in the First Epistle to the Corinthians had plainly declared that the wife could be a believer in her sense ('sanctified'), and the husband an unbeliever ('unsanctified'). Why would he have advised husband or wife not to leave an unbelieving spouse if the Apostle had not at least envisaged the possibility? Furthermore St Paul also envisaged some unbelievers wishing to depart and added: 'A brother or a sister is not under bondage in such cases.'

Still, Katherine Chidley was careful to make it clear that an 'unsanctified' husband was not robbed of his ordinary rights, only of control of his wife's beliefs: 'It is true he hath authority over her in bodily and civil respects, but not to be a Lord over her conscience.' On the primacy of conscience, Katherine Chidley was unalterably strong, denying utterly the claims of the 'magistrate' to rule over it: 'I know of no true Divinity that teacheth men to be Lords over the Conscience.' (Although she herself would not tolerate the Catholics – but that, she declared, was because they had attempted by plots and treachery to 'ruinate the land'.)

At the end of the *Justification* Katherine Chidley challenged Edwards to a parley on the subject of Independency, each speaker to choose six people who in the presence of a moderator would thrash out the matter in 'fair discourse'. The sting was in the tail. Katherine Chidley was confident that she would defeat

Thomas Edwards, but if by any chance she did not, that would represent no triumph for him: 'for I am a poor woman and unable to deal with you'. It was perhaps that thought which led Edwards to reject the encounter.

Katherine Chidley's second pamphlet, *A New Yeares Gift, Or A Briefe Exhortation to Mr Thomas Edwards*, contended that Independency alone followed the primitive pattern of Christ, and she argued that it should thus be instituted as the State religion, controlled by Parliament (not the Westminster Assembly of Divines) to form 'one entire government established upon sound principles, unalterable'. *Good Counsell to the Petitioners for Presbyterian Government that they may declare their faith before they build their Church*, of November 1645, which suggested that 'there is but one true Religion', attacked Presbyterianism for not being according to God's Word. The Chidleys, mother and son, were also said to have written the famous independent tract *Launseters Launse* together; and Katherine Chidley may have had a hand in the composition of *The Petition of Women* in 1649.[12]

Unlike the retiring Elizabeth Warren, who said of herself that she disliked controversy (and about whom as a result nothing is known beyond her pamphlets), Katherine Chidley led a robust existence outside the confines of the printed page. In August 1645, for example, she rose up in church in Stepney, preached the tenets of Brownism and attacked various ministers 'with a great deal of Violence and bitterness'. Her particular grievance was the meeting of people in churches and other places where 'idolatrous services' had previously taken place. The incumbent minister, a Mr Greenhill, tried to rebuke her. Was no worship to take place in a church just because it had once been dedicated in the name of saints or angels? Did that imply that this church had been for ever 'set apart' for 'idolatry'? This encompassed the whole of England, which had been 'set apart' or dedicated to St George. At this Katherine Chidley's outburst of indignation was so overriding that Mr Greenhill was obliged to retire.[13]

In 1646 when Thomas Edwards issued his celebrated attack on Independency, *Gangraena*, he spared time to denounce the whole idea of women preaching, as well as the audacious

Katherine Chidley in particular. As for claims of spiritual equality, this would mean that 'all women at once were exempt from being under government'.[14] In fact, as we have seen, Katherine Chidley had specifically excepted such a claim from her demands; nevertheless the fear remained and Edwards, in voicing it, exercised a more potent influence on public opinion than Katherine Chidley in denying it.

In contrast to the 'preacheress', the prophetess had always been treated with a certain nervous respect by society – remember Jane Hawkins, 'a poor woman (and she but a pedlar)', who in 1629 had for a period prophesied before 200 people (see p.187). Claiming direct inspiration from God, the prophetess might challenge accepted notions concerning religion and society but she did not necessarily in her own person challenge the accepted order. What differentiated the Civil War period was the substantial increase in the number of prophetesses and allied female seers. In this time of hopes and dreams and visions, the attitude of authority itself – the new authority: Army, Council, new Parliament, new rulers such as Cromwell – was equally more responsive.

In 1654 an Independent church congregation would debate at length whether the average man had that dominion over prophetesses such as he had over 'all Widows and Maids that are not Prophetesses'. The eventual conclusion relied upon St Paul's remark in his First Epistle to the Corinthians that 'every woman that prayeth or prophesieth with her head uncovered dishonoureth her head'; from this admonition it was deduced that St Paul, since he did not explicitly forbid them, conceived of and tolerated the existence of prophetesses, so long as their heads were covered. So it was decided that 'a Woman (Maid, Wife or Widow) being a Prophetess may Speak, Prophesy, Pray with a Veil. Others may not.'[15]

It was the good fortune of Lady Eleanor Davies, she whose desperate rambling prophecies concerning the fate of King Charles I had brought her first to the Gatehouse prison and then to Bedlam (see p.191 ff.), to survive into this more imaginative age. In 1648 she sought out Oliver Cromwell. With her predilection for anagrams, Lady Eleanor was from the first well disposed towards a man whose very name – O. CROMWEL – suggested the words HOWL ROME. The 'O' of Oliver she envisaged hopefully as the splendid round sun, in contrast to the sickly crescent moon which was the 'C' of Charles I. When the Army was at its headquarters at St Albans in 1648, Lady Eleanor presented to him a book of her prophecies first printed (with dire results) in 1633. She superscribed the book *The Armies Commission*, adding the verse: 'Behold he cometh with ten thousand of his Saints to execute judgement on all.' The splendid sun showed not only more tolerance but more humour than the sickly moon – but then of course Cromwell was not compared to Belshazzar as Charles I had been. Smiling at the superscription, and putting on his 'specticles' [sic], Cromwell gently observed: 'But we are not all Saints.'[16]

As a result of this newly permissive atmosphere towards prophetesses, Lady Eleanor was able to spend her last years in a state of happiness and honour she can scarcely have expected in the bad old days of the King's reign. She also had the sweetness of revenge; her old enemy Archbishop Laud, 'horned like the lamb', was executed in 1645. When Charles I was in prison in January 1649, shortly before his own execution, Lady Eleanor took it upon herself to write to him: 'For King Charles, Prisoner, These'. She reminded him of her sufferings at his behest 'because [I] took upon me to be a Prophetess' and suggested that he make public acknowledgement of his 'high offence'. He should also implore her forgiveness, 'if so be you expect to find Mercy in this world or the other'.

In August that year, when the King, for better or for worse, had long exchanged worlds, Lady Eleanor's pamphlet was reprinted. In 1651 appeared *The Restitution of Prophecy*, restoring all her original revelations, and at her death in 1652 the Anglican divine Peter Du Moulin suggested she had indeed been 'favoured with some beam of divine knowledge of future things', while being in general '*erudita supra Sexum, mitis infra Sortem*': learned above her sex, humble below her fortune. The official epitaph put up by Lady Eleanor's family congratulated her on having 'in a woman's body, a man's spirit'.[17]

What was more, despite these Cromwellian connections, a dutiful daughter saw to it that Lady Eleanor's reputation was not blackened for ever after the Restoration. Lucy Countess of Huntingdon and her friend Katherine Stanley, Marchioness of Dorchester joined together to protest to Thomas Dugdale over the historical inaccuracies in his 1660 *Continuation* of Sir Richard Baker's *Chronicle*.[18] As has been noticed (see p.204), Lady Dorchester succeeded in removing the slur against the courage of her own mother, Charlotte Countess of Derby, based on false Parliamentary reports. Lady Huntingdon's task was more delicate. Lady Eleanor Davies could hardly be whitewashed entirely but it was a matter of just how she was presented. Dugdale's statement that she was 'generally reputed little better than a mad woman' caused much distress; in particular Lady Huntingdon was anxious to rescue her mother from the charge that in predicting the death of the Duke of Buckingham she had been associated with the notorious popular astrologer of the time, Dr Lambe.

In the end Lady Huntingdon, supported by her young son Theophilus, seventh Earl of Huntingdon, was successful. Lady Eleanor's name was expunged from the account of the Duke of Buckingham's death. Even Peter Du Moulin's eulogy – learned above her sex, humble below her fortune – was removed from the new edition as being presumably distasteful to the Countess. One wonders what Lady Eleanor herself would have thought of that omission. More pleasing to her perhaps would have been her grandson Theophilus's measured yet tender judgement of her career.

Lord Huntingdon wrote that his grandmother – 'one not a little enthusiasticall' – had 'obliged' his mother to give him his unusual Christian name (this occurred very shortly before Lady Eleanor's death, for Theophilus, the longed-for male heir to replace three dead sons, was not born until 1650).[19] He showed no signs of holding this against her. On the contrary, he accepted her own account that 'she heard voices supernatural, [so] that she was endowed with the gift of prophecy', but for censuring the ecclesiastical government and the Queen's Catholic practices, 'and her obstinate refusing any submission', wrote Lord Huntingdon, she was sentenced in the Court of High Commission 'as one that was out of her wits'.

Lord Huntingdon's chief indignation was reserved for the historian Sir William Sanderson, who in his account of the reign of Charles I had passed 'his own censure on this Lady as if she was either mad or possessed with delusions from the Devil'. This was indeed a 'Barbarous' judgement for a historian to deliver to posterity, complained Lord Huntingdon, 'considering her [Lady Eleanor's] extraction from a family of Ancient English Nobility...'

Lady Eleanor Davies was an eccentric and an exception. The social standing of the other prophetesses of the period made it at least conceivable – by Lord Huntingdon's standards, that is – for them to be considered mad or deluded. Yet on the whole respect obtained. At Bodmin in February 1647, for example, a young girl was said to be busy foretelling things to come, most of which were said already to have 'fallen out true'. (Although one of her prophecies, that Charles I would shortly enjoy his own again, being revenged on his enemies, was less successful). She lived off a diet of sweetmeats, which were brought to her by 'small people clad in green, and sometimes by birds'. This girl was said to cure most diseases, as well as specializing in broken bones, which she mended with a touch of her hand. Examined by three divines, she gave a good account of herself, having the Scriptures by heart 'very perfectly'. Now under guard, she was seen to be fasting entirely, except on Christmas Day, when she had a feast of 'bread and water'.[20]

The prophetesses who interrupted the councils of Cromwell, the Army and later his colleagues in the new Government of England were an even more remarkable phenomenon. The point has been made that at least half a dozen times between 1647 and

1654 important deliberations were put aside, while some obscure prophetess (or prophet) delivered a message generally relayed by the Almighty via an apocalyptic vision.[21] Nothing underlines more clearly the weird atmosphere of these times. In the 1630s King Charles I showed first irritation, then outright anger, faced with the revelations of Lady Eleanor Davies. At the end of December 1648 – the most crucial period for the Army Council as the King's future swayed in the balance – an unknown woman named Elizabeth Poole appeared in front of them to communicate her visions concerning 'the presence of God with the Army'. She declared that the Army had appeared to her in the shape of a man and the country as a whole as a woman 'full of imperfection, crooked, weak, sickly'. The man it seemed was destined to heal the woman. This revelation was taken extremely seriously by the Army Council and much discussed. Elizabeth Poole's visions were described by Colonel Rich as 'that testimony which God hath manifested here by an unexpected Providence'.[22]

On 5 January God instructed Elizabeth Poole to return to the Council. There she handed in a paper arguing against the execution of the King, which was formally debated by the Council's members in her absence, She was then called back for further discussions. Elizabeth Poole repeated her conviction that the King should not be executed: 'you may bind his hands and hold him fast under' she announced, but he should not be put to death. She referred to the Scriptures to enforce her case, quoting the text: 'Vengeance is mine, saith the Lord.' She also described the King as the husband or head of the people; as such, citing the precedent of Nabal among the Israelites, he might be restrained but not cut down by his 'wife'.

Henry Ireton – the most intellectual of the Army leaders – questioned Elizabeth Poole at length about her revelations. If this King was not to die, was no King ever to die? Had she seen an angel or a vision? (The answer was: a vision.) A later Royalist pamphlet accused Cromwell of stage-managing the whole incident, coaching the woman in her answers to the Council; but this is manifestly absurd, especially in view of the King's fate at the hands of his 'wife' less than a month afterwards. The true significance of Elizabeth Poole lay in the exalted audience this humble woman was able to secure without difficulty, by invoking the awesome role of the prophetess.

The most extreme language was used by those prophetesses connected with the Fifth Monarchy movement. This was a millenarian sect so called because it looked forward to the establishment of the 'Fifth Monarchy' – that of Christ after his second coming. Among the Fifth Monarchists themselves particular reverence was accorded to any woman who 'appeared to be endowed with divine grace' – although no other category of woman other than a prophetess was in the end granted special rights within their church; nor, contrary to popular accusation did the Fifth Monarchists attempt to elevate the status of the woman within the family, asking only for freedom of conscience from the husband's control.[25]

The determination of the Fifth Monarchists that the second coming of Christ would establish His political power brought them into natural conflict with the current rulers of England. The movement got under way after 1651 when it became clear that neither Parliament (nor Cromwell) was likely to set up the 'Rule of the Saints', as had once been hoped. In 1653 Cromwell's elevation as Protector was construed as a further insult to the true dominion of Jesus Christ, since to Him alone belonged the prerogative of single rule. Cromwell, hailed by Lady Eleanor Davies as a splendid sun in the early stages of his leadership, now found himself identified with something far less pleasant called the 'Little Horn', an odious excrescence on the head of the Beast. Despite this, and despite the violence of the prophetesses' invective, for some time the civil powers showed quite remarkable restraint towards them, genuinely hampered by their claims to be reporting the true intentions of God. The treatment of Mary Overton, dragged through the streets of London on 'cudgels' with her baby at her breast, and thrown into Bridewell among the vagrants and harlots for helping to sew up her husband's political pamphlets, contrasts remarkably, as we shall see, with that of the fervent Fifth Monarchist Anna Trapnel, including the comparative comfort allowed to the prophetess when she finally did reach Bridewell.

Anna Trapnel was the daughter of a shipwright in Poplar, and lived in Hackney.[24] By her own account, *A Legacy for Saints, being several Experiences of the dealings of God with Anna Trapnel,* her piety came to her early, 'when a child, then the Lord awed my spirit', and was encouraged by her 'godly mother'.[25] By the time she was fourteen, she was eager to hear the words of the Lord and to pray for herself, and it was while listening to the famous independent preacher Hugh Peter on a text of Isaiah that her eyes were opened to 'the marriage covenant...between God and his spouse'. Thereafter Anna went from minister to minister, and from sermon to sermon daily, but still did not find further elucidation. She could not sleep or even rest. In her depression she was even tempted to suicide, to which the devil tempted her by showing her a sharp knife. Her spiritual aridity only increased as she wrestled with the doctrine that Christ came not only to the righteous, but to all sinners. Finally she found herself able to accept it.

After this time of protracted perplexity, Anna enjoyed her true moment of revelation on New Year's Day 1642. It was a Sunday and she was listening to the Baptist minister of St Botolph's Church in Aldgate, John Simpson (later a prominent Fifth Monarchist), preaching on the text: 'Now if any man have not the spirit of Christ, he is none of his.' Suddenly Anna found herself saying: 'Lord, I have the spirit.' Then what joy she felt! 'Oh what triumphing and songs of Hallelujah were in my spirit.' Anna felt 'a clothing of glory' over her and saw angels, a clear flame without smoke and other 'christal appearances'. Sometimes 'the golden trumpet sounded higher, and sometimes lower, yet still it was sounding, and caused an echo to follow it'.

Thereafter there were still moments when Anna felt buffeted by Satan, as when she learnt of her mother's death. Yet many 'raptures' followed: sometimes she would fall down on the ground in public, at other times, alone in her room, she felt grace pouring over her 'like a fountain'. John Simpson, visiting Anna at home when she was sick, and her 'earthly tabernacle' – her body

– was shaking with a fever, issued a caution: she might be deluded regarding the presence of God within her, as others in the past had been. But Anna had no such doubts. She knew that the Lord had chosen her so that 'out of the mouths of babes and sucklings he would perfect his praise'. She had a series of visions which ranged from the sun itself to Jesus taking up Peter and John into the Mount, the Transfiguration, and 'Revelations concerning the Government of the Nation, the Parliament, Army and Ministry'.

It was important to Anna Trapnel, as it was to an earlier prophetess and pamphleteer, Mary Pope, to point out the divine source of such outpourings. Mary Pope, author of *A Treatise of Magistracy*, referred to 'God having made me a Mother in Israel' and God 'as it were forcing me on ... for helping to settle these unsettled times'. Anna made a similar point. She felt a strong personal identification with 'that approved Hannah', the prophetess in the book of Samuel, which sometimes led to her being described as Hannah, not Anna, Trapnel (in fact she herself always signed her name Anna).[26]

The importance of the connection with the biblical Hannah, whom she declared herself desirous of imitating, was that Hannah too had been judged to be 'mad, under the administration of evil angels, and a witch'. Even the priest Eli had at first assumed Hannah to be drunk when he saw her lips moving – in prophecy – and no sound coming forth. Hannah had issued a dignified reproach to Eli telling him not to confuse 'thy handmaid' with 'a daughter of Belial'. In an age rich in citation of biblical precedent, all of this was very much to the advantage of any latter-day Hannah, who might expect to encounter several Elis, and even more unsympathetic individuals, in the course of her divinely-ordained career as a prophetess.

Anna Trapnel prided herself on two other aspects of her character, in both of which one can detect a certain feminine defensiveness, as though to meet predictable charges in advance. First, she was concerned to make it clear that she was in no way a whore, being on the contrary, as her friends put it, of 'beautiful and unblameable conversation'. Second, she prided herself on the fact that she had not received any ordinary education, since 'Christ's scholars', amongst which she included herself, were endowed with a far better type of learning 'from above'. Consciously or not, this was a smart attitude to adopt for one who could well claim to be one of 'Christ's scholars' but not the duller sort who had merely attended an earthly university. So Anna, in her long rambling verses of prophecy, preempted one accusation commonly made against the women who preached – that they were silly uneducated females:

> Thou shalt not read what's spoke of Dragon and Beast
> With University-art;
> But thou shalt read with Kings seven eyes,
> And an enlightened heart.
>
> Thou shalt not run to Antichrists Libraries
> To fetch from thence any skill
> To read the Revelation of Christ,
> But be with knowledge fill'd.[27]

As for the other common charge – that the rise of women preaching demonstrated the sheer foolishness of giving them an education – Anna Trapnel, being untutored, was not liable to that. She after all had received her education from the great university in the sky.

Anna Trapnel first came into public prominence as part of the violent Fifth Monarchist reaction to the installation of Oliver Cromwell as Protector on 16 December 1653. On the eve of the event, she had had a vision of Cromwell in the shape of a bull amidst a large herd of cattle: 'and of a sudden there was a great shout of those that followed him, he being singled out alone, and the foremost, and he looking back, they bowed themselves unto him, and leaped up from the earth, and shewed much joy that he had become their Supreme'. However, all did not end happily for the joyful herd, for after mistakenly 'running at the Saints', they found themselves scattered, with their horns broken, and finally they fell into their graves.[28]

Three days later a Welsh preacher named Vavasour Powell announced in a sermon that Cromwell's Government could only be temporary (in view of the expected coming of Christ) and 'a small matter should fetch him down with little noise'. It was not the kind of remark calculated to reassure a nervous new regime, and in January Powell was summoned to Whitehall to explain himself before the Council. Along with him went 'a maid called Hannah'.

Anna Trapnel sat just outside the Council chamber in a little room with a fire, awaiting Powell's return from his examination. Just as Powell emerged, intending to go home, Anna was 'as it were seized by the Lord' and 'carried forth in a spirit of Prayer and Singing, from noon till night'. When she finally fell into her bed at Mr Roberts's lodging house near the Palace of Whitehall, at eleven o'clock at night, she lay there for twelve days. For the first five of these Anna remained without eating or drinking; thereafter she took a little toast soaked in small beer every twenty-four hours, sometimes merely to moisten her mouth. During all this period her eyes were shut, while out of her mouth issued a stream of prophecies, for two, three or even four hours at a time, by day or by night, and sometimes both.[29]

The sensational effect of such a daily performance in the heart of Whitehall, so close to the seat of the Protectoral power, may be imagined. 'Many hundreds' were said to be flocking to see her. Although very little of what she was saying could be understood when Anna was singing, her prayers were reported to be 'in exceeding odd method and order', and phrased in 'good language'. The effect of her 'excellent words and well placed' was that 'all that come, do much admire what they hear from her'. In view of some of Anna's topics for prayer – that the Lord Protector should be 'delivered from Carnal Councils' and should not be 'vain, nor regard earthly pomp and pleasure' – perhaps the obscurity of her singing was to be preferred, at least from the point of view of the Government. After twelve days of this, Anna rose up from her bed at Mr Roberts's lodging house and went home 'speedily and lustily'.[30]

Of course the sensation did not stop there. Since 1650 Anna

Trapnel had belonged to the congregation of John Simpson, the minister of St Botolph's, now a leading Fifth Monarchist, who was one of the 'lecturers' at Allhallows Church. At the end of January Simpson was arrested and sent to prison at Windsor, along with other ministers, for making public a vision which predicted the fall of Cromwell within six months. At Allhallows, however, the new Protectoral regime continued to be denounced. Marchamont Nedham, the Commonwealth journalist, reported on this to Cromwell personally in February, making the point that 'This meeting much diminishes your reputation among foreigners, who expect changes, because they are proclaimed from the pulpit, and great things are made of it, though it is but a confluence of silly wretches.' Moreover, there was a plan to print Anna Trapnel's discourses 'which are desperate against your person, family, children, friends and the government', as well as sending her all over England to proclaim them. She is much visited, wrote Nedham, doing 'a world of mischief' since 'the vulgar dote on vain prophecies' such as she proclaimed daily in a trance.[31]

Still no action was taken against Anna Trapnel personally despite these subversive sentiments. Not everyone accepted the source of her visions without reservation: 'some say that what she doth is by a mighty inspiration, others say they suppose her to be a troubled mind'. Yet the general impression given was of some sort of communion with God, as one correspondent wrote who confessed himself baffled by the precise nature of her revelation and 'under what sort to rank it'.[32]

As for the attention Anna Trapnel received, Dorothy Osborne referred, humorously perhaps, but with a wry note beneath it all, to the prophetess's success in the world compared to her own. In March 1654 she wrote to her lover, William Temple: 'I am coming into my preaching term again. What think you, were it not a good way of preferment as the times are? If you advise me to do it, I'll venture.' After all, the woman (Anna Trapnel) 'was cried up mightily'. Dorothy Osborne's father had recently died, which affected the question of her long-delayed marriage (see p.40); now Dorothy had to await her brother's arrival to know 'how I shall dispose myself'. Once more, Dorothy advocated patience to William Temple.[33] At the same time, rather more excitingly, Anna Trapnel awaited the arrival of the spirit of God and needed apparently very little other guidance as to how she should dispose herself.

The guidance which arrived from the Lord was that Anna should accept an invitation to tour the West Country.[34] When she first received the invitation, Anna exclaimed: 'There's a far journey indeed!' But the Lord over-persuaded Anna. As a preliminary she visited Simpson in his Windsor prison, having a vision of 'high rocky hills' at Hillingdon near Uxbridge on the way, and knowing that was how Cornwall would be. Still Satan tempted her not to set out; however, in the nick of time the birds singing outside the window of her chamber in the early morning reminded Anna of God's care for sparrows and restored her to her purpose.

The journey to the West Country certainly justified Anna's original reaction. She got a place in a coach at an inn but it took six days for the coach to reach Exeter; fortunately its 'rattlings' could not disturb her inner tranquillity. In the West Anna stayed at Tregasow near Truro with Captain Langdon, a Fifth Monarchist who had been a member of the recently defunct Barebones Parliament.

A later report would sum up the purpose of her visit as 'to asperse the government'. That was certainly too crude a summary from Anna's point of view, and she wrote back to the congregation at Allhallows denying that she had ever tried to stir up the people. However, her language on the subject of the Protector could hardly be interpreted otherwise. From the Government's point of view it was equally relevant that Anna, together with other Fifth Monarchists, took the line that the 'Saints' were not bound by legal precepts but by the commands of the Gospel 'and in this sense they are dead to the law, by the life of Christ in them'. People who considered themselves 'dead to the law' were not likely long to survive at liberty once they started to break it in any way that outraged the community. Thus when the local Presbyterian clergy showed themselves notably hostile to Anna and her prophecies, they were easily able to secure a warrant against her for subversion.[35]

On 11 April 1654 an order was given to take Anna Trapnel 'quickly' and send her up to the Council in London.[36]

Anna spent the eve of her apprehension in an all-night session of prayer and singing. She was still in a trance, and still singing the next afternoon when the constable with the justices came for her. Captain Langdon pleaded for her to be allowed to remain one more night, but the response was merely to pull the entranced woman from her pillow, first lifting up her eyelids to see if she was shamming. From the doorway a Presbyterian minister commented grimly: 'A whip will fetch her out.' Then at last Anna awoke and saying that she had had 'a sweet day', inquired if anyone had visited her.[37]

According to Anna, the people round about were on her side, telling the justices who came to take her that they would have to fetch their silk gowns and perform the deed themselves 'for the poor would not do it'. However, on her way to the sessions, a less enlightened mob of men and women, boys and girls, pulled at her as she passed and shouted: 'How do you now? How is it with you now?' And in the session house she was, as she put it, 'a gazing stock'.

One of those who gazed at her steadfastly in the face was the 'witch-trying woman'. But Anna survived this ordeal and although she heard whispers all round her that she would reveal herself to be a witch by being unable to answer her judges, afterwards it was agreed by this same crowd of whisperers that she could not possibly be a witch, since she had spoken so many 'good words'. All the same the accusation of witchcraft – at least by the ignorant – was never totally abandoned. Later, at Plymouth, words like 'witchcraft' and 'a white Devil' were thrown at her.

In the main Anna Trapnel was courteously treated by her judges, despite the fact that she refused to read aloud one of her own passages concerning the Little Horn. A soldier who smiled when Anna related one of her visions was sent out of court. Two women were produced who swore that Anna had been well aware of the people's presence during her trance. One of her judges termed Anna, not uncharitably, 'a dreamer. ('So Joseph was called', retorted Anna.)

Anna's true sufferings began in the course of her journey back to London. There was no proper vessel to convey her to Portsmouth so that Anna spent more than fifteen weeks in a 'man's prison' before being shipped along with some prisoners-of-war (although she did have a maid with her). When a storm blew up, Anna was accused by her shipmates of causing the winds through witchcraft 'and they curst me there'. The same storm caused an injury to her leg. Her company in the coach from Portsmouth was rather more agreeable: a clutch of partridge eggs on its way to the Protector as a present. The sight of the eggs inspired Anna. To her companions in the coach 'I often told of a present from heaven', she wrote afterwards, 'which was much better than the present of partridge eggs, yea, it was costlier than the gold of Ophir, or Rubies and Pearls from a far country'. Another comparison she was inspired to make was between 'the Great Protector' in heaven and the inferior man who had assumed the same title in England in the December of the previous year.

On 2 June Anna Trapnel was committed to Bridewell.[38] She reached the prison at eleven o'clock at night. The Matron told her sharply that she had dealt with other 'ranting sluts', before admitting she had never received one quite like Anna, since she had performed no 'base actions'. Anna now insisted on sending for her friends, who would collect the maid that she had brought from Cornwall to attend her. Despite the Matron's protests, the friends arrived at midnight, and inspected Anna's lodging. They found it large, but with only 'a hard flock-bed' and one little window in the corner; the common 'shore' (sewer) ran beneath 'which sink smelt grievously'. The rats 'that abode much in that room', running about like cats and dogs, also contributed to the smell. Everyone, including Anna herself, was horrified. The Matron however was inexorable, denied Anna's right to a maid, and refused to leave her a candle, saying that she did not trust a prisoner to put it out.

To poor Anna, alone in the stinking darkness, Satan now returned. He suggested that everyone would point at her when she went out, saying 'There goes a Bridewell bird'; decent people would not associate with her 'because of Bridewell reproach'. The hard cold bed and the damp sheets gave her a fever. It was not until Anna's friends had clubbed together to buy a copy of the order against her for 16d that the Matron was convinced nothing had been laid to her charge. Thereafter, because Anna was not a criminal, the Matron allowed flowers and herbs to be strewn, to sweeten the room; her friends were now allowed to stay.

On the day Anna was supposed to appear in court, she was too weak to rise. The Matron showed a flash of her old form by threatening to send the man to fetch her who conveyed the harlots and thieves to beat hemp. Under the circumstances Anna's friends persuaded her to appear. Once again, she was treated courteously in court and allowed to sit down. After that relations between Anna and the Matron never progressed much further than an uneasy truce, the Matron accusing Anna of telling tales 'to wrong her', and Anna much resenting the Matron's suggestion that Anna wanted 'men to come at her'. Explaining herself, Anna said that her delight was not and never had been in men's company 'but in all people as they are godly'.

Yet compared to most criminals – that of course being the very comparison which she detested – Anna Trapnel was well treated. There was no question, as there had been with Mary Overton and Katherine Hadley, of suggesting that she belonged to their number. She was allowed to rent her own chamber at 5s a week – expensive but convenient – and when she was supposed to beat hemp, the other women did it for her. Seven out of the eight weeks she spent in gaol, Anna was accompanied by her sister Ursula Adman. For all that, she could hardly sleep because of 'such scolding' among the prisoners, especially when they were brought in at night. It was no 'pleasant prison' to those 'brought up tenderly', reflected Anna.

Anna Trapnel was released on 26 July after nearly eight weeks in Bridewell.[39] She had declared of herself: 'while I have tongue and breath it shall go forth for the Fifth Monarchy Laws, teaching and practice'. Nor would she give any undertaking about her public pronouncements on her release: on the contrary, she announced she would continue to speak out whenever the spirit moved her. Anna visited the West Country again the following year and with 'three young fellows' went to see the Fifth Monarchist John Carew in St Mawes prison. One of these fellows had a sword, and a soldier taxed him with it, saying that he was on the look-out for Cavaliers, and unless it was accounted for, he would remove it. Anna Trapnel and the young fellows together denied his authority: 'The Lord Protector we own not, thou art of the Army of the Beast.' But when the Governors of Pendennis Castle and the justices sent for her, Anna went into a convenient trance.

A quantity of her verses, which were probably given extemporaneously, were taken down by a reporter in 1657 or 1658.[40] Some of the imagery with Anna as the 'wife' of Christ recalls that of the Catholic mystics (whom Anna would have sternly condemned):

> For they did tear and rent the veil
> Of Christs beloved wife,
> She doth complain unto her King,
> What injuries and smites
> O spouse my Love, saith he, still sing... [41]

Some of it, which has been compared to the early hymns of the Methodists, touches with its simplicity:

> I shall be enclosed and kept
> I shall be very secure
> Unto eternity itself
> And through many strokes, endure.
>
> Though many strokes of death doth pain
> And make the body smart
> Yet thy presence, dear Jesus, doth
> Refresh and raise my heart.

Anna Trapnel did not however display much spirit of Christian forgiveness to her enemies:

> ... Bedone by as they did
> O they have laid them on the rack
> They have tormented by degrees
> And as they have done, so shall it be
> Saith Christ, done unto these ...[42]

In *Voice for the King of Saints* of 1658 she developed the theme further:

> O come with vengeance, come Dear Lord,
> That their blood may drop out,
> That do now rob and steal from thee.

Nor did she regard the godly and the ungodly as in any way equal in an ideal society: under the 'Rule of the Saints', the godly alone would have been constituted 'earls and potentates'.[43]

Anna Trapnel was attacked in print as late as 1660, at which point, with the turn-about of the Restoration, she vanishes from history.†

After 1660 the voices of the prophetesses died away except for a few lonely exclamations; the female clamour of the Commonwealth, both sonorous and serious, gave way to the merry prattle of the ladies of King Charles II's England. The bells rang out for the restored King on 29 May, the cannons roared, and over 20,000 people jostled to greet him in London, so that the noise of it all was so great that it made Charles 'prodigiously dazed'.[45] Women were amongst these 20,000, as there had been women watching the execution of his father eleven years earlier. But the age when the female voice might be listened to with general respect — at least if it claimed to come from God — was over.

Did nothing remain — except memories, painful or otherwise — of this time when women had been 'stronger grown'?

†Although she is just possibly to be identified with Anna Trapnel who married in Woodbridge in Soffolk in 1661.[44]

It has been mentioned that among those women who caused public disturbances some of the wildest had been those 'eerie spirits' surrounding the strange Quaker enthusiast and preacher James Naylor. In some ways Quaker women, who were prominent in the sect from the start (giving rise to rumours that the sect was entirely composed of them), coincided in their behaviour with the worst prejudices concerning the uncontrolled female. Disruption of services, for example, by persistent crying out and 'quaking' during a minister's sermon – hence the popular nickname for what was in fact the Society of Friends – whenever moved by the spirit to do so, was not calculated to win the respect of the male authorities.

'Good Mistress Fell, go into your own pew, or else go your way', exclaimed a local justice to Margaret Fell concerning her repeated interventions at the local 'steeplehouse', in the course of which she called him 'a caterpillar' to be swept aside (and she was the sect's most respectable member).[46]

'Little Elizabeth' Fletcher, as she was generally known for her tiny physique, arrived in Oxford in June 1654 at the age of fourteen, on a self-imposed mission to speak to the undergraduates. After some ugly horse-play from her 'flock', which led to Little Elizabeth's being pushed under the pump 'with other shameful abuses', this 'virtuous maid of considerable family', 'contrary to her own Will or Inclination. In Obedience to the Lord' ran naked through the streets of Oxford 'as a sign of the Hypocritical Profession they made there'. In the end, since she still persisted in speaking, the Vice-Chancellor of Oxford had Little Elizabeth whipped for blasphemy.[47]

There was however another aspect to the Quaker religion at its inception which was of more profound importance to the weaker vessel than these manifestations of unrest. George Fox, the founder of the Society of Friends, was a weaver's son from Leicestershire, whom William Penn described as 'an original, being no man's copy'. One of the marks of his originality was to face up to the uncomfortable implications of Christianity, that sex was not necessarily relevant where religion was concerned. Whereas an individual prophetess such as Anna Trapnel had merely claimed a special position for herself, in 1656 George Fox published the first defence in English of the spiritual equality of women since the Reformation. As for testifying, wrote Fox in 1652, 'I said that if the power of God and the Seed spoke in man or woman it was Christ.'[48]

Since Quaker testifying was dependent upon the arrival of the spirit of Christ in the breast, this doctrine of Fox's cast an entirely new light on the whole subject of women speaking in public. We shall meet the heroic if turbulent Quaker women again, their voices at least unstilled, their steps vigorous and defiant in adversity, as they not only travelled their own land but ventured to the New World of Puritan Massachusetts and the old world of the Sultan's Turkey. These women at least were confident that 'in the restoration by Christ' they were equal partners once again: 'Man and Woman, as they were before the Fall'.[49] Thus the most enduring claim made for woman during the period when the world was turned upside down proved to concern her soul, but that of course was invisible, as woman herself was sometimes supposed to be.

References

Prologue: How Weak?

1 e.g. Hieron, *Helpe unto Devotion*, p.270.
2 Wilkinson, 'Merchant-Royal', p.130.
3 Rowse, *Shakespeare's Dark Lady*, p.103.
4 Perkins, *Discourse of the Damned Art*, p.168.
5 Josceline, 'Mothers Legacy', BL Add MSS, 27.467.
6 Swetnam, *Arraignment of Women*, p.15.
7 See Camden, *Elizabethan Woman*, pp.23–4.
8 *Fox Journal*, p.8.
9 Austin, *Haec Homo*, p.5.
10 Allestree, *Ladies Calling*, Preface.
11 *As You Like It*, Act II, scene IV; Sharp, *Midwives Book*, p.250.
12 cit. Illick, *Child-Rearing*, p.320; *Ladies Dictionary*, p.136.
13 cit. Stone, *Family, Sex and Marriage*, p.495.
14 *Letters In Honour of the Dutchess of Newcastle*, p.166; Newcastle, *Worlds Olio*, Preface.
15 *Lawes Resolutions*, p.6.
16 *Lawes Resolutions*, p.6.
17 Salmon, *Aristotle's Masterpiece*, p.3.
18 *Hoby Diary*, p.47.
19 Dante's *Inferno*, Book 1, Canto III.

Chapter 1: A Wife Sought for Wealth

1 Wilkinson, 'Merchant-Royal', p.20.

2 Nichols, *Progresses of King James I*, pp.105–21.

3 Wilkinson, 'Merchant-Royal', p.18; Dedication.

4 Gataker, 'Good Wife Gods Gift', p.8.

5 *Lawes Resolutions*, p.144.

6 HMC, Hastings MSS, IV, p.332; *Cromwell Writings*, I, pp.585–92; II, p.8.

7 *Hatton Correspondence*, I, pp.15–16.

8 Kenny, *History of the Law of England*, Part III, Chapter III.

9 Powell, *Domestic Relations*, p.5 and note 2.

10 *Lawes Resolutions*, p.146.

11 Willson, *King James VI and I*, p.388.

12 Willson, *King James VI and I*, p.286.

13 The 'courtship' is dealt with at length in Norsworthy, *Lady Hatton*; Lockyer, *Buckingham*, adds the findings of modern scholarship.

14 Ben Jonson, *The Gypsies Metamorphosed*, p.139.

15 *Hic Mulier: Or, The Man-Woman*.

16 cit. Norsworthy, *Lady Hatton*, p.55; Gardiner, *History of England*, III, p.87.

17 Norsworthy, *Lady Hatton*, p.39.

18 See Stone, *Family, Sex and Marriage*, pp.31, 33–4.

19 Norsworthy, *Lady Hatton*, p.43.

20 Norsworthy, *Lady Hatton*, pp.49–50.

21 cit. Norsworthy, *Lady Hatton*, p.29; HMC, Salisbury MSS, XXII, p.52.

22 MacDonald, *Mystical Bedlam*, p.21; CSP Domestic, 1619–23, p.405.

23 Lockyer, *Buckingham*, p.408.

24 May, *Social Control of Sex Expression*, p.132.

25 Norsworthy, *Lady Hatton*, p.125.

26 On 20 October 1624 according to Burke's *Extinct Peerages*, p.559; Lockyer, *Buckingham*, p.285, gives the birth as 'early in 1625'.

27 Norsworthy, *Lady Hatton*, p.151.

28 *Conway letters*, p.25.

29 Burke's *Extinct Peerages*, p.559.

30 For the marriage of Mary Blacknall see *Verney papers*, pp.138–46.

31 See Stone, *Family, Sex and Marriage*, pp.30–37.

32 *Verney Memoirs*, II, p.421.

33 *Verney Memoirs*, III, p.30.

34 CSP Domestic, 1637, p.422.

35 CSP Domestic, 1637, p.423.

36 CSP Domestic, 1637, p.423.

37 CSP Domestic, 1637, pp.404, 547.

38 CSP Domestic, 1637, p.565.

39 CSP Domestic, 1637–8, p.499.

Chapter 2: *Affection Is False*

1 cit. Schücking, *Puritan Family*, pp.25–6; Rogers, *Matrimoniall Honour*, p.32.

2 See Sensabaugh, *Love Ethics in Platonic Court Drama*; Ben Jonson, *The New Inn*, Act I, scene V.

3 *Houblon Family*, I, Appendix A, p.346.

4 cit. *Collins' Peerage*, II, p.491.

5 HMC, Salisbury MSS, XXII, p.239.

6 Swetnam, *Arraignment of Women*, pp.12–13; Gataker. 'Good Wife Gods Gift', p.18.

7 cit. Scott Thomson, *Noble Household*, p.28.

8 McElwee, *Murder of Overbury*, pp.238–41.

9 cit. Scott Thomson, *Noble Household*, pp.28, 30.

10 Scott Thomson, *Noble Household*, pp.28, 30.

11 Duncon, *Vi-Countess Falkland*, p.149; Duncon, *Returns of Spiritual Comfort*, p.1.

12 Duncon, *Vi-Countess Falkland*, p.152.

13 *Clarendon Life*, I, p.44.

14 *Clarendon Life*, I, p.45.

15 Clarendon, *History of Rebellion*, III, p.180.

16 Duncon, *Vi-Countess Falkland*, p.153; Aubrey, *Brief Lives*, ed. Powell, p.335. I discount Aubrey's secondhand gossip concerning Falkland's death (p.356), preferring the account given by Clarendon, who knew him intimately.

17 Clarendon, *History of Rebellion*, III, pp. 189–90.

18 Duncon, *Vi-Countess Falkland*, pp.155, 157.

19 Duncon, *Vi-Countess Falkland*, pp.176, 195.

20 Duncon, *Vi-Countess Falkland*, p.205.

21 Newcastle, *True Relation*, p.12.

22 cit. Grant, *Margaret the First*, p.81.

23 See E. A. Parry's edition for the letters and Lord David Cecil's biography of Dorothy Osborne in *Two Quiet Lives*.

24 *Osborne Letters*, pp.181–2, 182.

25 *Osborne Letters*, p.197.

26 *Osborne Letters*, p.163.

27 Newdegate, *Muniment Room*, p.36.

28 *Lismore Papers*, V, p.101; *Warwick Autobiography*, p.3.

29 *Warwick Autobiography*, p.8.

30 See Gardiner, *Oxinden and Peyton*, pp.xxvi–xxvii and 'Oxinden Correspondence', V, BL Add MSS, 28, 003.

31 Fell Smith, *Warwick*, p.336; *Osborne Letters*, p.115.

32 'Oxinden Correspondence', V, BL Add MSS, 28, 003, fo. 147, 143.

33 'Oxinden Correspondence', V, BL Add MSS, 28, 003, fo. 143.

34 'Oxinden Correspondence', V, BL Add MSS, 28, 003, fo. 173.

35 'Oxinden Correspondence'. V, BL Add MSS, 28, 003, fo. 173.

36 See Gardiner, *Oxinden and Peyton*. pp.113–14, 155, 171.

37 Woolley, *Gentlewomans Companion*, p.104.

38 MacDonald, *Mystical Bedlam*, p.90.

39 *Martindale Life*, p.16.

40 See Laslett, *World we have lost* (1983), pp.81–3.

41 cit. Duffy, *Inherit the Earth*, p.88; *Overbury Works*, pp.169–70.

42 *Herrick Poems*, pp.229–30.

43 *Osborne Letters*, p.85.

Chapter 3: Crown to her Husband

1 Walker, *Holy Life*, p.39 quoting Proverbs, 12, VS. 4; Hieron, *Helpe unto Devotion*, p.386; Walker, *Holy Life*, p.40; Hookes, *Amanda*, p.116.

2 Knevet, *Funerall Elegies to the memory of Lady Paston*; Ballard, *Memoirs of Several Ladies*, p.285.

3 Markham, *English Huswife*, II, p.3.

4 Brathwaite, *English Gentlewoman*, p.397.

5 Walker, *Holy Life*, p.39.

6 *Houblon Family*, Appendix A, p.346; *Evelyn Diary*, II, pp.237, 128, 173.

7 i.e. *Pepys Diary*, VI, p.316; IX, p.204; *Hic Mulier: Or, The Man-Woman*.

8 cit. Notestein, *English Woman*, p.94; Bridenbaugh, *Vexed Englishmen*, p.119 and note; Fuller, *Worthies*, II, p.294.

9 Gardiner, *Oxinden Letters*, pp.40–41.

10 cit. Notestein, *English Woman*, p.94.

11 Howell, *Familiar Letters*, p.76; *Memoriae Matris* in Herbert, *Works*, p.422 (translation by Edmund Blunden in *Essays and Literature by Members of the English Association*, XIX, pp.32–3).

12 cit. Clark, *Working Life*, pp.44–5.

13 *Stout Autobiography*, p.3.

14 cit. Fussell, *English Countrywoman*, p.62; Clark, *Working Life*, p.51.
15 *Queens Closet Opened*, Preface; see especially pp.7, 44.
16 Kent, *Choice Manuall*, see especially pp.107–8, 174, 4.
17 Kent, *Choice Manuall*, p.198.
18 Brathwaite, *English Gentlewoman*, p.397.
19 Walker, *Holy Life*, pp.14, 67.
20 Walker, *Holy Life*, p.67.
21 Walker, *Holy Life*, p.72.
22 Walker, *Holy Life*, pp.67, 88.
23 Ambrose, *Works*, pp.117–18.
24 Fell Smith, *Warwick*, pp.322–41; *Warwick Memoir*, pp.292–4.
25 Walker, *Holy Life*, p.27.
26 Evelyn, *Mundus Muliebris*, Preface; Gardiner, *Oxinden Letters*, p.299.
27 Nash, *Worcestershire*, I, p.500.
28 See Stone, *Family, Sex and Marriage*, pp.489–90; Sharp, *Midwives Book*,
    p.33.
29 Gouge, *Domesticall Duties*, p.223; Milton, *Paradise Lost*, Book IV,
    lines 338–9.
30 cit. Bowle, *Evelyn*, p.177.
31 Capp, *Astrology*, pp.120–21.
32 *Oglander Notebook*, p.5.
33 Whitelocke, *Memorials*, III, p.32.
34 See Christie, *Shaftesbury*, p.lii.
35 Fell Smith, *Warwick*, p.302.
36 *Heywood Autobiography*, I, pp.61, 177.
37 *Harley Letters*, pp.1, 3.
38 Denbigh, *Royalist Father*, pp.197, 202, 199.
39 *Lovelace Poems*, p.17.
40 See Lady Fanshawe's account in *Halkett and Fanshawe*, pp.110, 102.
41 *Halkett and Fanshawe*, p.114.
42 *Halkett and Fanshawe*, p.115.
43 *Halkett and Fanshawe*, pp.115–16.
44 *Halkett and Fanshawe*, pp.123, 128.
45 *Halkett and Fanshawe*, pp.130–31.
46 *Halkett and Fanshawe*, p.103.
47 *Halkett and Fanshawe*, p.103.
48 Fanshawe, *Shorter Poems*, p.6.

Chapter 4: The Pain and the Peril

1 See Schücking, *Puritan Family*, p.67.

2 Hookes, *Amanda*, p.1.

3 Walker, *Holy Life*, pp.44, 33.

4 See Appendix, 'A Chronology of Sir Richard Fanshawe', *Halkett and Fanshawe*, pp.95–9.

5 Hieron, *Helpe unto Devotion*, p.148; I Timothy, 2, VS. 14–15.

6 Hieron, *Helpe unto Devotion*, p.148.

7 *Halkett and Fanshawe*, p.22.

8 Sermon, *Ladies Companion*, p.7.

9 *Cust Family Records*, series II, p.97; *Pepys Diary*, V, p.222.

10 Grant, *Margaret the First*, p.96; Newcastle, *CCXI Letters*, p.94.

11 Sackville-West, *Clifford*, p.107; Newcastle, *CCXI Letters*, p.95.

12 *Heywood Autobiography*, I, p.70.

13 *Mordaunt Private Diarie*, p.21.

14 *Mordaunt Private Diarie*, p.3; Clarendon, *History of the Rebellion*, VI, p.59.

15 HMC, Salisbury MSS, 1612–88, p.433; see Fraser, *Cromwell*, pp.478–82.

16 *Mordaunt Private Diarie*, pp.28, 38, 152, 183.

17 Himes, *Contraception*, pp.168–70, 183, 191–2; *Pepys Diary*, VIII, p.318.

18 See Schnucker, 'Elizabethan Birth Control'; 'New Bill in Reply to the Ladies and Batchelors', p.449.

19 Defoe, *Conjugal Lewdness*, p.155; Capp, *Astrology*, p.122.

20 Capp, *Astrology*, p.122; Schnucker, 'Elizabethan Birth Control', p.657.

21 Schnucker, 'Elizabethan Birth Control', pp.657–9; Eccles, *Obstetrics in Stuart England*, pp.26–32.

22 Macfarlane, *Josselin*, p.201.

23 cit. Wrigley, 'Family Limitation', p.105, note 3.

24 See Wrigley, 'Family Limitation'; Henry, *Anciennes Familles Genevoises*.

25 *Warwick Autobiography*, p.32.

26 Josceline, 'Mothers Legacy', BL Add MSS, 27, 467; Reynolds, *Learned Lady*, p.29.

27 Josceline, 'Mothers Legacy', BL Add MSS, 27, 467: Reynolds, *Learned Lady*, p.29.

28 Sharp, *Midwives Book*, p.170; Newcastle, *CCXI Letters*, p.189.

29 *Harcourt Papers*, I, p.106; Pilkington, *Celebrated Female Characters*, p.199.

30 See Evelyn, *Mrs Godolphin*, for her story; esp. pp.79, 144–51.

31 Black, *Folk-Medicine*, pp.162–3; *Pepys Diary*, IV, p.339 and note 2; Eccles, *Obstetrics in Stuart England*, p.20.

32 Evelyn, *Mrs Godolphin*, p.156.

33 Hartmann, *King's Friend*, p.205.

34 Hieron, *Helpe unto Devotion*, p.270; Cartwright, *Sacharissa*, p.74.

35 Gardiner, *History of England*, IX, p.80; Higgins, 'Women in the Civil War', p.50.

36 See Stone, *Family, Sex and Marriage*, esp. pp. 105–14; MacDonald, *Mystical Bedlam*, pp.77–82.

37 *Verney Memoirs*, II, p.296; *Heywood Autobiography*, I, p.45; Souars, *Orinda*, p.89.

38 *Cholmley Memoirs*, p.31.

39 Clarke, *Lives of Eminent Persons*, p.158.

40 Duncon, *Vi-Countess Falkland*, p.175; Sidney, *Diary*, I, p. lxxxv.

41 *Cust Family Records*, series II, p.120; see Stone, *Family, Sex and Marriage*, p.60 for 'an average family' of four, five, or six children of whom two or three would die young.

42 *Thornton Autobiography*, p.126.

43 *Thornton Autobiography*, p.94.

44 *Thornton Autobiography*, p.145.

45 Peter Laslett, in *World we have lost* (1983), p.129; cit. Illick, *Child-Rearing*, p.305 and note 10, p.333; Stone, *Crisis of the Aristocracy*, p.619.

46 See McLaren, 'Nature's Contraceptive'.

47 *Stout Autobiography*, p.14; McLaren, 'Nature's Contraceptive', p.432.

48 Ross, *Margaret Fell*, p.335; *Collins' Peerage*, II, p.81; *Conway Letters*, p.124.

49 Fildes, 'Infant Feeding Practices', seminar.

50 Sharp, *Midwives Book*, pp.349, 365; *Verney Memoirs*, II. p.94.

51 *Heywood Autobiography*, I, p.58; Clark, *Working Life*, p.27; CSP Domestic, 1661–2, p.221; 'Farthing affidavit', *Notes and Queries*, V, 11th series, 1912, p.508; Fildes, 'Infant Feeding Practices', seminar.

52 McLaren, 'Nature's Contraceptive', p.433.

53 Schnucker, *Puritans and Pregnancy*, p.648; Sharp, *Midwives Book*, p.353.

54 Newdegate, *Muniment Room*, pp.20, 88.

55 See 'Lincoln's Nursery', esp. pp.25, 27, 205, 31.

Chapter 5: Are You Widows?

 1 'Warwicke Specialities', BL Add MSS, 27, 357.

 2 Duncon, *Returns of Spiritual Comfort*; Clarke, *Lives of Eminent Persons*, II, p.148.

3 Newdegate, *Muniment Room*, pp.86, 156, 126.

4 Macfarlane, *Marital and Sexual Relationships*, pp.120, 213.

5 *Herbert Autobiography*, pp.xix, 10 and note 3.

6 See Cartwright, *Sacharissa*, for the story of Dorothy Sidney; *Waller Poems*, I, p.128; Cartwright, *Sacharissa*, p.74.

7 Cartwright, *Sacharissa*, pp.104–6.

8 *Osborne Letters*, p.44.

9 *Pepys Diary*, I, p.60.

10 Laslett, *World we have lost* (1983), Table 10, p.108, gives 38.1 in 1601, declining to 35.7 in 1661 and 32.5 in 1721.

11 Stone, *Family, Sex and Marriage*, p.56.

12 *Verney Memoirs*, I, p.242.

13 *Verney Memoirs*, I, p.257.

14 *Verney Memoirs*, I, pp.265, 268.

15 *Verney Memoirs*, I, p.274; *Warwick Autobiography*, p.27.

16 Fell Smith, *Warwick*, p.11.

17 Fell Smith, *Warwick*, pp.109–10.

18 *Herbert Autobiography*, pp. 46–7.

19 Blundell, *Cavalier's Notebook*, p.242; Brailsford, *Quaker Women*, p.137; *Harley Letters*, p. 117.

20 Notestein, *English Woman*, p. 107, note 16.

21 *Osborne Letters*, p.123.

22 Kirkman, *Unlucky Citizen*, p.163.

23 Price, *London Bankers*, pp.151, 31; Price, *Marygold*, p.23.

24 See Lang, 'Greater Merchants of London', Chapter V; *Chamberlain Letters*, II, pp.572, 576; *Pepys Diary*, VI, p.215.

25 See the Rev. L.B. Larking in *Proceedings, Principally in the County of Kent, In Connection with the Parliaments called in 1640*, for the story of the Widow Bennett.

26 Philip Massinger, *City Madam*, Act IV, scene IV.

27 John Webster, *Duchess of Malfi*, Act I, scene I; Swetnam, *Arraignment of Women*, p.31.

28 Larking, *Proceedings*, p.xxxiii.

29 See *Verney Papers*, pp.199–223 for the second marriage of Margaret Poulteney.

30 *Verney Papers*, p.221.

31 Allestree, *Ladies Calling*, p.42.

32 'Twysden Notebooks', BL Add MSS, 34, 163, fo. 211.

33 'Twysden Notebooks', BL Add MSS, 34, 163, fo. 211.

34 'Twysden Notebooks', BL Add MSS, 34, 163, fo. 210, 28.

35 G.E.C., *Complete Peerage*, XII/2, p.775, note D.
36 Sackville-West, *Clifford*, p.xxxviii; Rowse, *Shakespeare's Dark Lady*, p.139.
37 Notestein, *Four Worthies*, p.128; Sackville-West, *Clifford*, p.28.
38 Sackville-West, *Clifford*, p.xxxix; Whitaker, *History of Craven*, p.277; Cocke, 'Clifford'.
39 Notestein, *Four Worthies*, p.149; cit. Ballard, *Memoirs of Several Ladies*, p.317.
40 Notestein, *Four Worthies*, p.154; see Ballard, *Memoirs of Several Ladies*, p.314, writing within living memory of Lady Anne.
41 Even if these rights, up till the end of the seventeenth century, were only effective in practice in the City of London, the province of York and Wales (see Stone, *Family, Sex and Marriage*, pp.195–6).
42 *Thornton Autobiography*, p.247.
43 See Stenton, *English Woman*, pp.100–105.
44 See Clark, *Working Life*, pp.10, 150, 104.
45 Clark, *Working Life*, pp.20–31, 233, 215; cit. Thompson, *Women in Stuart England*, p.217, note 86.
46 Stenton, *English Woman*, p.219; Clark, *Working Life*, p.161.
47 Brathwaite, *English Gentlewoman*, p.332.

Chapter 6: Poor and Atrabilious

1 HMC, Hastings MSS, IV, p.325; the third Earl of Warwick was the proposed bridegroom, cit. Fell Smith, *Warwick*, p.145.
2 See Laslett, *World we have lost* (1983), pp.90–98; Thomas, *Religion*, pp.560–67.
3 Pearl, 'Social Policy', p.129.
4 cit. Smith, 'Growing Old in Early Stuart England', p.127.
5 Ballard, *Memoirs of Several Ladies*, p.361; *Collins' Peerage*, IV, p.106; Smith, 'Growing Old in Early Stuart England', p.127.
6 John Milton, *Comus*, l. 453; John Ford, *'Tis Pity She's a Whore*, Act II, scene V; *Hic Mulier: Or, The Man-Woman*.
7 cit. Thomas, *Religion*, p.464.
8 Perkins, *Discourse of the Damned Art*, p.168; Burton, *Anatomy of Melancholy*, I, p.210; Quaife, *Wanton Wenches*, p.152.
9 See Ewen, *Witchcraft*, Index (Marks); also Macfarlane, *Witchcraft*, p.19 for increasing stress placed on marks at trial; Thomas, *Religion*, pp.445–6.
10 cit. George, '"Goodwife" to "Mistress"', p.161; Eyre, *Dyurnall*, p.46; Proverbs, 25, VS. 24, cit. for example in Allestree, *Ladies Calling*, p.48.

11 Roberts, *Social History*, p.156; see Capp, *Astrology*, pp.124–5.

12 Bridenbaugh, *Vexed Englishmen*, pp.357–8.

13 Thomas, *Religion*, pp.503–5; Dekker, Ford and Rowley, *Witch of Edmonton*, Act II, scene I.

14 Woolley, *Gentlewomans Companion*, p.42; see Burstein, 'Psychopathology of Old Age'.

15 Thomas, *Religion*, p.557; Macfarlane, *Witchcraft*, p.161; Stearne, *Discovery of Witchcraft*, p.12.

16 Thomas, *Religion*, p.565; Burstein, 'Psychopathology of Old Age', p.65.

17 Scot, *Discoverie of Witchcraft*, Epistle to Readers, p.xxiii.

18 See *Complete History of Magick, Sorcery and Witchcraft* (1715), I, pp.177–95 for a version of the Belvoir witches' story written when witchcraft was still part of contemporary belief.

19 Ewen, *Witchcraft*, p.231; Scot, *Discoverie of Witchcraft*, p.5.

20 *Macbeth*, Act I, scene I; Dekker, Ford and Rowley, *Witch of Edmonton*, Act V, scene I; Nichols, *Leicestershire*, p.49, note 12; see Ewen, *North Moreton*, p.4.

21 *Complete History of Magick*, I, p.179.

22 Ewen, *Witchcraft*, p.233.

23 Notestein, *Witchcraft*, p.134, note 19.

24 See *Complete History of Magick*, I, pp.177–95; Ewen, *Witchcraft*, pp.232–3.

25 Nichols, *Leicestershire*, p.49, note 12.

26 Nichols, *Leicestershire*, p.49.

27 *Complete History of Magick*, I, p.193.

28 Ewen, *Witchcraft*, p.233; *Complete History of Magick*, p.195.

29 HMC, Rutland MSS, 12th Report, IV, pp.514, 516.

30 CSP Domestic, 1619–23, p.71; Lockyer, *Buckingham*, p.58.

31 Lockyer, *Buckingham*, p.59; Stone, *Family and Fortune*, p.197.

32 *Wilson Life*, p.476.

33 See Larner, *Enemies of God*, p.20, for a summary of recent work on the subject.

34 Macfarlane, *Witchcraft*, p.163; Stearne, *Confirmation of Witchcraft*, p.10; Scot, *Discoverie of Witchcraft*, p.42; Larner, *Enemies of God*, p.20; Burton, *Anatomy of Melancholy*, I, p.210.

35 e.g. *Middlesex County Records*, III, p.287; Ewen, *Witch Hunting*, p.33; cit. Burstein, 'Psychopathology of Old Age', p.64.

36 cit. Notestein, *Witchcraft*, p.272, note 6.

37 See Ewen, *Witchcraft*, pp.365–7, for the trial.

38 cit. Ewen, *Witchcraft*, p.372.

39 Notestein, *Witchcraft*, p.272, note 6.

40 cit. Macfarlane, *Witchcraft*, p.114, and see pp.114–30 for 'cunning folk' in general; *Verney Memoirs*, IV, p.172.

41 cit. Burstein, '*Psychopathology of Old Age*', p.64; Gardiner, *Oxinden Letters*, pp.220–21.

42 Hill, *Intellectual Consequences of the Revolution*, p.64.

43 *Athenian Oracle*, III, p.336.

44 Dekker, Ford and Rowley, *Witch of Edmonton*, Act II, scene I.

Chapter 7: Unlearned Virgins

1 Josceline, 'Mothers Legacy', BL Add MSS, 27, 467, *Mordaunt Private Diarie*, Appendix, p.228; *Harcourt Papers*, I, pp.153, 173.

2 Quaife, *Wanton Wenches*, p.95.

3 *Verney Memoirs*, II, p.76; IV, p.255.

4 Newcastle, *Worlds Olio*, Preface; p.72.

5 Newdegate, *Muniment Room*, p.150; Josceline, 'Mothers Legacy', BL Add MSS, 27, 467; Reynolds, *Learned Lady*, p.29.

6 *Osborne Letters*, p.100.

7 *Letters in Honour of the Dutchess of Newcastle*, pp.4–5, II.

8 *Bradstreet Works*, p.361; Oman, *Elizabeth of Bohemia*, p.22.

9 Fraser, *Mary Queen of Scots*, p.180.

10 Reynolds, *Learned Lady*, pp.9, 23; cit. Notestein, *English Woman*, p.82.

11 Clark, *Lives of Eminent Persons*, pp.201–2.

12 Eyre, *Dyurnall*, p.34; Duncon, *Vi-Countess Falkland*, p.152; Fell Smith, *Warwick*, pp.170–71; *Cholmley Memoirs*, p.52.

13 Leigh, *Mothers Blessing*, pp.4, 56.

14 cit. Gardiner, *Girlhood at School*, p.194.

15 Matthew, *Lady Lucy Knatchbull*, p.xiv.

16 Memo of Mary Ward, cit. Chambers, *Mary Ward*, I, p.376, note iii.

17 For the life of Mary Ward, see M.C.E. Chambers' biography (1885), and post 1945 shorter studies, pamphlets and articles by James Brodrick SJ, Joseph Grisar SJ, Margaret Mary Littlehales IBVM, Pauline Parker IBVM, and Immolata Wetter IBVM.

18 cit. Littlehales, *Mary Ward*, p.13.

19 Chambers, *Mary Ward*, I, pp.410–13.

20 cit. Littlehales, *Mary Ward*, p.14.

21 Wetter, *Apostolic Vocation*, p.89.

22 Littlehales, *Mary Ward*, p.27.

23 cit. Wetter, *Apostolic Vocation*, p.91.

24 *Italian Life* (probably written by Mary Poyntz), cit. Littlehales, *Mary Ward*, p.28.

25 *Heywood Autobiography*, p.49; Walker, *Holy Life*, p.96; Ballard, *Memoirs of Several Ladies*, p.310.

26 *Thornton Autobiography*, pp.233, 342; *Verney Memoirs*, II, p.228.

27 Cressy, *Literacy*, pp.119, 128, 145.

28 Scott Thomson, *Noble Household*, p.120.

29 Scott Thomson, *Noble Household*, pp.75–6.

30 Scott Thomson, *Noble Household*, p.305.

31 Reynolds, *Learned Lady*, p.266; *Hearne Remains*, p.307.

32 *Oglander Notebook*, p.74.

33 *Conway Letters*, pp.15, 5.

34 Masson, *Milton*, V, p.232; *Collins' Peerage*, VII p.167.

35 Fell Smith, *Warwick*, p.38.

36 *Warwick Autobiography*, pp.14, 22.

37 Masson, *Milton*, V, pp.233–4.

38 Fell Smith, *Warwick*, p.37; Budgell, *Lives of the Boyles*, I, Appendix, p.5; I, p.147.

39 Masson, *Milton*, V, p.457.

40 Fell Smith, *Warwick*, p.315.

41 Fell Smith, *Warwick*, p.357.

42 *Locke Correspondence*, II, p.219; Fell Smith, *Warwick*, p.347.

43 Walker, *Holy Life*, p.39; Clarke, *Lives of Eminent Persons*, p.201.

44 Halkett and Fanshawe, pp.10, 110; *Thornton Autobiography*, p.8.

45 *All's Well That Ends Well*, Act I, scene III.

46 See Lucy Hutchinson, *Memoirs of Col. Hutchinson*, ed. James Sutherland, pp.28–35 and 288–9 for her account of her education.

47 cit. Hutchinson, *Memoirs*, pp.278–89.

48 Hutchinson, *Memoirs*, p.33.

49 Hutchinson, *Memoirs*, p.48.

50 Roberts, *Social History*, p.378; Thompson, *Women in Stuart England*, p.204; Gardiner, *Girlhood at School*, pp.276–94.

51 Thompson, *Women in Stuart England*, pp.192–3.

52 Mulcaster, *Positions*, cit. Cressy, *Education*, pp.109–11.

53 Thompson, *Women in Stuart England*, pp. 189–90.

54 Gardiner, *Girlhood at School*, p.181.

55 Gardiner, *Oxinden and Peyton*, p.128; *Thornton Autobiography*, p.8; Gardiner, *Girlhood at School*, p.159.

56 F. P. Verney, 1892, *Verney Memoirs*, I, p.xiii; Dorothy Gardiner 1933, *Oxinden Letters*, p.xxviii.

57 cit. Goreau, *Aphra*, p.31.

58 Lambley, *French Language*, pp.263–4, 299; *Harley Letters*, p.13.

59 *Artamenes*, Dedication.

60 *Verney Memoirs*, III, p.66.

61 *Verney Memoirs*, III, pp.72–4.

62 *Verney Memoirs*, III, p.74.

63 Dr Denton had sat on the Council of the Girls' Public Day Schools Company, *Verney Memoirs*, I, p.72.

Chapter 8: Living under Obedience

1 See Batchiler, *Virgin's Pattern*; Gardiner, *Girlhood at School*, pp.211–13.

2 Batchiler, *Virgin's Pattern*, Epitaph.

3 Theodore Spencer in 'History of an Unfortunate Lady'.

4 Batchiler, *Virgin's Pattern*.

5 Batchiler, *Virgin's Pattern*.

6 Batchiler, *Virgin's Pattern*.

7 Milton cit. Goreau, *Aphra*, p.76; Clarke, *Lives of Eminent Persons*, p.135; Chambers, *Mary Ward*, I, p.210.

8 Newcastle, *CCXI Letters*, p.124; Evelyn, *Mrs Godolphin*, pp.75, 121.

9 See *Halkett and Fanshawe*, pp.12–20.

10 Gibbon, *Decline and Fall of the Roman Empire*, I, Chapter 3; Chambers, *Mary Ward*, I, pp.203–5; Clarke, *Lives of Eminent Persons*, p.135.

11 Warner, *Alone of All Her Sex*, pp.246–7.

12 Stafford, *Femall Glory*, pp.25, 32.

13 Stafford, *Femall Glory*, p.168.

14 Laslett, *World we have lost* (1983), p.27, describes the gentry class and above as one twenty-fifth or at most one twentieth of the population; OED; Bridenbaugh, *Vexed Englishmen*, p.147.

15 *Pepys Diary*, VII, p.193 and note 2; Ashley, *Life in Stuart England*, p.27; HMC, Salisbury MSS, 1612–88, p.394.

16 Laslett, *World we have lost* (1983), p.12.

17 Chambers, *Mary Ward*, II, p.33.

18 I Corinthians, 14, VS. 35; *Verney Memoirs*, III, p.74.

19 Macfarlane, *Josselin*, p.147; Laslett, *World we have lost* (1983), p.13.

20 Laslett, *World we have lost* (1983), p.82, suggests a 'mean age' of about twenty-three and a half.

21 Wage of £2 cited for 1685 by Goreau, *Aphra*, p.73; *Cust Family Records*, series II, p.63; Scott Thomson, *Noble Household*, p.301.

22 Fell Smith, *Warwick*, p.348; Stuart, *English Abigail*, p.40.

23 For *Mary Woodforde's Book*, see *Woodforde Papers*, pp.3–34.

24 Blundell, *Cavalier's Notebook*, p.158; Halifax, *Complete Works*, p.292.

25 *Twysden Diary*, pp.119, 122, 134; Scott Thomson, *Noble Household*, p.120.

26 *Wilson Life*, p.462.

27 Scott Thomson, *Noble Household*, p.309.

28 Kirkman, *Unlucky Citizen*, p.127; HMC, Salisbury MSS, XXII, p.425.

29 Kirkman, *Unlucky Citizen*, p.99.

30 *Thornton Autobiography*, p.277; *Diary of Robert Hooke 1672–1680*, cit. Stone, *Family, Sex and Marriage*, pp.561–3.

31 See *Martindale Life*, pp.6–8, 17–18.

32 See Spufford, 'Portraits of Society'.

33 Hogrefe, *Tudor Women*, pp.89–90; *Mistress Mary Firth*.

34 See CSP Domestic, 1628–9, pp.530–1.

35 Thomas, *Religion*, p.137.

36 Carte MS, Vol. LXXVIII, fo. 410, no. 175.

37 For the career of Lady Eleanor Davies see especially Spencer, 'Unfortunate Lady', and 'Dougle Fooleries'.

38 Spencer, 'Unfortunate Lady', p.43.

39 CSP Domestic, 1619–23, p.400.

40 'Dougle Fooleries', p.95.

41 HMC, Hastings MSS, IV, p.343.

42 Spencer, 'Unfortunate Lady', p.48.

43 CSP Domestic, 1633–4, pp.266, 345; 'Petition of Lady Eleanor (Davies)', Thomason Tract, 669, fo. 10/2.

44 CSP Domestic, 1633–4, p.261.

45 Spencer, 'Unfortunate Lady', p.51.

46 CSP Domestic, 1633–4, p.346.

47 'Dougle Fooleries', p.97.

48 'Dougle Fooleries', p.94.

49 Tract no. 18, HMC, Hastings MSS, IV, p.344.

Chapter 9: Courage above her Sex

1 Newcastle, *Worlds Olio*, p.215.

2 cit. Bankes, *Dorset Heritage*, p.55; Washbourn, *Gloucestrensis*, part I, p.lxxxvii.

3 HMC, Bath MSS, I, p.27; still to be seen on the wall of the chancel in St Martin's Church, Ruislip, Middlesex.

4 *Cholmley Memoirs*, p.42; *Cholmley's Narrative*, p.583.

5 cit. Coate, *Social Life*, p.30; *Cromwell Writings*, II, pp.378–9.

6 'Lathom Siege Journall', p.163.

7 'Dyve Letters', p.67.

8 See Fraser, *Cromwell*, p.335; 'Dyve Letters', p.73; Foster, 'Digby', p.23.

9 Denbigh, *Royalist Father*, p.224.

10 *Harcourt Papers*, I, p.168; see the anonymous 'A Briefe Journall of the Siege against Lathom', Ormerod's *Civil War Tracts in Lancashire*, pp.159–86, for a first-hand account of its course.

11 'Lathom Siege Journall', p.167.

12 'Lathom Siege Journall', p.177.

13 See Powicke, 'Hastings Manuscripts', pp.262–7.

14 Lloyd, *Memoires of Noble Personages*, p.572; Blundell, *Cavalier's Notebook*, p.151; *Fox Journal*, p.464.

15 See Godwin, *Civil War in Hampshire*, pp.84–370.

16 Clarendon, *History of Rebellion*, III, p.410.

17 Godwin, *Civil War in Hampshire*, p.347; *Cromwell Writings*, I, p.341.

18 Lloyd, *Memoires of Noble Personages*, p.586; Clarendon, *History of Rebellion*, II, p.536.

19 Hutchins, *Dorset*, I, pp.504, 488–9.

20 Hutchins, *Dorset*, I, p.495.

21 Hutchins, *Dorset*, I, p.489; for a contemporary account of the siege, see *Mercurius Rusticus*, No. XI, cit. Hutchins, *Dorset*, I, pp.504–7.

22 Hutchins, *Dorset*, I, p.507.

23 Hutchins, *Dorset*, I, p.506.

24 Hutchins, *Dorset*, I, p.508; Vicars, *Burning-Bush*, p.372.

25 Hutchins, *Dorset*, I, p.509.

26 cit. Bankes, *Dorset Heritage*, p.94.

27 HMC, Bath MSS, I, p.4.

28 *Harley Letters*, p.xiii.

29 *Harley Letters*, pp.7–9, 13, 16, 20.

30 *Harley Letters*, p.24.

31 *Harley Letters*, pp.104, 158, 167, 178, 181.

32 *Harley Letters*, p.183.

33 *Harley Letters*, p.186.

34 *Harley Letters*, pp.188–90.

35 *Harley Letters*, p.204; HMC, Bath MSS, I, p.8.

36 HMC, Bath MSS, pp.8–9.

37 HMC, Bath MSS, pp.12–13.

38 HMC, Bath MSS, pp.4, 6.

39 HMC, Bath MSS, pp.14, 17.

40 HMC, Bath MSS, p.17.

41 HMC, Bath MSS, p.27.

42 *Harley Letters*, pp.206–7, 209.

43 The exact date of her death is not known; see her entry in DNB.

44 HMC, Bath MSS, pp.29–32.

45 *Harley Letters*, pp.230, xxxv.

46 Washbourn, *Gloucestrensis*, Part II, p.227; Butler, *Hudibras*, p.148.

47 Higgins, 'Women in the Civil War', p.38; Burghall, 'Providence Improved', p.166.

48 Bayley, *Civil War in Dorset*, p.174; Strong, *Joanereidos*, 1645; 'Tobie Trundle', in *Joanereidos*, 1674.

49 Bayley, *Civil War in Dorset*, p.127; Kaufman, *Conscientious Cavalier*, p.154.

50 Kaufman, *Conscientious Cavalier*, p.154.

51 Bayley, *Civil War in Dorset*, p.150 note 1, p.172.

52 'Tobie Trundle', in *Joanereidos*, 1674.

53 Bayley, *Civil War in Dorset*, p.191.

54 Vicars, *Gods Arke*, pp.246, 259.

Chapter 10: His Comrade

1 *Verney Memoirs*, II, p.96; 'Scourge of Civil War', Thomason Tract, 669, fo. 10/27.

2 Higgins, 'Women in the Civil War', p.29; *Cromwell Writings*, I, p.248.

3 CSP Domestic, 1645–7, p.260; Gregg, *Charles I*, p.361; *Athenae Oxonienses*, I, p.xxviii.

4 *Athenae Oxonienses*, I, p.xxviii; IV, pp.15–41.

5 Gregg, *Charles I*, p.411.

6 *Lilly's History*, p.139.

7 Hillier, *Narrative*, pp.142, 130, 140.

8 Note by P. Bliss, *Athenae Oxonienses*, I, p.xxix; Gregg, *Charles I*, p.443.

9 See J. Loftis, Introduction, *Halkett and Fanshawe*, p.xii.

10 See *Halkett and Fanshawe*, pp.23–30.

11 *James II Memoirs*, p.41.

12 *Verney Memoirs*, I, p.293.

13 *Warwick Autobiography*, p.20.

14 See Denbigh, *Royalist Father*, pp.165–95.

15 *Crashaw Poems*, p.236.

16 *Staffordshire and Great Rebellion*, p.132.

17 Everitt, *Kent and Great Rebellion*, p.26.

18 Quaife, *Wanton Wenches*, pp.125, 133.

19 cit. Clark, *Working Life*, p.80.

20 *Verney Memoirs*, II, p.176.

21 *Verney Memoirs*, II, pp.199–200.

22 *Verney Memoirs*, II, p.203.

23 *Mercurius Aulicus*, 9 September 1643.

24 cit. Godwin, *Civil War in Hampshire*, pp.121–2.

25 Godwin, *Civil War in Hampshire*, p.122.

26 On the exaggeration of horrors including this incident, Brig. Peter Young to the author; *Luke Letter Books*, p.204.

27 Bayley, *Civil War in Dorset*, p.188 and note I.

28 Young, *Edgehill*, p.11; Whitelocke, *Memorials*, I, p.188.

29 BL Harleian MSS, 6804, fo. 75/6.

30 Higgins, 'Women in the Civil War', pp.46–7; Firth, *Cromwell's Army*, pp.298–9.

31 Young, *Marston Moor*, p.166, and letter to the author.

32 Lacy, *Old Troop*, pp.150, 141, 155.

33 Lacy, *Old Troop*, p.141; 'Gallant She-Souldier', *Roxburghe Ballads*, VII, pp.728–9.

34 Higgins, 'Women in the Civil War', p.42.

35 Firth, *Cromwell's Army*, pp.80, 73–4, 116–17; 'Female Warrior', *Douce Ballads*, I (79); 'Famous Woman Drummer, *Roxburghe Ballads*, VII, pp.730–32.

36 Higgins, 'Women in the Civil War', p.45.

37 Higgins, 'Women in the Civil War', p.42; CSP Domestic, 1639, pp.146, 282.

38 *Mrs Christian Davies' Life*, pp.2, 20.

39 HMC, Leyborne-Popham MSS, p.112 for Col. Sawrey's letter; extensive researches in local records have unfortunately failed to produce an Anne Dymoke of the right age.

40 *Verney Memoirs*, IV, p.256.

41 *Venables Narrative*, p.102.

42 Firth, *Cromwell's Army*, pp.259–60.

43 Hutchinson, *Memoirs*, p.99.

44 Macdonald, *Alkin*, p.21; CSP Domestic, 1652–3, p.xxxi; Frank, *English Newspaper*, p.204.

45 Firth, *Cromwell's Army*, p.264; Clark, *Working Life*, p.243.

46 Firth, *Cromwell's Army*, p.265.

47 *Halkett and Fanshawe*, p.75.

48 *Halkett and Fanshawe*, p.82.

Chapter 11: A Soliciting Temper

1 Makin, *Essay on Education*, p.25; Newcastle, *True Relation*, p.20.

2 Gardiner, *Civil War*, I, pp.100–101, 244.

3 Higgins, 'Women in the Civil War', p.110 and note I.

4 Gardiner, *Civil War*, III, p.197; Higgins, 'Women in the Civil War', p.15.

5 Fraser, *Cromwell*, p.504.

6 Beard, *American Civilization*, I, p.25; Nash, *Worcestershire*, I, p.492; Foster, 'Digby', p.4.

7 CSP Domestic, 1640–41, pp.249–50; Clark, *Working Life*, pp.23–4.

8 Gardiner, *Civil War*, III, pp.197–9.

9 *Knyvett Letters*, p.147.

10 See *Twysden Family*, pp.172–3 and *Cholmley Memoirs*, pp.44–8.

11 *Twysden Family*, p.148.

12 For the story of Dame Isabella Twysden, see her *Diary*, ed. by the Rev. F.W. Bennet, and 'Twysden Notebooks', BL Add MSS, 34, 163.

13 See *Twysden Diary*.

14 'Twysden Notebooks', BL Add MSS, 34, 163, 1, fo. 332.

15 'Twysden Notebooks', BL Add MSS, 34, 163, 1, fo. 332.

16 *Verney Memoirs*, II, p.238.

17 *Verney Memoirs*, II, p.225.

18 *Verney Memoirs*, II, pp.231–2, 234–5.

19 *Verney Memoirs*, II, pp.239–40.

20 *Verney Memoirs*, II, p.239.

21 *Verney Memoirs*, II, pp.244, 253.

22 Newcastle, *True Relation*, p.20.

23 Newcastle, *True Relation*, p.20; *Verney Memoirs*, II, p.248.

24 *Verney Memoirs*, II, pp.249–58.

25 See *Verney Memoirs*, II, pp.255–82, 292–3, 316–17 for Mary Verney's dealings with the Committee, visit to Claydon and return to France.

26 *Verney Memoirs*, II, p.411.

27 *Verney Memoirs*, II, pp.414–16.

28 *Verney Memoirs*, II, pp.422–3.

29 *Verney Memoirs*, III, p.30.

Chapter 12: Sharing in the Commonwealth

1 Higgins, 'Women in the Civil War', p.146.

2 Neville, *Ladies Parliament; Ladies, A Second Time, Assembled; Commonwealth of Ladies.*

3 CSP Venetian, 1643–7, p.135; *Venables Narrative*, p.xl.

4 Gibb, *Fairfax*, p.181; *Mercurius Pragmaticus*, 26 December 1648.

5 Clarendon, cit. Stone, *Family, Sex and Marriage*, p.340; *Verney Memoirs*, III, pp.318, 341.

6 Newcastle, *Worlds Olio*, pp.74–5.

7 Taylor, *Sex in History*, p.277; Knox, *Enthusiasm*, p.140.

8 Brailsford, *Quaker Women*, p.246; Ross, *Margaret Fell*, p.108.

9 cit. Stone, *Family, Sex and Marriage*, pp.627, 626.

10 cit. Owen, 'Lincolnshire Women', p.34; Fraser, *Cromwell*, p.54; Higgins, 'Women in the Civil War', p.142.

11 Kerridge, 'Revolts in Wiltshire', pp.68–9; Higgins, 'Women in the Civil War', p.144.

12 George, '"Goodwife" to "Mistress"', p.152; *Womens Sharpe Revenge*, pp.37–42.

13 See Mitchell and Leys, *London*, pp.397–8; Herbert, *History of Livery Companies*, p.21.

14 Lupton, *London Characters*, pp.91–4.

15 See OED (see also Mary Ward's use of Billingsgate, p.128 *ante*); Timbs, *Curiosities of London*, pp. 54–5; Butler, *Hudibras*, p.44.

16 Higgins, 'Women in the Civil War', pp.154–67; 'Certaine Informations', E. 65 (8); Gardiner, *Civil War*, I, p.187.

17 *Kingdomes Weekly Intelligencer*, E. 65/11; Higgins, 'Women in the Civil War', p.168.

18 Carlyle, *Critical Essays*, IV, pp.327, 333.

19 See Hirst, *Representative of the People?*, pp.18–19.

20 Chapman and Chapman, *Status of Women under Law*, p.23; Hirst, *Representative of the People?*, p.18.

21 Coke, *Institutes*, Part 4, p.4.

22 Fieldhouse, 'Parliamentary Representation in the Borough of Richmond', pp.207–8.

23 *Clarke Papers*, I, pp.299, 302; Gregg, *Free-Born John*, p.215.

24 Thomas, 'Women and Sects', p.56.

25 Astell, *Reflections*, pp.43–5.

26 cit. Appendix C, Berens, *Digger Movement*, p.252.

27 *Middlesex County Records*, III, pp.xxii, 287.

28 Gibb, *Lilburne*, pp.171, 174; Gregg, *Free-Born John*, on the other hand, makes no such suggestion: see p.215.

29 Higgins, 'Women in the Civil War', pp.178–87.

30 'Overton Appeal and Petition', E. 381/10, pp. 3–4, 6–9, 174.

31 Gregg, *Free-Born John*, p.398.

32 Gregg, *Free-Born John*, p.90.

33 Gregg, *Free-Born John*, p.103.

34 Lilburne, *Freemans Freedome Vindicated*, p.6.

35 Gibb, *Lilburne*, p.192.

36 Gibb, *Lilburne*, p.192.

37 Rushworth, *Collections*, VIII, p.1257.

38 *Mercurius Militaris*, 22 April 1649.

39 *Petition of Women*, 1649, E. 551(14).

40 Gibb, *Lilburne*, p.174; Higgins, 'Women in the Civil War', p.178; *To the House of Commons for Lockier*, 5 May 1649, BL 669, fo. 14/27.

41 Higgins, 'Women in the Civil War', pp. 180–81; *To the Parliament for Mr J. Lilburn*, 24 June 1653, BL 669, fo. 17/24; *Unto every individual Member of Parliament*, 26 July 1653, BL 669, fo. 17/37; Clarendon MSS, Vol. 46, fo. 110.

42 Clarendon MSS, Vol. 46, fo. 131.

43 Gibb, *Lilburne*, pp.272–3

44 Gregg, *Free-Born John*, p.314.

45 Gregg, *Free-Born John*, p.321.

46 CSP Domestic, 1655, pp.263–4; Gregg, *Free-Born John*, p.340.

47 Gregg, *Free-Born John*, p.340.

48 Gibb, *Lilburne*, p.342.

49 *Petition of Elizabeth Lilburne*, CSP Domestic, 1657–8, p.148.

50 CSP Domestic, 1658–9, pp.260–61.

51 Pauline Gregg, *Free-Born John*, p.348, thinks he would not have approved.

52 Lilburne, *Jonah's Cry*, p.4.

Chapter 13: When Women Preach

1 Duncon, *Vi-Countess Falkland*, p.205; Brathwaite, *English Gentlewoman*, p.82.

2 *Verney Memoirs*, III, p.72.

3 Thomas, 'Women and Sects', p.47; Higgins, 'Women in the Civil War', p.88; Williams, 'Women Preachers', p.563.

4 Higgins, 'Women in the Civil War', p.93; Edwards, *Gangraena*, cit. Higgins, 'Women in the Civil War', p.89.

5 Williams, 'Women Preachers', p.563.

6 Vicars, *Schismatick Sifted*, p.34; Edwards, *Gangraena*, p.84.

7 BL Add MSS, 31, 116, fo. 254–4V (I owe this reference to
   Dr Maurice Ashley); cit. Williams, 'Women Preachers', p.564.

8 cit. Higgins, 'Women in the Civil War', p.83; Thomas, 'Women and
   Sects', pp.50, 60, note 66.

9 Warren, *Old and Good Way vindicated*, Preface; Warren, *Spiritual Thrift*,
   p.81.

10 Williams, 'Women Preachers', p.563; Ballard, *Memoirs of Several
   Ladies*, p.281; Edwards, *Gangraena*, p.170.

11 Williams, 'Women Preachers', p.566; Chidley, *Justification*, p.26.

12 Chidley, *New Yeares Gift*, E. 23(13); Chidley, *Good Counsell*, 669,
   fo. 10/39.

13 Williams, 'Women Preachers', pp.567–8.

14 Edwards, *Gangraena*, cit. Weigall, 'Women Militants', p.437.

15 'Puritan Congregation Minute Book', 1654, Rawlinson MSS, D.828,
   fo. 30/32.

16 Spencer, 'Unfortunate Lady', pp.56–8.

17 Ballard, *Memoirs of Several Ladies*, p.280; Spencer, 'Unfortunate Lady',
   pp.56–9.

18 See Powicke, 'Hastings Manuscripts', pp.267–74.

19 See Carte MSS, Vol. LXXVII, fo. 201, 417.

20 Clarendon MSS, Vol. 29, fo. 102.

21 Thomas, *Religion*, p.139 and note I.

22 See *Clarke Papers*, II, pp.150, 154, 163–5; Fraser, *Cromwell*, pp.227–8.

23 Capp, *Fifth Monarchy*, p.174.

24 See Capp, *Fifth Monarchy*, Appendix I, p.266 for summary of Anna
   Trapnel's career.

25 See Trapnel, *Legacy for Saints*, pp.1–43.

26 I Samuel, VS. 12–18; *Trapnel's Report and Plea*, Preface.

27 Trapnel, *Legacy for Saints*, Preface: Trapnel, *Cry of a Stone*, p.42;
   Burrage, 'Trapnel's Prophecies', p.531; 'Anonymous Folio Volume',
   Bodleian Library, S.1.42. Th; Dobell, 'Unique Book: Trapnel',
   p.221.

28 *Strange News from Whitehall*, pp.4–6.

29 *Cromwelliana*, p.133.

30 *Strange News from Whitehall*, p.8.

31 Capp, *Fifth Monarchy*, pp.262, 101; CSP Domestic, 1653–4, p.393.

32 'B.T. 21.10.54' cit. Burrage, 'Trapnel's Prophecies', pp.531–2;
   Thurloe Papers, XXI, Rawlinson MSS, A 21, fo. 323.

33 *Osborne Letters*, p.222.

34 See *Trapnel's Report and Plea*, pp.1–20.

35 Trapnel, *Legacy for Saints*, p.49.

36 CSP Domestic, 1654, pp.86, 89, 134.

37 *Trapnel's Report and Plea*, pp.21–37.

38 CSP Domestic, 1654, p.436; *Trapnel's Report and Plea*, p.38.

39 CSP Domestic, 1654, p.438; Trapnel, *Legacy for Saints*, p.59.

40 See 'Anonymous Folio Volume', Bodleian Library, S.1.42. Th; note
   by Bertram Dobell, 'Unique Book: Trapnel', p.221.

41 'Anonymous Folio Volume', Bodleian Library, S.1.42. Th, p.1.

42 Dobell, 'Unique Book: Trapnel', p.223; 'Anonymous Folio
   Volume', Bodleian Library, S.1.42. Th, pp.256, 649, 697.

43 cit. Capp, *Fifth Monarchy*, p.142.

44 Capp, *Fifth Monarchy*, p.266.

45 *Charles II Letters*, p.92.

46 *Clarendon State Papers*, II, p.383; Ross, *Margaret Fell*, p.39.

47 See Brailsford, *Quaker Women*, pp.103–6.

48 *Fox Journal*, p.96.

49 cit. Thomas, 'Women and Sects', p.47.

Index